The Thirteenth of May

PROBLEMS IN EUROPEAN HISTORY:
A DOCUMENTARY COLLECTION

The Thirteenth of May
The Advent of de Gaulle's Republic

EDITED BY

CHARLES S. MAIER
DAN S. WHITE

Harvard University

New York
OXFORD UNIVERSITY PRESS
London   Toronto   1968

Grateful acknowledgment is made to *Le Monde*, *Le Figaro*, and the European edition of the former New York *Herald Tribune* for permission to translate or reproduce articles and copyright material and to *The New Yorker* magazine for permission to reprint the "Letters from Paris" by Genêt (Janet Flanner), copyright 1953, 1954, © 1955, 1956 by The New Yorker Magazine, Inc.

FOREWORD

Problems in European History: A Documentary Collection has arisen out of a collective teaching experience. The series seeks to overcome a shortcoming which the authors believe persists in college history instruction. Certainly the restricting confines of the traditional textbook have been expanded as numerous collections of "readings" have appeared. But the undergraduate still remains at a distance from the historian's workshop. A compilation of heavily edited "significant documents" does not make for the sense of contact with the past that the study of history ought to promote. And the predigested selections from contending historians, neatly arrayed on either side of "classic" controversies, does not get the student to probe the underlying evidence; in fact, these academic disputations often leave him bewildered.

The conviction that students learned little of the way in which historians actually worked prompted a group of young Harvard historians five years ago to develop a new approach. The course that resulted — Social Sciences 3: Problems in Modern European History — represented an attempt to focus intensively on a small number of problems. Each problem would involve careful analysis of a wide variety of original source material. The student could develop the skills and understanding of historical explanation. In learning to compare evidence, make and test hypotheses, and judge critically earlier accounts, he would encounter some of the problems of historical research as experienced by the working historian.

In Social Sciences 3 eight studies in historical analysis are presented in a year. Our intention here is to make these documentary collections available, not necessarily as a series except in their underlying aim, but as separate problems that can be studied individually in connection with courses in European history. Each book has been edited and introduced with that purpose in mind. Thus the student can wrestle with the problems inherent in historical writing and judgment while he studies intensively a segment of the history of the country or period being taught.

Social Sciences 3 has developed over the past four years through the efforts of our collaborators, who share in the creation of these books beyond what we can gratefully acknowledge. Individual problems were prepared or substantially recast by the respective authors, but each case study was discussed and scrutinized by the entire staff of Social Sciences 3. To all of them, to the Committee on General Education of Harvard College, which has generously given of its time and efforts, and to our students — whose criticisms and suggestions were a fundamental guideline — we extend our thanks.

Cambridge, Mass.   RICHARD BIENVENU
August, 1967   JOHN F. NAYLOR

CONTENTS

The Thirteenth of May

INTRODUCTION

The Thirteenth of May 1958 is the most recent of the *grandes journées,* the "great days," which mark the turning points of modern French history. Like earlier "great days" it refers not only to the date of a particular crucial episode but signifies as well the whole development that pivoted around this event. The crucial event of May 13 was the forcible establishment of a Committee of Public Safety in Algiers as a counter-government in opposition to the parliamentary authority. Its ultimate result—the meaning of May 13 in the larger sense—was the end of the Fourth French Republic and the advent of the Fifth, the Republic of Charles de Gaulle. It is an event well worth studying through documents. The fall of a political system has always been one of the most compelling of historical dramas. But it carries an atmosphere of urgency which is difficult to convey through a secondary account. This collection seeks to take the reader to the heart of the crisis and to allow him to understand it not only in retrospect, but as it developed.

A crisis like that of the Thirteenth of May throws into stark relief the fragile points in a political structure, but it does not come upon a country overnight. The weaknesses of the France of 1958 had developed over a long period of time. Some had existed from the inception of the Fourth Republic, in 1946. Still, the regime had lived on with them—or despite them—until May 13,

1958. It is the historian's task to determine why in this final crisis these weaknesses became fatal, which ones became fatal, and whether they were indeed fatal. One need only scan a list of titles on the subject to see how differently the events of May 1958 have been interpreted: *The Suicide of the Fourth Republic, The Coup d'État of May 13, The Algerian Revolution, De Gaulle's Revolution.*

An event complex enough to provoke such a variety of interpretations demands close reading of its source materials. There is no other way to keep track of the interlaced and overlapping issues and personalities, or to catch the nuances and changes of reference which so often signified switches of policies or of loyalties. The documents do not, however, tell the story by themselves. They do not yield ready-made conclusions. The reader must reach his own judgments about the Thirteenth of May, and as experience has shown, the documents of this collection permit widely divergent opinions and interpretations.

The events of the Thirteenth of May took place only a decade ago. Are they, then, being so near to us, proper material for historical analysis? An earlier generation of historians was fond of saying that we could not really have perspective on anything which had occurred since Napoleon's defeat at Waterloo in 1815. Nevertheless, this same generation greatly admired ancient historians such as Thucydides and Tacitus, who were direct contemporaries of many of the events they described. Not the perspective granted by intervening years, but the incisiveness of their analyses made these ancient historians the first masters of their craft. Thucydides was no further from the battles of the Peloponnesian War than we are from the crisis of the Thirteenth of May. In that respect he may serve us comfortably as a model.

Still, in believing that they could not view recent events objectively, older historians had a point that deserves consideration. They wanted to wait for all the documents to become available; only then, they believed, could they tell a true and complete story. From the standpoint of the present, this outlook attributed a false impartiality to the sources; it was still the historian, after all, who interpreted them. But the older view did expose the inevitable problem of contemporary history: that many of the documents relevant to a problem will be locked up. With respect to the Thirteenth of May in particular, government archives are still closed, many private accounts still unwritten or unpublished. The most reliable sources at hand are speeches, press statements, open debates, on-the-spot reporting and analysis—the public record. Often enough the public record is all that is available even a century after the event; the imperfect state of documentation is a common problem for historians. The result is an absence of information about aims, motivations, and intentions—private thoughts as opposed to public words. These things must be judged with particular care.

Most of the documents in this collection do not require special comment, but a word about the newspapers is necessary. Save for *L'Écho d'Alger* all the French journals represented in the documents were Parisian papers. Among them *Le Monde* is the most important and convenient source and has been used most often here. *L'Écho d'Alger* was the chief French daily of Algiers. As the press organ of Alain de Sérigny, a key political figure in Algiers, it reflected many of the sentiments of the French population in Algeria. *L'Écho d'Alger* and, in Paris, *Le Figaro, Combat,* and *L'Humanité* were morning papers. The other journals used here— *Le Monde, La Croix, L'Information, France-Soir*—appeared in the afternoon and carried the following day's date.*

Although the first two sections of *The Thirteenth of May* illuminate much of the background of the crisis, some aspects of the problem merit further attention here. In particular we might take a closer look at the state of the French army, at the history of the Fourth Republic, at the problem of Algeria, and at the personality of Charles de Gaulle. All were essential elements in the crisis, and

*This manner of dating can be confusing if not kept in mind. For example, the issue of *Le Monde* dated May 15 actually appeared on the afternoon of May 14; Maurice Duverger's references to "yesterday" in this May 15 issue (reprinted below, pp. 237–9) therefore refer to May 13. It will be helpful to remember this point as French newspapers often print their reports without a dateline.

no assessment of May 13 is possible without gauging the effect and importance of each of them.

The revolt of May 13 in Algiers began with cries of "The army to power," and by the morning of May 14 the army had taken over effective power in Algeria. This French army of 1958—the professional army, the generals, and officers—was an unhappy collection of men. It lived in an atmosphere of past defeat in Europe and Indochina and of present frustration in Algeria. It wanted victory badly, but victory was proving difficult against an adversary who struck at his own choosing and then melted away into the population or across the Tunisian or Moroccan borders. French officers had been developing new conceptions of the army's role—conceptions which required not only military, but also political judgments. Against a past tradition of loyalty to civil authority and non-involvement in politics, these new doctrines represented a sharp change in the French military attitude, and ultimately they were to force many officers to face the classic problem of military obedience: whether it was to be possible for the army to accept a political solution with which it did not agree. The idea of negotiation with the Moslem National Liberation Front (FLN) placed the entire effort of the army into question: soldiers did not wish to achieve military superiority and thereupon concede power peacefully to the Algerian insurgents, and they clearly did not want to give up before the fight was won. Military leaders certainly had no objections to the government's taking a hard line in Algeria, but many were prepared to resist a ministry that they believed would negotiate an "abandonment" of the territory. Their attitude was to play its part in the background and outcome of the Thirteenth of May.

At the outbreak of the crisis, the government in Paris was to appeal to Frenchmen to rally to the defense of the Republic. But in 1958 many Frenchmen saw little in the Republic that they wished to defend. Public opinion soundings indicate this indifference and dissatisfaction. Late in 1957 a group of thirty-five hundred army draftees was asked to identify both the French premier and the year's winner of the Tour de France bicycle race. Fifteen per cent made the first identification correctly; 97 per cent the second. Another survey, a few months later, asking persons what they would do in case of a military rising against the government, found that 90 per cent chose non-involvement in one form or another. Only four of every one hundred persons asked said they would fight for the regime. As the documents of this book show, not only large segments of the public, but many political leaders desired changes in the system. The regime was in question long before the revolt in Algiers challenged its authority.

When the French people went to the polls in October 1945 to decide the form of their postwar government, 96 per cent voted in favor of creating a new, Fourth Republic. Few Frenchmen wished a return to the old system of the Third Republic, discredited by the memories of bitter partisan strife in the 1930's and the defeat by the Germans in 1940. Most hoped for the construction of a better order out of the ruins of World War II. It might seem, considering the overwhelming majority of the referendum, that these hopes were to be fulfilled. But very quickly many Frenchmen were to become deeply dissatisfied with the way in which the new Republic was being constructed.

The problems of the regime-to-be were rooted in the unique political situation of postwar France, a situation in which the long-standing party alignments of the Third Republic had been thrown out of balance. On the right, the so-called moderates, a traditionally strong conservative force in French politics, were in disarray, many of them in at least temporary disgrace because of their acceptance of the collaborationist Vichy government. The political center of gravity had swung to the left. In the elections to a constituent assembly, which immediately followed the referendum of October 1945, the French Communist and Socialist parties each won approximately one quarter of the votes and seats. Another quarter went to the new, socially progressive Catholic

Popular Republican Movement (MRP). Each of these three dominant groups had been associated with the wartime Resistance movement; each was strongly in favor of immediate economic and social reforms. On these matters there was room for co-operation—known under the formula of *tripartisme*—and the Constituent Assembly was able to pass a series of basic reforms. But on constitutional questions *tripartisme* did not work, and serious differences separated the three major groups. A similar relationship existed between the parties and General de Gaulle, whom they had confirmed as head of state following the referendum. De Gaulle joined them in their efforts at social reform. But his vision of a desirable constitution was very different from those the parties held.

As the referendum of October 1945 indicated, the general sentiment in postwar France was for a strong government. Frenchmen wished to get away from the parliamentary stalemates of the Third Republic, in which expediency and the search for a majority too often had taken the place of policy. Yet each of the possibilities for strong government was crippled by the distribution of political forces. All three of the partners of *tripartisme* disliked the idea of a powerful executive, for in the existing circumstances such an executive could only be General de Gaulle, who had shown as head of the 1944–45 provisional government that he had little use for parties. The MRP and some Socialists also feared an overly powerful legislature, in which the Communists, who approved such a system, might become dominant. Because the framing of the constitution was in the hands of the parties, de Gaulle was not able to influence it, and partly for that reason he resigned as chief of state in January 1946. The Communists were initially more successful, securing, with help from the Socialists, a constitutional draft incorporating a strong unicameral legislature. But with the MRP agitating against it, this draft constitution was rejected by referendum in May 1946. It was left for a new Constituent Assembly, elected in June 1946, to draw the lesson, and the constitution it produced avoided any preponderant concentration of power. With two chambers of parliament (although the upper house was not significant) and a weak presidency, the new draft very much recalled the system of the Third Republic. It was adopted by referendum in October, but the vote showed the degree of popular dissatisfaction: 9,263,416 for, 8,143,981 against, with 8,467,537 abstaining.

To understand why so many Frenchmen refused to endorse the new Republic, it is necessary to look back at the political system of which the Constitution of October 1946 was reminiscent. It was a regime that stood for the individual in both the abstract and the concrete sense: justice for every man, advantage for every constituent. The guiding philosophy of the Third Republic came to be that of keeping government out of the individual's life, save when it could benefit him. The duty of the deputy, in the words of the Radical publicist "Alain," was "to represent the ordinary citizen against the eternal conspiracy of the strong, the rich, the powerful." In the Third Republic's early decades, between 1870 and the First World War, a majority of Frenchmen found this system and its outlook preferable to the more authoritarian alternatives represented by royalists, Bonapartists, and the Catholic Church. The Republic, moreover, inherited a "mystique" from the revolutionary past and presided over an era of economic stability and cultural brilliance. When corruption became visible, the system could appear shabby and encourage cynicism. But in times of crisis the republican tradition roused strong and generous loyalties.

Nonetheless, the workings of government under the Third Republic corresponded only partly to the ideals of its supporters. After a conflict between the legislature and executive in the late 1870's—one also named after a great day: the Sixteenth of May— the presidency of the Republic was kept weak. No longer would a president ever dissolve a legislature, and the elected National Assembly became the supreme organ of government. But the parliamentary system did not function as democratically as its appearance indicated. With the president too weak to dissolve the legislature the deputies were virtually irremovable for the four years between elections. Defeat of a government did not, as in

England, bring on new elections, and so deputies could topple a
premier without fear of an immediate accounting of their actions
before the voters. The results were frequent changes of ministries
and a fragile continuity of policy in the Assembly, and much actual government by the permanent bureaucracy. Ironically, the
system which "Alain" and his fellow Radicals espoused often
favored in practice the arbitrary rule they so disliked.

This negative government of the Third Republic suited French
society in the decades before World War I. France was still pre-
dominantly a country of the little man—farmer, artisan, shopkeeper—whose economic activity corresponded to his individual-
istic politics. Industrialization was not as rapid or as disruptive to
society as it was, for example, in Germany. Industrial concentration was less pervasive, and the transition from rural to urban life
came slowly. Frenchmen were also reluctant to give up their existing way of life in order to plunge into a highly competitive and
large-scale capitalistic economy. Entrepreneurs aimed at security,
not expansion; a limited market with high prices and high profits
satisfied most of them. Industrialization did progress, of course. In
1914 France was the fourth leading manufacturing nation in the
world. But aside from giving rise to a moderate-sized socialist
movement, industrialization did not greatly affect the country's
politics, which remained anchored in the France of the small town
and the small operator. It was this France whose predominant
political grouping during the years between the turn of the century
and 1914 was the so-called Radical Socialist Party, which combined a militantly secular, democratic faith with a dislike of newer
collectivist tendencies.

From the outbreak of World War I, these foundations of the
Third Republic grew increasingly shaky. There was a constant
erosion of the society and attitudes that had made the political
system so well suited to the nation. Between 1914 and 1940 the
costs of war and national defense, the experience of inflation, the
shock of economic depression, and the revival of a threatening
Germany strained France's resources and morale to a degree un-

imaginable in the early, sunnier days of the Republic. And as sacrifice became the order of the day, more and more Frenchmen questioned whether their sacrifice should be for the existing order. To the growing industrial working class, which had learned that organization was its best economic and political weapon, the idealized individualism of the Republic seemed out of date. More surprisingly perhaps, individualism had also lost its appeal to many on the political right, who had come to believe that national defense and the protection of the middle-class order demanded values different from those the Republic embodied. The Radical Socialists, symptomatically, oscillated between alliances with the socialist left and with the "moderate" *laissez-faire* right—their celebrations of secularism and individual liberty apparently irrelevant to the new and harsh realities.

Negative government similarly found critics on both left and right. Although disagreeing on the particular remedy, socialists and communists, right-wing authoritarians and fascists all argued that parliamentary democracy had proven its inability to meet the demands of war and postwar, and that a strong, interventionist state power was essential to the health and future of the country. Manifested on the right by the appearance of fascist groups and the spread of antidemocratic sentiment among former "moderates," manifested on the left by the growth of the French Communist Party and the 1936 electoral success of the Socialist-Communist-Radical Popular Front, this tide of dissatisfaction reached its peak in the 1930's. The parliamentary Republic came to suggest stagnation, deep division, and demoralization. By its death in 1940 the Third Republic had become a widely unpopular regime. It ended its days with a disastrous military defeat and the surrender of its powers to an aged, politically retrograde general, Pétain. Thus the specter of its resurrection through the Constitution of 1946 predictably rekindled the long-standing dissatisfaction of many Frenchmen with the way their country was ruled.

As during the 1930's, opposition to the new regime in postwar France came from both the left and the right. The left-wing foes of

the Fourth Republic were the Communists, who became a permanent opposition of roughly one-fourth of the electorate and
Assembly following their ouster from the government—and the
end of *tripartisme*—in May 1947. Between 1945 and 1947 the
Communists belonged to the government as one of the heirs of the
Resistance, apparently hoping for an opportunity to take over
power from the inside. Once out of the cabinet, they attempted to
bring the regime of their ex-partners to its knees through a series
of major strikes. But government firmness, embodied by the tough
Socialist Interior Minister Jules Moch, broke the back of this strike
offensive in 1947 and 1948. From that point the French Communists were loud of voice but ineffective in action, save as allies
of those who wished to bring a government down. They maintained their strength in the country and in parliament, but they did
not succeed in broadening their influence. The party was damaged
by its official approval of Soviet repression of the Hungarian revolution late in 1956, but more among intellectuals than among ordinary voters. Despite Hungary, despite the dullness of its leaders,
the Communist Party remained the collecting-point for thousands
of workers, white-collar employees, and farmers who wanted to
protest the inequalities they saw in the Fourth Republic. Protest
was the most the party organization itself could do in many cases;
but with their 25 per cent of the electorate and their dominance
over France's largest labor-union federation, the CGT, the French
Communists appeared to their opponents as a continual danger
to the existing order.

The first serious opposition to the Republic from what is most
easily termed the right came, as could be expected, from General
de Gaulle. In April 1947, one month before the Communists were
ousted from the government, de Gaulle appealed to Frenchmen to
join him in a new movement, the Rally of the French People
(RPF). The response was immediate and impressive. In municipal
elections the following October, RPF candidates won 40 per cent
of the vote and captured the mayoralties of the thirteen largest
cities of France. Like its leader, the RPF was not easy to charac-

terize. Its members generally showed a stronger sense for social justice than moderates or Radicals; they were pronouncedly anti-Communist; above all they possessed an unshakeable faith in de Gaulle and his ability to restore the nation's well-being—and to defend it in the face of growing American-Russian rivalry. The RPF was not at first a party, but instead a union of Gaullist supporters from among several groups—moderates, Radicals, MRP. De Gaulle did not want a party. It has been argued that he founded the RPF in anticipation of a diplomatic showdown, even war, between the United States and Russia, expecting in that case to be quickly returned to power. The loose structure of the early RPF might have sufficed for such a prospect, but its leader's desire not to have a party was impossible to uphold over a longer period of time. In the elections of 1951 the RPF ran its own slate of candidates. It was strikingly successful and with 120 seats became the largest party in the new Assembly. Success in elections, however, was not of real use to de Gaulle, who called on his deputies to boycott the parliament rather than have any share in the "system." The faithful obeyed him; many others began to defect from the RPF. What appeared desirable to the austere general did not seem practical to all elected deputies, particularly when other groups were wooing their allegiance. As the defections increased, de Gaulle became disillusioned. In 1953 he abruptly dissolved the RPF and withdrew from the political scene.

After the General's departure, the survivors of the RPF who remained loyal to de Gaulle grouped together as the Social Republican Party. But they were reduced to a small delegation of twenty deputies in the elections of January 1956. The new thunder on the right came from the movement led by Pierre Poujade, a storekeeper from St. Céré (Lot) in southwest France. Insofar as Poujade combined nationalism and antiparliamentarism in his message, he echoed the sentiments of the Gaullists. But his agitation also included much of the "hands-off" philosophy of the earlier Radical outlook, in a caricatured and extremist guise. Likewise Poujade found his followers mostly in the small-town and rural

sections of the South and West, by the 1950's a backwater area
that was lagging economically and subject to depopulation. In this
respect he differed from the Gaullists, who had good connections
with the new technocrat class of the Fourth Republic. Poujade's
movement, *Union et Fraternité Française,* won fifty-one seats in
the 1956 elections, but as an antiparliamentary group in parliament
it also suffered defections. By 1958 only thirty-one deputies still
belonged to the UFF.

The attitudes of the Fourth Republic's outright opponents thus
exposed most of the characteristic critiques of the regime. All disliked parliamentary government and viewed it as the device of a
particular ruling clique—"those princes who govern us," as the
Gaullist senator Michel Debré sarcastically called them. All found
the state too weak: either in its direction of economic life (the
Communists), in its defense of national interests (the Poujadists),
or in both (the Gaullists). And from both left and right, Communists and Poujadists, came the complaint that the "system"
favored inequality and did not do enough for the little man. In
reality, however, the record was not so black. The Fourth Republic
made much progress between 1945 and 1958. In these thirteen
years France experienced a dramatic rise in the national birth rate
and a jump of population from forty to forty-four million in a
decade. It was a younger country than before the war. It was also
a more prosperous country. Production had surpassed prewar
totals; nationalization, long-term planning, and participation in the
Common Market contributed to a more dynamic economy than
had existed under the Third Republic. Wages were up in the mid-
1950's, and social services expanded. The problem, however, was
that these accomplishments, as before, were mostly the work of the
permanent bureaucracy. The government parties of the Fourth Republic may have shared much of the modern outlook responsible
for these improvements, but under the constitutional system they
had inaugurated in 1946 they were unable to transform their views
into working legislation. The visible regime, the coalitions of the
National Assembly, seemed confined to the same old instability;
with rare exceptions they radiated no élan, awoke no loyalties.

Workaday politics appeared condemned to *immobilisme* in large part because of the even fragmentation of parties. The party system of the Fourth Republic has often been described as hexagonal. On the extreme left were the Communists, on the right, the Gaullists and later Poujadists, all of whom leveled the most fundamental criticisms at the regime. In between were the four major republican parties who shuffled in and out of the ministries: the domesticated Socialists on the left-center; then the Radicals, who were now the reduced and fragmented remnants of the once great party of the Third Republic; in the center the Catholic-Democratic MRP; and on the right the "moderates," now grouped officially as the Independents, who were economically conservative and nationalist but not so fundamentally hostile to the regime as were the Gaullists or Poujadists. These were the governing parties after the end of *tripartisme* in 1947. Between 1947 and 1951 governments based themselves on the so-called Third Force—a middle-of-the-road combination of MRP, Radicals, and Socialists. Premiers fell often during this period, for the Third Force could not hold together on three major areas of legislation. The Socialists opposed the orthodox financial measures of their partners, the Radicals were against new state social services and retained residues of anticlericalism, the MRP fought all legislation intended to limit the influence of the Catholic Church. After the 1951 elections there was a shift to the right. While the SFIO joined the opposition, the ruling coalition became one of Radicals, MRP, and Independents, under the Independents' leader, Antoine Pinay. The new combination was nearly as unstable as the old, however, particularly when financial and foreign policy questions came under debate. Disagreements and bickering slowly ate away unity, not only among the partners but also within individual parties; by late 1955 the pivotal group of the coalition, the Radicals, were split into warring factions under the coalition's last two premiers, Pierre Mendès-France and Edgar Faure. In the hope of producing a new, more stable parliamentary line-up Faure dissolved the Assembly six months before its official termination and ordered new elections for January 1956.

Contrary to Faure's hope, these final elections of the Fourth Republic made parliamentary division still worse than before, and the *immobilisme* of government all the greater. After 1956 the good will of both the Socialists and conservative Independents simultaneously was necessary for a government to survive; the Assembly was that evenly fragmented.* One result, paradoxical in appearance, was that the deputies were reluctant to overthrow a cabinet because of the probable difficulty of forming a new one. The Socialist Guy Mollet, who formed the first government after the 1956 election, thus held office longer than any of his predecessors had done. But Mollet's tenure only testified to the stalemate

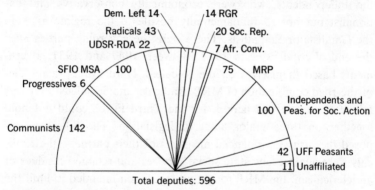

Divisions in the National Assembly as of April 15, 1958.

of parliament. In the accompanying diagram one may survey the numerical possibilities for a majority at the moment the crisis of May 13 broke out. But each of these possibilities demanded a unity that had become hard to achieve by 1958. One issue above all was to impede it—Algeria.

*The Radicals were now divided into three groups: the *Radical Party*, whose most prominent figure was Mendès-France; the *Rassemblement des Gauches républicaines* (RGR), under Mendès-France's rival Edgar Faure; and the Democratic Left, led by Henri Queuille and André Morice and distinguished by its support for an unyielding policy in Algeria. Between the Radical factions and the Socialists was still another group, the Democratic and Social Union of the Resistance (UDSR), a home for left-wing and mildly leftist leaders who did not possess strong organizational backing. François Mitterrand and René Pleven were the most notable of its members.

Abroad as well as at home the Fourth Republic faced harsh dilemmas between 1945 and 1958. Chief among them was the question of France's overseas possessions. Like the other postwar colonial powers, France had pledged herself to the improvement of her territories. De Gaulle had made this commitment even before the Liberation, at an imperial conference at Brazzaville in French Equatorial Africa, in 1944. In the 1946 constitution the French Empire became a French Union with an advisory council in Paris, and overseas subjects of France were granted the "quality of French citizen." But there were no measures in the direction of self-government. As the Brazzaville conference had declared, "the aims of the work of colonization which France is pursuing in her colonies exclude any idea of autonomy and any possibility of development outside the French empire *bloc*." Postwar experience was to show, however, that an ever greater number of French colonial subjects were to reject this assimilationist viewpoint of their masters.

Three postwar revolts in widely separated outposts of the French Union—Indochina in 1945, Algeria in 1945, Madagascar in 1947—showed the mood for independence. The latter two uprisings did not last long; the army repressed them quickly and with much loss of life among the native population. But the Indochinese revolution persisted until it became the consuming problem—and after the 1954 French defeat at Dien Bien Phu the most humiliating disaster—of French foreign policy in the decade after 1945. Dien Bien Phu and the subsequent Geneva Conference, granting Vietnamese independence, marked a turning point in French perspectives, a realization by many Frenchmen that sooner or later France would have to give self-government to her overseas possessions. This viewpoint found a champion in the Radical leader Pierre Mendès-France, who, as premier, had given up Indochina at the Geneva Conference rather than subject France to further losses of men in Southeast Asia. Under Mendès-France and his successor Edgar Faure, France granted virtual independence to the North African protectorates of Tunisia and Morocco in 1954 and

1955. But the change in outlook in Paris, whatever might have been its effect in Algeria, came too late for the Moslem nationalists of the FLN. On All Saints' Day, November 1, 1954, the National Liberation Front launched an armed revolt from strongholds in the Aurès Mountains.

Algeria was not legally a colony in 1954, but a part of France, with over a century of French settlement and history behind it. Algeria had been considered a possible refuge for the French government before the surrender to the Germans in 1940, and it had become the headquarters of de Gaulle's Free French movement of 1942–44. More than a million of the country's ten million inhabitants were Europeans, of Italian and Spanish as well as of French origin. A good percentage of them had been born and raised in North Africa. Although from the beginning of settlement the majority of Europeans had lived in the cities along or near the Mediterranean, many had begun their life in Algeria as farmers. They had worked hard under difficult conditions to make good on the North African land. They were largely successful, however, and from their effort and sacrifice, French Algerians, as the Europeans were called, derived the view that the settlers had made the country into what it was, that Algeria belonged to them fully as much as it belonged to the Moslems who were there when the first French arrived in 1830. Nevertheless, in spite of this historical picture, the drift of Europeans to the cities was a constant phenomenon. In 1956 only 12.5 per cent of them were occupied in agriculture, while 80 per cent lived in the cities—in particular, the three largest urban settlements: Algiers, Oran, and Constantine.

Europeans in Algeria had always had the rights of French citizenship. Before 1944 all but a small percentage of Moslems were not citizens, but only "subjects" and lived under a "native code." Wartime and postwar governments did away with these distinctions. The native code gave way to formal equality before the law in 1944; the division between citizen and subject disappeared with implementation of the 1946 Constitution. But the apparent equality guaranteed to Algeria remained weighted in favor of the Euro-

peans. Of the thirty deputies and fourteen senators Algeria sent to
the National Assembly, one half were elected by a Moslem electoral college. Had the Moslems elected as many deputies as their
numbers would have warranted in metropolitan France, they would
have had about one hundred out of about six hundred deputies.
Or to see the problem another way, had the Moslem electoral
college chosen a number of representatives proportionate to the
Moslem percentage of the Algerian population, they could have
chosen twenty-seven of the thirty deputies, and twelve or thirteen
senators. Similarly, in home rule, the Algerian Statute of 1947
granted the Moslems equality by race and not by numbers, that is,
permitted them to elect half the members of an all-Algerian Assembly. In practice there was not even equality by race, for in
1948 and 1951 the French rigged the elections to the Moslem
electoral college, which under the Statute was to choose the
Moslem members of the Algerian Assembly. Only following the
outbreak of the FLN revolt were there serious attempts at reform,
first under Jacques Soustelle, governor-general in 1955–56, then
under Guy Mollet and his resident minister for Algeria, Robert
Lacoste. The *loi-cadre* of 1958, which figures in the events of May
13, was the most recent of these reforms.

After 1954 the fundamental problem in Algeria was whether
there existed any solution for the country's future which could
appear equitable to both Europeans and Moslems. Most Europeans
felt they were modest people, not oppressors. But few would settle
for anything less collectively than an equal share of wealth and
power, notwithstanding the fact that the corresponding Moslem
share would have to be divided among nine times as many people.
For these Europeans the FLN's goal of independence—an Algeria
without the protection of France—posed an intolerable prospect.
Yet they were not able to defend themselves alone; once the rebellion had broken out, they had to rely on the government in
Paris. And relying on the regime, they lived in constant fear that
its resolve might weaken—a possibility that lurked each time a
new government had to be formed. "Abandonment" by metro-

politan France became the nightmare of the Europeans of Algeria. It was also a fate which most refused to accept passively. The Algerian problem was not only a question of what those in metropolitan France thought and did about Algeria. It also depended upon what Frenchmen in Algeria thought and did in regard to France.

It was only in 1956, under the government of Guy Mollet, that the French began an all-out effort to defeat the FLN and its guerrillas. Mollet hoped to secure a quick end to the rebellion by coupling the offer of a cease-fire with the application of overwhelming military force. To achieve this goal he took the politically sensitive step of sending draftee reservist units across the Mediterranean. Conscripts had never been sent to Indochina. Mollet's strategy allowed the army to take the offensive against the FLN, but it did not end the war, and metropolitan France began to feel the effects of the conflict. The war disrupted an already weak French financial situation, and it diverted funds from social projects desired at home. It took the lives of two hundred to three hundred French soldiers and police each month. And the war cost France sympathy abroad, even among her allies, and most hurtfully in the United States.

In 1958 the conflict in Algeria was a war that Frenchmen did not like and were not winning. However, it was also a war they did not want to lose. Militarily, the battle to seal the frontiers against infiltration from Tunisia and Morocco had succeeded the battle to secure Algiers from FLN terrorism, and the end of fighting was not in sight. Politically, peace seemed impossible to reach; the FLN refused any settlement short of independence, while no French government was ready to forsake its obligation to protect the Europeans and loyal Moslems among the population. The leaders of the Fourth Republic seemed incapable of breaking the stalemate in Algeria; the compromises of *immobilisme* stood in the way of new initiatives. In the National Assembly were reflected all the divisions and conflicting sentiments—the desires for both peace and victory—which precluded public consensus on Algerian policy.

Debate could quickly degenerate into accusations of betrayal. The premier who attempted to change existing policy immediately risked losing his majority, no matter whether he proposed more force or more negotiation. Until 1958 the Fourth Republic, with all its weaknesses, had overcome a succession of domestic and foreign crises. One of the chief problems of the Thirteenth of May is to understand how and why the Republic could not overcome the particular problem of Algeria.

Although Charles de Gaulle had turned his back on politics in 1953, by 1958 his name was figuring increasingly in speculation about Algeria and about the future of the Fourth Republic. For many Frenchmen de Gaulle offered an alternative preferable to the system of government then present. His desire for stronger executive powers in the constitution was well known; he appeared to stand for a French Algeria; and he possessed the trust of much of the army. De Gaulle, however, was reported to be pessimistic about his chances for a return to power. He had not commented publicly on the political situation in recent years, and he would not comment. Both friends and opponents, he complained, would misinterpret whatever he said. But while de Gaulle remained silent, his partisans were not so withdrawn. The General's abstention from politics contrasted with the activities of several important Gaullists, such as Jacques Soustelle, Michel Debré, and Léon Delbecque, who encouraged a tough policy in Algeria and the replacement of the Fourth Republic at home. De Gaulle certainly kept himself informed of these activities before May 13, and he maintained even closer touch with his allies once the revolt was under way, with Gaullists prominent in its leadership. At issue, however, remains the question of de Gaulle's participation and his aims. These sprang out of past courage, and past frustrations.

Few persons have made a more dramatic entrance onto the stage of their country's history than did Charles de Gaulle, speaking over BBC Radio on the evening of June 18, 1940, the day after his government had asked Nazi Germany for armistice terms.

But has the last word been said? Must we abandon all hope? Is our defeat final and irremediable? To these questions I answer—No! . . .

Mistakes have been made, there have been delays and untold suffering, but the fact remains that there still exists in the world everything we need to crush our enemies some day. Today we are crushed by the sheer weight of mechanized forces hurled against us, but we can still look to a future in which even greater mechanized force will bring us victory. The destiny of the world is at stake.

I, General de Gaulle, now in London, call on all French officers and men who are at present on British soil, or may be in the future, with or without their arms; I call on all engineers and skilled workmen from the armaments factories who are at present on British soil, or may be in the future, to get in touch with me.

Whatever happens, the flame of French resistance must not and shall not die.

The name of Charles de Gaulle was virtually unknown to the French public before June 18, 1940. But it was already familiar in military and some political circles. At the age of forty-nine, just promoted to brigadier, he was the youngest general in the French Army. Since June 7 he had belonged to the cabinet as Undersecretary of State for War, an appointment he owed to his most important political friend, Premier Paul Reynaud. De Gaulle was an unusual military type—not only a successful commanding officer but also a respected theorist and historian. He had been the pet of his future antagonist Marshal Pétain during the 1920's, and the subject of many glowing predictions by both other superiors and men of his own rank in the officer corps. De Gaulle, never a man of false modesty, was quite conscious that he might some day play a high role, and in his lectures in the late 1920's, later published as Le Fil de l'Épée (The Edge of the Sword), he appears to have been bringing together his conceptions of leadership. For de Gaulle, realism and aloofness characterized the great men of history. Great men knew how to listen to advice; they always kept themselves informed of the actual possibilities of their time and situation. But they sovereignly reserved decisions to themselves, and they de-

manded full loyalty in the execution of those decisions. As keys to
de Gaulle's later career, these ideas were just as important as his
more well-known advocacy of offensive mechanized warfare. De
Gaulle was prepared for leadership when the opportunity to lead
came to him.

In 1940 de Gaulle was ready to give way to other government
leaders, should they escape from France to carry on the fight from
overseas. But none came, and so he continued at the head of what
was initially called the Fighting French movement. In the early
stages of his leadership he acted in effect as the defender of the
Third Republic—the legal government as opposed to the Vichy
regime which had been established in France following the armistice. From 1942, however, he advocated the creation after the war
of a new, purified Fourth Republic. Despite the roadblocks put up
by the Americans and British, he gradually became the undisputed
leader of all his anti-Vichy compatriots. The creation in 1941 of a
French National Committee under his presidency established his
control over Frenchmen abroad, while he secured pre-eminence
within France through an agreement with the underground National
Council of Resistance in June 1942. The Allies might wish to ignore the supremacy he was winning, but Frenchmen did not. In
1943 he went one step further toward a true government-in-exile
by combining the French National Committee and the liberated
North African administration into a French Committee of National
Liberation, based at Algiers. A year later he re-entered France as
head of the Provisional Government, with a position too strong for
the Allies or the French Communists, the strongest Resistance
group, to challenge. As we have seen, the 1945 Constituent Assembly confirmed de Gaulle as head of the Republic. But he was
already unhappy in office when he received this vote, and a few
months later, in January 1946, he resigned.

In the years after 1946, de Gaulle's perspectives on the world
remained a mixture of the old and the new. Alongside his inde-
finable faith in France was a recognition, not shared by all his
critics, of the importance of technological advancement. Tech-

nology was not an end in itself for de Gaulle. It was a means
enabling the state to maintain its independence, and in de Gaulle's
view, the independent state was still the basic element of politics.
Without a state free to go its own way, no people could be its own
master or follow its own promptings. Technological advancement,
with its dividends in industrial power and weaponry, was one
guarantee of independence. Complementing it there had to be a
political order which allowed the state to employ its power:
France's government had to give a strong hand to the executive. In
his speech at Bayeux in June 1946, during the interval between
the defeat of the first draft constitution and the drawing up of the
second, de Gaulle gave perhaps the fullest description of the constitutional order he desired. It is clear from this address how little
the constitution adopted the following October could have pleased
him.

De Gaulle hoped that the RPF could become the instrument of
the reforms he desired. But the RPF was ultimately a failure, and
in 1953 de Gaulle quit politics. He withdrew to his estate, La
Boisserie, at Colombey-les-Deux-Églises; he wrote his memoirs; he
visited some of France's overseas territories. Previous to the events
of the Thirteenth of May, his most recent public statements had
been at a press conference on June 30, 1955.

In the first volume of his *War Memoirs,* published in 1954,
Charles de Gaulle suggested that Providence had created France
to undergo either brilliant successes or exemplary misfortunes.
Whether or not they expressed the workings of Providence, the
1950's were a time of misfortunes for France. The parliamentary
regime was in trouble, criticized as ineffective and unresponsive to
the nation; the democratic liberties the Fourth Republic guaranteed seemed not to count against the shortcomings many Frenchmen found in their government. Abroad, the Fourth Republic had
extracted itself from one trauma of decolonization, only to fall into
another, more serious one. If these difficulties were not enough, the
nation was also discovering an army increasingly at odds with its
civilian leaders, increasingly restive as the instrument of policies

which it neither influenced nor controlled. France had become the proverbial "sick man of Europe."

At his final press conference, de Gaulle had concluded: *"Au revoir, messieurs, à longtemps!"* In the documents which follow, we may see why it was not so long until he faced the press—and the nation—once again.

Suggested Readings

The Fourth Republic
Jacques Fauvet. *La Quatrième République*. Paris, 1959.
Stanley Hoffmann et al. *In Search of France*. Cambridge, Mass., 1963.
Herbert Luethy. *France Against Herself*. Translated by Eric Mosbacher. New York, 1955.
Duncan MacRae, Jr. *Parliament, Parties and Society in France 1946–1958*. New York, 1967.
David Thomson. *Democracy in France Since 1870*. Fourth Edition. New York and London, 1964.
Philip M. Williams. *Crisis and Compromise: Politics in the Fourth Republic*. Hamden, Conn., 1964.

The Army
John Steward Ambler. *The French Army in Politics, 1945–1962*. Columbus, Ohio, 1966.
George Armstrong Kelly. *Lost Soldiers: The French Army and Empire in Crisis, 1947–1962*. Cambridge, Mass., 1965.
Paul Marie de La Gorce. *The French Army: A Military-Political History*. Translated by Kenneth Douglas. New York, 1963.
Jean Lartéguy. *The Centurions*. Translated by Xan Fielding. New York, 1962.
———. *The Praetorians*. Translated by Xan Fielding. New York, 1963.

Algeria
Michael K. Clark. *Algeria in Turmoil: A History of the Rebellion*. New York, 1959.
Albert Memmi. *The Colonizer and the Colonized*. Translated by Howard Greenfield. Boston, 1967.

Dorothy Pickles. *Algeria and France: From Colonialism to Cooperation*. New York, 1963.

Jules Roy. *The War in Algeria*. Translated by Richard Howard. New York, 1961.

Jean-Jacques Servan-Schreiber. *Lieutenant in Algeria*. Translated from the French by Ronald Matthews. New York, 1957.

Germaine Tillion. *France and Algeria: Complementary Enemies*. Translated by Richard Howard. New York, 1961.

De Gaulle

A. W. DePorte. *De Gaulle's Foreign Policy 1944–1946*. Cambridge, Mass., 1968.

Jean Lacouture. *De Gaulle*. Translated by Francis K. Price. New York, 1966.

David Schoenbrun. *The Three Lives of Charles de Gaulle*. New York, 1966.

Jean-Raymond Tournoux. *Sons of France: Pétain and De Gaulle*. Translated by Oliver Coburn. New York, 1966.

The Thirteenth of May

Merry and Serge Bromberger. *Les Treize Complots du Treize Mai*. Paris, 1959.

Jean Ferniot. *De Gaulle et le Treize Mai*. Paris, 1965.

Alexander Werth. *The de Gaulle Revolution*. London, 1960.

Motion Picture

The Battle of Algiers. Screenplay by Franco Solinas and Gillo Pontecorvo. Directed by Gillo Pontecorvo. Produced by Antonio Muso-Igor Films of Rome, 1966.

I
"THE BANKRUPTCY OF ILLUSIONS"

Introduction

The selections of this first section introduce us to the Fourth Republic as it labors through from its early days to the Algerian war. In style as well as content General de Gaulle's *War Memoirs* are noteworthy for what they reveal of their author and his views of France's problems; and in the context of the Thirteenth of May they are particularly interesting for de Gaulle's description of his "departure" in January 1946—a subject to which both the General and others frequently referred in 1958. De Gaulle's major constitutional pronouncement, the Bayeux speech of June 1946, appears immediately before the 1946 Constitution, and the sequence invites a comparison. How the Fourth Republic worked— or appeared to work—in practice is conveyed by the "Letters from Paris" of Janet Flanner (Genêt), a longtime observer of French affairs.

The programs of the three heads of government and the following summary of the 1958 *loi-cadre* illuminate the Algerian problem. As the new foundation for government in Algeria, the *loi-cadre* deserves particular examination. It was meant to appeal to both French and Moslem Algerians. Whether it could do so depended, however, on the degree of real change it would produce in Algerian institutions and on the effect of the single electoral college, which departed from the former practice of separate balloting by

27

Europeans and Moslems. It was France's political pacification program—discussed interminably during 1957. But when the *loi-cadre*
was finally passed under Gaillard, could it still be effective? How
much change did it indicate France could allow in Algeria?

Charles de Gaulle: Disunion and Departure

The road to greatness lay open before us, but what condition France
was in to follow it! While the reactions from every part of the globe,
the conversations with statesmen, the ovations of foreign crowds conveyed the world's appeal to France, the graphs and statistics laid on
my desk, the reports furnished by our services, the spectacle of devas-
tation offered by our territory, the councils, where I heard our ministers describing the extent of our misery and the penury of our means,
gave me the measure of our debilitation. No power now contested our
right to play a major role in the world's destiny. But at home, France's
condition was expressed in a balance sheet of ruins.

One third of our nation's wealth had been annihilated. In all forms,
in all regions, devastations covered our territory. Naturally, that of
buildings was the most spectacular. As a result of the battles of 1940,
later the Allied bombings and finally the liberation itself, 500,000
buildings had been completely destroyed, 1,500,000 seriously damaged.
It was the factories which had chiefly suffered, causing an additional
delay in our economic recovery. We also lacked housing for six million
Frenchmen. And what could be said of the ruined railway terminals,
the lines cut, the bridges exploded, the canals blocked, the harbors
choked? The engineers whom I asked for an estimate of the time
necessary to restore our edifices and communications replied, "It will
take twenty years!" As for the land, a million hectares had been reduced to nonproductivity, spoiled by explosions, strewn with mines,
pitted with entrenchments; fifteen million more yielded scarcely anything, since our farmers had been unable to cultivate them properly
for five years. Everywhere there was a shortage of tools, fertilizers,
plants and seeds. The livestock was reduced by half.

Though less apparent, the damages caused by theft were heavier
still. We had been pillaged, so to speak, regularly. In the text of the

From Chapters 6 and 7 of *The War Memoirs of Charles de Gaulle*, Volume III,
Salvation 1944–1946. Translated from the French by Richard Howard. Copy-
right 1959–60 by Charles de Gaulle. Reprinted by permission of the publisher,
Simon and Schuster, Inc.

"armistice," the Germans had specified that the "expenses of the occupation troops will be met by the French government." Under this rubric the enemy had laid hold of exorbitant sums, thanks to which he not only supported his armies, but also purchased (with our money) and shipped to Germany huge quantities of machinery and consumer goods. Further, a so-called "compensation agreement" had imposed on the French treasury the settlement of the differences between the value of the exports "freely made" to Germany and the cost of imports of coal and raw materials the Reich sent to France to supply the factories it was maintaining in operation for its own advantage. Since there were virtually no such exports and, on the other hand, such imports continued to be considerable, the "agreement" had been a terrible burden for us. In addition, all kinds of German purchases on the black market, partial requisitions, local fines, and qualified thefts had completed the spoliation of France. And how evaluate the millions of days of labor imposed on French workmen to the enemy's profit and diverted from our production, the lowering of physical value inflicted on our people by undernourishment, the fact that during five years everything in France had deteriorated without our being able to maintain, repair, renew? All in all, the occupation cost us more than 2,000 billion 1938 francs, that is, 80,000 billion today. Peace found our economy deprived of a large part of its means of production, our finances crushed beneath a colossal public debt, our budgets condemned to bear the enormous expenses of reconstruction for a long time.

This disappearance of our resources and instruments of labor was all the more ruinous in that it followed close upon the ravages of the First World War. The interval of twenty years between the end of the First and the start of the Second had not been long enough for us to recoup our lost wealth. In particular, the accumulated capital the French possessed in France and abroad before 1914 had evaporated, while the 500 million shells we fired from the Somme to the Vosges exploded over a period of fifty-one months. To reconstruct, afterward, all that had been destroyed, to pension off the wounded, widows and orphans, to pay the war's innumerable expenses, we had been forced to borrow continually, to devaluate our currency, to abandon renovation and modernization projects. In 1939, it was a poverty-stricken, outmoded France who entered the conflict; and in the course of the latest ordeal, a large share of what remained had been engulfed. To bind up her wounds and repair her ruins once again, she had only minimum reserves at her disposal and a cruelly reduced credit. How manage if we were reduced to our own poor means? How maintain independence if we had recourse to others?

In this as in all domains, what we lacked could be compensated for, up to a point, by human values. But our losses were heavy here too. More than 635,000 Frenchmen had died as a result of enemy action, 250,000 in combat, 160,000 in bombardments or executed by the occupiers, 150,000 victims of maltreatment in concentration camps, 75,000 as prisoners of war or forced laborers. Further 585,000 men had become invalids. In relation to the total population, the percentage of French losses had not reached that of the Germans or the Russians. But it was higher than that of the British, the Italians, or the Americans. Most important, the losses suffered by our nation were relatively higher than the figures indicated. For it was among our scant youth that death had reaped this harvest. Again, during the First World War, twice the number of victims had fallen—that is, the highest proportion among all the belligerents—and at a period when our birth rate was the lowest in the world. In sum, the French people, their average age the highest among nations and their death rate the only one to exceed the birth rate since the beginning of the century, not yet having made good the losses of the preceding hecatomb, had just suffered an extremely critical amputation of its rare active elements. Indeed those it had lost were the most enterprising, the most generous, the finest of its number.

In addition, the diminution of substance and consequently of power inflicted upon France during two world wars had only accentuated the abasement she had suffered in the space of two human lifetimes. At the beginning of the last century—quite recently, in historical terms—our country was the most populous in Europe, the strongest and richest in the world, and her influence unequaled. But disastrous causes had combined to drive her from this dominant position and to start her down a slope where each generation saw her stumble lower. Mutilated of the territories nature intended her to have, grotesquely costumed in artificial frontiers, separated from a third of the population springing from her stock, France had been living for a hundred and thirty years in a chronic state of infirmity, insecurity and acrimony. When the economic capacity of the great nations depended chiefly on coal, France had virtually none. Subsequently, when petroleum controlled everything else, France had been without any supply of her own. During the same period population doubled in England, tripled in Germany and in Italy, quadrupled in Russia, decupled in America; in France it remained stationary.

This physical decline went hand in hand with a moral depression. The disasters which put an end to Napoleon Bonaparte's attempt at hegemony and later the defeat inflicted upon the nation by the might of Prussia and her German satellites had submerged the French beneath such waves of humiliation that henceforth they were to doubt themselves. Certainly the 1918 victory revived their faith, for a moment. But it cost so dear and bore fruits so bitter that such hopes died at once under the shock of 1940. The soul of France died a little more. Thanks to the wakening of the resistance and to the miracle of our victory, it still survived, but lame and, so to speak, sclerotic. Moreover, so many disasters had not failed to inflict terrible wounds upon national unity. Fifteen regimes had supervened since 1789, each in turn installed by revolution or *coup d'état,* none succeeding in insuring equilibrium, all swept away by catastrophes and leaving ineffaceable divisions behind them.

And today I was at the head of a ruined, decimated, lacerated nation, surrounded by ill will. Hearing my voice, France had been able to unite and march to her liberation. She had subsequently accepted such order until the war was over. Meanwhile, the nation had gladly received the reforms which spared it social strife and permitted its recovery. Lastly, it had permitted me to carry out the foreign activity which assured the recovery of its status. This was a great step, in relation to the disasters that had almost engulfed us. But it was minuscule in comparison to all that we must achieve before recovering our power, without which we would ultimately lose even our reasons to exist.

I had conceived a plan which was nothing more than common sense. First, we must procure what we had so long lacked in respect to sources of energy. As for coal, union with the Saar, now virtually accomplished, and the annual fifty million tons we were about to obtain from the Ruhr would afford us twice what our own mines produced. As for petroleum, there was every likelihood that the research group we had just established would discover reserves in the immense French possessions, since we had territories in each of the world's major geographical groups. As for the nascent atomic energy production, the resources of uranium which seemed abundant in our territories, as well as our scientific and industrial capacities, offered us an opportunity of reaching an exceptional level. The High Commission created to this effect was to get the project under way. Further, and whatever our actual penury, a careful policy of modernization and supply would replace our outmoded machinery. The High Commission on Planning had charge of this task. But of all our projects, those tending to increase the population were the most necessary; the measures already taken—assistance to families, allowances—would henceforth produce their effects. Finally, the social harmony to be established by the association of capital, labor and technology, the national independence maintained in any event, could cause a climate favorable to pride and effort to prevail in France.

Our country was in a position to achieve these goals if it remained united and the state led it forward. For how could it advance if it were divided against itself, if it were not guided in its progress by an authentic government? Yet, as France became free again, I realized with chagrin that her political forces were making great efforts to divide her and that on various levels everything was attempting to sever the nation from me.

I had every apparent justification for prolonging the sort of monarchy which I had recently assumed and which the general consent had subsequently confirmed. But the French people was itself, and not any other; if it did not desire such a regime nothing could impose it. To what upheavals would I condemn France by claiming to impose my absolute authority officially and for an unlimited period, once the danger which had put it into my hands had vanished? During the conflict, my declarations had deliberately left no doubt as to my resolution to restore its power to the French people once events would permit elections. If my power had been increasingly recognized, it was to a large degree because of this commitment. To refuse to fulfill it now would stamp my mission with a fraudulent seal. But it would also gradually turn against me the nation which would no longer distinguish the reasons for this despotic action; the Communists, then at the peak of their energy and influence, would gain control of the opposition and simultaneously designate themselves as my necessary successors.

Opposition would be all the more certain since, save in periods of public danger, there can be no such thing as a lasting dictatorship, unless a single faction, resolved to overpower the rest, supports it against all comers. As the champion of France rather than of any class or party, I incited hatred against no one and had no clientele who favored me in order to be favored in return. Even the men of the resistance, if they remained emotionally loyal to the ideal that once united them, had already, to a large degree, abandoned me politically and split into various factions. Only the Army could furnish me the means of controlling the country by constraining the recalcitrant elements. But this military omnipotence, established by force in peacetime, would soon appear unjustifiable to adherents of every tendency.

Fundamentally, what was, what could be dictatorship's resource if not great national ambition or the fear of a people imperiled by foreign powers? France had had two empires. She acclaimed the first when she felt capable of dominating Europe and when she was exhausted by disorder and confusion. She consented to the second in her desire to efface the humiliation of treaties which had sealed her defeat and in the agony recent social upheavals had forced upon her. Yet how had each of these Caesarean regimes ended? Today, no conquest, no revenge tempted our citizens; the mass of the people feared neither invasion nor revolution. Public safety was now a *fait accompli,* and I had no desire to maintain the momentary dictatorship which I had exercised in the course of the storm and which I would not fail to prolong or resume if the nation were in danger. Therefore, as I had promised, I would let the people make their choice in a general election.

Yet even as I dismissed the notion of my own despotism, I was no less convinced that the nation required a regime whose power would be strong and continuous. The parties were evidently unqualified to provide such power. Apart from the Communists, who intended to dominate by any means whatever, whose government would ultimately be infiltrated by an alien organization, who would find in France the resolute support of a portion of the population and of the Soviets abroad, but who would bring France to servitude, I observed that no political formation was in a position to assure the leadership of the nation and of the state. Although some among them could obtain the votes of an important fraction of the citizens, not a single one was thought of as representing public interest as a whole. Each would gather only the voices of a minority, and many electors would vote not so much *for* one party as *against* the others. In short, no organization commanded either the power or the credit which would permit it to lay claim to national authority.

To the parties' fractional character, which infected them with weakness, was added their own decadence. The latter was still concealed beneath rhetoric, but the doctrinal passion which was once their source, their attraction and their greatness could not be maintained in a period of materialism so indifferent to ideals. No longer inspired by principles, no longer ambitious to proselytize since they found no audiences on these grounds, they were inevitably tending to degradation, shrinking until each became nothing more than the representation of a cate-

gory of interests. If the government fell into their hands again, it was
certain that their leaders, their delegates and their militant members
would turn into professionals making a career out of politics. The
conquest of public functions, of influential positions, of administrative
sinecures would henceforth absorb the parties and limit their activities
to what they called tactics, which was nothing more than the practice
of compromise and denial. Since all were minority representatives,
they would have to share the positions of command with their rivals
in order to accede to them at all. As a result they would proceed by
giving themselves the lie in relation to the electorate. While the constant juxtaposition, within the government, of conflicting groups and
men could result only in impotence.

As for me, considering France's immediate political realities and the
extent and difficulty of the state's task, I had determined what the
desirable institutions had to be; to realize them, I had naturally taken
into account the lessons of our recent disaster, still so painful, as well
as my experience of men and affairs, and lastly the role which events
enabled me to play in the establishment of the Fourth Republic.

As I saw it, the state must have a head, that is, a leader in whom
the nation could see beyond its own fluctuations, a man in charge of
essential matters and the guarantor of its fate. It was also necessary
that this executive, destined to serve only the national community, not
originate in the parliament which united the delegations of particular
interests. These conditions implied that the chief of state not belong to
a party, that he be designated by the people, that he be empowered to
appoint the Cabinet, that he possess the right to consult the nation,
either by referendum or by election of assemblies, that he receive,
finally, the mandate of insuring the integrity and independence of
France in case of danger. Beyond those circumstances when it would
be the President's duty to intervene publicly, government and parliament would collaborate, the latter controlling the former and authorized to cause its fall, but the national magistrate exercising his arbitration and having recourse to that of the people.

I could not overlook the fact that my project contradicted the
claims of every party. None among them, whether by conviction or
precaution, had as yet dared to oppose De Gaulle. Some who already expressed criticism and admonishment still refrained from
challenging him outright. The Communists themselves, while brandishing trumpets and drums, were careful not to cross swords with me.
But it was clear that in the crucial debate that was approaching, discord was inevitable. With various qualifications, all the parties intended
the future constitution to re-create a regime whose powers would

depend directly and exclusively on themselves and in which De Gaulle would have no place, unless he were willing to be merely a figurehead. In this regard, the lessons of the past, the realities of the present, the threats of the future had absolutely no effect on their point of view and their demands.

That the Third Republic had constantly failed to achieve equilibrium, finally collapsing in an abyss of capitulation, gave each party reasons to attack the others in its own behalf, but not the necessity to abjure the same weaknesses. That France could not re-establish herself with the cohesion of her people, the abnegation of factions, and the leadership of a recognized and continuous authority was a principle altogether alien to their universe. For them, on the contrary, it was a matter of opposing all competitors, of provoking those passions and claims by which they could support themselves, of seizing power not so much to serve the entire nation as to fasten their own particular program to it. That De Gaulle, having succeeded in uniting the nation and leading it to salvation, should now be kept at its head was not the way they envisioned the future, though they were careful to lavish their praises upon him now. For tomorrow, they conceded, his withdrawal could not occur without certain transitions. They even attempted to create some sort of decorative position to which he could be relegated. Yet none of them supposed that leadership could long remain in the hands of a person whose mere presence was evidently incompatible with their regime.

Nonetheless, though I did not expect the spontaneous support of the parties, it seemed conceivable to me that the nation's instinct and the confidence it had hitherto accorded me were sufficiently manifest to oblige the "politicians" to swim with the current. It was my task to sound out French opinion as to whether the state should be constructed as I proposed. If they responded affirmatively, the parties would adapt themselves to it, and the new Republic would have my participation. If not, I would not fail to draw the consequences.

But if I had always intended that the people should ultimately make the decision, I felt no less doubt and anxiety as to the result. For was this people, beneath the moving proofs of affection it lavished upon me which nevertheless expressed its distress as much as its affection—was this people not exhausted, discouraged, divided? And as for these enormous enterprises, this vigorous action, these strong institutions which I proposed to its effort, did they not exceed its means and its desires? And I myself—had I the capacity, the skill, the eloquence necessary to galvanize them, when everything was sinking into mediocrity? Yet, whatever the nation's eventual answer to the question which would be put to it, it was my duty, while I waited, to govern with all the authority it had accorded me. . . .

The 1946 budget was under discussion. For form's sake the government insisted that the final vote be taken on January first. But on that day, as the discussion seemed to draw to a close, the Socialists suddenly demanded a 20 per cent reduction of the credits assigned to National Defense. It was obvious that so sudden and summary a proposition, directed against an order of expenditures which evidently could not be reduced to such proportions from one day to the next, was inspired by both electoral demagogy and hostility toward me.

Since I was detained in the Rue St.-Dominique on New Year's Day by the visits of the diplomatic corps and the authorities, the Palais Bourbon debate dragged on without reaching an outcome. Though Minister of Finance Pleven, Minister of the Armies Michelet, Minister of Armament Tillon and Minister of State Auriol followed my instructions and declared that the government rejected the proposition, the Left—Socialists, Communists and the majority of the Radicals—which together comprised the majority, was prepared to vote it through. However, and as if to prove that the real issue was De Gaulle, the Assembly postponed any conclusion until I came in person to take part in the discussion.

I did so during the afternoon. In my presence, Messrs. Philip and Gazier led the attack with passion, supported by the applause of their Socialist colleagues, the Radicals counting the blows. Actually, the challengers protested their intention was not to destroy the government; they were taking action, they said, only to oblige it to yield before the parliamentary will. The Popular Republicans made it clear that they did not approve the aggression launched against me on such grounds, while the Right voiced its anxiety, but these fractions of the Assembly were careful not to condemn the opposition in explicit terms. As for the Communists, hesitating between the immediate imperative of demagogy and their tactics of the moment, they informed me that the assault had not been made with their agreement, but that if the Socialists were to bring the matter to vote, they themselves would be obliged to deny me their support.

That evening, probing hearts and hopes, I realized that the matter was already decided, that it would be vain and even unworthy to presume to govern when the parties, their power restored, had resumed their old tricks; in short, that I must now prepare my own departure from the scene.

In two brief interventions, I indicated to the Assembly the absurdity of the constraint they hoped to impose upon me and the frivolity with which the representatives of the people were preparing to cut into the national defense in order to give themselves the advantage of a partisan maneuver. Then, proceeding to the heart of the matter, I declared that this debate posed the entire problem of tomorrow's institutions. Once the government, acting in full knowledge of the case, had assumed its responsibility in so serious a matter, was it acceptable that the parliament should now wish to oblige it to contradict and humiliate itself? Were we imitating the regime of the Assembly? For my part, I refused to do so. If the credits requested were not voted that same evening, the government would not remain in office another hour.

"I should like to add a word," I said, "which is not for the present but, even now, for the future. The point that divides us is a general conception of the government and its relations with the national representation. We have begun to reconstruct the Republic. After me, you will continue to do so. I must tell you in all conscience—and doubtless this is the last time I shall be speaking to you from this place—that if you do not take into account the absolute necessities of governmental authority, dignity and responsibility, you will find yourselves in a situation which I predict will cause you bitter regret for having taken the way you have chosen."

As if the opposition wished to emphasize the fact that its attitude had been nothing but ruse and palinode, it suddenly fell silent. The order of the day, adopted virtually unanimously by the Assembly, imposed no conditions upon me. After which, the budget was passed without difficulty. But although my defeat had not been accomplished, the mere fact that it had appeared possible produced a profound effect. My government had been breached by the majority during a threat-crammed debate. Henceforth, perhaps, the same effect could be accomplished apropos of virtually any issue. It was apparent that if De Gaulle tolerated this situation in order to remain in office, his prestige would decline, until one day the parties would either no longer tolerate him or else relegate him to some harmless and decorative function. But I had neither the right nor the inclination to lend myself to such calculations. As I left the Palais Bourbon on the evening of January 1, I had determined upon my departure from office. All that remained was to select the date, without making any concessions whatever.

Certainly it would be before the end of the month. For the constitutional debate would then begin, and I was convinced that by remain-

ing in the nascent regime I would not have the possibility of imposing
my views nor even of supporting them. The draft which the committee created by the Constituent Assembly had prepared was precisely the converse of what I considered necessary, instituting as it did
the absolute government of a single and sovereign Assembly; the
executive having no other role than to apply what was prescribed; the
President of the Council being elected by the parliament and permitted to form his Cabinet only after passing a thorough examination
as to his tendencies and platform and assuming commitments which
would severely bind him beforehand. As for the President of the Republic, it was agreed, after many hesitations, that there might be one,
though he must be deprived of any political role and not have the
slightest effect on the machinery of state—in other words, be the
prisoner of his insipid symbolic function. This was probably the position intended for General de Gaulle by those who were calling the
tune. Moreover, the committeemen, as well as the parties, were careful
not to have any communication with me on the subject. Once, when I
summoned the chairman, M. François de Menthon, to inquire as to
the progress made, I was told that the Assembly and its committee
considered that I was not to participate in the debate, since I was not
a member myself. Under such conditions, to attempt to pursue my
goals in this crucial area as in all other respects, would be to invite
impotence and insult. . . .

Where was I to go? Contemplating the prospect of my resignation
from office, I had resolved to live in Colombey-les-deux-Eglises, and
had begun repairing my war-damaged house with this in mind. But
these arrangements would take several months. At first I thought of
traveling to some distant region where I could wait in peace. But the
tide of insult and invective launched against me by political dens and
the majority of newspapers determined me to remain in Metropolitan
France so that no one could suppose such attacks had affected me. I
therefore rented the Pavillon de Marly from the Service des Beaux
Arts, and lived there until May.

Nevertheless, while the regime's personnel gave itself up to the
euphoria of old habits regained, the mass of the French people, on the
contrary, sank back into distress. Gone was that atmosphere of exaltation, that hope of success, that ambition for France, which supported
the national soul. Every Frenchman, whatever his tendencies, had the
troubling suspicion that with the General vanished something primordial, permanent and necessary which he incarnated in history and

which the regime of parties could not represent. In the sidetracked leader, men persisted in seeing a kind of capital of sovereignty, a last resort selected in advance. They supposed such legitimacy could remain latent in a period without anxiety. But they knew it could be invoked by common consent as soon as a new laceration threatened the nation.

My attitude, through the years, would be dictated by this mission which France continued to assign me, even when, in the immediate circumstances, many tendencies did not follow me. Whatever I said or was made to say, my words, real or supposed, would pass into the public domain. All those I dealt with reacted as if, invested with the supreme authority, I had received them in the national palaces. Wherever I happened to make an appearance, those present would burst into ardent manifestations.

It was this atmosphere which enveloped me during the course of the first public action I took once I had abandoned my official status; I made a speech in Bayeux, describing what our institutions should be. I spoke on many subsequent occasions, condemning the constitution wrung from the country's lassitude; appealing to the French people to unite in order to change the bad regime; launching ideas to deal with the future from many platforms; appearing before crowds in every French and Algerian department, at least twice in each and more in some, in order to keep the spark alight and to make contact with many affecting loyalties. It was these same tributes which were lavished upon me after 1952, when I determined to withdraw from the situation as it stood, the disease being too advanced for any remedy to affect it before the inevitable upheaval; when I occasionally presided at some ceremony; when I visited our territories in Africa and the Indian Ocean, traveling around the world from one French territory to the next, watching the oil gushers being brought in in the Sahara. At the moment of finishing this book, I feel the same countless hearts turning toward my simple house.

This is my home. In the tumult of men and events, solitude was my temptation; now it is my friend. What other satisfaction can be sought once you have confronted history? Moreover, this section of Champagne is imbued with calm—wide, mournful horizons; melancholy woods and meadows; the frieze of resigned old mountains; tranquil, unpretentious villages where nothing has changed its spirit or its place for thousands of years. All this can be seen from my village. Situated high on the plateau, near a wooded hill, it weathers the centuries among the fields cultivated by its inhabitants. The latter, though

I am careful not to force myself upon them, surround me with their discreet friendship. I know their families, I respect and love them.

Silence fills my house. From the corner room where I spend most of my daylight hours, I look out far into the west. There is nothing to obstruct my view for some fifteen kilometers. Above the plain and the woods, my eyes follow the long slopes descending toward the valley of the Aube, then the heights of the slope opposite. From a rise in the garden, I look down on the wild depths where the forest envelops the tilled land like the sea beating on a promontory. I watch the night cover the landscape. Then, looking up at the stars, I steep myself in the insignificance of earthly things.

Of course letters, the radio, the newspapers bring news of our world into this hermitage. During brief visits to Paris, I receive visitors, whose remarks reveal the course of men and events. During vacations, our children and grandchildren surround us, with the exception of our daughter Anne, who left this world before us. But how many hours slip by in reading, writing, dreaming, when no illusion sweetens my bitter serenity.

Yet, on our little property—I have walked around it fifteen thousand times—the trees, stripped by the cold, rarely fail to turn green again, and the flowers my wife has planted bloom once more each spring. The village houses are decrepit, but suddenly laughing girls and boys come out of their doors. When I walk to one of the nearby woods—Les Dhuits, Clairvaux, Le Heu, Blinfeix, La Chapelle—their solemn depths fill me with nostalgia; but suddenly the song of a bird, the sun through the leaves, or the buds of a thicket remind me that ever since it has existed on earth, life wages a battle it has never lost. Then I feel a secret solace passing through me. Since everything eternally begins anew, what I have done will sooner or later be a source of new ardor after I have gone.

As age triumphs, nature comes closer to me. Each year, in the four seasons which are as so many lessons, I find consolation in her wisdom. In spring she sings: "Whatever has happened, I am in the beginning! All is bright, even the snow flurries; young, even the wizened trees; beautiful, even the stony fields. Love raises the sap within me and with it certitudes so radiant and powerful they will never end!"

And in summer she proclaims: "Consider the glory of my fruitfulness. Striving, everything that nourishes life comes from me. Each life depends on my warmth. These seeds, these fruits, these herds the sun now floods with light are a victory nothing can destroy. Henceforth, the future belongs to me!"

In autumn, she sighs: "My task is near its term. I have given my flowers, my harvests, my fruits. Now, I retire within myself. See how beautiful I am still in my robe of purple and gold, beneath the brilliant sun. Alas, the winds and the frosts will soon tear away my vestments. But one day, upon my naked body, my youth will flower again!"

In winter, she moans: "Here I lie, barren and frozen. How many plants, animals and birds have I created and loved, who die now on my breast that can no longer feed or warm them! Then is my destiny sealed? Is death's the victory forever? No! Already, deep in my inert soil, a secret labor is being accomplished. Motionless in the heart of darkness, I foresee the marvelous return of light and life!"

Old Earth, worn by the ages, wracked by rain and storm, exhausted yet ever ready to produce what life must have to go on!

Old France, weighed down with history, prostrated by wars and revolutions, endlessly vacillating from greatness to decline, but revived, century after century, by the genius of renewal!

Old man, exhausted by ordeal, detached from human deeds, feeling the approach of the eternal cold, but always watching in the shadows for the gleam of hope!

Speech Delivered by General de Gaulle at Bayeux, June 16, 1946

In our beloved Normandy, glorious and maimed, Bayeux and the country surrounding it were witnesses of some of the greatest events in history. And they proved themselves worthy of them. Here, four years after the initial disaster of France and the Allies, the final stages of the victory of the Allies and of France began. The efforts of those who never yielded and around whom, since June 18, 1940, was gathered all that was best in the nation and that reforged the power of France, found their justification here at last.

It is here, also, on the soil of our ancestors, that the state was reborn! A legitimate state, since it was founded on the interests and the feelings of the nation; a state whose true sovereignty was born of war, liberty and victory, whilst servitude only had the appearance of it; a state upheld in its rights, its dignity and its authority in the midst of its vicissitudes of destitution and intrigues; a state saved from the interference of foreign powers; a state which was able to gather round itself again a united nation and a united Empire, to reassemble all the forces of the country and of the French Union and to carry itself to final victory together with its allies, to treat as an equal with the other great nations of the world, to maintain public order, to mete out justice and finally to begin the reconstruction of the country.

If this great work was carried on outside the earlier pattern of government, it was because the old pattern did not correspond to the needs of the nation and so had ceased to be operative in the general turmoil. Salvation was to come from another direction.

This came, at first, from a chosen few, sprung spontaneously from the heart of the nation who set aside any feelings of party or class and devoted themselves to the struggle for freedom and the greatness and the rehabilitation of France. A feeling of moral superiority, an almost religious sense of sacrifice and example, a love of risk and adventure, scorn of danger, of other claims and of being outbid, complete confidence in the strength and cunning of their mighty conspiracy as well as in the victory and the future of France, these were the heartfelt feelings of those chosen few. They sprang from nothing and despite heavy losses, led the Empire and all of France.

Their work would not have succeeded, however, without the approval of the whole French population. The people, with an instinctive desire for survival and victory, never saw the disaster of 1940 as anything other than a single vicissitude of the World War, in which France served as the vanguard. Though many bowed before the storm, there were very few who accepted the fact of defeat in their heart of hearts. France never thought for a moment that the enemy could be a friend; she never believed that her salvation could be achieved by anything other than the forces of freedom. As veil after veil was torn away, the people of the country saw the true dawn. Wherever the Cross of Lorraine was hoisted, the whole scaffolding of an authority which, though apparently founded on the Constitution was only ephemeral, crumbled away. It is a truism that power is worth nothing, *de facto* or *de jure*, unless it corresponds with the highest interests of the country and unless it is backed by confident support from the citizens. Unless the Constitution is built on this basis it might as well be built on sand. There would always be the risk of seeing the edifice collapse once more at the time of one of the crises to which, by nature, our country is often exposed.

For this reason, once the safety of the state was assured by its victory and the unity of the nation was upheld, the greatest and most

urgent task of all became the establishment of a new French Constitution. As soon as it was possible, the people of France were invited
to elect their representatives, fixing a limit to their mandate and re-
serving for themselves the final vote. This settled, we retired from the
scene, not only so as to avoid embroiling in quarrels the party which
by virtue of events we can symbolize and which belongs to the nation
as a whole, but so that no consideration relative to one man, whilst he
directed the state, should be able to falsify the work of the legislators.

The nation and the French Union, however, are still awaiting a
Constitution, made for them and of which they fully approve. To tell
you the truth, though I regret the delay, I must admit that a successful
result, though a little different from the first idea, is worth more than
an unsuccessful one, conceived in haste.

Over a period of time only twice the normal span of a man's life,
France has been invaded seven times and has had thirteen régimes,
for everything is contained in the misfortunes of a people. So many
shocks to our public life have spread the poison that has exacerbated
the natural Gallic temperament, which is so prone to divisions and
quarrels. The unheard-of trials we have just passed through have
naturally only aggravated this state of affairs. The present situation in
the world, where behind their different ideologies the powers—between
which we are placed—face each other, cannot fail to introduce a great
element of trouble into our political struggles. Briefly, the rivalry of
parties in our country is a national characteristic, that of always questioning everything and thus all too often overshadowing the major
interests of the country. The national temperament, the vicissitudes of
history and the catastrophes of the present day, are established facts;
it is therefore essential for the future of the country and of democracy
that our Constitution show itself aware of this and takes care to preserve the law, and retain the cohesion of the Government and the
efficiency of the administration, as well as the prestige and authority of
the state.

In fact, any trouble in the state leads inevitably to the disaffection
of its citizens towards its Constitution. It needs, therefore, only the
slightest hitch for the menace of dictatorship to appear. All the more
so because the organization of modern society, which is to a certain
extent mechanical, makes good order in the direction and regular functioning of the machinery which makes its work more necessary and
more desirable every day. How and why did the First, Second and
Third Republics come to an end? How and why did Italian democracy,
the Weimar Republic in Germany and the Spanish Republic make

way for the régimes we know of? And yet what is a dictatorship but a great adventure? Its beginnings undoubtedly look advantageous. In the midst of the enthusiasm of some and the resignation of others, by the force of the order which it imposes, by its glamour and its government propaganda, at first sight it seems dynamic compared with the anarchy which it succeeds. But it is the destiny of all dictators to go too far in what they undertake. The more restrictions are imposed on people the greater their desire for freedom bcomes. Then bigger and better results must be offered them in compensation whatever the cost. The nation becomes a machine which its master accelerates ever more frenziedly. Whether it be a question of internal or external objectives, the aims, the risks and the efforts pass bit by bit beyond the realms of possibility. At every step, both within and without the country, obstacles are multiplied; and in the end the mainspring breaks. The great edifice collapses in blood and ruin, and the nation, broken, finds itself in a worse position than it had been when the great adventure began.

Pondering this is enough to make us realize how necessary it is that our new democratic institutions should themselves compensate for the effects of our perpetually ebullient policy. Moreover for us it is a matter of life or death in the world and century in which we live. The position, the independence, and the very existence of our country and of the French Union are definitely at stake. It is the very essence of democracy to express opinions and to strive, by suffrage, to orientate public action and legislation according to its concepts. But all the principles and all experience show that legislative, executive and judicial power should be sharply divided and soundly balanced, and that above political contingencies there should be a national arbiter to give continuity to the different combinations.

It is clearly understood that the original vote of our laws and budgets is dependent on an Assembly elected by universal and direct suffrage. But in its early stages such an Assembly is not necessarily gifted with clairvoyance or complete serenity. A second Assembly, therefore, elected and composed differently, should have the responsibility of publicly examining what the first had only considered, of formulating amendments, and of putting forward proposals. The main lines of general policy emanate from the Chamber of Deputies, but local interests also have inclinations and rights. These exist in Metropolitan France and, above all, they exist in the overseas territories, attached in various ways to the French Union. They exist in the Saar, which by the nature of things and in our victory is once more beside us, the sons of the Franks. The future of the 110 millions of men and women who live in the shadow of our flag is of a federal order, which time will gradually evolve, but the new Constitution must decide its beginning and organize its development.

Everything, then, points to the establishment of a second Chamber, whose members, for essential purposes, will be elected by the general and municipal councils. This Chamber will act as a complement to the first, by revising its plans, should need arise, by examining new ones or by respecting the importance of administrative competence within the framework of the law, which is so often neglected by a purely political body. It would be normal to add, too, representatives of economic, social and intellectual organizations, so that all the major activities of the country may have their spokesmen. United to those elected by the local assemblies from the overseas territories, the members of this Assembly will form the Grand Council of the French Union, qualified to debate laws and problems concerning the Union: budgets, foreign and internal relations, national defence, economy and communications.

It is obvious that the executive power cannot be dependent on a Parliament composed of two Chambers exercising legislative power unless we are prepared for a confusion of authority that would turn the Government into nothing more than an assembly of delegations. No doubt it was necessary, in the period of transition in which we find ourselves, for the National Constituent Assembly to elect the President of the Provisional Government, since with no other precedent to go by there was no correct procedure to be adopted. But this can only be a temporary measure. In fact our duty is consecrated to the unity, to the cohesion and to the internal discipline of the Government of France, unless we wish to see the direction of the country quickly becoming powerless and unqualified to rule. How, then, can this unity, this cohesion and this discipline be maintained in the long run, if the executive power emanates from another authority with which it must balance, and if each member of the Government, which is collectively responsibile to the entire nation, is only the representative of a single party?

It is therefore from the head of the state, placed above party feeling and elected by a college which embodies Parliament, but with a wider scope and composed in such a way as to make of him President of the French Union as well as of the French Republic, it is from him that executive power must flow. It must be his task to reconcile the various interests and to choose men who are acceptable to Parliament. His should be the task of nominating ministers and firstly, of course, the

Prime Minister, who is to direct the policy and work of the Government. To him would fall the task of promulgating laws and decrees, for these engage the citizens towards the whole state. To him belongs the task of presiding over the Councils of the Government, and to ensure that continuity which a nation cannot do without. He must also act as arbiter over the heads of the Council in any political contingency, normally through the Council or in moments of grave confusion by calling on the country to make its sovereign wishes known by means of elections. On him devolves the duty, if the nation is in danger, of safeguarding national independence and the treaties concluded by France.

A long time ago some Greeks asked Solon the Wise: 'What is the best form of Constitution?' He replied: 'First, tell me, for what nation and in which times.' Today, we are dealing with the people of France and the French Union, and the times are very hard and very dangerous! Let us see ourselves as we are. We must take the times as they are. We must succeed, despite enormous difficulties, in reconstructing the country so that every man and every woman belonging to us will get a little comfort, security and happiness, and so that we may increase in numbers, in power and in feelings of brotherhood. We must preserve the freedom which we have safeguarded with so much suffering. We must ensure the destiny of France in the midst of all the obstacles that stand in our path and in that of peace. With our fellowmen, we must use every talent of which we are capable to help our ageless, wretched Mother, the World. Let us be lucid and strong enough both to make for ourselves and to keep to rules of national life which will tend to gather us together at a time when we are driven ceaselessly to division amongst ourselves! Our whole history is the alternation of the immense sorrows of a divided people, and the fruitful grandeur of a free nation grouped under the aegis of a strong state.

Constitution
of the French Republic

The National Constituent Assembly has adopted,
The French people has approved,
The President of the Provisional Government of
the Republic promulgates the Constitution that follows:

Preamble

On the morrow of the victory of the free peoples over the regimes that attempted to enslave and degrade the human person, the French people proclaims once more that every human being, without distinction of race, religion or belief, possesses inalienable and sacred rights. It solemnly reaffirms the rights and freedoms of man and of the citizen consecrated by the Declaration of Rights of 1789 and the fundamental principles recognized by the laws of the Republic. . . .

The French Republic, faithful to its traditions, abides by the rules of international public law. It will not undertake wars of conquest and will never use its arms against the freedom of any people.

On condition of reciprocity, France accepts the limitations of sovereignty necessary to the organization and defense of peace.

France forms with the people of its overseas territories a Union based upon equality of rights and duties without distinction of race or religion.

The French Union is composed of nations and peoples who wish to place in common or co-ordinate their resources and their efforts in order to develop their civilization, increase their well-being and ensure their security.

Faithful to her traditional mission, France proposes to guide the people for whom she has assumed responsibility toward freedom to govern themselves and democratically to manage their own affairs; putting aside any system of colonization based upon arbitrary power, she guarantees to all equal access to public office and the individual or collective exercise of the rights and liberties proclaimed or confirmed above.

.   .   .

Title II
The Parliament

ARTICLE 5

The Parliament shall be composed of the National Assembly and the Council of the Republic.

ARTICLE 6

The duration of the powers of each Assembly, its mode of election, the conditions of eligibility and the bases of ineligibilities and incompatibilities shall be determined by the law.

However, the two Chambers shall be elected on a territorial basis, the National Assembly by universal, direct suffrage, the Council of the Republic by the communal and departmental bodies by universal, indirect suffrage. The Council of the Republic is renewable one-half at a time.

Nevertheless, the National Assembly may itself elect by proportional representation councillors whose number shall not exceed one-sixth of the total number of members of the Council of the Republic.

The number of members of the Council of the Republic may not be less than 250 nor more than 320.

ARTICLE 7

War may not be declared without a vote of the National Assembly and the concurrent opinion of the Council of the Republic.

ARTICLE 8

Each of the two Chambers shall pass upon the eligibility of its members and the regularity of their elections; it alone may receive their resignation. . . .

ARTICLE 13

The National Assembly alone shall adopt the laws. It may not delegate this right.

ARTICLE 14

The President of the Council of Ministers and the members of the Parliament shall have the initiative in legislation.

Bills and proposed laws introduced by members of the National Assembly shall be filed with its secretariat.

Proposed laws introduced by members of the Council of the Republic shall be filed with its secretariat and sent without debate to the secretariat of the National Assembly. They may not be received if they would result in the reduction of revenues or the creation of new expenditures.

ARTICLE 15

The National Assembly shall study the bills and proposed laws submitted to it in its committees, of which it shall determine the number, the composition and the jurisdiction.

ARTICLE 16

The proposed budget shall be submitted to the National Assembly. This bill may include only such provisions as are strictly financial.

An organic law shall regulate the method of presentation of the budget.

ARTICLE 17

The deputies of the National Assembly shall have the right to initiate appropriations.

However, no proposals which would tend to increase appropriations already decided upon or create new ones may be presented during the discussion of the budget and of prospective or supplementary appropriations. . . .

ARTICLE 20

The Council of the Republic shall examine, in order to give its opinion thereon, the bills and proposed laws passed on first reading by the National Assembly.

It shall give its opinion not more than two months after a measure is sent to it by the National Assembly. When the budget law is under discussion, this time may be reduced, if need be, to such time as does not exceed that taken by the National Assembly for its consideration and vote. When the National Assembly has adopted a rule for emergency procedure, the Council of the Republic shall give its opinion within the same time as that provided for debate by the rule of the National Assembly. The time limit specified in the present article shall be suspended during interruptions of the session. It may be extended by a decision of the National Assembly.

If the opinion of the Council of the Republic is in agreement with that of the National Assembly or if it has not been given within the time limit specified in the preceding paragraph, the law shall be promulgated as passed by the National Assembly.

If this opinion is not in agreement with that of the National Assembly, the latter body shall examine the bill or proposed law on second reading. It shall dispose definitively and absolutely of the amendments proposed by the Council of the Republic, accepting or rejecting them in whole or in part. When these amendments are completely or partially rejected, the vote on second reading of the law shall be by roll call and by an absolute majority of the members of the National Assembly, if the vote on the whole has been taken under the same conditions by the Council of the Republic.

ARTICLE 21

No member of the Parliament may be prosecuted, sought by the police, arrested, detained or tried because of opinions expressed or votes cast by him in the exercise of his function.

ARTICLE 22

No member of the Parliament may be prosecuted or arrested during his term of office for a criminal offense except with the authorization of the Chamber of which he is a member, or in the case of a major crime. The detention or prosecution of a member of the Parliament shall be suspended if the Chamber of which he is a member requests it. . . .

Title V
The President of the Republic

ARTICLE 29

The President of the Republic shall be elected by the Parliament.

He shall be elected for seven years. He shall be eligible for re-election only once.

ARTICLE 30

The President of the Republic shall appoint in the Council of Ministers the Councillors of State, the Grand Chancellor of the Legion of Honor, the ambassadors and special envoys, the members of the Superior Council and the Committee for National Defense, the rectors of the universities, the prefects, the chiefs of the central administrative services, the general officers and the Government representatives in the overseas territories.

ARTICLE 31

The President of the Republic shall be kept informed of the progress of international negotiations. He shall sign and ratify all treaties.

The President of the Republic shall accredit ambassadors and special envoys to foreign powers; foreign ambassadors and special envoys shall be accredited to him.

ARTICLE 32

The President of the Republic shall preside over the Council of Ministers. He shall order the minutes of their meetings to be recorded and shall keep them in his possession.

ARTICLE 33

The President of the Republic shall preside in the same capacity over the Superior Council and the Committee for National Defense, and shall have the title of Commander-in-chief of the armed forces.

ARTICLE 34

The President of the Republic shall preside over the Superior Council of the Judiciary.

ARTICLE 35

The President of the Republic shall have the right of pardon in the Superior Council of the Judiciary.

ARTICLE 36

The President of the Republic shall promulgate the laws within ten days after their text, as finally adopted, has been sent to the Government. This interval may be reduced to five days if the National Assembly declares an emergency.

Within the time limit fixed for promulgation of law, the President of the Republic, in a message stating his reasons, may ask that it be reconsidered by both Chambers; this reconsideration may not be refused.

If the President of the Republic does not promulgate a law within the time limit fixed by the present Constitution, the President of the National Assembly shall promulgate it.

ARTICLE 37

The President of the Republic shall communicate with the Parliament by means of messages addressed to the National Assembly.

ARTICLE 38

Every act of the President of the Republic must be countersigned by the President of the Council of Ministers and by a Minister. . . .

Title VI
The Council of Ministers

ARTICLE 45

At the opening of each legislative session, the President of the Republic, after the customary consultations, shall designate the President of the Council.

The latter shall submit to the National Assembly the program and the policy of the Cabinet he intends to constitute.

The President of the Council and the Ministers may not be formally appointed until the President of the Council receives a vote of confidence from the National Assembly by a roll call vote and by an absolute majority of the deputies, except when force majeure prevents the National Assembly from meeting.

The same procedure shall be followed during a legislative session in the event of a vacancy caused by death, resignation or any other circumstance, except in the case set forth in Article 52 below.

No ministerial crisis occurring within the fifteen-day period after the appointment of the ministers shall require the application of Article 51.

ARTICLE 46

The President of the Council and the Ministers chosen by him shall be formally appointed by a decree of the President of the Republic.

ARTICLE 47

The President of the Council shall ensure the execution of the laws.

He shall appoint all civil and military officials except those specified in Articles 30, 46 and 84.

The President of the Council shall assume the direction of the armed forces and shall coordinate all measures necessary for national defense.

The acts of the President of the Council mentioned in the present article shall be countersigned by the Ministers concerned.

ARTICLE 48

The Ministers shall be collectively responsible to the National Assembly for the general policy of the Cabinet and individually responsible for their personal actions.

They shall not be responsible to the Council of the Republic.

ARTICLE 49

A question of confidence may not be put except after discussion by the Council of Ministers; it can be put only by the President of the Council.

The vote on a question of confidence may not be taken until one full day after it has been put before the Assembly. It shall be taken by a roll call.

The Cabinet may not be refused a vote of confidence except by an absolute majority of the Deputies in the Assembly.

Refusal to give such a vote shall automatically result in the collective resignation of the Cabinet.

ARTICLE 50

Passage of a motion of censure by the National Assembly shall automatically result in the collective resignation of the Cabinet.

The vote on such a motion cannot be taken until one full day after it has been made. It must be taken by a roll call.

A motion of censure may be adopted only by an absolute majority of the Deputies in the Assembly.

ARTICLE 51

If in the course of an eighteen-month period two ministerial crises occur under the conditions set forth in Articles 49 and 50, the Council of Ministers, with the concurrence of the President of the Assembly, may decide to dissolve the National Assembly. Its dissolution shall be proclaimed by a decree of the President of the Republic in accordance with such decision.

The provisions of the preceding paragraph may not be applied before the expiration of the first eighteen months of the Legislature.

ARTICLE 52

In case of dissolution, the Cabinet, with the exception of the President of the Council and the Minister of the Interior, shall remain in office to carry on current business.

The President of the Republic shall appoint the President of the National Assembly as President of the Council. The latter shall appoint the new Minister of the Interior with the approval of the secretariat of the National Assembly. He shall appoint as Ministers of State members of party groups not represented in the Government.

General elections shall take place not less than twenty and not more than thirty days after the dissolution.

The National Assembly shall convene by right on the third Thursday after its election.

Janet Flanner: Letters from Paris

December 30, 1952
In one way, anyhow, French politics stuck to a pattern in 1952. In the first week of the year France lost her government, and in the last week of the year France lacked a government once more. It has lately looked as if France would have no government for New Year's Day of 1953, either. The new government, when it does turn up, will be the eighteenth—a dozen and a half of them—since the postwar Fourth Republic was founded, in 1945. The present hiatus is regarded by the French as the most profoundly serious of all, if only because it proves for the seventeenth time that something is wrong with the system, which it is now admitted must be fixed. Until recently, the demand for constitutional revision was suspiciously considered exclusively the product of the ideological mysticism of General Charles de Gaulle and his followers in the Rassemblement du Peuple Français. Today, few politicians would disagree with the General—not even those who

wrote the Fourth Republic's constitution. The main trouble with the document is that it makes better provision for the fall of governments than it does for the coördination of their limited postwar powers.

It is significant and astonishing that after Premier Antoine Pinay's fall last week, de Gaulle's Rassemblement was given—if only in vain—its first chance to form a government. It was too much to expect that the "Trojan Horse" (which is what jeering anti-Gaullists, in disapprobation and fear, call the General's Party) would be able to take the preliminary jumps, let alone stay the course, loaded as it is with the weight of his remarkable personality and the personalities of those devoted to him. But that the Gaullists were asked at all showed a new Parliamentary attitude toward Gaullism, and certainly showed a new attitude on the part of the Gaullists toward themselves. Previously, their General had declared that his group should not even aim at taking power unless he could be the governmental chief, preferably President of the Republic; today he is not even a deputy—is, indeed, nobody but the fantastic head of his own Party, living in secluded campestral concentration in his country house southeast of Paris. He also instructed his deputies to vote nothing but no in Parliament, where they sat like monuments of obstruction until recently, when thirty-one of them revolted and were thrown out of the Party as rebels. In accepting an offer to try to form a government last week, the Gaullists, on the General's orders, emerged at last from their mysterious isolation, really with the object of reviving the faith of their voters, who were tired of the General's dignified policy of patiently waiting for France to collapse and then summon him as savior. What the other politicians hope they have gained from letting the Gaullists have a nibble at reality and power is that the Rassemblement will now permanently abandon its position of negation and help form a more stable coalition majority, without which no party is strong enough to found and hold a government in France today.

Jacques Soustelle, the Gaullist deputy who failed to become the new premier, is one of the group's several noted intellectuals, having been a distinguished ethnologist and the assistant director of the Musée de l'Homme before he took up a political career. As one accustomed to dealing with various species of man, he expertly interviewed ten former French premiers, of ten party mixtures, all of whose short-lived governments had fallen like houses of cards. Premier Pinay, in his bitterness over his recent fall, angrily described the French Parliament as a "bear garden" and declared that he would take part in no more governments. Experts opine that before long he will probably be called to take part in a government of his own again. The Banque de France warned last March that the state was in danger of bankruptcy, and it was the theretofore unknown Pinay who came in as a little business-man to save the franc. In the one week since he left, the franc has fallen and the dollar has risen. Financially as well as politically, Pinay may be the only premier France can now afford.

February 17, 1953
It is too well-known a fact that governments in France fall too often. Everyone is also fully aware that there is a connection between govern-ment falls and the plethora of French political parties, of which right now there are eleven, six of them being major. To Americans, with their old-fashioned system of two parties, and even to the British, with their three parties, there seems to be something comic in France's hav-ing nearly a dozen. Obviously, the fact that there are eleven parties here is a tragedy. Since 1953 is bound to be filled with the acute argu-mentative decisions looming on both sides of the Atlantic, the prestige of France as West Europe's leader can ill support the strain of crumbling governments. Some sort of reform—under Premier René Mayer, if he doesn't fall before or during the attempt, or under who-ever comes next—is regarded as inevitable, for to remain in power now is like trying to walk on marbles. The Fourth Republic's constitution, in memory of Marshal Pétain and in terror of General de Gaulle's position of solitary eminence just after the liberation, was expressly created weak, to prevent dictatorship. It was carefully written to give too much power to Parliament and not enough to the executive govern-ment. In Mayer's inaugural speech, he said he would single out for revision Article 13, which, if reformed, would permit a premier, under exceptional circumstances, to pass unpopular, needed laws (such as a law to tackle the French citizenry's tax evasions) by himself, thus re-lieving the deputies from having to answer for them to their angry electors; and Article 51, which, if reformed, would make it easier for a premier to dissolve Parliament. Then if a government fell, Parlia-ment could fall with it, which, of course, would put the fear of God into deputies, and into political parties, too. But while these reforms may increase stability, they will not reduce the number of parties.

The Rassemblement du Peuple Français, General Charles de Gaulle's party, now has eighty-five deputies. In the 1951 elections, the R.P.F. became the largest Parliamentary party of France, by a margin of fourteen deputies. Recently it lost thirty-two members (and three affiliates), who bolted, or were ousted as heretics, after they had voted for Pinay's financial measures in defiance of de Gaulle's orders that his deputies sit like monuments, voting no to all government proposals. In 1946, General de Gaulle dramatically abandoned the Presidency of the Provisional Government in order to keep "the spiritual national investment," which he said the French Resistance and Liberation symbolized in him, from being sullied by party politics. The part of the French public and French politicians that has feared his later aims as being toward a *coup d'état* are still unable to explain why, if he desired dictatorial power, he did not seize it at the war's end, when France was at his feet. His R.P.F. political party was founded in 1947 not by him but by admirers, who gave it to him and the public like an extraordinary gift. What draws his followers is his conviction that France has rotted, socially, financially, and politically, and needs a drastic upheaval. Formerly, the General seemed to believe that a low-grade Parliament would bring about national collapse, which would thus allow what he calls *le pays réel* to vote him in as a savior. But since last month everything has changed. His party, originally "above party politics" and thus sitting in Parliament in a dignified vacuum, is now tentatively playing the parliamentary game. De Gaulle's aspiration is to be President of France, but a sort of idealized American President, with strong powers, a firm executive hand, and a Parliament reduced to a purely legislative role. As President, de Gaulle would treat the Communists, who obey Moscow, as treasonable criminals. He has consistently declared that the Fourth Republic's constitution demands a reform, which nearly everybody now admits. De Gaulle, as the incarnation of French patriotism, says that NATO has turned France into an American protectorate without adequate American protection; he wants France's defense run by Frenchmen, not by the United States. He is against a Federated Europe as being the death-blow to the sacred French nationality; what he does want is a Confederated Europe. General de Gaulle has lately been sending the Paris press frequent, lengthy communiqués on his newest political formulas. Even in addressing the newspapers, his language remains that of Bossuet, Bishop of Meaux nearly three hundred years ago. If the international situation deteriorates greatly, it is always possible that de Gaulle will make history again.

The French say that all their eleven parties and differing ideas—when they do differ—spring from the characteristic individualism of the French mind; that this double-edged genius for variety is the basis for the overdevelopment of the democratic principle of choice, now swelled through logic to the point of functional weakness. Even

French deputies of the same party vote individualistically, as do some American congressmen. There is no party discipline, as in England, of obeying the whips. It is impossible to prophesy, for instance, how the French deputies and parties—except for the Communists, who will vote no, and the M.R.P.s, who will probably vote yes—will ballot when the European Army project comes up. French citizens who are disheartened by French politics think their politicians have become professionals, who deal in power as a business, like trading in eggs or real estate, as if their responsibilities were not the whole fabric of people's lives.

It is curious that the Third Republic, of which the Fourth is the descendant, started out in 1871 with hardly any party system at all.

May 6, 1953

If some of the French nowadays feel helplessly cut off from what goes on in the national government—in Parliament and inside their deputies' heads—most of the citizenry still feel close indeed to their local functionaries, the city or village mayor and councillors who do the neighborhood governing right under the citizens' noses. Accordingly, seventy-eight per cent of the voters actually voted the other day in the municipal elections in France's thirty-eight thousand communes. At least eleven councillors are elected in every municipality—even in villages with a population of a few hundred—which meant that all over France something like one voter in twenty-five was running for office. In small towns, mayors are paid merely a token salary, but they get to drape themselves in the official tricolor sash, which is worth a fortune in dignity; the councillors receive nothing at all. In a Hérault hamlet called Pégairolles-de-l'Escalette, all eleven councillors refused at the last minute to run again, because they had had too much trouble governing the one hundred and eighty inhabitants (and each other), so since Election Day the place has had no councillors at all, and heaven knows what may happen. At Montagnard-Dieu, in the Ardennes, all nine voters, who were using the mayor's cooking pot for the ballot urn, voted early so his wife could cook lunch on time. The daughter of Nancy's mayor was fined for nocturnally pasting posters around town that libelled her father's political rival. At Bessuéjouls, the mayor, who was up for reëlection, his wife, and one of his sons were all murdered during election week, and the addled local politicians failed to present a new candidate to take his place. More Balzacian incidents and characters are connected with France's municipal elections than with the voting for the national job of deputy, a big plum and sterner stuff. Among the special figures recently elected to office in their home towns were one member of the Académie Française; two actors, including one from the Comédie-Française; the president of the French Rugby Federation; American Ambassador C. Douglas Dillon's cousin Weller Seymour, of the village of Neaufles-St.-Martin; two Communists in prison, including Comrade Henri Martin of *"Libérez Henri Martin"* slogan fame; and the former noted Cabinet minister Georges Bonnet, who was not even a candidate.

The outstanding political result of the elections was the destructive defeat of General de Gaulle's party, Le Rassemblement du Peuple Français. Ever an unpredictable, Cartesian leader, in an amazing statement just printed in his party paper, *Le Rassemblement,* he dissolved the party itself. The old R.P.F. deputies and the few newly elected ones may no longer call themselves R.P.F.s. He does not disavow them as his *compagnons,* but as politicos they are now nameless, and on their own. (About thirty rebellious deputies of his achieved this personal liberty for themselves last year by backsliding out of the party.) The original salvational Gaullist movement, conceived to rescue France from the corruption of too many political parties, was itself transformed in 1947, by successful elections, into one more political party—against the General's wish. It is this party that, after these disastrous 1953 elections, he has just dissolved. The Gaullist Rassemblement movement itself he has by metamorphosis just restored to its exalted, unpractical form—a kind of patriotic political cult. Disdainful, as ever, of politics per se and interested only in the art of governing, the General scathingly said in his R.P.F. dissolution statement that in France "neither the Left nor the Right can govern alone. Acting together, they neutralize each other. The world sees this as it watches our sad political circus parade. The French regime is sterile and for the moment cannot change—a series of combines, bargains, majority votes, and office investitures that make up the games, the poisons, and the joys of the system." But he foresees, as he has been foreseeing for the past seven years, that France is facing a serious shakeup, and that with it will come what he bitterly called "the bankruptcy of illusions." "The safety of France," he continued, "and the state will be at stake. *Il faut préparer le recours.*" And who will furnish the means that will save? Le Rassemblement, whose ex-R.P.F. candidates just lost the municipal elections.

June 18, 1953
France has been four weeks without a government, although nine politicians have been offered a change at the premiership by President

Vincent Auriol. An acid newspaper cartoon by blasé old Sennep shows Auriol wondering whom to ask next and murmuring, "Maybe a well-known woman—Danielle Darrieux or Martine Carol . . ." Assembly President Edouard Herriot, aged eighty-one and sick in bed, received at his bedside his Radical Party leaders, whom he belatedly warned to stop playing party politics, saying, "At the close of my life, with all my soul I implore you to think now of nothing but France." The politicians had better think of their own skins, too. According to Article 51 of the Constitution, this Parliament can be dissolved and the deputies sent hunting for their jobs in general elections if they overthrow one more government on a question of confidence or censure between now and November, 1954. To the French public, the present crisis fundamentally shows just what the seventeen other crises since the Liberation have shown, but with a strange air of finality. It shows that if a French Premier is to govern with any continuity today, he must be given special powers. For the first time in a crisis, there is practically a sitdown strike among designate-Premiers, who will not lift a finger unless they are promised better Premier working conditions. Above all, this crisis, like a magnifying glass grown seventeen times stronger, makes ultravisible the fact that France's multi-party system and her disparate ways of looking at political matters—a disparity upheld by French logic and French republican liberty—have reached a point where, through habit and through shortsighted human psychology, political greed, and Gallic precedent, party-minded men, both in and out of politics, are concerned only with their differences in thinking, instead of with developing the ideas they have in common.

Considering all the pressures besieging France—the delayed Bermuda conference, the old unsettled business of the European Army, the new influential, softening Soviet policy that almost daily is seeping out from behind the Iron Curtain, and France's vital need for a revived diplomacy and some set foreign policy, even about its own war in Indo-China—considering all these exterior semi-crises, the ridiculous aspect of this present crisis is that it began in France's hip pocket over a question of money, although France is the richest country in Europe. There has always been the comforting theory that France's financial troubles come merely from the fact that her citizens don't· pay their taxes. According to the last Finance Minister's Report on the Economic Budget of the Nation, the state revenue would admittedly be billions of francs higher if the citizens paid all the taxes they owe—that is, if French businessmen did not classically keep two sets of books and pay only on the lesser book. But the report says, nevertheless, that more than a third of the national income does wind up in the tax channels.

Yet with all that money rolling in, Premier René Mayer had to borrow money from the Banque de France, which, in a way, is why he fell and why the crisis began. Then the Banque de France, dunning for a payment on the debt, knocked on the government's door and found nobody home.

June 30, 1953
If—as was certainly not the case—France had been able to afford her recent record-breaking five-week political crisis, during which she was without a government, the crisis would have done almost nothing but good because it so harmed the present kind of parliamentary regime in the estimation of the French people. Unbearably costly as the crisis was in lost prestige and even financially, it seems, at any rate, to have proved to France's citizens a fact they had to make sure of, once and for all—that the present constitution absolutely must be reformed, so Parliament will not have the power to do again what it has just been doing, and so the executive will be able to sit in the seat of state long enough to govern. According to experts, if anything is sure right now in French politics, after the incomprehensible choice of an obscurity like the Calvados deputy Joseph Laniel as Premier, it is that Parliament will undertake a revision of the constitution, if only to save itself from possible dissolution.

The outstanding salutary human element to emerge during the critical month was the bold, harsh intelligence and the uncompromising personality of the youngish politico Pierre Mendès-France, as revealed in his unaccepted program for saving the country through economic and social reforms. Plenty of French have got into the habit of thinking that their country cannot be saved. Mendès-France's program, outlined in the speech he delivered in Parliament when he was trying to get support for his bid for the Premiership, set a standard by which all other programs have since been judged. Though the parliamentary majority turned his program down, millions of French accepted it in their own minds and remember it as the one notable declaration among the millions of words of *blah-blah-blah* (French for "yackety-yack") spoken here. A lawyer and a banker trained by the Rothschilds, yet a representative of the younger-generation reform wing in the liberal, if money-conscious, old Radical Socialist Party, Mendès-France remains the dominant figure of the crisis and, with luck, he could be the new leading man of France, which certainly still needs one.

The crisis reminded one of Alice and the Red Queen when they started running, not to get anywhere but merely to stay on the same spot. With the crisis ended, France is just where she was before it began, though more winded. As ex-Premier Antoine Pinay, one of the unsuccessful candidates, remarked bitterly, there are two hundred and five Marxists on one side of the Assembly, and, on the other, four hundred and twenty-two anti-Marxist deputies, whom it is impossible to pull together into an unselfish, non-party national coalition that could put France back on her feet. And as the semi-Socialist afternoon paper *France-Soir* pointed out, still to be solved are France's interior and exterior financial deficits, the European Army problem, the Indo-China war, the Moroccan troubles, rising unemployment, inadequate salaries, a stagnant economy, investment difficulties, and insufficient housing. The height of Parisian editorial indignation at Parliament's feeble choice of the inexperienced new Premier—after its five weeks of lionlike roaring—was reached by the independent *Combat*. "The cowardly relief felt by the deputies in seating M. Laniel is not shared by the rest of the country," it fulminated. "They are making another grave mistake if they think it is."

During the five critical weeks, the Paris newspapers kept printing, if merely from habit, what the parliamentarians thought about politics. Only one paper extensively printed what the French citizens thought about Parliament. This was *L'Express,* the new Paris political weekly edited by Jean-Jacques Servan-Schreiber, who previously was one of the noted younger political experts writing for *Le Monde.* What he printed in *L'Express* was a culling from the famous regular reports on what the French feel and think about life and politics which are gathered (according to a shrewd system started by Napoleon Bonaparte) by the prefects' offices in each of the ninety departments of France; the reports are sent to Paris and boiled down into a synthesis, which is available to three officials—the President of France, the Premier, if there is one, and the Minister of the Interior. *L'Express's* own editorial analysis of its selection of nationwide prefectural reports was that the French are so sick of Parliament they might even accept some single leader to save France "if only he gives an impression of being honest, brutal, and courageous." Unquestionably most of the citizens' opinions, as represented in the prefects' reports, were scathing. In and around Rouen, people wrote three times the average budget of monthly letters to their prefect, all full of complaints. They charged that their deputies had shilly-shallied deceitfully in abstaining from voting on all the candidates for Premier put before Parliament, and in not stating clearly on the Assembly floor whether they were for or against Mendès-

France's program, and why. They also said that Parliament ought to be dissolved, but only after passing an electoral reform, since "otherwise the same deputies would turn up again and the muddles would continue." In Compiègne, a leading citizen declared that "the deeply disgusted French people demand a dictator with a pitchfork and broom." In Boulogne, a businessmen's petition asked that "the nation choose new representatives, who would really work to restore France." In Lyon, home of Parliament's president, old Edouard Herriot, there was an increased wave of antiparliamentarianism. In the northern coal region, workers thought the high cost of living more important than politicians, "who never change anyhow." In the south, the major theme was again dissolution of Parliament, preceded by electoral reforms to prevent the reëlection of *"les incapables,"* along with prophecies of serious social troubles this autumn if there is not a new government atmosphere and crew. The prize reaction to the crisis came from a citizen of Marseille, who wrote to President Auriol (the President declared that his bulging private letter bag showed him how dangerous and profound is the malaise of the French people) demanding the dissolution of Parliament and of all eleven political parties in favor of a tricolor format of only three authorized groups: a blue party for the Republicans, or right; a white party for the center; and a red party for all the left. It was a sensible, if impossible, plan.

The major post-crisis worry now is just plain money. According to the caretaker govenment's report, the crises cost France the equivalent of two hundred and eighty million dollars in unfloated loans and other losses. The state coffer is bare and is taking another massive loan from the Banque de France to pay state employees their end-of-June salaries. What the French people now want to know is by which of the two customary agonies will the deficit be met—by extra taxation or by printing more inflationary money.

Obviously, France has had so much history that it necessarily keeps repeating itself. Apropos to today's terrible deficit, there has been recalled, like an echo from the past, Louis XVI's financial dilemma, during which Marie Antoinette supposedly asked the Royal Finance Minister, "What will you do about the deficit, Monsieur le Ministre?" "Nothing, Madame," he replied. "It is too serious."

June 30, 1954
The victory of Pierre Mendès-France in becoming Premier, if only for the four weeks he gave himself to perform what are beginning to look like obtainable miracles, has had an extraordinary effect on the

country. On all sides there exists "a more or less general hopefulness, even though it may be discolored by skepticism," as one newspaper phrased it. Informal polls have been hastily taken to find out what the citizens feel and think about their new leader, as if for once their reactions mattered. The findings are illuminating. The *populo,* or poorer class, and the topmost educated class are the most enthusiastic about him, the middle class the least. There is more incredulity among businessmen and industrialists about his chance of fulfilling his month's promises than there is among the intellectual and technical cadres; high-profit and low-output French business and industry have been screaming for reform, mostly on taxation, but they already suspect that in his economic-reform program he may try to reform them, too, and, naturally, believe that he cannot succeed. On the other hand, in a wave of curiosity, a recent conference of thirty highly educated technical experts in Paris industry took a vote on its feeling for the Premier, and the returns were twenty-seven for, only three against. And a recent reunion of lycée and university professors recorded a nearly unanimous outburst of confidence in the Premier. The students at the Ecole Normale Supérieure and at the Polytechnique, who are the cream of young French brains, are mostly for him, because they think he has an excellent mind, clear formulations, no tergiversations, and is honest, and because he is only forty-seven and full of sap, and has chosen six men under forty as Cabinet Ministers and State Secretaries. The Army brass tends to be for him, because he named as Minister of Defense General Pierre Koenig, who fought the Laniel Defense Ministry over the poor pay of combat officers in Indo-China and also over its conduct of the war. The support of Mendès-France that is closest to bedrock is probably that of the *fonctionnaires,* or civil-service employees, who keep France running for whatever government comes along—and even when there is no government at all—and who have a correspondingly poor view of politicians generally. Lower and middling *fonctionnaires* are out-and-out for him as the exceptional politician, and among the mature chiefs, men of importance in the state machinery, are many who might be kindled by him into hope for a renewed, cleansed France—a France they could more gladly serve.

Mendès-France's Parliamentary base is certainly shaky. The political parties represented by the men now in his Cabinet have a total of only about two hundred and seventy-five Assembly votes—and the parties involved would not, any more than his own Radical Party, necessarily support him generously. He even has two fence jumpers from Bidault's

M.R.P. Party, which gave its members strict instructions against taking office with this newcomer, the first Premier since the war to put the M.R.P., as well as Bidault, after his long, faithful, uneasy seasons as Foreign Minister, on the shelf of the opposition. The M.R.P.'s votes against him will be triply bitter.

Mendès-France's contract time is nearly half up. He has already created a Cabinet post new to French history—that of Minister for Moroccan and Tunisian Affairs—as the first step in carrying out his plan for new relations with those riotously inflamed protectorates. He has done what in his *Premier-désigné* speech in Parliament he warned the French Communists he would do whether his cease-fire offer ended the war or not—ordered reinforcements to be made ready for the Far East expeditionary force. He has called both on prior governments and on his own to present to the Assembly early in July definite proposals for reforming the constitution. His first fiscal-reform project, just announced, aims at strengthening and enforcing last year's half-hearted law taxing manufacturers' markups, which, if made to work, would enormously bolster the national economy. Though some of the French, especially the wealthy, feared unorthodox novelty reforms from him, he seems so far merely to be reforming the weak or inapplicable reforms other men passed as lip service to necessity or in order to keep previous reformers quiet.

The first, and most compelling, item on Mendès-France's program—to obtain a cease-fire—now looks closer, since, to everyone's surprise, Sir Winston and the President have announced that the United Kingdom and the United States will press forward with their security plans for Southeast Asia whether or not France negotiates an acceptable agreement in Geneva. This is probably the best incentive the Anglo-Saxons have yet given France in her efforts to get such an agreement at the peace conference. As France waits for the Indo-China project—physically the most vital issue to the French people, as war and truce issues always are—to be finished one way or the other, the great and almost philosophical French issue of the European Defense Community is close to boiling. It is the most nearly insurmountable problem in Mendès-France's program, because it will have to be settled by the French themselves, now and finally and at last. After twenty-five months of waiting, Belgium's Henri Spaak, speaking for the exasperated Benelux group, and Chancellor Adenauer, speaking for West Germany, this week began bringing pressure on the Premier, and the American Ambassador, C. Douglas Dillon, transmitted to him Washington's urgent demand that France ratify at least a European defense community. In an effort to get a compromise plan that French Parliamentary partisans of E.D.C. and those who are its enemies would both accept, the Premier had already set General Koenig, who is anti-E.D.C., and Maurice Bourgès-Maunoury, the Minister of Industry and Commerce, who is for it, to working on it together. Between this compromise E.D.C., which doubtless no one but the French would accept, and the old, original E.D.C., which other Atlantic nations have long since accepted, Parliament must finally make up its mind during the last week of the Premier's contract—and perhaps, of course, of his Premiership.

Mendès-France is nothing of an athlete in appearance, and nobody dreamed that he had the gift of drawing on himself the vast public eye as a politician. But as Premier he is like a runner running a unique, exciting political hurdle race while the citizens of France watch him closely, lap after lap. As far as real racing is concerned, this has been the high point of the horse-racing season in Paris, with well-dressed women, fine, sensitive animals, thin jockeys, and great crowds at Longchamp, Auteuil, Enghien, and St.-Cloud. But the Premier's race against time is the strangest historical contest anybody has ever seen run here, and France has her eyes on it.

November 9, 1954
Many of Mendès-France's well-wishers wish, for his sake and theirs, that he would stay at home right now, rather than distribute his energies visiting Canada, Washington, and New York. He has been demonstrating in his speeches, activities, weekly fireside radio talks, journeys, and projects on the home front the same talent for programmed momentum that distinguished him in his early, dramatic dealings with vital foreign affairs at Geneva and London, when he molded a new diplomacy for France. He has so much under way that those who believe in the possibility of his renewed France, uprooted from its immobility, feel that he should not drop his hold even for ten days in America, for fear that something may start slipping into reverse behind his back now that his political ill-wishers are recovering their wits and organization. During his five months of power, he has governed in a new kind of political space that he created for himself—above the political parties—and what has upheld him has been public opinion. His popularity with the dominant majority of the French people and with the younger element of Parliament—for he is the leader of the young-generation postwar politicos who are daring to try to do what the old politicos have only talked about—is what has given

him the elevation he needed in order to operate in his new political style. But to set in motion the economical, social, and administrative reforms that undoubtedly are his greatest aims, and that Parliament has voted him special powers to tackle, he will have to come closer to earth and will have to rally support in the parties and give pledges somewhere—always the fatal danger of French parliamentarianism on the lower level. Mendès-France is now passing from his first stage, the phenomenal, into his second stage, the actual.

The French say that in addition to having Bidault's M.R.P. party, which has now become Right Wing, and the Communists bitterly opposed to him, Mendès-France has two elements in society against him. First are the all too numerous small manufacturers, whose poor organization, low production, and abnormally high profits make them a losing proposition for the national economy, and whom his reforms would first wipe out and then relocate more usefully. Second are certain high-tariff, power-lobby, and monopoly groups, some of which have been receiving enormous government subsidies; he has already collided with the beet-sugar-alcohol group and a number of big textile interests. He may soon have against him the *bistro* owners and barkeepers, to judge by his strong feelings about the disaster of France's rising alcoholism. A recent graph in *Le Figaro* shows that the French annually consume more than three times as much alcohol as Americans, with all their dry Martinis, do. Mendès-France is the first French Premier ever to drink milk in public, which his wife says he learned to do in the United States in the course of his short stay during the war. His announcement that, beginning with the New Year, France's surplus milk will be distributed to schoolchildren and to the boys in the French Army has caused consternation among French mothers, for the French think that no drink is as bad for the liver as milk. The *Mendésistes*, as his supporters are called, believe that the next three months will tell the story of how far his courage, lucidity, and exceptional intellectual grasp of economic affairs will be permitted to go in making the up-to-date France that everybody has been telling the French they ought to have.

December 7, 1955

Till now, post-war French governments have collapsed with such ease that their twenty falls in ten years constituted the major connecting parliamentary history of the Fourth Republic. Last Tuesday's twenty-first fall became a harsh crash, through the consequent dissolution of Parliament itself—for the first time since May 16, 1877, a date made memorable by the unpleasant, autocratic Marshal de MacMahon, then President of the Third Republic. After Premier Edgar Faure's government was overemphatically voted from power the other night, there was a long moment of fatigued silence, and no emotion, no hate, no grief—Faure being a chilly sort of leader—such as made the impressive climax to the fall of Pierre Mendès-France and his government last February. That was the occasion on which Faure started his astonishing rise to fame. As the Mendésist junior Premier, he set up his government to carry on the policies of his fallen chief, and ended it trying to drive him into the wilderness.

In this struggle, Faure has won. Mendès-France—and maybe France herself—has lost. Instead of winning by overthrowing Faure that final Tuesday, the Mendésists lost through somebody's overshooting—*une erreur de tir,* as it was sportingly called here. Somebody arranged that seven more anti-Faure votes should be cast than were needed for a simple defeat, and thus made the anti-government majority—by six votes—greater than half the total roll of the Assembly. (Ironically, a similar too heavy parliamentary majority overthrew Mendès-France himself ten months back.) Mendès-France is the only anti-Marxist who has ever bothered with youth, the future of France. He calls his new movement the Front Républicain, to distinguish it from the Front Populaire idea, which would include Communists.

After the terrific sensation caused by Faure's dissolution of Parliament, Mendès-France achieved a second-best sensational riposte by having Faure expelled from the Radical Socialist Party. In France, party expulsion leaves a politician as disgraced and homeless as an Englishman who has been pitched out of his club. With all these melodramatic surprises erupting here, the front pages of the Paris newspapers have looked like chapters from serialized thrillers. The episode the Parisians liked best was the Assembly's being booted out, for Parliament is mostly a despised institution today. Among the excitements have been the violent denunciations of Faure's dissolution order as a reactionary plot, an anti-democratic *coup de force,* and a piece of political chicanery that served him rather than the nation for whose aid it should have been intended.

Mendès-France has also been painfully criticized—at least in private—by some of his too exalted followers of last year. He has been reproached by them for the disillusioning, irascible demagogy he has displayed in *L'Éxpress,* the Mendésists' weekly paper, where, in his brief signed editorials, he has fulminated about "tricked elections," "guilty men," and "a plot against La Patrie." Perhaps the worst of the

many ill results of his and Faure's destructive struggle is that the toga
of Mendès-France seems to have slipped, or at least to be showing
discouraging signs of wear and tear.

December 20, 1955
This must be the funniest election campaign—unfortunately reflecting
the dire gravity of the whole parliamentary situation—that either of
the two modern Republics of France ever saw. It is as if the nation's
former genius for old-fashioned farce were finally taking over the
nation's politics, which have too long invited it. The fact that the cam-
paigning to elect an entire new Assembly on January 2nd is restricted
to a single month makes for a ludicrous situation in itself, and it is
complicated by the uproarious confusion of five thousand-odd candidates struggling for five hundred and forty-four deputies' seats on
nearly a thousand electoral lists presented by twenty-eight national
political parties and scores of minor local groups. It is this overcrowd-
ing and hustling that gives the comic touch—this frantic haste of mobs
of politicos, all on the run after being caught short, all spouting
speeches and promises as they hurry in and out of the public view in
a helter-skelter of cross-directions and cross-purposes. Invectives are
being hurled, and even objects. While being televised at a country
political meeting the other night, ex-Minister and present candidate
François Mitterrand was hit on the nose by a pear, and bled freely
before the camera. Already eleven of the national political parties have
dropped from sight, as if they had fallen through a trapdoor. Even the
names of the fantasy midget parties that only Frenchmen could father
seem unusually odd this year. One outside Paris that has half a dozen
candidates running is called the Witness of Christ Party, and is
politically opposed to people's taking medicine. Another party calls
itself the League of Consumers in Favor of Lowering the Cost of
Living and Stabilizing the Franc. Still another, more vengeful, is
named Social Solidarity Against Former Deputies. The most optimistic
little party is simply called the Fifth Republic.

It was well known in advance that Mendès-France would lead a
new Left—his Republican Front—in a try for a majority to effect the
vitally needed reforms in whatever sort of Parliament is hatched out
in 1956. Nobody realized that a new extreme Right was also about to
burst into the campaign—the Poujadistes. Pierre Poujade will be recalled as the husky, belligerent, thirty-five-year-old shopkeeper from
St-Céré in southwestern France, who last winter roused a popular
revolt among other little businessmen against paying what they call

unfairly high taxes. Since then, his followers have cut their political eyeteeth pretty well all over France by getting into the Chambers of Commerce, which are elected bodies here. This month, exactly like Hitler when he was still a Fascist débutant, Poujade is shouting that his party is neither Left nor Right but only national. It is also anti-Semitic, anti-Communist, anti-democratic, anti-parliamentary, and pro-violence. A week or so ago, at a hysterical mass meeting, Poujade thundered, "When we come to power, if the deputies don't do their job right, we will hang them!" At Mendès-France's Salle de la Mutualité meeting for women voters, the well-organized Poujadiste strong-arm squad of hecklers yelled, "Mendès to the scaffold, Mauriac to the jackals [because of his democratic Moroccan sympathies], and Herriot to the Panthéon!," this last meaning that the octogenarian Radical Socialist leader is so old and dead that he should be entombed. At Poujade's Salle Wagram meeting, on mounting the platform he immediately did his regular striptease act, pulling off his windbreaker, scarf, and sweater and then rolling up his shirtsleeves, before firing his hearers with the declaration that "Our ancestors cut off the head of a king for doing far less than the men who govern us today!" As enthusiasm mounted, a woman devotee screamed, "Poujade is Jeanne d'Arc and Henri Quatre both!" In the tough style he affects, he finally called not only on his shopkeeeprs but on underpaid workmen and the ever dissatisfied peasantry to vote the Poujade ticket, "to save their guts and France." It is now expected that the Poujadistes will elect about ten deputies to the new Parliament—not bad for a beginning.

Registration has been the heaviest in the history of the two modern Republics, and the voting should be, too. Once more, it is Mendès-France who has galvanized the whole political scene. His speeches are dramatic and damning against the late government leaders. He is still attacking the curse of drink in France, and "the kingdom of alcohol" ruled by the industrial-alcohol trust. Though middle-class Left liberals are always saying that what France needs is a leader, some now say that they are afraid to vote for leader Mendès because he may be too autocratic. Others, being anti-Semitic, say that they are afraid to vote for him because voting for him, a Jew, will increase anti-Semitism here—a fine case of upside-down logic. The best anti-Communist political wisecrack of the campaign was made by Socialist chief Guy Mollet, who said disdainfully, "French Communists are not Left, they are East." Conservative Antoine Pinay, addressing a small, refined group of youths in a salon at the Hotel Lutétia, opened by remarking, "Someone has said that politics is the art of making possible that which is necessary." "Valéry—Paul Valéry, the poet—said it!" one listening youth shouted impatiently. Pinay, who was pinch-hitting for his more important and now ultraconservative running mate Edgar Faure, also told the young men, "Military service is out-of-date —just a few months of it will be enough." As further flattering planks in the Faure youth program, he promised them scholarships and organized part-time jobs, poverty among university students and the need to earn while studying being a terrible education problem here. He also promised government loans so that youth could get married while still young enough to enjoy marriage, with the loans being repaid in part, on a sort of installment plan, by the birth of each child. Oh, this is undoubtedly an extraordinarily entertaining French election campaign!

January 5, 1956
The Tour Eiffel caught fire the day after the elections. It was something that no one in France expected and that could hardly be believed when it happened—and it was a perfect symbol of the election results. Nobody had been able to imagine anything worse than that the new Assembly should turn out to resemble the old one. Neither politicians nor voters had any advance notion of the curious monster they were creating between them, with its body paralyzed in the middle and with swollen, extraneous wings on its left and right. It was the wild success of the Poujadists that upset all predictions and calculations and has left in its destructive wake nothing but explanations as strange as the victory itself. According to *Figaro*, it is now clear—too late—that the Poujadists are the myriads of little forgotten and discontented men, anti-parliamentarian and leaderless, who rose with a shout in 1951 to follow the nobilities of General de Gaulle and this year settled for the fisticuffs of the stationery-shop keeper of St.-Céré, who thus inherited de Gaulle's leadership in an illegitimacy of descent such as no previous political campaign has ever seen. There was certainly nothing secretive or hidden in the Poujadists' campaign, animated as it was by shouting hecklers at rival meetings, yells, fights, threats, and a violence of language and sentiment that echoed in every corner of France. Maybe all this deafened the Institut Français d'Opinion Publique, the French Gallup Poll, which heard nothing at all to indicate that Poujade's men would come out of their fights with fifty-one Assembly seats. It was predicted that the Communists would win a couple of dozen additional seats, but no

one dreamed they would win fifty-two new ones, which makes them the dominant party, with a hundred and forty-five deputies, and, furthermore, the only established party in all France to win new seats, every other party having lost in strength. Never before in the electoral history of the four Republics have all the parliamentary parties slid downhill together this way, in a crumbling decline set going by a kick from the discontented voters, and never before have the only parties to pick up new seats been two anti-parliamentary parties.

On Tuesday night, with the returns mostly in, *Le Monde* went straight to the heart of the matter. "The problem of tomorrow" it stated, "is to ascertain whether, outside of the Communists and Poujadists, a government majority can be located." On Wednesday, two days after the election, the Communist paper *Humanité* suddenly ran an enormous headline : "VIVE LE FRONT POPULAIRE!" *Huma*'s idea of the Popular Front today is a kind of Communist houseparty where everyone is welcome to stop in and make common cause against the reactionaries, and since both the Socialists and Mendès-France's adherents have refused the invitation, it now appears that the guests for whom *Humanité* is hanging out the latchstring must be the reactionary Poujadists themselves, though they are considered by everybody else the fiercest and most ignorant reactionaries now going. Nobody in the center is blind to the fact that the two parties, rigged up in an unnatural plurality, would be a terrible combination. The Faurist majority no longer exists, and the strict Mendésists, too, are a minority. The number of Mendésist deputies elected is probably around a hundred and fifty, and of Faurists perhaps two hundred; nobody can tell exactly, because a baker's dozen or so on each side are affiliates who defy positive categorizing until tried and proved. The only optimistic prophecy given out so far on the future of this new Parliament is that it cannot last more than six months before being dissolved.

The thing that is clearest now is the picture of the voters—of their energy and determination to express themselves, and their definite frame of mind, which is largely discontent with what they have been receiving from the government as it has been set up recently, and also over the past ten years. This is considered the only reading possible for the dwindling number of seats they gave the old-line, established French parties. It is the key reading for the big gain they gave the Communists and for the landslide sendoff they proffered the Poujadists —votes representing, to an unidentifiable degree, social protest, dissatisfaction, and hopes for change, rather than any recent flood of dialectical conversions or any great historical conviction as to Poujade's odd notion of reviving the Etats Généraux of 1789 (which, he would have discovered if he had read a little farther in Larousse, resulted in a governmental paralysis that led to the creation of a National Assembly, which is what France has now and which has long been paralyzed in its turn). This time, the voters were voting for what they thought they and France ought to have now, not someday, and for the politicians or groups most likely to be able to provide at least part of it—and, above all, for men who would get something, almost anything, done.

In an expectedly heavy turnout, over eighty per cent of the voting population went to the polls—a figure that makes American election intensities look puny. There has not been a winter national election in France since 1876, winter being considered a poor time to get people out to vote. And the day after New Year's, the biggest annual family holiday, is the worst day for an election in the whole year. Parisians who had gone off on the traditional holiday cut their pleasures short in the civic resolve, rare in any democracy, to get back and do their duty. The state railways assisted, with more than a hundred extra so-called voters' trains coming into the Gare de Lyon alone on Sunday and Monday mornings from the South—especially from the Riviera. Beginning on Monday, motor routes leading to Paris were reported thick with family cars of all grades, bringing the adults —generally accompanied by country baskets of Brussels sprouts and pale winter butter, about the only farm produce available just now— to the *urnes*. The importance of this big turnout was that it constituted a grave warning. One of the most bitterly popular slogans was *"Sortez les sortants!"* ("Throw out the outgoing deputies!"), and a hundred and forty-six of them were so thrown into political oblivion. The Gaullist Social Republican Party was almost wiped out, Bidault's M.R.P.s took a bad drubbing, and the theory and functioning of Parliament itself once more suffered a hard beating. However, according to Wednesday night's *Le Monde*, Parliament will have its new chance in the hands of the Socialists and of Mendès-France, on both of whom the majority and the government of tomorrow will depend. That can well be a lot better luck than Parliament and a great many voters deserve.

OFFICIAL POLICIES OF THE PREMIERS

Premier Guy Mollet's Governmental Program

Excerpts From the Statement of Policy
Delivered by Premier-Designate Guy Mollet
Before the French National Assembly on January 31, 1956

M. Mollet dealt first with those problems "which are more a matter of parliamentary then of governmental initiative, but whose solution is nevertheless a pre-condition for any lasting improvement of the situation in France.

"In particular, although an at least controversial use of the right of dissolution has just been made, we must not on that account give up the idea of changing the Constitution in this respect, in such a way as to increase the stability of the executive power and thus strengthen the authority of the State. I hope the Assembly will take up without delay the proposals already submitted by several of our colleagues. I should like to point out that, however much it wishes to respect the Parliament's full sovereignty, the Government would consider it its duty to intervene if the Assembly did not reach a swift decision.

"The second problem before the Assembly is that of electoral reform. The country wants a clear and simple system. I welcome in this respect the initiative just taken by the group to which I have the honor of belonging, and I hope the National Assembly will consider it as soon as possible.

"The third problem concerns parliamentary procedure or, more precisely, the rules of the Assembly. Although I thoroughly disapprove of the unfair attacks which certain people have made against the system itself or against elected representatives, I must admit that the methods of operation of this Assembly are often faulty, that they paralyze and wear out the members. . . .

Algeria
"The most urgent, the most painful (of the problems currently facing France) is that of Algeria. The Government must give it priority. It dominates all those which France has to solve. The President of the

French Embassy, New York, *Speeches and Press Conferences*, No. 55, February 1956.

Council will devote his first efforts to it and give it his personal attention.

"The sending to Algiers of a Resident Minister—an office which has
been entrusted to a distinguished personality to whose selflessness I
wish to pay tribute—and the presence at his side of two Secretaries of
State are evidence of the Government's determination to act swiftly
and to have its decisions rigorously respected.

"During recent weeks, and particularly in the last few days, I have
inquired into all aspects of the question. The first conclusion I have
come to is that we must exclude from the debate any bickering over
words: assimilation, integration, association, federation, etc. Besides,
we would soon realize that, whatever choice we made in principle, for
a long time the measures would be the same and would tend toward
a greater degree of freedom and equality. The important thing today
is not to set one theory against another, but to give evidence of determination, to define objectives, intentions and, if possible, a method.

"France's objective, the Government's resolve, is first and foremost
to restore peace, to free the minds of men on both sides from the
burden of fear, and for that purpose, to put an end to terrorism and
repression. The next step is to continue organizing the institutions on
a democratic basis, to establish coexistence between the two sections
of the population which history has brought together and which we
shall not allow to be separated, and to ensure the country's economic
and social development. Our goal, therefore, is to maintain and
strengthen the indissoluble union between Algeria and Metropolitan
France.

"Need I insist on what France would become without Algeria,
Algeria without France? History, human contacts and economic ex-
changes have created between them ties which are essential and
profitable to both.

"France's goal is at one and the same time to recognize and respect
Algeria's individuality and to establish full political equality among all
her inhabitants.

"Whom are we addressing? Algeria consists of two principal groups.
First, there is an important minority of European origin, which is
itself divided: besides a few men, whose short-sighted selfishness is to
a great extent responsible for the present situation, it comprises persons
of modest origin, conscientious workers devoted to their country: it is
by them, through them, that France is present in Algeria. Second,
there is a native population daily increasing in number. Although it
includes unfortunately, a minority of fanatics and criminals, its

immense majority desires only to maintain its ties with France. Yet the latter must ensure full equality of rights to those Moslems whose equality of responsibilities no one has ever contested. Knowing the facts, having set our objectives, let us try to define our methods. The National Assembly must solemnly affirm that Algeria's ultimate fate will never, in any case, be decided unilaterally.

"We shall then assert unequivocally—and this follows from our first principle—that we shall not allow any solution to be imposed by force or ever permit one section of the population to dictate its views to the other.

Free Elections With a Single Electoral College—"It is the Government's intention that the people should be consulted as soon as possible, by means of free elections under a single college system, and this implies electoral reform.

"I do not want to say anything today on the chronological order in which the contemplated elections are to take place: elections to the French Parliament, to the Algerian Assembly, which will have to be dissolved, and to the local assemblies.

"The Government will shortly submit to the Assembly the texts giving it the necessary powers for putting into effect certain preliminary reforms, especially municipal reform and the reform of the civil service and administration in Algeria. The fundamental decisions that I have just outlined will bring about a change of climate.

"Although the military potential of the forces deployed in Algeria cannot be reduced in the immediate future, their efficiency will be increased by means of simple reforms in their structure and use, which will improve their adaptation to local conditions. The troops' needs will be met and their relief assured.

"While safeguarding the security of persons and property, the Government intends to prove that France is determined to bring about the necessary relaxation of tension. Besides the indispensable reforms in the administration and the civil service, which I have already mentioned, it will undertake the immediate release of political prisoners, no confusion being possible between the latter and those persons convicted through regular penal procedure.

"It will also undertake a series of urgent and indispensable measures in the economic and social fields, designed especially to continue and expand the large-scale public works program and to combat poverty by distributing food and clothing. The Government also attaches the greatest importance to agrarian reform.

"In this Algerian drama, where France is staking her destiny, it is the Government's duty to tell the country the truth and to act. Otherwise, events might lead to the irreparable, and this France can and must prevent through initiative and will power.

Economic and Financial Policy
"The political, economic and social policy of the Government will bar, on the one hand inflation and devaluation, on the other social injustice. Inflation ruins the wage earners and the economically underprivileged; it destroys savings and benefits only the speculators. Economic expansion, coupled with a rigorous financial policy, is the only way of saving the currency: it must therefore be pursued tenaciously. . . .

Tax Reform
"The Government will not undertake any new expenditure without at the same time proposing to the Assembly the necessary measures for financing it, coupled with the maximum savings which can be effected on budgetary items not connected with equipment and public works. It will not be sufficient, however, to ensure the balance of new expenditures; a patient effort must be made to reduce a budgetary deficit so great that it may one day affect the state of our currency.

"Of course we must utilize as extensively as possible, and for carefully chosen purposes, the capital that is currently plentiful on the market. Savings must be used for producing and not for spending. That is why the ordinary expenditures of the State must be covered by ordinary resources. The Government will propose to the Assembly a fiscal reform—which the previous Assembly had already heard about—a reform based on simplification, efficiency, and justice. It will provide in particular for the complete suppression of the tax collecting duties attributed until now to small tradesmen and artisans—each one here should know, were he better informed, that this is an old project—and for a complete transformation of the system of local finances.

"The Government will determine to what extent it will have to ask Parliament for certain special powers in economic and social matters. It will do its best to limit these powers and to resort as much as possible to the procedure of the 'lois-cadres*', which has often been defined before the National Assembly. . . ."

*[A loi-cadre is a general term for an act by which parliament authorizes an over-all policy but leaves detailed decisions of implementation to the executive —Eds.]

Principles of French Policy in Algeria Defined by Premier Guy Mollet

Main Excerpts of Statement
Made by French Premier Guy Mollet Before the National
Assembly on February 16, 1956

" . . . I took the feelings of Algeria's European population into consideration when I had to make my decisions. Under the Constitution, I alone was responsible for these decisions, and I accept full responsibility. . . .

"The Minister Residing in Algeria, General Catroux, with his unusually high ideals, would not allow his name to become a cause of discord between himself and his former comrades-in-arms. He asked me to release him from his duties. I made my choice. I refused to let some people make martyrs of themselves. I denied them the victims which they had already announced. I accepted General Catroux's resignation and I assume full responsibility for my decision.

The Military Situation in Algeria
"The rebels are operating mainly on the political and psychological levels. Purely military action is of only relatively minor interest for them; it is merely the basis for an infinitely broader propaganda campaign.

"The undeniable effectiveness of this political and psychological action accounts for the far-reaching disturbances which relatively small bands have been able to cause throughout Algeria, in spite of the military measures put into effect by France. France's answer will remain inadequate so long as it rests solely on a military basis.

"I have been told this by the military leaders themselves: the army can keep terorism in check. It cannot eliminate it alone, if the terrorists have the support of a large section of the population.

"The Government will therefore take all necessary measures to ensure order and respect for the laws of the Republic, but at the same time, it will give the Moslems grounds for hope and will in turn make use of political and propaganda weapons.

"To ensure the security, to protect the lives of both the Europeans and Moslems of Algeria, such is France's prime duty.

French Embassy, New York, *Speeches and Press Conferences*, No. 56, February 1956.

"It is not, however, the solution to the Algerian problem, which lies in the economic, social and political fields.

"The Government is determined to make a considerable effort in order to develop Algeria's economy and raise the standard of living of its population. It will wage war on poverty, but will not confine itself to that: to do so would be to resign itself to a kind of social paternalism and to disappoint a population which yearns for human dignity as much as for bread.

Social Reforms
"All our reforms will be dominated by this one concern: to provide work and livelihood for a million men. We shall begin with an immediate measure, the emergency distribution of basic foodstuffs, to be furnished by Metropolitan France.

"This aid will be supplemented by appropriations which will make it possible to provide manual labor for the greatest number of unemployed, and by strict limitations on immigration.

A Huge Financial Effort
"These measures, of course, are not enough to renovate the Algerian economy. A large-scale equipment program will mobilize all of the country's natural resources. It will be supplemented by an industrialization program. This implies a huge financial effort on the part of Metropolitan France, an effort which will best prove France's determination to remain present in Algeria.

"Our action will deal first with agricultural investments designed to bring the farm population to an advanced stage of economic development. The Government intends to carry out, in the words of a prominent expert, a large-scale program of small-scale works: soil restoration, small irrigation projects, water supply points, development of the rural improvement centers and of the centers for the technical training of the Moslem farm population. At the same time it will work out a vast plan of agrarian reform, to which it attaches the greatest importance. . . .

Political Measures
"Let us consider first Algeria's European population. Some—I think it is a mistake—have tried to make colonialists out of all of them. If that was once my attitude, it no longer is. There is among them a small, selfish—fiercely selfish—minority of propertied people, relentlessly defending their own interests and political position. I have

already mentioned their financial power. These men have taken their precautions. They willingly gamble on the worst. Unfortunately, they back the extremist organizations and the shock-troops which some have tried to set against the Government. They take an unfair advantage of the good faith of patriots for interests which are in no way French.

"The Government is determined to take all necessary measures to ensure due respect for the laws of the Republic. My talks with different people in Algeria have convinced me that the great majority of Europeans is not ready to follow the extremists. We must restore confidence to all these Europeans by ensuring their security: both an inner feeling of security—France will never abandon them, she will never abandon Algeria—and physical security for themselves and their families.

"We must next convince them that immobilism never pays, that to cling to the status quo is to have already lost.

"There is a certain parallelism between the situation I have just described and that of the Moslem community. Everything can yet be regained by France, but we no longer have the right to delay. Each day the extremists try to widen the gap between the two communities. . . .

"France must regain the initiative. She must supplement economic and social measures with others designed to fulfill the undeniable political aspirations of the Moslem population. It will be all to her credit to recognize and satisfy these aspirations.

"The Moslems yearn for social, economic and political justice. But they want this justice to be fair, to guarantee the freeing of the innocent as well as the punishment of the guilty. Above all, they want it to be the same for all.

The Algerian Personality

"To both Europeans and Moslems, I once again solemnly declare that the union between Metropolitan France and Algeria is indissoluble. The Government will fight to keep France in Algeria, and she will remain there. There is no future for Algeria without France.

"To both Europeans and Moslems, I solemnly declare that France recognizes and respects Algeria's personality.

"To both Europeans and Moslems, the Government solemnly announces that what is meant by Algeria's personality will not in any case be determined unilaterally. It will be determined by free discussions with the authentic representatives of the population, chosen

through fair and supervised elections. We shall not choose our inter-
locutors: they will be chosen by popular vote.

"One of the very first concerns of the Government is to hold free
elections as soon as possible.

"The Government will give priority to the election of the Deputies
from Algeria to the National Assembly. It will next organize elections
to the Algerian Assembly.

"The freedom and fairness of these elections will be strictly guaranteed and controlled by all the means at the disposal of the Government and the Parliament.

"In order to put its policy into effect, the Government does not
exclude the possibility of asking Parliament for the special powers
which it might consider necessary for swift and forceful action. It
is waiting to be informed of the details of the program now being
worked out by the Minister Residing in Algeria.

"Internal action will be supplemented by international action. Confronted with the painful problem of Algeria, France must be able to
count on the unqualified support of her friends and know how to
obtain respect for her rights from all the other nations. I do not
think I have to say more.

"Our objective will be to replace by a confident co-operation the
tête-à-tête between two communities now firmly rooted in their positions and often lined up against each other in mutual distrust. It will
be to create a fraternal Franco-Moslem community, in which Europeans and Moslems will work together for the prosperity of Algeria."

Premier Bourgès-Maunoury Outlines His Governmental Program

> Following are the main excerpts of the policy
> statement made by Premier Designate Maurice
> Bourgès-Maunoury before the French National
> Assembly on June 12, 1957. The new Premier
> obtained investiture by a vote of 240 to 194.

The Algerian Question

"The Algerian drama is my first concern. Let us, first of all, do away
with a false dilemma. We do not have the choice today between two
courses, one being the continuation at all costs of an unending and

French Embassy, New York, *Speeches and Press Conferences*, No. 96, June 13,
1957.

absurd struggle, and the other leading suddenly, as by a miracle, to peace and prosperity.

"We must wage the struggle as long as it is forced upon us, and at the same time, we must help millions of men to build together a new Algeria.

"The officers of our army, the soldiers of France, have a right to our gratitude. This army has watched, day and night, over the security of millions of men and women whose very lives and property are in danger. It has paid heavily. I should like to pay tribute to the victims of terrorism and their families, as well as to those who fall on the field of battle.

"These sacrifices will not be in vain. The rebels know now that they will never win by force of arms. For a while they had hoped to have us condemned by the United Nations. They failed in this attempt. After all the acts of terrorism, whatever their origin, after the monstrous massacre of the 300 male inhabitants of Melouza, world public opinion knows what they are capable of.

"Our weariness is their last hope. In that, too, they are mistaken. I say this solemnly to all the people of Algeria: our country will continue in its effort as long as necessary. It can and wants to do this.

"We hereby make another solemn commitment: to undertake— without waiting any longer for our adversaries to show their willingness —to undertake the building of a new Algeria. For that is the problem now confronting us. Confident in the future which we can guarantee to it, and tired of being criticized by the rebellion, the population must isolate this rebellion and work with us for its final elimination.

"The previous Government set an end goal: to maintain and strengthen the indissoluble union between Metropolitan France and Algeria; and at the same time, to recognize and respect Algeria's individual character, while providing political equality for all its inhabitants.

"By our uninterrupted determination and action, we shall prove to Algerian public opinion, and to world opinion as well, that our promise to establish a new state of things in Algeria is not a short-lived statement of intentions.

"The strategy of the rebels is quite clear. They reject the cease-fire. Thus, they avoid holding free elections, hence discussing the statute. At the same time they turn to world opinion to say that no progress has been made and that France's promises have not been kept. The assassinations, the bloody events of the last few days make a tragic thing of this hypocrisy. We shall not let ourselves be overwhelmed by such a maneuver. We shall not let ourselves be hindered in the construction of a new Algeria.

A "Loi-Cadre" for Algeria—"That is why, while retaining all the objectives which Premier Guy Mollet had defined in his declaration of investiture, and while the appeal for a cease-fire remains valid, I have decided to introduce as soon as possible a draft 'loi-cadre' to serve as a basis for the gradual establishment of new political structures. They will be set up first on the local level, then in the Departments, and lastly on a regional level. Each region will become a provincial political unit.

"The provinces and their special political organs will be the starting point for elaborating the structure of the Algerian entity. When it becomes possible to hold elections, the elected representatives of the population will be called upon to study this 'loi-cadre' in order to adopt it or to suggest the changes which they would consider desirable. It will thus be put into effect with the support of all men of good will.

"This political reform will be preceded by a far-reaching administrative reform for which the groundwork has already been laid and which will result essentially in bringing closer together the administrative organs and the populations for which they are responsible. These reforms will lead to the gradual elimination of the General Government of Algeria and to the transfer of powers from the central to the regional level. . . .

"I do not think that outbreaks of whipped-up nationalism are inevitable in the evolution of the peoples of the French Union. In a country like Algeria which derives its unity solely from the French presence, such a phase could only be one of confusion, marked by a series of disastrous upheavals. It is this which, properly speaking, would be retrogression.

"The truth is that the Europeans and Moslems of Algeria have a great task to perform together and that this country, which belongs to both groups alike, must be able to ensure in the future equality of living conditions and status for all. The truth is that the maintenance of the French presence there will prevent decades of groping and mistakes for the greatest good of the population."

The Financial Situation

"We cannot escape the necessity of asking the Bank of France for a new advance. Nor can we any longer avoid drawing on the gold reserves of the Bank at the end of June in order to meet our external obligations."

"We are thus obviously passing through a very difficult period. The study which I have made of the accidental and underlying causes of this situation has convinced me that the remedies were not beyond our reach. They presuppose at one and the same time very drastic immediate action and patient longer term action. The program presented by my Government will be guided by this twofold requirement.

"It is fallacious to single out one budgetary item among others as responsible for the deficit. In this respect, the inflationary effect of our military expenditures in Algeria has often been overestimated.

"Our military budget today, including operations in Algeria, is about $3.7 billion. It accounts for a smaller share of the over-all public expenditures than it did five years ago—a time when, it is true, we were engaged in operations in Indochina, but a time also when the national income was far from its present level. If the operations in Algeria were to stop, the savings that might gradually be anticipated could not exceed that figure. In addition the return of peace in Algeria should not lead us to make that budgetary economy.

"The funds released should for the most part be devoted to economic development and to improving the standard of living of the populations of North Africa. . . .

Institutional Reform
Referring to the problems of France's governmental institutions, M. Bourgès-Maunoury pointed out that, in the light of ten years' experience, the strengthening of the Executive is a pressing need. It must come about as a result of a revision of the Constitution. The Committee on Universal Suffrage has done a sizable job, but owing to lack of agreement on several important points, their work threatens to bog down.

"At this point, it is the Government's duty to intervene in an attempt to reconcile the various points of view. The State's authority must be reinforced and the institutions of the French Union adopted. . . ."

M. Bourgès-Maunoury added that his Government would have no intention of putting pressure on the Assembly to adopt this or that system of voting, but that it did seem necessary to him to remove an obstacle by a clear vote on principles and to dispel a source of conflict between closely related groups which are often in agreement on other important questions.

"We must not wait for the end of Parliament's term of office for that body to discuss, in the last minute rush, the manner in which the country will be called upon to vote."

Premier Felix Gaillard Outlines His Governmental Program

Following are the main excerpts of the policy statement made by Premier-Designate Félix Gaillard before the French National Assembly on November 5, 1957. The new Premier obtained investiture by a vote of 337 to 174.

"Since the beginning of the year, that is to say during the past ten months, France has undergone two ministerial crises.

"For a total of two months, she was without a Government.

"Nothing was able to prevent these crises, not the threat of a double financial failure, nor the need for unity in the face of events in Algeria, nor the concern to keep a place for our country among the nations of the world.

"Our young men are fighting with honor in Algeria. Our homes are brightened by the presence of many children. Our engineers are discovering immense riches beneath the desert sands. France is working, producing and progressing.

"And yet, the exercise of power falls prey to instability and to the opposition between parties.

"The healthy and vigorous body of our country is stricken with a purely political malady, which prevents us more and more from accomplishing the great tasks of the State.

"The very gravity of this malady has made it imperative for me not to constitute just any kind of Government that might gain acceptance as a result of your weariness and your resignation, but—in short—to resolve the crisis and not to camouflage it. . . .

"The leaders or representatives of the various political groups will be asked to form a permanent delegation to the Government.

"This body will have as its mission to deal with the political and national problems confronting our political life, to compose the differences that arise among its members instead of allowing these differences to be settled in a way always negative for the opposition.

"The day when the Government finds itself unable to settle these differences and to enforce its policy, it would be logical—but only then—for it to yield its place to another, for then it would have shown that it can no longer fulfill its mission.

"We are determined to restore the fundamental rules of the func-

French Embassy, New York, *Speeches and Press Conferences*, No. 101, November 5, 1957.

tioning of parliamentary democracy. You must help us if you do not wish to see citizens, in ever-increasing numbers, lose faith in the regime and confine themselves to the pursuit of their personal interests alone, to the detriment of the nation's interest. . . .

"The priority and the importance of the problems that assail us is so obvious that the Government could not allow minor projects to stand in its way.

"In the months to come, we will be engaged in a contest—and if we do not work together we will surely lose it—a contest on which depends, at one and the same time, the safeguarding of our currency and the prosperity of our economy, the future of Algeria and of the Franco-African community, the possibility of organizing a truly effective democracy and of joining as major partners in the Europe that is becoming united.

"These problems will have to be taken up according to a rigid schedule. The majority that I wish to form today around the Government will have, with its very first vote, to pledge itself to close its eyes and ears to minor problems, to silence all impatience, to endure with us the difficulties that we cannot foresee at this time but that will certainly come to block our way.

"Beginning tomorrow, the Parliament must make up for a lost month.

"It must first renew the special powers relating to Algeria that were granted the previous Government, and resume the debate on a draft 'loi-cadre' defining the principles on which our country's Algerian policy is based.

"This text must indicate unequivocally that our country is not satisfied with the necessary action of wiping out terrorism but that it seeks a political solution of the Algerian problem.

"Within the framework of indissoluble ties between Metropolitan France and this territory, the personality of Algeria must be able to develop fully. It will succeed in this only by respecting the ethnic communities of which it is composed and by ensuring equitable representation for all the human and economic components of its population on all the administrative bodies of the territory.

"The desire to ensure the coexistence of the Algerian communities must be reconciled with equality of the rights of individuals within a single electoral college. To this end the Government will draft an electoral law taking into account the reservations expressed by certain members of the Assembly at the time of the previous debates on the 'loi-cadre.' The two bills will be submitted to the Parliament at the same time.

"The Assembly will thus proclaim not only to Algeria but to the world that its policy is not limited to the reestablishment of order but also, and above all, that it provides for the political future of a territory that cannot but remain closely associated with France.

"As of now, the Government renews its appeal for a cease-fire on terms which have remained valid. It is ready to give guarantees that as soon as the fighting has ended, as soon as calm has been restored, free elections can take place. The new Algerian representatives will discuss the future organization of Algeria with the Government. My Government will be ready to make all the necessary contacts, at any time, with those who are fighting against us in order to bring about a cease-fire.

"I should like from this very rostrum to appeal to our adversaries. They must understand that three years of fighting have not weakened France's determination. For three years, more than a million young men have been doing their duty in Algeria. They did not only fight, they built roads. Back in Metropolitan France, far from criticizing France's work and action in Algeria, they have extolled it wherever they went. Thus all the people of France feel Algeria closer to their hearts each day.

"Therefore our weariness should not be relied upon to force us to give up. Nor will terrorism in Metropolitan France—which the Government has decided not to tolerate—alter our determination.

"And tomorrow, when peace is restored, France again—as she did yesterday—will provide the indispensable and brotherly assistance required by a young and rapidly growing people.

"The rebel leaders know our centuries-old traditions. From what other country can they expect so much understanding, so much unselfish support? How long will they put hate before the obvious interest of Algeria?

"I cannot believe that this appeal will remain unanswered.

"Silence would show that the F.L.N. leaders are the worst enemies of the Algerian people by imposing terror, murder and war upon them; by depriving them of an era of prosperity heralded by the exploitation of the wealth of the Sahara; by continuing to burden Tunisia with the dreadful problem of the occupation of part of her territory by the armed bands of 'fellaghas.'

"France offers peace in Algeria, and at the same time offers to Tunisia, Morocco and the other neighboring territories of Black Africa and Arab Africa, an association in the exploitation of the wealth of the Sahara.

"Today, she is ready to put all her own resources into this immense task, and tomorrow, to enroll the cooperation of the countries with whom she will be associated in the European Common Market.

"The choice is now between war and peace. In either case, France will not fail in her mission.

"As soon as Parliament has approved the 'loi-cadre,' it will have to discuss the budget for 1958.

"The Government wants every possible means to be used so that the budget bill be promulgated by January 1st, thus eliminating the need for a provisional monthly appropriation. We can best show our determination to recover financially by voting a budget providing for greatly decreased expenditures and new sources of revenue. . . .

Transformation of the Political Institutions of Algeria
The Loi-Cadre and the Electoral Law

The "Loi-Cadre" on the Institutions of Algeria and the Electoral Law* outline a program that makes it possible for Algeria's political institutions to evolve in the direction of greater democracy. These new institutions were designed to answer the need for peaceful coexistence of the various communities living side by side in Algeria.

The first concern of the Government was to ensure absolute equality of citizens and communities. This is evidenced by the abolition of the double electoral college and by the institution of universal suffrage with a single college for elections to all representative assemblies; all voters, regardless of the community to which they belong, will be listed on a single electoral roll, will cast their votes in the same polling places with the same ballots, and will choose between the same candidates.

The second concern is expressed by the establishment both of legislative and executive organs, in regions defined by physical, economic, and human geography, and of central bodies for Algeria as a whole. Each region will have its Assembly elected by universal suffrage and a single college, its Council of Communities, and its responsible Government. In Algiers, the corresponding organs will be created according to the procedure which has almost always been followed for the setting up of federative institutions. The powers of these organs will be determined with a view to as great a decentralization as possible and

French Embassy, New York, *French Affairs*, No. 52, February 1958.

*The Electoral Law was adopted in its final form by the French Parliament on January 28, 1958, and the "Loi-Cadre" on January 31, 1958.

will permit the Moslems to manage their own affairs on the various administrative levels.

Concerning the powers reserved to the French Republic, these will, to a certain extent, still be exercised by the populations of Algeria, since they will also have their representatives in the parliamentary assemblies of Metropolitan France.

The third concern is shown by the evolutionary character of the "Loi-Cadre," which provides machinery for the evolution of the Algerian institutions and permits the adaptation of the various powers devolving upon the different legislative and executive organs. Thus, it is not a question of a statute drawn up once and for all; free discussions will take place between France and the validly appointed representatives of the Algerian populations on the very meaning of their institutions.

GENERAL PRINCIPLES

These two laws express, on the institutional level, the fundamental principles which must govern the new Algeria:

> To ensure the coexistence of the communities which make up Algeria, with due respect for the rights of each;

> To ensure strict equality of rights and just representation of all the inhabitants, regardless of their origin or their religion;

> To define the Algerian personality, while maintaining the necessary ties between Metropolitan France and Algeria.

For almost a year now, the French Government has stated categorically that, as soon as a cease-fire has been achieved, it would hold free elections in Algeria and that it would negotiate with the freely elected representatives of Algeria. This offer remains valid. The refusal with which this proposal of a cease-fire has been met by the leaders of the rebellion, however, must not result in crippling the political evolution necessary to Algeria and in delaying the setting up of these institutions. That is why the lawmakers stipulated that temporary structures could be established right away. These structures will serve as a basis for discussion by the elected Algerian representatives as soon as free elections can be organized.

The Government wrote into the very body of the text itself the determination of the French Republic to contribute to the economic and social development of Algeria. This will be done through the Fund for Economic Development, which was established by decree in August 1957. (Title V of the "Loi-Cadre")

Finally, the Government thought it advisable to make it possible for the institutions to evolve. It is stipulated, therefore, that modifications of the "Loi-Cadre" can take place if the desire for this is expressed concurrently by both the Territorial Assemblies and the Federative Assembly of Algeria. (Title VII of the "Loi-Cadre")

DESCRIPTION OF THE INSTITUTIONS

The institutions provided for reflect the desire to respect the existence in Algeria of different communities. These communities must live together in harmony if Algeria is to develop. This presupposes that each of them be given the assurance that it will not be crushed by the other. For this reason, it was decided to have recourse to a federative system.

The Territories

Algeria will be divided into a certain number of territories.

Each territory will manage its own affairs freely and democratically by means of an elected *Territorial Assembly* and a *Government* responsible to that Assembly. They will be competent to handle all questions except those enumerated in Article 9 of the "Loi-Cadre" as coming under the jurisdiction of the central organs of the French Republic or their representatives, or the local collectivities. (Article 3, paragraph 2)

In each territory a *Council of Communities,* comprising an equal number of citizens of French civil status and citizens of other personal status, will be set up. This Council can give its opinion on the decisions of the Territorial Assembly. When these two bodies fail to agree within a given time limit, the Minister for Algeria may either promulgate the decision of the Territorial Assembly, or refer it to the Council of State.

The Federative Institutions

The setting up of a Federative Assembly and a Federative Council will serve as an expression of the Algerian personality.

Certain interests of each territory must be co-ordinated with those of the other territories. Other interests must be brought into harmony or co-ordinated with those of Metropolitan France and the French Union.

The "Loi-Cadre" provides that, two years after its election, each Territorial Assembly may transfer some of its attributes to federative organs. These organs will be set up as soon as the majority of the Territorial Assemblies have expressed their intention to transfer certain attributes.

The Federative Assembly will comprise two sections composed, respectively, of delegates from the Territorial Assemblies and delegates from the Councils of Communities. These sections will sit together, but will vote separately. In the case of disagreement, the same procedure of arbitration will be used as in cases of disagreement between the Territorial Assemblies and the Councils of Communities.

The Federative Council, composed of delegates elected in equal number by each of the Territorial Assemblies, will be charged with carrying out the decisions of the Federative Assembly.

National Sovereignty

The exercise of national sovereignty in Algeria will be consistent with the following conditions:

> The Algerian voters will be represented in the French Parliament as well as in all the other assemblies provided for by the Constitution;
>
> Competence in a certain number of matters enumerated in the "Loi-Cadre" (Article 9) will be reserved to the French Republic. The Republic will be represented in Algeria by a Minister and in the territories by delegates. The Minister will be the depositary of the powers of the Republic and the guardian of the federative institutions.

THE ELECTORAL SYSTEM

The Electoral Law which accompanies the "Loi-Cadre" solemnly enacts into law the principle of a single college and that of the equitable, true, and obligatory representation of the various communities.

With regard to the *territorial and departmental elections,* the law establishes the uninominal list with a single ballot.* The candidate in each district who obtains the greatest number of votes is declared elected. (Articles 1 & 6 of the Electoral Law)

Nevertheless, in order to prevent the oppression of minority communities, a certain number of candidates will be elected at large from

*The uninominal list means that each political group presents one candidate for each seat in the Assembly.

the Department or the territory, according to the formula of proportional representation. (Articles 3 & 4)

With regard to the *municipal elections*, the law provides for proportional representation, as it is established by the electoral code of Metropolitan France. Nevertheless, in all the communes where there are 100 or more residents with a civil or customary status different from that of the majority, the commune must be divided into electoral sections and each section will elect a number of councillors in proportion to the number of its voters. (Article 10) One of the councillors from each section will be designated by his colleagues to record all vital statistics such as births, marriages, and deaths.

TEMPORARY PROVISIONS

The statute will go into effect immediately. As the present situation makes it impossible to hold elections at this time, temporary organs will be set up on a transitional basis. (Title VI of the "Loi-Cadre")

Most of the new communes have already been provided with special delegations whose members were appointed on the basis of consultations with the heads of families and the traditional Moslem assemblies. Eighty per cent of their members are Moslem. Until elections can be held, the Territorial Assemblies will be composed of persons designated by the Municipal Councils and the General Councils.

In Algiers, a temporary Consultative Council, composed of an equal number of delegates from each territorial Government and presided over by the Minister for Algeria, will assist the latter in transferring to the organs of the territories the powers which previously had devolved on the General Government of Algeria; the General Government is abolished by the "Loi-Cadre."

II

"THE MEMORY OF VAIN SACRIFICES"

Introduction

The readings here spotlight the background of the military role in the crisis. They raise the question of how the army was changed by more than a decade of colonial fighting; what had to be promised the army to preserve its loyalties in Algeria; what lessons the army itself drew about communism, revolutionary movements, and its own role in fighting them; finally, what the army would demand of France to continue its mission. The directives of the Algerian Resident Minister, Robert Lacoste, offer a glimpse of how much spokesmen for the regime promised in order to convince the military that it would not sacrifice in vain. But, it must be asked, what were the dangers of Lacoste's approach? The article by General Allard shows how the military conceived of the larger stakes of its African mission. Raoul Girardet attempts to synthesize the impact of the whole Fourth Republic experience. To avoid prejudicing the reader, we have omitted Girardet's summary and final conclusions about the Thirteenth of May. What remains is testimony that conveys an image of the army's mood by a writer sensitive to its notions of honor and empathetic with its conflict in loyalties. Finally, the tract by Roger Trinquier, of which the more general portions are reprinted here, reflects the conclusions about actual fighting that some veterans of Indochina and Algeria were reaching in the later 1950's. In this case the authorship is of special interest, for Trinquier himself was involved in the events of the Thirteenth of May and thereafter with the movement to retain French Algeria. Trinquier's manual leaves the student with sobering inquiries both about the relationship of means and ends in counter-insurgency warfare, and about the possible costs of pursuing "modern warfare" to the political values of supposedly democratic regimes. Taken together, the selections should expose the potential conflict in loyalties among the military as the immediate crisis of the regime opened during the winter and spring of 1958—over an issue involving the exercise of military power.

DIRECTIVES FROM THE RESIDENT MINISTER OF ALGERIA

General Directive No. 1

To the Officers and Noncommissioned Officers
of the Army, Navy and Air Force Stationed in Algeria
Issued by Robert Lacoste, Minister Residing in Algeria,
at Algiers on May 19, 1956

In order to enable you to act at all echelons with the maximum efficiency, I deem it necessary to define for you personally, as precisely as possible, the political course that I intend to follow in Algeria in the name of the Government of the Republic. This directive is only the first example of the constant contact that I wish to establish with all the officers and noncommissioned officers of the regular forces or of the reserves in service here.

France's Inalienable Rights in Algeria

I want to state at the outset, with absolute clarity, that the inalienable rights of France in Algeria do not, in my opinion, admit of any equivocation.

The memory of the vain sacrifices agreed to in the Far East, certain press campaigns, regrettable intrigues, even threats from abroad may have led the Army to think that, embarked on a hopeless venture in North Africa, it enjoyed neither the backing of public opinion nor the full support of the public powers.

I want to take this opportunity, therefore, to assert unquestionably

French Embassy, New York, *French Affairs*, No. 39, January 1957, 2–6, 8–10.

that the troops of Algeria may at all times count on my unconditional support in their action for the re-establishment of order and pacification of this country. In return, I ask them to have full confidence in my efforts to guide it gradually in the direction that I shall outline below. Finally I think there is very great hope that national public opinion, warned of the importance of the Algerian problem, will increasingly support our efforts to re-establish peace with justice in this land.

Yet we must have no illusions regarding the ease with which we shall solve the Algerian problem; this problem is tremendous and of a complex nature, at once political and military. We must not expect any miracles. But I am absolutely sure that it can be solved and that our country is equal to the task. This will no doubt demand time and great effort in all fields, as well as much faith and abnegation. I know that the Army can give all this; I ask more of it: it must serve as an example to all sections of the Algerian population.

The New Forms of Association
Between Metropolitan France and Algeria

It is necessary for you to know the general ideas underlying the political and psychological action in which the Army must co-operate.

First of all, there is the problem of the forms of association between Metropolitan France and the Algerian territory. The Parliament has explicitly recognized a certain "Algerian personality." All Frenchmen, furthermore, agree that the *département* of Oran, for example, cannot have the same status as Ardèche or Lot-et-Garonne.

Furthermore, the presence of two communities (one of French ancestry, the other of Moslem ancestry) living side by side, makes a special statute for Algeria necessary.

Such a statute has existed since 1947 but we must have the courage to recognize that it has never been applied completely. Nevertheless, it is outmoded today. It is therefore necessary to establish a new one. The Government has solemnly undertaken not to decide on it without the co-operation of elected representatives of Algeria—in order to lead the local population to discuss, not its presence within the French community (which is laid down as a formal postulate), but the forms of association between Metropolitan France and Algeria.

We must contrive to reach a period of decreased tension in Algeria in order for this basic reform to be realized.

The Elements of a New Policy

Do we have to wait for that moment, which will undoubtedly be long in coming, in order to promote a new policy? I do not think so, because it is largely insofar as we apply this policy that Algeria will be able to regain a stability which—I wish to make this absolutely clear—may in no way result in a return to the former state of affairs.

An inescapable fact compels our attention today. A mass of some 8,000,000 French-Moslems*—many of whom are underdeveloped, underadministrated, underemployed and undernourished—is growing at a rate which will increase it by 25 per cent in ten years. This mass is undermined by a line of propaganda from abroad which is xenophobic and fanatical. This propaganda, unfortunately abetted by innumerable errors or hesitations on our part, has begun to create an enormous gulf between this mass and a French community called "of French stock" which, although in the minority, is dynamic, lively and jealous of the rights it has acquired under the legitimate pretext of efforts made for the country's development. And these rights have sometimes been translated into fact, through the existence of a preferential system.

Both of these communities have a tendency to withdraw within themselves. In certain regions this is now an accomplished fact.

For the Frenchmen "of French stock" often have reflexes of self-preservation which make them forget that coexistence is imposed on them and that this coexistence cannot validly rely on force alone. It is absolutely necessary that they assimilate this fact.

The French-Moslems, under the influence of readily disseminated propaganda, do not stop to consider that the forms under which certain people want them to develop are incompatible with modern life, the material advantages of which, however, they are demanding more and more. Subjected to a propaganda campaign conducted from abroad, which tries, under the pretext of religion, to fan xenophobic agitation, they are closely watching the very rapid—too rapid—development of two young neighboring states, wondering whether the fact that they have the same faith does not give them *ipso facto* a different nationality from ours. Terrorized by crimes of an atrocious savagery, they lapse into total passivity, while questioning France's determination and her justice.

From these observations it is possible to define the rudiments of a course of action that is quite obviously part of an over-all international policy, which it is not my function to define here, but which implies the abandonment of a certain number of outworn slogans that, by an unfortunate chance, often run counter to our interests, and also an interallied solidarity which it has sometimes been possible to doubt.

*M. Lacoste uses this expression to stress the fact that all Algerians are *ipso facto* citizens of France.

What is happening in Algeria is only one aspect of a gigantic world conflict in which certain Moslem countries, before falling into anarchy, are seeking, by Hitlerian methods, to set up an encroaching dictatorship in part of the African continent.

In this country we are engaged in a struggle which is that of the West, that of civilization against anarchy, of democracy against dictatorship. It is necessary to assimilate this idea in order to understand its full significance. We are defending not only the rights acquired by France in Algeria but also the right of peoples to determine their own destiny otherwise than through fear. We are fighting for liberty.

The Dominant Concern of My Policy is Determined by the Necessity of Bringing the Two Local Communities Closer Together by Restoring Their Confidence in Each Other and in Metropolitan France.
In view of the actual and inadequate condition of the French-Moslems, it is only natural that great political, economic, and social efforts should be made on their behalf.

These efforts must be along the following lines:

1. The economy of this country must undergo a revolutionary transformation in order to enable it to:

> furnish a livelihood to all its inhabitants according to adequate standards;

> meet the demands of a "run-away" increase in the population, which it is morally and physically impossible to curb.

2. This country must be transformed socially in order to bring it gradually to a level comparable to that of the Western countries by overthrowing an outworn framework. It is necessary, for this purpose, to:

> give it an administration which is not overconcentrated at the head but, on the contrary, well developed in all its branches throughout the land;

> combine the two communities within this administration, in order to prevent one of them from having the impression that it is governed exclusively by the other.

3. Finally, the underdeveloped masses must be given an elementary political education in order to enable them later to take a valid part in the management of Algerian affairs and, at a still further date, in those of the national community.

All this presupposes, therefore, the promulgation of political, administrative, and economic reforms, the broad lines of which I now propose to give you.

Political Reforms

I intend to promote very shortly (and without waiting for calm to be restored throughout the country) reforms of the municipal or communal institutions which will be put into effect immediately in all the regions that are calm or pacified.

The aim is to divide the present mixed communes into groups of "douars" or villages which will elect local delegates on the lowest level; in the troubled zones, these delegates can be appointed instead of elected. It is at this stage that we shall be able to give the civic education mentioned above. There will continue to be municipal councillors in these groups of villages but the corps of caids will be abolished.

If total pacification is long in coming, I plan to propose to the Government that—working through these local officials and according to a method of designation yet to be worked out—it seek the representatives we may need to draw up the general statute referred to above, which would replace that of 1947. This statute should fit into an overall pattern, of which we should already be thinking, and which would give the Republic a more flexible framework, allowing Algeria in particular to preserve all its originality.

I should like, in this connection, to make it perfectly clear that the fact of having once been a spokesman for Algeria in discussions with the French Government, does not in my opinion entitle a person to be in any way a representative of this country in the future. . . .

The Army's Role

But none of this can be accomplished unless confidence is re-established, and as a result, order restored.

To this end, the Army's action is decisive and vital.

First by its presence, then by its firmness, the Army must re-establish order in this country. I am sufficiently familiar with its spirit and its traditions to know that it could not possibly abuse this directive.

I am sure that it will be your own wish to remain humane at all times, as the honor of France demands. Furthermore, it is absolutely necessary to be on one's guard against provocation by the rebels, who, by increasing terrorism, are trying to provoke uncontrolled acts of reprisal which they exhibit in order to create the appearance of a war of extermination and to marshal international opinion and the great powers against us, while seeking their support in the diplomatic field. Terrorism must be met with conscious and unfailing discipline and concerted action.

Although it is the instrument of force, the Army is in fact one of the most valid elements of contact I have with the population.

I want each officer and noncommissioned officer to be, in his own sphere, the defender of the ideas which I have set forth here (and which I shall supplement), even if he gives only limited moral support to them himself. I shall even go further: it is my wish, in agreement with your superiors, that you supervise the execution of some of these measures by seeing that they are publicized and even applied.

I have no intention of explaining to you here how I should like your military action to be conducted in the field. Although I am not indifferent to it, your action in this domain is the responsibility of your leaders. I am already seeking with them the best ways of winning more rapidly this war of nerves that is forced on us, and I think that your action must be given as much meaning as possible.

It has been said and reiterated that every conflict is, basically, a conflict of ideologies. But contrary to what may happen in other places, and even if behind them the disturbing Communist propaganda and the conquering passion of Islam may be discerned, our adversaries of today, the terrorists, the rebels, have no ideology other than the wish to evict France from Algeria.

In this "internal" conflict which they want to transform into an "external" conflict, they have no valid theory or framework. They are trying to make up for the absence of any political doctrine by a real racism (which the unconscionable action of certain Frenchmen has, unfortunately, sometimes encouraged). They are seeking to justify, on the grounds of religious kinship, the inadmissible interference of foreigners.

Against this absence of ideology, we can offer not any particular political ideology, but that which the present crisis may reinvigorate, the "national" ideology, the love of France. Our country's enormous resources of culture and generosity have indeed been barely tapped for Algeria. It is up to you to help me draw them here. For we shall build a new Algeria only by giving this Franco-Moslem population, often still backward, complete equality of rights and duties with Metropolitan France in order to satisfy its dignity and legitimate self-respect.

We must take these three words, "Liberty, Equality, Fraternity," sprung from the French Revolution, as the definition of our presence here. No one can claim that we could give anything better to Algeria.

No Foreign Interference in Algeria

I cannot pass over in silence the considerable influence on Algeria of what is happening in Tunisia and Morocco. It is obviously very tempting for all these young neighboring states to seek, at our expense, spectacular distractions to the often unpleasant realities of an independence which they have so loudly demanded. However, it is very dangerous for them thus to seek a certificate of pan-Arabism from donors who grant them no support other than incitement to hatred and arms for assassins.

I can emphatically state that the maintenance, in its entirety, of the French presence in Algeria expressly conditions the existence of the Tunisian and Moroccan regimes which, without it, would fall into anarchy, and I know that their leaders know it, even if they cannot admit it.

Finally, I know the distance which separates Algiers from Algeria and my office from the daily vicissitudes of all the inhabitants of this country. I am attempting, beginning this week, to overcome this by sending out special envoys who are familiar with my intentions and provided with broad powers.

As far as you are concerned, I think I know your difficulties, your worries, your doubts and even your vexations. When I am not told of them, I think I can guess them, and, as a veteran of 1914–1918, I am reminded in thinking of you of that famous caption to one of Forain's drawings, "If only THEY hold out!"

In order to give you confidence, I want to tell you that my own is immense. Undoubtedly, we shall still have, in the days to come, very great trials to overcome in this country in which calm will not suddenly return. But these trials must not frighten you since, like me, you believe in our country and since that faith is your main reason for wearing a uniform.

I see in the Algerian ordeal a reason for believing in a rebirth of France. Something great always has come out of the storms of our history.

General Directive No. 2

To the Officers and Noncommissioned Officers
of the Army, Navy and Air Force Stationed in Algeria
Issued by Robert Lacoste, Minister Residing in Algeria,
on August 18, 1956

Three months ago, in my first general directive, I sketched the broad lines of the course of action I intend to follow with you in Algeria.

We must now take our bearings, by considering first, carefully and honestly, how this action has been put into effect so that we may next determine what direction it must take in the future.

The Support of Metropolitan France
Something outstanding has taken place during the past three months—the whole of Metropolitan France, aware of the importance of this struggle, put forth a tremendous effort to ensure its success. Battalion after battalion—almost two hundred thousand men, carrying full pack—arrived in Algeria, thus doubling the number of troops already stationed in this territory.

All these men were taken away from their homes and their jobs. They might have been disheartened by subversive or defeatist propaganda but, as soon as they arrived, they understood the meaning of their presence and showed such courage and devotion that I wish to pay tribute to them once again.

The Frenchman's nature is such that perilous times regenerate and strengthen his patriotism.

A massive effort has been made: a financial effort and, above all, a human effort. But everyone must know that France unanimously intends to continue it: we have taken the path of no return. . . .

French Embassy, New York, *French Affairs*, No. 39, January 1957, 10.

General Directive No. 4

To the Officers and Noncommissioned Officers
of the Army, Navy and Air Force Stationed in Algeria
Issued by Robert Lacoste, Minister Residing in Algeria,
at Algiers on April 3, 1957

We have fallen into the habit of periodically taking stock of the situation together. I shall try, therefore, to tell you today as precisely as possible what the present conditions are in Algeria. . . .

French Embassy, New York, *French Affairs*, No. 39a, April 1957, 1–2, 4–6.

The Situation Today

As a matter of fact, the leaders of the rebellion have failed in their plan to internationalize the Algerian problem. Not only did the Assembly of the United Nations not pass any resolution hostile to French policy but, what is more, their endeavor strengthened France's national consciousness, which is aroused each time foreign powers want to interfere in our affairs.

Above all, it should be noted that our American friends have at last understood the sincerity of our plans and the significance of our efforts, and explicitly opposed the ventures of the countries supporting the rebellion.

It was easier to achieve this important result because of the failure of the general strike and of the insurrectional plans, a failure that was followed by a rigorous offensive conducted against the rebel bands and the political and military organization of the rebellion. This offensive culminated in the destruction of an important part of its central control system and the capture of a considerable amount of weapons and war equipment. This resulted chiefly in an unquestionable relaxation of tension in the large urban centers where school enrollment, for example, has been restored to normal. Along the borders, our system of observation and defense is now steadily improving.

In Metropolitan France, I note once again that although certain supposedly responsible circles remain morbidly in favor of solutions requiring abandonment and engage in unremitting opposition to our action, the majority of public opinion, however, has confidence in our efforts.

The number of exactions demanded by the rebels has been steadily declining for the last two months and extensive military and police activity in Algiers itself has completely altered the atmosphere of that city. The "battle of Algiers," which the rebels forced upon us in February, was won by drastic action. This victory prevented a bloody insurrection. We should be thankful that we have thus escaped serious dangers which might have reversed the general situation at our expense.

It would be dangerous, however, to relax our efforts just because of this general and substantial improvement; our task is still difficult but I hope that everyone is now convinced that we shall ultimately succeed. . . .

But the psychological and political work that I expect from the Army in Algeria today is just as important as its purely military activity.

You must start with a simple but categorical assumption: we must ask only one thing of a suffering French-Moslem population terrorized by the rebellion—recognition of the French homeland and of our flag and that is all. We can certainly understand that the inhabitants of this country may be hostile to the Government's policy, opposed to the methods of the Administration and unfavorable to the various drafts which have been worked out for a statute of Algeria. That is their right since we intend that our fellow countrymen, wherever they may be, retain the right to think and to express their opinions. But it is absolutely necessary for them to recognize that they cannot live without a mother country, with which they have essential ties that cannot be broken. . . .

A New Factor in The Problem

An event of paramount importance, finally, is likely substantially to change the destiny of Algeria and France: the discovery of considerable mineral—especially petroleum—deposits in the Sahara. These discoveries, which are significant in terms of the world market, will bear out our country's mission in Africa and justify even further all the efforts of Metropolitan France to restore calm to Algeria, which is the key to the Sahara.

As a matter of fact, the Algerian Sahara, where up to now almost all the new discoveries have been made, will become part of a vaster French economic community whose expansion will considerably help the development of northern Algeria.

This will enable our country to recover the elements of power and independence which it has lacked for a long time. With this new power and independence, it will be able to resume the place that rightfully belongs to it in Europe and the world.

In the ordinary course of events, all of North Africa is destined to turn toward the "West" and our civilization alone is capable of keeping it from chaos. Furthermore, only an Algeria which is closely united to France can prevent the neighboring countries from being engulfed by disorder and then by communism, which now semi-officially encourages subversion.

Today, more than ever, the French Army is the best guarantee of our presence in Africa. It is almost alone in shouldering the burden of the struggle against the Algerian rebellion and I believe that it is aware of this. This task will give it the opportunity of becoming one of the best initiated armies in the world in the modern concepts of "surface warfare" and "revolutionary warfare," while remaining at the same time thoroughly humane.

The eyes of the entire country are on the troops in Algeria—and today, through you, France is recovering that patriotic spirit which some thought had disappeared. Let me assure you once more of all the affectionate confidence I have in you. We shall remain in Algeria, not because we are the stronger, but because we are in the right.

General Directive No. 5

To the Officers and Noncommissioned Officers
of the Army, Navy and Air Force Stationed in Algeria
Issued by Robert Lacoste, Minister of Algeria
at Algiers on August 12, 1957

The Tasks That Lie Ahead
Despite the rigors of an Algerian summer, your efforts must not cease. On the contrary, you should intensify them. Reinforcements are arriving at the present time from Metropolitan France, from Tunisia and from Morocco; they should make it possible for you to achieve further results. One of the first results to be achieved is the tightening up of our frontiers.

Last November, I told you how I felt about the behavior of the Tunisian and Moroccan Governments, which were tolerating the presence on their territories of troublesome elements engaged in constant violations of our frontiers. We hoped for a long time that an appeal to reason would be all that was needed to lead these two states to a more wholesome concept of the duties of independence. We have been disappointed.

The interference of our neighbors in our internal affairs is on the increase; the arms traffic has grown in volume, the outrages committed against our forces and lines of communication by bands, which, having struck their blow, find refuge in the bases they have established on neighboring soil, are now too numerous to keep track of. Just recently, armed bands coming from Tunisia indulged in wholesale kidnapings of populations which they carried off with them, thus hoping to give rise to a problem of Algerian refugees, a problem that would then be exploited on the international level.

In order to meet this situation, the Minister of National Defense and I decided to set up, on the Algerian frontiers, a continuous line of barriers that would be strictly patrolled. On the Moroccan frontier, this device, which has been in effect for several months, has given proof

French Embassy, New York, *French Affairs*, No. 39b, September 1957, 1, 3, 7.

of its effectiveness; it will be reinforced and improved. On the Tunisian frontier, a strong defensive line, 185 miles in length, is now under construction. Combined with the necessary and legitimate exercise of the right of pursuit, this will not fail to strike a mortal blow at the scandalous arms traffic which is being carried on there at the present time.

The leaders of the rebellion, fearing these measures that are placing the outlaws in danger of being cut off, have undertaken an intensive logistic effort which has assumed even greater importance than military action as such. This is coupled with an effort to improve the organization of their units.

This battle of the frontier—whose outcome will be decisive for the fate of Algeria—must be won. I am counting on your vigilance and your energies bent toward this end. . . .

Be confident. Confidence: that is the key-word for the summer of 1957. If confidence remains always lively here, where the storm is unleashed, if it is not lost by our brothers in Metropolitan France, if it is impressed on those who are in charge of leading public opinion or of deciding the country's policies, then all will be saved and saved quickly.

Should there be any flinching on the other hand, should Frenchmen, by their bearing, their attitude, their remarks, show that France, weary, refuses to make the effort demanded of her and should she, betraying her duties, desert, then we would see our adversaries retrieve their hopes, resume their intrigues, renew their efforts, multiply their crimes. . . .

Be confident therefore and Algeria will be safeguarded and with her, all the territories over which our flag flies, territories that are often far away and where, at the moment, a bold and generous experiment is being tried, which can bear fruit only if we prove here, from Tlemcen to Bône, from Algiers to Tamanrasset, that France knows the meaning of determination. . . .

Certainly we have not yet reached the end of the road but already the way is less rough; I can already catch sight of the end of our difficult journey. One more effort and we shall be able to say with pride that we have saved Algeria and, with her, France.

Lieutenant General Jacques Allard:
NATO and North Africa

It frequently occurs that an officer who is newly assigned to one of the great interallied general staffs of NATO asks the following question: How is it that the field of action of allied strategy is limited in the South by the Mediterranean? Nothing seems foreseen in the defense plans for confronting an encirclement of Europe via North Africa. Could not the potential enemy, Russia, shunning the risks of a total war, realize this encirclement indirectly by helping to generate limited conflicts and internal subversion with the goal of eliminating Western influence and gradually leading under her domination the underdeveloped peoples that a prematurely granted independence will deliver defenseless to Marxism?

The answer to this question, I have heard it said many a time, can be summarized as follows: the field of activity of the Supreme Allied Command in Europe is limited to the defense of member countries. Or else: beyond the frontiers within which NATO strategy is exerted member countries have full liberty to carry out their own policies. Our general staffs need not concern themselves about this.

This answer is not satisfactory. It conceals the principal weakness of the organization. The North Atlantic Pact, which was signed in the grip of the great fear that seized the free world in the postwar years when it was faced with the imbalance of forces and Soviet expansionist designs, had only one goal: to re-establish the equilibrium in order to secure the world from the mortal risk of a new world war.

The union of the twelve, then fifteen, countries of NATO, achieved in an instinctive leap for defense and survival, and the prodigious effort effected by everyone under the American aegis checked this threat. "Deterrent power" carried the day. The "defensive shield," stretched from the North Cape to and including the Mediterranean, allied with the power of atomic retaliatory forces, removed the specter of total war.

The Russians did not delude themselves, but they did draw some lessons. Might not the objective that could not be attacked directly be outflanked and finally neutralized? In their eyes the Middle East, Egypt, North Africa now took on considerable strategic importance.

Translated and reproduced with the permission of the publisher from the *Revue de Défense Nationale*, Nouvelle Série, 14e Année, May 1958, 907–11. A similar résumé was presented to NATO's Supreme Command in November 1957.

If this part of the world where Westerners were incapable of co-ordin-
ating their policies, where even these policies clashed in an under-
handed struggle of divergent interests and ideologies, if this part of
the world could escape from Western influence, the objective would
be attained without striking a blow. Is eliminating Western influence
from the Middle East and North Africa a more difficult enterprise
for the masters of the Kremlin than the one that in less than ten
years attained the same objective in the Asiatic world? Certainly not.
It is also quite conceivable that for the strategists of the cold war
in Moscow this is a question of a plan meticulously prepared. A plan
whose stages unfold strictly as foreseen thanks to the assistance that
the Western powers unwittingly provide because of the differences
among their own policies and a misunderstanding of realities and dangers that history will judge later—when it shall be too late—as short-
sighted.

The importance of North Africa, particularly in the strategic domain,
cannot, however, be overemphasized. A vast prolongation of this little
European peninsula where two hundred million inhabitants are cornered
with their back to the sea, North Africa is its safeguard. The recent
discoveries of enormous economic possibilities reinforce even more
the importance of North Africa's strategic position. It would be idle
to recall the degree to which the defense of Europe would be inconceivable without North Africa. Deprived of the naval bases at Bizerte
and Mers-el-Kebir, or the Strategic Air Command and French air
bases, dispossessed of the African Atlantic ports, ousted from the
North African hinterland that is so remarkably situated geographically
in respect to the European theater and indispensable both for logistic
maneuver and the use of reserves, European countries would not have
further possibilities of maneuver once engaged in a war. An early defeat in Europe would be irremediable, all the more so because liberty
of action in the Atlantic would be gravely compromised. And when
one speaks about the possible loss of North Africa, one must equally
contemplate that of the entire African continent.

The maintenance of North Africa in the Western camp is thus vital
for Europe, that is for NATO and consequently for the entire free
world.

It would be good, moreover, if the countries concerned with NATO
could be convinced of this, but they disagree on the means needed
to assure this maintenance, and these disagreements—dramatic in their
consequences—run a strong risk of leading to a result at cross pur-

poses with the desired objective. The recent experience of the Middle East (without mentioning the hardly older one of the Far East) does not seem to have opened their eyes. It is clear in fact that Russia alone can be the winner, especially since she is now present in the eastern Mediterranean by virtue of the influence that she exerts on the Arab peoples to the detriment of the traditional Western influence.

The essential conceptions that divide the West can be summarized as follows:

Some estimate that a France who is victorious in Algeria, who resumes her role as a leader on both shores of the Mediterranean, allied with a reviving Germany and the other countries adhering to the Common Market organization and as the foremost exploiter of the Saharan riches, would endanger their role of economic arbiter and defeat their traditional oscillating policies.

Others who feel a sort of divine calling to govern the free world by virtue of their wealth, their numbers, and the uncontested role that they have played for twenty years, as well as by their separation from the old Europe are persuaded that their "doctrine"—a mixture of a subjective anti-colonialism and an imperious need for economic expansion—is infallible and will permit them to win to the Western cause those who will owe them independence and material aid while at the same time not discouraging their allies on the old continent.

Finally, others estimate in contrast—and they are paid to know these matters—that one cannot violate the law of time with impunity when it comes to the evolution of peoples, even in the century of the atom and artificial satellites.

In short, for the impartial observer as for the historian of the future, everything takes place as if there were hidden the less avowable demands of a new form of colonialism under the cover of ideologies that in themselves are perfectly respectable and enjoy such names as "support for the peoples under guardianship who aspire to independence" or "aid to underdeveloped countries." No longer is it to be a question of pushing them in the name of the right of peoples to self-determination, to accede to a political independence that a minority claims but for which the masses are not prepared, in order better to make them economic colonies afterward. Incapable of confronting the multiple tasks of a modern state, without roots or traditions, these young states will inevitably fall into dependence on the money-lenders and will submit to their conditions. Those who think and act in this way risk being christened by tomorrow's historians with the sad name of sorcerer's apprentice. For the experience exists—and the same causes always produce the same effects—to prove that an independence prematurely seized engenders dictatorship, anarchy, and regression in the evolution of the masses, thus preparing the way for communism, whether or not one passes through the stage of an opportunist neutralism.

It is high time that the Western Powers take hold of themselves, that they realize that for thirteen years they have played the game of their adversary and proceeded from defeat to defeat. The threat has changed form, but the situation of the free world is presently as grave as when the great fear led twelve nations to unite and sign the North Atlantic Pact in 1950. Time is pressing. France, once again alone, is already engaged in combat—an avant-garde struggle, not in the classically foreseen screening battle along the Iron Curtain but on the subversive-war front opened by the foreigner in North Africa. The meaning and the stakes of this battle do not yet seem comprehended by the allies of France. And yet, while fighting so that Algeria remains French in order to safeguard the influence of Western civilization in North Africa, France is fighting for NATO. Her troops, withdrawn from metropolitan France and Germany, have not been diverted from the defense of Europe, for without North Africa European defense retains no further meaning. However, having labored for more than a century on the southern shore of the Mediterranean, France alone is capable of being the cement that holds North Africa in the Western edifice.

Raoul Girardet: Civil and Military Power in the Fourth Republic

I: INTRODUCTION

Throughout the nineteenth century and during the first part of the twentieth, the definition of the relations between civil and military power in France was based on two simple and essential principles.

Translated by Martha Finkelstein, Columbia University, from R. Girardet, "Pouvoir Civil et Pouvoir Militaire en France sous la Quatrième République," paper, 7th Round Table, International Political Science Association (Opatija, Yugoslavia), September 1959, and R. Girardet, "Pouvoir civil et pouvoir militaire dans la France contemporaine," *Revue Française de Science Politique*, 10 (March 1960), 5–38. The parts of the article appearing in this volume are reproduced

The first was the complete subordination of military power to the authority of legal government. Summing up the tradition of French civil law on this matter, M. Duguit, a lawyer, writes:

> The military must be a passive tool in the hands of government. The latter can only fulfill its mission if it has the military completely at its disposal, so that the government may use it as an unconscious material force. This excludes all possibility of military leaders in any way refusing to comply with governmental orders. . . . The state would no longer exist if military leaders were allowed to question its orders. The ideal armed force would be one that government could activate simply by pressing a button.

This first fundamental principle logically led to the second essential rule—the military must never interfere in politics. At the beginning of the century it was taught at St. Cyr that, "The army's loyalty and devotion to legal government must be absolute. There is no other formula that would as securely safeguard the soldier's honor." Thus, the army must have no feelings, no opinions, and no inclinations; if these do exist, the army must be unaware of them and act as if they were nonexistent. During the nineteenth century neutrality, or rather political passivity, was considered one of the principal tenets of military ethics. In this way, an attempt was made to free the soldier from any doubt, interior struggle, or pangs of conscience. In time of political upheaval he would "stand by his flag," taking orders from his superiors, who in turn would defer to the final decisions of the Minister of War then in power. Thus, the political fidelity of the army would be at once revocable and perpetual. The military would be loyal to the state irrespective of changing governments. In short, the army should always be "la Grande Muette. . . ."

It would be premature to venture into a field where all the existing documentation amounts to a few journalistic accounts. In a more limited manner I shall endeavor only to follow and to interpret the *change of attitude* that has marked the history of the French army from 1945 to the present, a change of attitude with regard to government and to certain essential values. In the last fifteen years the French military has undergone a very great psychological, intellectual, and

moral change; I shall attempt to investigate and outline the reasons
for this change.

In effect, three factors seem to stand out:

1. The very grave psychological and moral repercussions that the
   French army has felt because of the colonial wars it has had to
   wage since the end of World War II.
2. The development by a few military theoreticians of a new doctrine
   of "revolutionary war," and the spread of this doctrine throughout the military community.
3. The French army's assumption of administrative power in Algerian departments and the transformation of Algeria into a
   "military province."

In the convergence of these factors lies the essential explanation for
the gradual establishment of a new type of relations between civil and
military power. . . .

II: "THE UNREST OF THE ARMY"

The Fourth Republic will necessarily hold an important place in the
moral history of the French army: to many officers it was a period of
re-evaluation. "Twenty years of war have changed us," states a "forty-
year-old officer." Lacking assurance from those in a position to give it,
the soldier has become a questioning man. "For almost twenty years,
without understanding why or how, France has been at war," says a
member of the same generation. "But those to whom the country has
given arms, those who kill and those who die have a right to question."
In fact, a complete revision of certain fundamental values has affected
many military minds in the past fifteen years. This has incurred the
often distressing repudiation of certain essential conventions, an often
harrowing abandon of elementary postulates that for more than a century were the basis of the rules of military ethics. The old imperatives
of the honor of the military, codified and handed down by the nineteenth century, no longer seem capable of answering the questions and
problems which arise from France's situation in the middle of the
twentieth century. Other rules are sought, other assurances are demanded with uneasiness and often in confusion. This moral revolution
slowly has upset the customs and way of thinking of military society.
And it is this moral revolution that constitutes the most often mis-
understood but essential aspect of the "unrest of the army," which
was noted by the French press in the last years of the Fourth Republic.

In order to understand this crisis, the very important heritage left by the World War and the occupation cannot be neglected. Since 1940, traditional principles of military ethics, notably that of total and absolute obedience to political power, have been suddenly questioned. How can the imperative of submission to legal power be invoked when three governments have simultaneously laid claim to the exclusive privilege of legitimacy? How can we distinguish between what is rebellion and what is loyalty since, by their contradictory use, they have necessarily lost all meaning? For the first time, the soldier has had to choose among many opposing duties. In a moving book Air Commander Jules Roy evokes the drama of the Army in Africa in November, 1942. He writes of the divergences in the communiques from Vichy, Algiers, and London, of the orders, the doubts, the contradictory demands, and "the collapse of old disciplines which could no longer hold us together." "There no longer was any virtue," writes M. Roy, "which could be called discipline. At the same time, I was condemned not to rely on anyone." These lines seem to indicate the breakdown of the abstract, impersonal, legalistic concept of military duty as it had been defined in the nineteenth century. The fleet, scuttled at Toulon, had wanted to obey. However, it was condemned to disappear from the battlefields where the destiny of the world hung in the balance. On the other hand, those who erased the humiliation of 1940 were those who agreed to break the bonds of discipline, those who were seditious toward the established order. The existence of a wealth of references, memories, and experiences from this period could not help but count in the years to follow. After World War II had ended, the army, on the whole, did not feel it necessary to draw any definite lesson from these past events. It even appears that the military kept silent about the moral crisis which they considered to be linked with exceptional circumstances that were unlikely to occur again. The right to vote, granted to the military by a decree of August 7, 1945, did not seem to prevent the army's return, during peacetime, to its traditional policy of nonintervention in politics. In fact, there was a wait of about six years, until the unfolding of the war in Indochina, before the problem of relations between civil and military power was brought to the fore by the army as a whole. Only then were new awarenesses and new attitudes more precisely and more systematically defined.

Tension with the Government and the Crisis of Authority
In 1957, General Navarre, former Commander-in-Chief of the French expeditionary force in the Far East which was defeated at Dien Bien

Phu, declared, "The real reasons for the defeat in Indochina are political." This statement summarizes perfectly (in spite of its author's lack of popularity with his troops) the conclusion which the army seems to have drawn from its unfortunate Indochinese venture. A simple but unshakable conviction developed. After the Geneva armistice, the fighting men in Indochina placed the responsibility for the particularly bloody eight-year war which ended in humiliation on governmental policy, or rather the lack of it.

Many blamed the government for improper handling of the war, the dispersion of governmental authority (Indochinese affairs were the concern of nine ministries), unclear decisions, lack of continuity in the definition, and the pursuit of a policy. The government was also blamed for never having supplied the expeditionary force with necessary technical means for successful conduct of the conflict, for the shortage of men, for the mediocrity and depletion of war material, and for the fluctuations in prestige. The government was also reproached for never having stated any coherent or precise purpose for the war, and for having provided only very insufficient effort when victory seemed possible and then uselessly continuing the fight when the situation was irreparably compromised. Civil power was finally blamed for not protecting the fighting force from its "enemies from within," for not dealing severely with the divulgence of military secrets, and for having silently tolerated numerous financial dealings, all of which illustrated the scandalous chronicle of the Indochinese conflict. The army had been "stabbed in the back"; it had been betrayed more by the institutional disorder than by the weakness of men in power.

There existed a feeling of betrayal by the government, and also a feeling of abandonment by the nation. The fighting force in Indochina felt it was carrying on the fight alone, on the margin of the French community; it was neither understood nor supported by public opinion. With bitterness and sometimes with morose delight, the army recalled all the facts which pointed to the nation's indifference or hostility: the campaigns by the extreme left against "this filthy war," the sympathy expressed by some of the press for the cause of the adversary, the secrecy surrounding the army's suffering, the clandestine atmosphere imposed on the embarkation of reinforcements and the return of wounded, the numerous harassments consciously or unconsciously inflicted.

> They wanted him to be alone, to fight alone [one officer writes, speaking of the position of the soldier in contemporary France.] They refused to dirty their hands less from scruples than from a

sluggishness of mind, an obsession for peace at home and intellectual comfort. . . . If the whole business was to turn out badly, then the army would naturally take the blame. Thus, the soldier was sent to fight a war for which no one wanted to shoulder the responsibilities.

I breathed the air of defeat, lived through the months feeling abandoned [a contemporary novelist, trying to retrace a psychological pattern, has an officer say]. We were appropriately beaten but not for lack of courage. However, we were ashamed of this unreasonable, ignoble war that our country's leaders had forced us to wage without foreseeing the fatality of its failure and our humiliation.

This state of mind handed down by the Indochinese conflict—this bitterness, rancor, and humiliation—was to be aggravated even more by events after 1954, such as the abandonment of Morocco and Tunisia, the failure of the Suez expedition, the difficult and uncertain beginnings of the fight against the Algerian rebellion. A strong sentimental attachment bound the army to the Moroccan protectorate, which it considered its own creation. The discontinuance of the Suez operation was even more humiliating to the troops that had conducted it, since they were aware of having achieved a perfect technical success. The atmosphere in which the task of pacification in Algeria was undertaken at last seemed tragically confused. A repetition of the errors of Indochina seemed inevitable. The army felt badly adapted to this mission; its daily efforts seemed inevitably menaced or compromised by the government's weakness. "It would be a pleasure to be the victors every once in a while," declared a colonel in 1954 upon seeing the victorious troops of Viet Minh advance on the port of Hanoi. To many of the most sorely tried officers, who bore the essential weight of the fighting in Indochina and North Africa, the ethic of "useless service" —of gratuitous and total devotion to obedience (a principle often invoked by their elders)—was not enough to justify their sacrifices or give meaning to their work. "Success is the only military rule," states a publication read by young military personnel. "Military servitude" is the motto of a sick poet. Servitude no longer exists; there is only success or failure. One does not study to serve but to win. This is the only way to serve with honor. These ideas are worth remembering: convinced that it would have to pay with its blood and honor for errors made by the government, the army found it absolutely necessary to substitute for the traditional duty of obedience *new imperatives based solely on the effectiveness and success of its fight.*

Therefore, it is not surprising that from 1953 to 1958 there was a considerable change in the traditional form of military discipline. On several different occasions officers publicly expressed disagreement with certain governmental decisions. In 1954 Marshal Juin, the highest official in the military hierarchy, took issue with the government project pertaining to E.D.C. and attacked it with violence. In 1956 General Guillaume, chief of the armed forces general staff, and General Zeller, chief of staff of ground forces, resigned in protest against the brutal "reconversion" of NATO divisions sent to Algeria by the government. In 1956 and 1957 sanctions were taken against Generals Faure and Bollardière, both found guilty of acts regarded as insubordination. Then came the resignation of General Dufourt, inspector general of the artillery, who scored certain appointments that he considered unjustified. Tensions were sharpest and most numerous at the very core of the military hierarchy. World War II, Indochina, and then the Algerian ordeal had created a young generation of officers for whom the values of obedience were visibly less important than they had been for their elders. These young officers had borne the principal weight of the fighting in the Far East and in North Africa, where the very violence of the fight had given them exceptional initiative and had forced them to assume uncommon responsibilities. It was these young captains and commanders who most strongly expressed their feelings of anger and humiliation. However, it was not only the government, the regime, and its institutions that they held responsible, but also the high command, the unwieldiness and sclerosis of the military apparatus, and the conformism and routine into which many of their leaders had sunk. They tended to include the established political order and the structure of military society in their attack; as a group they condemned the men in power and some of their own chiefs. One may read the following in an inquiry into the "crisis in the army" published in December, 1956:

> There is a general crisis of authority which manifests itself as much by a lack of discipline as by a lack of confidence in leaders. This has led to a serious rupture between generations. In the same direction, a feeling of failure and ineffectiveness in the face of the army's recent, present or future tasks has given rise to a desire for reorganization which in itself seems almost impossible to achieve.

This break between generations, remarked by many other observers—this internal crisis in the military—added to the general feeling of discontent and fever, gave the French army in the spring of 1958 a very peculiar character, which, until that time, had hardly ever appeared in its history.

III: THE BIRTH OF A REVOLUTIONARY FORCE

The period from 1947 to 1958 saw not only the growth of constantly aggravated tension between the army and governmental power, but also what was at first a vague and later a precise change in the relations that traditionally united military society with the national community. Today the military is no longer integrated in the French social system as it was on the eve of World War II. A new way of life has come into being; new habits, new ways of thinking and feeling, have developed.

The first fact is the constant devaluation of the military profession. A comparison of a captain's pay in 1900 and 1950 shows a decrease from 161 to 95 gold francs. This is an even more drastic reduction than it seems, since the added resources from which many officers' families benefited (other income, returns from landed property and real estate) also have been reduced considerably. Significantly, as reported in a recent journalistic account, a majority of the students at the Academy of St. Cyr want to marry a woman who has a job of her own.

The French officer cannot help but make bitter comparisons between his pay and that of foreign armies. It has been calculated that in 1953 a commanding officer in France earning 95,000 francs per month would have earned 120,000 if he were English, 220,000 if he were Russian, and 280,000 if he were American. He also cannot help but feel at a disadvantage in relation to other civil servants. There is no doubt that the decree of January 13, 1948, which fixed the scale of civil service salaries, greatly lowered military classifications in relation to those of civil employees, both of which had previously been homologous. (The few modifications of internal details have not greatly improved the position of superior cadres.) It is true that substantial bonuses were added to the pay of the fighting forces in Indochina. But it is no less certain that the great majority of French officers feel condemned to a mediocre and impecunious existence. They are all the more distressed, since the devaluation of their material situation is accompanied by a parallel devaluation of their social prestige and moral standing. An even graver problem, however, is the almost

permanent *nomadism* of military personnel since World War II. Aside
from colonial troops, the life of the professional soldier, under the
Third Republic, differed little from that of any other public servant.
It was not unusual to find officers whose entire careers had been spent
in no more than three or four garrisons at home. Today the entire
army has shared the fate once reserved for only the colonial officer.
It is important to note that a large number of captains serving in
Algeria in 1959 had previously had two tours of duty of twenty-seven
months in Indochina and then a first tour of duty of two years in
Algeria (without prejudice for those who had spent several rather
active months in Tunisia or Morocco); they were then fulfilling a
second Algerian tour of duty of at least thirty months, according to
official expectations. It can be estimated that since 1947 these officers
have spent an average of 88 months (including travel time) out of 144
outside of metropolitan France and separated from their families. For
many officers who completed their studies on the eve of World War II
and who today are in their forties, the fighting, interrupted only rarely,
has lasted since 1939. This kind of existence most assuredly has taken
its toll on family life; there are long separations, problems in the rear-
ing of children, and the like. It is even more distressing in the face
of the grave housing problem confronting the career officer during
his stays at home. In 1957 a journalist estimated that 52,000 apart-
ments were lacking for military personnel. About twenty per cent
of the officers assigned to France would have to stay at hotels with
their families; more than thirty per cent (forty per cent according to
Jean Planchais) would be separated from their families. The inevitable
consequences of such a state of affairs were the inability of the military
to establish or expand the circle of its social relations, the breaking
or loosening of certain traditional ties, and the creation of a military
"island" within the national community.

Thus, greatly cut off by its very way of life from the rest of the
national community, the military tended to withdraw into itself. It was
gradually forced to establish its own ethics, its own particular set of
values in opposition to existing social standards. Many young officers
did not hesitate to express their contempt for bourgeois conventions,
for luxuries, for the pursuit of security and profit, as well as their
pride in being different in a country that, in their opinion, had lost its
sense of grandeur and adventure. They opposed their values to those
of a "bourgeois" France.

> I am not a clerk [a young military novelist has an officer in
> Indochina say]. I do not wage war in an office from nine to five.

Paid vacations do not interest me, nor does a salary. I don't give a damn for an old age pension since I may be killed before I can collect it. . . . I have no house to build in the suburbs or at the seashore and no garden to tend on weekends. I have neither the time nor the opportunity to enjoy the luxuries which have become the only goal in life for my compatriots. . . . I feel no bitterness or regret. I love my country and my profession. This is perhaps the only thing which has permitted me to escape from a nine to five existence, from weekends and from the automobile showroom.

The anger inherent in these lines is even more apparent in the fictionalized account of one commanding officer of colonial paratroopers evoking the life of his comrades in Indochina:

It was successively suggested that he sell aperitifs, nylon stockings, automobile accessories, perfumes, watches. He consistently turned down these suggestions. He wanted a job that would mean more than a salary. . . . [He] was not yet prepared to struggle for existence in the commercial civilization of the twentieth century. . . .

Schooled in an atmosphere of war, he also feels alien to the mass which surrounds him.

Children leave school, women go shopping, a cop awaits relief, the delivery boy whistles on his rounds, auto horns assault your ears, the retired recount their memories. . . . We don't even know such people; we hardly see them. We can do nothing with them; we're not of the same world.

Finally, with a feeling of relief, the young officer sets off again for Indochina.

On second thought, [he later realizes] the stay in France was the most painful. His furlough in France was worse than the tour of duty in Indochina. War was more logical; he felt at home although on foreign soil.

Because of the vehemence of tone, the two preceding accounts are typical of extreme cases. In less aggressive and more subtle form, the feelings they convey, however, were shared by a great number of young army personnel.

We have drawn into ourselves [states a captain, writing of his experiences in Indochina]. We have lived close together and have become as sensitive and sore as whipped animals. How

great was our despair at being rejected by our country and
how great was our need for fraternity!

In the new French military literature of the 1950's one often heard
an echo of the romanticism expressed by *Les Réprouvés* (*The Outcasts*) of Ernst von Salomon after World War I. It would be foolish
to consider it just as literature. In effect, the voluntary, aggressive non-
conformity affected by many young officers was linked with a gap
between the important intellectual values commonly accepted by
French opinion and the intellectual values by which the unity of the
army is maintained. France embodied a curious paradox. In a conservative society—where class tensions were increasingly less violent
and where the general trend was toward granting an ever greater place
to the pursuit of material well-being and the need for security—the
army in 1958, even more than the proletariat whose way of life was
in the process of change, tended to appear as one of the most extraordinary forces, perhaps the only revolutionary one capable of men-
acing the established order.

IV: FACTS AND MYTHS OF REVOLUTIONARY WAR

The growth of a revolutionary spirit within the French army is strongly
linked with the war in Indochina. This conflict is equally inseparable
from another important occurrence in the military history of contemporary France—the army's discovery of a new type of warfare—
causing the formulation of a new doctrine which was soon to dominate
the thoughts and behavior of its intellectual élite.

> Some of us who have returned from this war [writes an officer]
> look back on the recent past and find that no other period in
> our military career has shaped our destinies as much, because
> we never before felt the need to think about our problems, to
> reject the formulas given us and to uncover new ideas and
> solutions each time.

The doctrine formulated by the French army since its Indochinese
experience is that of *revolutionary war*. With this new doctrine, certain
traditional values had to be re-examined, leading to a concept of the
role of the military within contemporary society that was considerably
different from earlier concepts.

The Tactics and Strategy of Revolutionary War

The elaboration of the doctrinal concepts of revolutionary war is a
direct outgrowth of a study of tactical methods employed by the Viet

Minh forces in Indochina. In effect, the army in Indochina was confronted by an unknown adversary which it could not defeat, in spite of recognized material superiority. The enemy had deliberately planned its strategy to thwart the French. The plan called for "war among the masses," in the words of Mao Tse-tung. Its main objective was the conquest of people, not the taking of territory or the domination of a battlefield. The victor was the one who knew how to take hold of a population morally, then materially mobilize its strength. To achieve this end, the enemy in Indochina employed very specific techniques which were completely effective. They were constant propaganda, systematic terrorism, the deliberate dismemberment of existing social structures, and the establishment of "parallel hierarchies," which slowly replaced the hierarchies of legal order and enslaved the population in an increasingly tight web of steel. The French army was forced to admit that in such a struggle military action should be secondary to psychological action, propaganda, the collection and exploitation of political as well as operational information, police action, liaison with the people, and economic and social action. The French army discovered that its men not only had to be experts in the use of arms, but also, and perhaps above all, had to be political agitators, organizers, and leaders of partisans. In the end, the qualities and methods of the ideological crusader were more effective in obtaining final victory than the qualities and methods of the soldier. . . .

Revolutionary War and the Political Vocation of the Army
From 1954 to 1958, four decisive years in the intellectual history of the army, the theory of revolutionary war spread rapidly in military circles. The expeditionary forces in Indochina were the crucible in which the new doctrine was formed. After their return from the Far East, some officers devoted themselves to the publication of their memoirs and their reflections. General Chassin, former commander of the air forces of the expeditionary corps and author of various works on Mao Tse-tung, is responsible, it seems, for the first studies on this subject, published in the October, 1954, issue of *Revue militaire d'information* and in the December issue of *Revue de défense nationale.* In June, 1955, Captain Souyris published an important article on the "self-defense of the masses" in the same journal. In December of the same year *Message des forces armées* made these significant remarks in its editorial:

> The military must fully understand the techniques of the war imposed upon it; it must realize that these techniques are not at all like those employed in '40 and '45 nor are they the ones

learned at military school. . . . Traditional warfare is not the
only possible answer. The disciples of Lenin are masters in two
other types of conflict. These are psychological war and revolutionary war; the latter is being launched right now.

A few months later Commander Hogard published the results of his
research in the *Revue de défense nationale*. Finally, in February-March
1957, a special issue of *Revue militaire d'information* was devoted
entirely to a discussion of the doctrine of revolutionary war. From
that time the army's intellectual élite, especially young officers, seems
to have accepted the new idea. In every issue of the various military
publications there is discussion or study of some new aspect of subversive, psychological, or revolutionary war. At the same time, new
concepts were officially propagated in military echelons. In 1956 an
Instruction Center in Psychological Warfare was created in Paris,
where military specialists were trained. In 1957, courses in "psychological instruction" were instituted in all military schools. These courses
include a thorough study of Marxist-Leninist doctrine, the techniques
of its penetration, and methods of combating them. A completely new
terminology has appeared in the military vocabulary. New trends of
thought and new attitudes have taken shape.

The first consequence of the generalization of the concept of revolutionary war is the often uncertain and anxious search by young military
personnel for the metaphysic of political conflict.

> In the present war of ideas waged by Marxism [writes the
> spokesman for a group of officers] we cannot win if we have
> no truths in which to believe, no values to defend. Today, every
> officer is convinced of this. . . .
>
> In the past, the nation needed men traditionally devoted to a
> career of arms. . . . Political preoccupations had no place in a
> narrowly specialized army. However, since the concept of war
> has changed—we are now faced with ideological warfare—
> the military must change as well. . . . It must be capable of
> establishing, effecting and assimilating a coherent plan.

The search for an international doctrine capable of effectively opposing Marxist-Leninist theories, the pursuit of a system of values strong
enough to unite and stimulate national energies, will henceforth play
a great part in military preoccupations. Some, perhaps the majority,
will attempt to define an ideology based on the exaltation of the traditional values of Western humanism: the dignity of man, patriotism,
respect for spiritual values, the desire for justice and progress. (This

is mainly the "doctrine" taught in courses on "psychological action" at the *École spéciale militaire*—that is, a synthesis of the ancient precepts of democratic idealism and the teachings of Christian morality.) Others overtly express their espousal of the principles of a strict type of Catholicism, finding the answer to the revolutionary menace in the establishment of an authoritarian, traditionalist Christian order which explicitly repudiates the postulates of liberal individualism. Finally, others lean toward an anti-Marxist, as well as anticapitalist, national collectivism. Needless to say, there is much confusion and hesitation, along with many contradictions, in this systematic quest for a doctrine. However, the mere existence of the quest is more important than the results it produces: it does not presuppose political commitment on the part of young officers; it does not involve any militant action from within a party or group. (Contrary to what has been written and said, adjustments of this sort occur only in isolated and rather rare cases. The military jealously wants to preserve its autonomy and avoid anything which might disrupt its unity.) It is no less true that the intensity of these doctrinal, ideological preoccupations has led the military further and further away from the elementary and simply defined precepts on which was founded its traditional position of nonintervention in politics. . . .

V: THE ALGERIAN AFFAIR

The war in Indochina marked the beginning of a grave period of tension between civil power and the military. The precepts of revolutionary war gradually tended to draw the military away from its traditional policy of political nonintervention. Algeria, however, was the decisive affair in which the army was to stand up to the government. This event cannot be fully understood unless an important fact, which seems to have escaped the majority of political observers, is considered. That fact is the progressive establishment, between 1954 and 1958, of a veritable "military province" in Algerian departments, the progressive assumption by the army of almost complete authority and administrative responsibility for this vast territory.

The Militarization of Algeria

When the Algerian rebellion broke out at the end of 1954, the task assigned to the army was relatively simple: re-establish order—that is, suppress uprisings, and chase, destroy, or subdue the F.L.N. bands.

However, since it was limited to a strictly military operation, the army's effort was doomed to almost irremediable failure. Deprived of information and cut off from any contact with the Moslem population, the "forces of law and order" wore themselves out thrusting at an elusive adversary. The experience of more than a century of colonial wars, the lessons of Galliéni and of Lyautey placed emphasis on the necessity of a policy of "pacification," closely coordinating military, psychological, and administrative action under one authority. The Indochinese precedent, constantly evoked by the doctrinaires of revolutionary war, was an indication of the dramatic conclusion that awaited combat unadapted to the methods of the adversary. The F.L.N., like the forces of Viet Minh, conducted a war "among the masses." Instead of hoping to achieve immediate military coups, the F.L.N. attempted to spread the network of its political and administrative structures over the entire Algerian population. Therefore, the French goal should have been, not the pursuit of its guerrillas, but the destruction of its political organization through the establishment of an opposition, through substitution of another political organization. The government could not help but recognize the validity of these observations. The police and traditional judiciary apparatus, accustomed to handling occurrences of an average criminal nature, were ridiculously impotent in the face of the systematic practice of terrorism carried on by the F.L.N. Algeria had only known inadequate administrative institutions, and in many places the all-too-weak existing structures began to crack at the beginning of the rebellion. There was an almost complete administrative void. At that time, only the army was in a position to fill it. Thus, gradually, from 1956 on, under the impetus of M. Lacoste, the resident Minister, increasingly greater responsibilities were confided in the military. The result was that, at least on a local level, the army had within its authority almost all repressive and administrative power.

The most important innovations were perhaps the S.A.S. (Special Administrative Sections) and the S.A.U. (Urban Administrative Sections) created in 1956. They led, in fact, to the establishment of a new administrative sectoring that was superimposed upon existing districts without destroying them (prefects and subprefects carried on their work until the crisis of May 13, 1958). The commanding officer of the S.A.S., usually a captain, was entirely responsible for the administrative affairs of the district under his command. His job was to take a census of the people, supervise them, and guide them. He supervised the economic development of the area, granting medical and social assistance. He also endeavored to reduce deficiencies in education.

This one man was mayor, teacher, and engineer. He directed and supervised the work of the medical staff and social workers under him, initiated work projects, levied taxes, established a small police force, and sparked local political activities. In 1958 there were more than 600 S.A.S. officers in Algeria, as a rule in areas cleared of rebel bands. Of course, in so-called operational districts most of the officers had to assume similar administrative tasks more or less empirically.

Faithful to the principles of "parallel hierarchies" dear to theoreticians of revolutionary war, the army also attempted to increase the number of organizations and groups under its supervision. In Algiers and its outskirts the fight against terrorism led to the establishment of a tight surveillance network based on the designation of some men responsible for whole neighborhoods and others for small groups of houses. But it was on the civic, moral, and professional level that the most interesting groups were formed. In every built-up area there were servicemen's canteens, places for gatherings and discussions, where the men could bring their sons. There were women's clubs led by social workers; even Moslems gathered there. The army even created and supervised trade schools; there were twenty-six of them by the end of 1957, with instructors coming from the *Centre de formation* at Dellys, which was itself established under military authority. There were even centers for the education of the future leaders of douars. Here basic administrative procedures were taught, along with enough military training to provide for the self-defense of villages.

In line with this effort to hold the population together, the army created a powerful apparatus for the gathering of information and the direction of public opinion. The latter was supervised by the Fifth Division of the Tenth Military District, which, since the beginning of the rebellion, had worked unceasingly to expand its field of activity. Its beginnings were relatively modest. Loudspeaker and leaflet campaigns were employed to spread French propaganda. Then better methods were perfected. A corps of itinerant officers (O.I.) was created. Advisory groups of these officers, expert in psychological action, traveled from district to district. Military publications increased. Movies and, above all, radio were more widely used. All in all, extremely diversified methods of propaganda were employed by the army in Algeria. These tasks added to the reasons for the almost complete change in the concept of the officer's traditonal role:

> This army . . . which in '39 sadly abandoned its horses . . . to dirty its hands in the mechanics of tanks and machine guns, becoming accustomed to the smell of oil and gas, . . . was now

plunged in a war in which these very tanks and guns would soon join the horses as museum pieces. The men now learned that they had to take care of the people, learn to swab mercurochrome, administer antibiotics and sulfa drugs, supervise the population, take the census, dole out work, talk of bulldozers, bridges and roads, highways, credit, enter into local politics, etc. . . . In a word, the army was the housekeeper of the nation.

In fact, on the verge of the crisis of May 13, 1958, the army had not only supplanted civil administration in districts where the latter was incapable of handling its job, but the precepts of revolutionary war had also taken over from old colonial traditions, extending and developing them. With its newspapers, schools, teams of social workers, youth organizations, and women's clubs, the army tended to appear as an omnipotent party, even monopolizing public power in some regions of Algeria. The army had its own propaganda machine, and its own surveillance and repression system. At least on the local level, it controlled and animated the most dynamic elements of that part of the Moslem population that had escaped the claws of the rebellion. In short, the army had given Algeria many new institutions.

Determination of an Algerian Policy

How can we avoid concluding that techniques of psychological action and of rehabilitation of the people are not, and cannot be, politically neutral? In reality, the mere fact that the army waged "a war among the masses," or, in more traditional terms, substituted "pacification" for "repression," inferred, even to the lowest echelons of the military hierarchy, the recognition of the development of a *particular Algerian policy*. Of course, the need for an all-inclusive policy attacking the entire Algerian problem was not immediately apparent to military circles. For a long while many officers refused to see beyond the narrow limits of the task assigned to them. For a long time as well the army in Algeria waited for the government to define and propose this sorely needed policy.

> Several of our comrades in Algeria [stated an editorial in *Message des forces armées* of August, 1956] have informed us of the difficulty of their position due to the complete absence of any governmental decision. In this psychological combat the army is asked to gain the popular confidence without the implacable weapon of a well-defined policy.

It is quite evident that, because of the great division in political parties and public opinion, the government was powerless to promote the well-defined policy demanded by the above military editorialist. What was demanded was a plan of action for Algeria completely without ambiguity, containing a sufficiently broad outlook for the future. The government's indecision in this matter was not the only cause for discontent with civil power that existed in the military. The necessities of the struggle forced the army to determine this political program for itself. However, it does not seem, in spite of some assertions, that there was systematic agreement or a co-ordinated and deliberate quest on the part of its officers. The methods of pacification and their logical implications gradually led to the almost spontaneous elaboration of a coherent Algerian policy based on several essential assertions.

The first of these was the continuing presence of the French on Algerian soil. The essential task of pacification was, in effect, to win over, or to win back, the adherence of the Moslem population, which was basically insecure, hesitant, vacillating, and dominated by concern for the future. The reservations created by this situation were due more to fear of compromise than to open hostility. Any vagueness as to the future, any ambiguity as to France's will to maintain her sovereignty, ran the risk of irreparably paralyzing any action aimed at persuading and involving the country. Therefore, every French officer serving in Algeria, in order to properly fulfill his mission, of necessity had to declare that those remaining loyal would never be abandoned. Because of this, it can be understood why the army had to disagree with the policy of "cease fire, elections, negotiations" as defined in 1956 by the government of M. Guy Mollet. This formula was not aimed at securing the future; it allowed for the greatest diversity of solutions and left the way open to all possibilities. The "pacifying" officer, bound by the daily difficulties of his task, was led to believe, on the contrary, that future security was the first and most important condition for the effectiveness of his work. He had to proclaim that any retreat was unthinkable. Any break in the expression of his will or in the manifestation of his resolve would greatly compromise the pursuit of goals he had been ordered to achieve.

It was not, however, just a question of obtaining the resigned or passive assent of the majority of the population. Even when secured, a guarantee of the continuance of French sovereignty was not enough to stand up to the mystique of the rebellion. Another faith and vision of the future had to be set in opposition to the faith and vision that sparked the adversary. This in turn led to a second, equally political, assertion: the need for the civic, economic, and social progress of the Moslems in Algeria. Since these Moslems were constantly dominated by a feeling of alienation from and frustration toward the population of European origin, the army thought that it would never win their deep faith or productively galvanize their energies and enthusiasm unless it offered them the concrete hope of a better and more dignified life. Thus, the army planned to concentrate on the most lowly, the outcasts.

> France's future in this country [writes *Contacts*, a journal of the Tenth Military District], lies in its concern for the lowly, and they are many. . . . Instead of maintaining the traditional self-seeking or distrustful contacts with informed or lettered people, thereby creating a barrier between the masses and France, we should study the lives of the small people, the poor, those who have been exploited without our knowledge.

An attempt was made to change the status of the Moslem woman and hasten her emancipation.

> Little by little [continued *Contacts*] we shall interest the women in our present struggle, giving them cause to turn their backs on the rebels. We would explain that women were the most downtrodden section of the population, that our goal is for the betterment of all, particularly the most unhappy.

Finally, a revolution of the Kemalist type, overthrowing old institutions and aimed at the destruction of traditional inequalities was proposed to the Algerian masses. A new Algeria would grow out of the struggle, an Algeria where all citizens would have identical rights and similar opportunities. It was said that the Algerians of tomorrow would be "completely independent Frenchmen."

The army was soon to summarize its vast program in one simple phrase, "l'Algérie française," and in one word, "integration." However, it would be a mistake to think that the officers using this word accorded it an extremely precise institutional meaning. A great diversity of opinion existed in military circles about the nature of future administrative ties which ought to unite Algerian and metropolitan departments. Some were in favor of complete assimilation, while others were aware of an Algerian "personality" endowed with its own institutions. In fact, as it was used by the army until May 13, 1958, integration essentially corresponded to a synthesis of three major elements, the fundamental imperatives of military policy in Algeria: maintenance of French sovereignty, the attainment by the Moslems of full civil equality, and economic and social progress.

> Integration [writes *Contacts*] means the recognition by Algerians
> and their metropolitan brothers of the equal rights of all citizens
> of Algeria; it means the pooling of all the material resources of
> both Algeria and the mother country.

Understood in this sense, integration constituted the idea-force, the
myth that the army intended to offer to the dreams of the Algerian
masses and oppose to the mystique of independence. "Our myth,"
declares Colonel Lacheroy, "involves telling the Moslem, 'You will be
like us.' " This may lead to a misconception. It was not just cold cal-
culation or a simple propaganda maneuver, but a profound desire by
the army to achieve an ideal condition. This condition involved the
complete abrogation of semicolonial statutes existing in Algeria until
1954, and the establishment of entirely new ties between Algerian and
metropolitan departments. At this point, the military were quite far
from their original task of re-establishing order. The army had set up
a goal in the Algerian fight that, without expressly contradicting it,
greatly transcended the goal sought by the government. On the basis
of experience the army developed a complete, coherent Algerian policy
closely linked to the imperatives and terms of the battle it had to
fight. It was a fitting policy, defined by the army itself, which remained
totally independent of the decisions of the government.

Sentimental and Moral Interests

Above all, the pursuit of this Algerian policy was connected, within
the ideological context of the French army, with a tenacious loyalty
to certain strong and influential values. It must not be forgotten that
the conquest of the French colonial empire, in the nineteenth century
and at the beginning of the twentieth, was almost entirely the work
of the army. It is not surprising that attachment to this empire occupied
an important place in the moral patrimony of the French officer, that
it was bound up with some of the most profound traditions inherited
by the officer. Ties binding the army to the heritage of a colonial
past were particularly numerous and strong in North Africa. How
could this fund of memories, images, legends and collective pride be
evoked? There were the legend of Lyautey and the great moments
in the Moroccan epic, all living realities talked about at mess and
taught at military academies. There was Algeria's role as a place of
refuge from 1940 to 1943. The divisions that had fought in Italy
and landed in France came to Algeria and found shelter. North African
garrisons were a kind of sanctuary during the first years of the postwar period. The officers there enjoyed a higher standard of living and
greater respect. Above all, there was great contact between the military

and the Moslem population. Many officers had led North African units or fought at their side. Ties of friendship in battle, of respect and affection, developed and remained strong. The army was also proud of having assured perfect equality of treatment within its ranks for both North Africans and Frenchmen. Many such factors combined to grant North Africa a privileged place in the "sentimental geography" of the French army.

But there were graver considerations. The pursuit of the task of pacification ineluctably obliged the French officer to compromise a number of loyal Algerian Moslems with French authority, for which he felt directly responsible. To evacuate Algeria would amount to abandoning the loyal to the reprisals of the rebellion. To the officer who had granted his protection, this would mean forfeiting basic duties of loyalty and honor. Many men had already returned from Indochina with a feeling of guilt, bearing a heavy burden for having betrayed the commitments they had made to the Vietnamese partisans fighting by their side.

> I knew a captain of the red hats [writes one witness] who was obsessed with the idea that he had lost his honor in Indochina because he had influenced hundreds of young Catholic Vietnamese to join him by repeating "we will never let you down," which he truly believed. At our departure the Viets had these young people shot for having believed the captain.

In Algeria, where the basic task was to obtain active, militant allegiance of the population, the problem was posed in a more general way. It is not surprising that it finally had a determinant place in the minds of a great many officers.

In this vein, there is no more significant example than this passage taken from the work of a former second lieutenant in the paratroopers, Jean Yves Alquier, where he relates his experiences as an S.A.S. officer. M. Alquier is about to return to civilian life. An old Moslem, once a fighter and now a douar leader is bidding him farewell:

> Lieutenant [says the old man], I want to speak to you for the last time before you leave us. It's about the young people of my *mechta*. I made them return from Algiers at your request so they could work with you and the captain. As long as you were here, they had confidence in France. But now I fear she is abandoning us. . . . You know that if Algeria is given her independence, all those who worked with France will be murdered. So, here is my request. As a trusting friend, I ask that you swear you will never abandon us, or that before leaving

> you will authorize the young people to go to work in Algiers
> or in France; they will be content there. I will stay behind with
> my sons and my people. . . .

Lieutenant Alquier then comments:

> While the old chief awaited my decision, I thought about all
> the people in Indochina who had been killed for believing that
> France, after having fought at their side, would never abandon
> them. I thought of those in Tunisia who, loyal to the end, had
> disappeared without a trace since our departure; and of those
> in Morocco. . . . And once again I wondered if one day we
> would not have the death of all those we had rallied and then
> betrayed on our conscience.

As it happened, Lieutenant Alquier refused to commit himself and
allowed the young people of the *douar* to leave for Algiers. But the
promise that he dared not make that day was made by many who
could not take any other stand without betraying their mission. In
the eyes of many officers the policy of pacification led to the establishment of a contract with the Moslem population, a personally binding
contract that they had no right to break. Thus, it seemed impossible
that the army should follow any policy other than the one to which
the government had so deeply committed it. In consequence, the government lost the possibility of defining and imposing another policy.
To the moral imperatives of obedience to legal government the army
opposed other stronger imperatives, which grew out of the execution
of the mission it had received. . . .

Colonel Roger Trinquier: Modern Warfare

THE NEED TO ADAPT OUR MILITARY
APPARATUS TO MODERN WARFARE

The defense of national territory is the *raison d'être* of an army; it
should always be capable of accomplishing this objective.

Since the liberation of France in 1945, however, the French Army
has not been able to halt the collapse of our Empire. And yet, the
effort the country has made for the army is unprecedented. No French
military man ought to rest until we have created an army at last
capable of assuring the defense of our national territory.

Selections from Sections 1, 2, 4, 5. 6, and 7 of *Modern Warfare* by Colonel
Roger Trinquier. Translated by Daniel Lee. Copyright 1964 by Frederick A.
Praeger, Inc., New York, N.Y. Reproduced by permission of the publisher.

We still persist in studying a type of warfare that no longer exists and that we shall never fight again, while we pay only passing attention to the war we lost in Indochina and the one we are about to lose in Algeria. Yet the abandonment of Indochina or of Algeria is just as important for France as would be the loss of a metropolitan province.

The result of this shortcoming is that the army is not prepared to confront an adversary employing arms and methods the army itself ignores. It has, therefore, no chance of winning.

It is a fact that in Indochina, despite a marked superiority in matériel and in troops, we were beaten. From one campaign to another, our commanders tried to drive the Vietminh into a classic pitched battle, the only kind we knew how to fight, in hope that our superiority in matériel would allow an easy victory. The Vietminh always knew how to elude such maneuvers. When they finally accepted the conventional battle so vainly sought for several years, it was only because they had assembled on the battlefield resources superior to our own. That was at Dien-Bien-Phu in May 1954.

Despite the record, our army is employing, with few exceptions, the identical combat procedures in North Africa. We are trying in the course of repeated complex operations to seize an adversary who eludes us. The results obtained bear no relation to the resources and efforts expended. In fact, we are only dispersing, rather than destroying, the attacked bands.

Our military machine reminds one of a pile driver attempting to crush a fly, indefatigably persisting in repeating its efforts.

The inability of the army to adapt itself to changed circumstances has heavy consequences. It gives credence to the belief that our adversaries, who represent only weak forces, are invincible and that, sooner or later, we shall have to accept their conditions for peace. It encourages the diffusion of dangerously erroneous ideas, which eventually become generally accepted. France is accused of having conducted rigged elections in Algeria, and one is led to believe that those carried out under the aegis of the (Algerian) National Liberation Front (F.L.N.) would be genuine. At the same time, it is well known that any threat that would subsequently confront the voters would be effective in quite a different way from the former, merely administrative, pressures.

All this is nonetheless what a large part of our own press tries to tell the public.

We know that it is not at all necessary to have the sympathy of a majority of the people in order to rule them. The right organization can turn the trick.

This is what our adversaries are accomplishing in Algeria. Thanks to a *specially adapted organization* and to appropriate methods of warfare, they have been successful in imposing themselves upon entire populations and in using them, despite their own desires in the matter, against us. Our enemies are submitting us to a kind of hateful extortion, to which we shall have to accede in the end if we cannot destroy the warfare system that confronts us. We would be gravely remiss in our duty if we should permit ourselves to be thus deluded and to abandon the struggle before final victory. We would be sacrificing defenseless populations to unscrupulous enemies.

MODERN WARFARE DEFINED

Since the end of World War II, a new form of warfare has been born. Called at times either *subversive warfare* or *revolutionary warfare,* it differs fundamentally from the wars of the past in that victory is not expected from the clash of two armies on a field of battle. This confrontation, which in times past saw the annihilation of an enemy army in one or more battles, no longer occurs.

Warfare is now an interlocking system of actions—political, economic, psychological, military—that aims at the *overthrow of the established authority in a country and its replacement by another regime.* To achieve this end, the aggressor tries to exploit the internal tensions of the country attacked—ideological, social, religious, economic—any conflict liable to have a profound influence on the population to be conquered. Moreover, in view of the present-day interdependence of nations, any residual grievance within a population, no matter how localized and lacking in scope, will surely be brought by determined adversaries into the framework of the great world conflict. From a localized conflict of secondary origin and importance, they will always attempt sooner or later to bring about a generalized conflict.

On so vast a field of action, traditional armed forces no longer enjoy their accustomed decisive role. Victory no longer depends on one battle over a given terrain. Military operations, as combat actions carried out against opposing armed forces, are of only limited importance and are never the total conflict.

This is doubtless the reason why the army, traditionally attracted by the purely military aspect of a conflict, has never seriously approached the study of a problem it considers an inferior element in the art of war.

A modern army is first of all one that is capable of winning the conflict in which its country is engaged. And we are certainly at war, because we run the risk of being finally defeated on the ground (as at Dien-Bien-Phu in May 1954) and because, in case of such a defeat, we shall have to cede vast territories to our opponents.

The struggle we have been carrying on for fifteen years, in Indochina as well as in Algeria, is truly a war. But what we are involved in is *modern warfare*.

If we want to win, it is in this light that we must consider it from now on.

Studies have been made in many countries of what is called subversive warfare. But they rarely go beyond the stage of guerrilla warfare, which comes closest to the traditional form.

Mindful of the Allied victory in World War II, and perhaps because it is more appealing to study successful combat methods than to dwell upon the reasons for a defeat, only the offensive use of the guerrilla has been considered. But the study of effective countermeasures has been neglected. Some authors have stressed the inadequacy of the means employed against the guerrilla; others have simply counseled reacting against the guerrilla—confronting him with the counterguerrilla to beat him at his own game.

This is to wish to resolve a problem quickly without having duly weighed it.

The subtlest aspects of *modern warfare*, such as the manipulation of populations, have been the subject of recent studies. But only some of the methods employed by an enemy to consolidate his hold over conquered populations in peacetime have been investigated, in particular the working of psychological action on the masses.

But the rallying of opposition and the study of effective means of protection have been neglected. More exactly, when the enemy's methods and their application have been recognized, propaganda and pressures have always been powerful enough to influence a poorly informed public and to lead it systematically to refuse to study or use the same methods.

We know that the *sine qua non* of victory in *modern warfare* is the unconditional support of a population. According to Mao Tse-tung, it is as essential to the combatant as water to the fish. Such support may be spontaneous, although that is quite rare and probably a temporary condition. If it doesn't exist, it must be secured by every possible means, the most effective of which is *terrorism*.

In *modern warfare*, we are not actually grappling with an army organized along traditional lines, but with a few armed elements acting clandestinely within a population manipulated by a special organization.

Our army in Algeria is in excess of 300,000 men supplied with the most modern equipment; its adversary numbers some 30,000, in general poorly equipped with only light weapons.

If we were to have an opportunity to meet this enemy on the traditional field of battle, a dream vainly pursued for years by many military commanders, victory would be assured in a matter of hours.

The war has lasted more than six years, however, and victory is still uncertain. The problem is more complex.

In seeking a solution, it is essential to realize that in *modern warfare* we are not up against just a few armed bands spread across a given territory, but rather against an *armed clandestine organization* whose essential role is to impose its will upon the population. Victory will be obtained only through the complete destruction of that organization. This is the master concept that must guide us in our study of *modern warfare*.

. . .

TERRORISM—THE PRINCIPAL WEAPON OF
MODERN WARFARE

The war in Indochina and the one in Algeria have demonstrated the basic weapon that permits our enemies to fight effectively with few resources and even to defeat a traditional army.

This weapon is *terrorism*.

Terrorism in the service of a clandestine organization devoted to manipulating the population is a recent development. After being used in Morocco in 1954, it reached its full development in Algiers in December 1956, and January 1957. The resultant surprise gave our adversaries an essential advantage, which may have been decisive. In effect, a hundred organized terrorists were all that was necessary to cause us to give up the game quickly to the Moroccans.

Terrorism, then, is a *weapon of warfare*, which can neither be ignored nor minimized. It is as a weapon of warfare that we should study it.

The goal of *modern warfare* is control of the populace, and terrorism is a particularly appropriate weapon, since it aims directly at
the inhabitant. In the street, at work, at home, the citizen lives continually under the threat of violent death. In the presence of this
permanent danger surrounding him, he has the depressing feeling of
being an isolated and defenseless target. The fact that public authority
and the police are no longer capable of ensuring his security adds to
his distress. He loses confidence in the state whose inherent mission
it is to guarantee his safety. He is more and more drawn to the side
of the terrorists, who alone are able to protect him.

The intended objective, which is to cause the population to vacillate,
is thus attained.

What characterizes modern terrorism, and makes for its basic
strength, is the slaughter of generally defenseless persons. The terrorist
operates within a familiar legal framework, while avoiding the ordinary
risks taken by the common criminal, let alone by soldiers on the field
of battle, or even by partisans facing regular troops.

The ordinary criminal kills a certain individual, usually only one,
for a specific purpose. Having achieved it, he may no longer constitute
a danger to society. His crime is based on an easily discernible motive
—robbery, vengeance, etc. To succeed, he quite often has to run risks
sufficient to cause his arrest. His crime is thus carried out within a
known framework. Well-defined police procedure can easily be applied,
which takes whatever time is necessary to obtain justice, while respecting the rights of both the individual and society.

The soldier meets his adversary on the field of battle and in uniform.
He fights within a framework of traditional rules that both sides respect. Aware of the dangers that confront him, the soldier has always
had a high regard for his opponent, because both run the same risks.
When the battle is over, the dead and the wounded of the two camps
are treated with the same humanity; prisoners are withdrawn as quickly
as possible from the battlefield and are simply kept from fighting again
until the end of the war.

For the partisan and the irregular who oppose a regular army, the
very fact that they violate the rules of warfare in fighting without a
uniform (avoiding the risks involved) deprives them of the protection
of these same rules. If taken prisoner while armed, they may be shot
on the spot.

But the case of the terrorist is quite otherwise. Not only does he
carry on warfare without uniform, but he attacks, far from a field of
battle, only unarmed civilians who are incapable of defending themselves and who are normally protected under the rules of warfare.

Surrounded by a vast organization, which prepares his task and assists him in its execution, which assures his withdrawal and his protection, he runs practically no risks—neither that of retaliation by his victims nor that of having to appear before a court of justice. When it has been decided to kill someone sometime somewhere, with the sole purpose of terrorizing the populace and strewing a certain number of bodies along the streets of a city or on country roads, it is quite easy under existing laws to escape the police.

In Algiers, during 1956, the F.L.N. set up the clandestine warfare organization already described, and it was impossible for the police forces to arrest a single terrorist. In the face of the ever increasing number of attacks, the police ought to have acknowledged their impotence and appealed to the army.

Without the massive intervention of the army (in particular of the Tenth Parachute Division) at the beginning of 1957, the entire city would have fallen into the hands of the F.L.N., the loss carrying with it the immediate abandonment of all Algeria.

In a large city, police forces can partly restrict the action of the terrorists and delay their complete control of the populace. Obliged to act secretly, the organization's functioning will be slow and difficult. Massive and drastic action by the army may even be able to stop it entirely, as in Algiers in 1957.

But in the unprotected regions that comprise the major portion of the national territory, particularly the vast area of inhabited countryside where police forces are small or nonexistent, terrorist action encounters no opposition at the beginning of a conflict and is most effective.

Isolated raids first reveal the existence of a partially organized movement. These attract attention and promote caution among the populace. Then, selective terrorism begins to eliminate lesser persons of influence, petty bureaucrats and various police officials who did not understand the first warnings or were slow in reacting to them. Administrative cadres are restrained or eliminated. The silence and collusion of the unprotected inhabitants have been won. Agents of the enemy have a free hand to organize and to manipulate the population at will.

From then on, within the midst of these people taken over by terrorism, the small armed bands whose task it is to wage guerrilla warfare are able to install themselves, in the phrase of Mao Tse-tung, like fish in water. Fed, informed, protected, they are able to strike without difficulty against the forces of order.

Modern warfare requires the unconditional support of the populace.

This support must be maintained at any price. Here again, terrorism plays its role.

An unceasing watch is exercised over all the inhabitants. Any suspicion or indication of lack of submission is punishable by death, quite often preceded by horrible torture.

The atrocities committed by the F.L.N. in Algeria to maintain its hold over the populace are innumerable. I will cite but one example to demonstrate the degree to which they were carried in certain areas.

In the month of September 1958, the forces of order took possession of the files of a military tribunal of one of the regions of the F.L.N. In the canton of Michelet alone, in the arrondissement (district) of Fort-National in Kabylie, more than 2,000 inhabitants were condemned to death and executed between November 1, 1954, and April 17, 1957.

Quite clearly, terrorism is a weapon of warfare, and it is important to stress it.

Although quite old, until recently it has been utilized only by isolated revolutionaries for spectacular attacks, principally against high political personalities, such as sovereigns, chiefs of state, and ministers. Even in Indochina, where guerrillas achieved such a remarkable degree of development that it permitted the Vietminh finally to win, terrorism has never been systematically employed. For example, the plastic bomb attacks outside the municipal theater in Saigon, which caused the greatest number of victims, were not carried out by the Vietminh (see Graham Greene's book *The Quiet American*).

The terrorist should not be considered an ordinary criminal. Actually, he fights within the framework of his organization, without personal interest, for a cause he considers noble and for a respectable ideal, the same as the soldiers in the armies confronting him. On the command of his superiors, he kills without hatred individuals unknown to him, with the same indifference as the soldier on the battlefield. His victims are often women and children, almost always defenseless individuals taken by surprise. But during a period of history when the bombing of open cities is permitted, and when two Japanese cities were razed to hasten the end of the war in the Pacific, one cannot with good cause reproach him.*

---

*Yassef Saadi, chief of the Autonomous Zone of Algiers (Z.A.A.), said after his arrest: "I had my bombs planted in the city because I didn't have the aircraft to transport them. But they caused fewer victims than the artillery and air bombardments of our mountain villages. I'm in a war, you cannot blame me."

The terrorist has become a soldier, like the aviator or the infantry-man.

But the aviator flying over a city knows that antiaircraft shells can kill or maim him. The infantryman wounded on the battlefield accepts physical suffering, often for long hours, when he falls between the lines and it is impossible to rescue him. It never occurs to him to complain and to ask, for example, that his enemy renounce the use of the rifle, the shell, or the bomb. If he can, he goes back to a hospital knowing this to be his lot. The soldier, therefore, admits the possibility of physical suffering as part of the job. The risks he runs on the battlefield and the suffering he endures are the price of the glory he receives.

The terrorist claims the same honors while rejecting the same obligations. His kind of organization permits him to escape from the police, his victims cannot defend themselves, and the army cannot use the power of its weapons against him because he hides himself perma-nently within the midst of a population going about its peaceful pursuits.

But he must be made to realize that, when he is captured, he cannot be treated as an ordinary criminal, nor like a prisoner taken on the battlefield. What the forces of order who have arrested him are seek-ing is not to punish a crime, for which he is otherwise not personally responsible, but, as in any war, the destruction of the enemy army or its surrender. Therefore he is not asked details about himself or about attacks that he may or may not have committed and that are not of immediate interest, but rather for precise information about his organization. In particular, each man has a superior whom he knows; he will first have to give the name of this person, along with his address, so that it will be possible to proceed with the arrest without delay.

No lawyer is present for such an interrogation. If the prisoner gives the information requested, the examination is quickly terminated; if not, specialists must force his secret from him. Then, as a soldier, he must face the suffering, and perhaps the death, he has heretofore managed to avoid. The terrorist must accept this as a condition inher-ent in his trade and in the methods of warfare that, with full knowl-edge, his superiors and he himself have chosen.* Once the interroga-

*In France during the Nazi occupation, members of the Resistance violated the rules of warfare. They knew they could not hide behind them, and they were per-fectly aware of the risks to which they were exposing themselves. Their glory is to have calmly faced those risks with full knowledge of the consequences.

tion is finished, however, the terrorist can take his place among soldiers. From then on, he is a prisoner of war like any other, kept from resuming hostilities until the end of the conflict.

It would be as useless and unjust to charge him with the attacks he was able to carry out, as to hold responsible the infantryman or the airman for the deaths caused by the weapons they use. According to Clausewitz:

> War . . . is an act of violence intended to compel an opponent to fulfill our will. . . . Self-imposed restrictions, almost imperceptible and hardly worth mentioning, termed usages of International Law, accompany it without impairing its power. Violence . . . is therefore the means; the compulsory submission of the enemy to our will is the ultimate object. . . .
>
> In such dangerous things as war, the errors which proceed from a spirit of benevolence are the worst. As the use of physical power to the utmost extent by no means excludes the cooperation of the intelligence, it follows that he who uses force unsparingly, without reference to the bloodshed involved, must obtain a superiority if his adversary uses less vigor in its application. . . .
>
> To introduce into the philosophy of war itself a principle of moderation would be an absurdity.*

These basic principles of traditional warfare retain all of their validity in *modern warfare*.

Although violence is an unavoidable necessity in warfare, certain unnecessary violence ought to be rigorously banned. Interrogations in *modern warfare* should be conducted by specialists perfectly versed in the techniques to be employed.

The first condition for a quick and effective interrogation is to have interrogators who know what they can ask the terrorist under questioning. For this, it is first of all essential to place him precisely within the diagram of the organization to which he belongs. A profound knowledge of the organization is required. It is useless to ask a funds collector about caches of weapons or bombs. Every clandestine organization is strictly compartmented, and he would know nothing about them. To ask him would be a useless waste of time. On the other hand, he does know to whom he remits the funds and under what conditions. This is the only subject about which he should be questioned.

*Karl von Clausewitz, *On War*, trans. Col. J. J. Graham (New York: E. P. Dutton and Co.), I, 2–3.

It is known that the ordinary terrorist operates as part of a three-man team; therefore he knows his comrade and his demi-cell superior. This is the only information he will be able to furnish, but he must give it quickly; otherwise, the individuals sought will have the time to disappear, the thread will be broken, and a lengthy search will quite often come to naught.

The interrogators must always strive not to injure the physical and moral integrity of individuals. Science can easily place at the army's disposition the means for obtaining what is sought.

But we must not trifle with our responsibilities. It is deceitful to permit artillery or aviation to bomb villages and slaughter women and children, while the real enemy usually escapes, and to refuse interrogation specialists the right to seize the truly guilty terrorist and spare the innocent.

Terrorism in the hands of our adversaries has become a formidable weapon of war that we can no longer permit ourselves to ignore. Tried out in Indochina and brought to perfection in Algeria, it can lead to any boldness, even a direct attack on metropolitan France. Thanks to the Communist Party, which is already on the scene and is familiar with underground operations, it would encounter no great difficulty.

Even a band of gangsters, lacking any political ideology at all, but without scruples and determined to employ the same methods, could constitute a grave danger.

In the light of present events, we can imagine in its broad outlines the unfolding of future aggression:

A few organized and well-trained men of action will carry out a reign of terror in the big cities. If the goal pursued is only to strew the streets nightly with a certain number of anonymous corpses to terrorize the inhabitants, a specialized organization would have no difficulty, within the framework of existing laws, in escaping the pursuit of the police. The numerous attacks being committed nightly in our large cities, which are nothing other than a prelude to facilitating the creation and training of an important warfare organization, demonstrate in a tangible way the inadequacy of a traditional police force against modern terrorists. Whenever a broad attack is unfolded, the police run the risk of being quickly overwhelmed.

In the countryside, and particularly in the hilly regions such as the Massif Central, the Alps, or Brittany, the population has no permanent protection. Small bands could easily block traffic through difficult passes by killing the passengers of the first two or three automobiles.

A few brutalities, such as savagely executed preventive assassinations in the surrounding villages, will cow the inhabitants into providing for the maintenance of the bands and will discourage them from giving useful information to the authorities.

Occasional police operations timidly carried out with inadequate forces will fail pitifully. These failures will encourage a goodly number of adventurers to team up with the original outlaws, who will rapidly develop into rebels.

In this fashion, immense zones will be practically abandoned to our adversaries and will be lost to our control. The way will be open to the guerrilla. With terrorism in the cities and guerrillas in the countryside, the war will have begun. This is the simple mechanism, now well known, which can at any instant be unleashed against us.

IDENTIFYING THE ADVERSARY

To carry out a war effectively, to win it, it is indispensable to identify the adversary exactly. This condition must be fulfilled so that our shots will strike home.

Formerly, this was a simple task. According to the period of our history, he was to be found on the other side of the Rhine or the other side of the Channel. He had his war aims, simple and precise, as we had ours. It would have been useless to attempt to convert him to our cause or to hope to cause him to give up the fight without having defeated him.

To gain a victory, the nation and its army put to work all material and moral resources. Any person who dealt with the enemy, or who favored his objectives in any way, was considered a traitor and was treated as such.

In *modern warfare*, the enemy is far more difficult to identify. No physical frontier separates the two camps. The line of demarcation between friend and foe passes through the very heart of the nation, through the same village, and sometimes divides the same family. It is a non-physical, often ideological boundary, which must however be expressly delineated if we want to reach the adversary and to defeat him.

Since *the military art is simply and completely one of action*, it is only when we have identified the enemy that the apparently complex problems posed to the army by *modern warfare* can be reduced to realistic proportions and easily resolved. The criteria for arriving at such a point will be difficult to establish; however, a study of the causes of the war and the aims pursued by the adversary will permit us to discover them.

The period of preparation before the opening of hostilities generally takes place under cover of a legally established political party; our opponents can thus get themselves within our frontiers and under the protection of our laws. Covered by legality, they will strive to create a climate favorable to their cause within the country and abroad and to establish on our own territory the essential elements of their warfare organization.

The fact that *modern warfare* is not officially declared, that a state of war is not generally proclaimed, permits the adversary to continue to take advantage of peacetime legislation, to pursue his activities both openly and secretly. He will strive by every means to preserve the fiction of peace, which is so essential to the pursuit of his design.

Therefore, the surest means of unveiling the adversary is to declare a state of war at the earliest moment, at the very latest when the first symptoms of the struggle are revealed in political assassinations, terrorism, guerrilla activities, etc.

At this stage the preparation of the opponent will be quite well advanced and the danger very great; to minimize this would be a disastrous mistake. Henceforth, any party that has supported or continues to support the enemy shall be considered a party of the enemy.

The nation attacked must fall in behind the government and its army. An army can throw itself into a campaign only when it has the moral support of the nation; it is the nation's faithful reflection because it is composed of the nation's youth and because it carries within it the hopes of the nation. Its unquestioned actions should be praised by the nation to maintain the nobility of the just cause it has been charged to make triumphant. The army, whose responsibility it is to do battle, must receive the unreserved, affectionate, and devoted support of the nation. Any propaganda tending to undermine its morale, causing it to doubt the necessity of its sacrifices, should be unmercifully repressed.

The army will then know where to strike. Any individual who, in any fashion whatsoever, favors the objectives of the enemy will be considered a traitor and treated as such.

In totalitarian countries, ideological boundaries are extended to the country's geographic limits, so that there may be no doubt as to the enemy to be struck. All enemies of the established power are eliminated or driven out of the national territory.

Although we should avoid these extreme measures, which are unquestionably incompatible with the ideals of liberty dear to us and to the civilization we are defending, we cannot, obviously, defeat an enemy we have not clearly identified.

We know that the *enemy* consists not of a few armed bands fighting on the ground, but of an organization that feeds him, informs him, and sustains his morale. This is a state of affairs that democracy tolerates within an attacked nation, but it enables the enemy to act secretly or openly in such a way that measures which might deal him a decisive blow are either never taken or are indefinitely delayed.

DEFENSE OF THE TERRITORY

Since the stake in *modern warfare* is the control of the populace, the first objective is to assure the people their protection by giving them the means of defending themselves, especially against terrorism.

We then have to create and train organizations capable of detecting the elements our enemies will strive to introduce into our territory preparatory to the open struggle.

Finally, if hostilities break out, if terrorism and guerrilla activity have established themselves over a large portion of our territory, we must combat them with the appropriate methods, which will be far more effective than those which would have been considered and used in peacetime.

The Inhabitants' Organization

Military schools teaching classic doctrines of warfare rely upon a number of decision factors—the mission, the enemy, the terrain, and the resources.

But one factor that is essential to the conduct of *modern warfare* is omitted—the inhabitant.

The battlefield today is no longer restricted. It is limitless; it can encompass entire nations. The inhabitant in his home is the center of the conflict. Amidst the continuing movement of military actions, he is the stablest element. Like it or not, the two camps are compelled to make him participate in the combat; in a certain sense, he has become a combatant also. Therefore, it is essential to prepare him for the role he will have to play and to enable him to fulfill it effectively on our side.

For the inhabitant to elude the threats of the enemy, to cease to be an isolated target that no police force can protect, we must have him participate in his own defense. To this end, we have him enter into a structured organization encompassing the entire population. No one shall be able to avoid this service, and each person at any moment will be subject to the orders of his civil or military superiors to participate in protective measures.

Control of the masses through a tight organization, often through several parallel organizations, is the master weapon of *modern warfare*. This is what permits the enemy to uncover quickly any hostile element within a subjugated population. Only when we have created a similar organization will we be able to discover, and as quickly eliminate, those individuals the enemy tries to introduce among us. . . .

Good will is never lacking even in the most troubled of times. Indochina and, later, Algeria have amply proven this. But we ought never to forget that ambition has always been a powerful incentive for a young and dynamic elite that wishes to get out of its rut and arrive. It is largely to this youth that we must appeal. We must bind them to us and compensate services rendered according to their worth.

Finally, of course, we may always assure ourselves of their loyalty by placing them within an organization it will be difficult to leave once admitted.

This inhabitants' organization certainly runs counter to our traditional spirit of individualism and may promote dangers to our liberties that we must not minimize. The analogy with certain totalitarian organizations will afford our adversaries easy opportunities to attack us.

But we cannot permit ourselves to be deluded. There is a fundamental difference. Our organization is a defensive one, the sole aim of which is to ensure the protection of the populace, particularly against the danger of terrorism. No individual entering it need abdicate a particle of his basic liberties; but in the face of a common enemy, each will give under discipline his total and unreserved assistance to his fellows and his superiors. Once the war is won or the danger has passed, our organization will have no reason to exist.

Abuses are always possible. The organization will have to be seriously controlled, so that it remains solely a means of protection against the external enemy and does not become a vehicle for internal political pressure. This cannot happen if it is created in a spirit of justice and if the burdens it necessitates are equitably shared among all the inhabitants of a given region, no matter what their social circumstances may be.

One should not lose sight of the fact that this is the sole means we have to assure the protection of peaceful citizens and to prevent terrorism from forcing them into a harsh and inhuman servitude.

Formerly, nations spent huge sums for the construction of fortifications designed to protect themselves against invasion. Today, the inhabitants' organization, the elite formation designed as a framework for protection and to give us information about the enemy's clandestine penetration of our territory, constitutes the modern means of defense against *modern warfare*.

Any country that does not create such an organization runs a permanent danger of being invaded. The financial outlays called for cannot be compared with those needed for the construction of elaborate fortifications. We have no excuse if we do not create such an organization. . . .

DIRECT ACTION ON THE POPULATIONS OF CITIES

. . . But the conduct of a police operation in the middle of a city raises numerous difficulties. We should note the main ones so that we may be able to overcome them.

1. *Modern warfare* is a new experience for the majority of our fellow citizens. Even among our friends, the systematic conduct of raids will run into opposition, resulting generally from a total lack of understanding of the enemy and his methods of warfare. This will often be very difficult to overcome.

For example, the fact that the enemy's warfare organization in a single city may consist of several thousand men will come as a surprise even to the majority of high administrative functionaries, who thought sincerely that they were dealing with only a few isolated criminals.

One of the first problems encountered, that of lodging the individuals arrested, will generally not have been anticipated. Prisons, designed essentially to accommodate offenders against common law, will rapidly become inadequate and will not meet our needs. We will be compelled to intern the prisoners under improvised, often deplorable conditions, which will lead to justifiable criticism our adversaries will exploit. From the beginning of hostilities, prison camps should be set up according to the conditions laid down by the Geneva Convention. They should be sufficiently large to take care of all prisoners until the end of the war.

2. By every means—and this is a quite legitimate tactic—our opponents will seek to slow down and, if possible, put an end to our operations. The fact that a state of war will generally not have been

declared will be, as we have already indicated, one of their most effective means of achieving this. In particular, they will attempt to have arrested terrorists treated as ordinary criminals and to have members of their organization considered as minor peacetime offenders.

On this subject, the files of the Algiers terrorist organization divulged some particularly interesting documents.

"We are no longer protected by legality," wrote the chief of the Algiers F.L.N. in 1957, when the army had taken over the functions of the police. "We ask all our friends to do the impossible to have legality re-established; otherwise we are lost."

Actually, the peacetime laws gave our enemies maximum opportunities for evading pursuit; it was vital to them that legality be strictly applied. The appeal was not launched in vain. Shortly thereafter, a violent press campaign was unleashed, both in France and abroad, demanding that peacetime laws be strictly adhered to in the course of police operations.

3. Warfare operations, especially those of a police nature in a large city, take place in the very midst of the populace, almost in public, whereas formerly they occurred on a battlefield, to which only armed forces had access.

Certain harsh actions can easily pass for brutalities in the eyes of a sensitive public. And it is a fact also that, in the process of extirpating the terrorist organization from their midst, the people will be manhandled, lined up, interrogated, searched. Day and night, armed soldiers will make unexpected intrusions into the homes of peaceful citizens to carry out necessary arrests. Fighting may occur in which the inhabitants will suffer.

People who know our adversaries will not protest in submitting to inconveniences they know to be necessary for the recovery of their liberty. But our enemies will not fail to exploit the situation for their propaganda needs.

Nevertheless, even if some brutality is inevitable, rigorous discipline must always be enforced to prevent wanton acts. The army has the means of demanding and maintaining firm discipline. It has at its disposal its own system of justice, precisely created to check quickly misdeeds or crimes committed by military personnel in the exercise of their duties. The army must apply the law without hesitation.

Under no pretext, however, can a government permit itself to become engaged in a polemic against the forces of order in this respect, a situation that can benefit only our adversaries.

Police action will therefore be actual operational warfare. It will

be methodically pursued until the enemy organization has been entirely annihilated. It will not end until we have organized the population and created an efficient intelligence service to enable it to defend
itself. This organization will have to be maintained until the end
of hostilities to prevent any return by the enemy to the offensive.
After the battle of Algiers in 1957, the French Government, under
pressure from our adversaries, permitted the dismantling of everything
the army had built up. Three years later, the enemy was able to re-
establish his organization and once again to take control of the population (December 1960). The victory of Algiers in 1957 had gone for
naught.

Our war aims must be clearly known to the people. They will have
to be convinced that if we call upon them to fight at our sides it
can only be in defense of a just cause. And we should not deceive
them. The surest means of gaining their confidence will be to crush
those who want to oppress them. When we have placed the terrorists
out of harm's way, the problem of pacification will be quickly resolved.

As long as we have not arrived at such a point, any *propaganda*,
any solution, however skillful, will be ineffective on a populace infected by clandestine organisms that penetrate like a cancer into its
midst and terrorize it. It is only when we have delivered it from
this evil that it will freely listen, think, and express itself. A just
peace will then be quite possible.

During the period of active operations, the role of propaganda action of the masses will have little effect. It will usually be limited to
making the people understand that the frequently severe measures
taken have no purpose other than to cause the rapid destruction of
the enemy.

With the gradual return to peace, however, propaganda will play
an important role in causing the sometimes impatient masses to understand the variety of problems that must be resolved before a return
to normal existence is possible. The inhabitants' organization will be
the most effective instrument of propaganda contact and dissemination.

The people know instinctively what is correct. It is only by substan-
tive measures that we will lead them to judge the validity of our
action.

War has always been a calamity for the people. Formerly, only
those inhabitants who found themselves in the paths of the armies had
to suffer the calamity. Today, *modern warfare* strikes the entire popu-

lation of a country, the inhabitants of the large cities as well as those of the most remote rural districts.

The enemy, infiltrated among the people, will always try to deprive the inhabitants of their means of subsistence. It is among the people that combat operations will take place, and their activities will be limited in many ways. They will have to suffer the exacting demands the enemy invokes to compel obedience, as well as the frequently severe measures the forces of order are led to take.

It will be the role of the *social services* to lessen the miseries war engenders.

But we must not lose sight of the fact that any material aid we give will only profit the enemy if the organization that permits his control and manipulation of the people has not first been destroyed. Aid must be prudently administered until the police operation has been completed; premature, uncontrolled assistance would be of no use to the inhabitants.

Once peace has been established, even in a small part of the territory, extensive and generous social assistance will be of prime importance in bringing to our cause many people who are unhappy and often disoriented by the military operations and who will not have always understood the underlying reasons for them.

The conduct of military operations in a large city, in the midst of the populace, without the benefit of the powerful weapons it possesses, is certainly one of the most delicate and complex problems ever to face an army.

To carry out effective police work, conduct operations among the citizenry, and cause the inhabitants to participate actively on its side, are obviously tasks for which the military generally has not been prepared. Some feel that these operations should be entirely carried out by the police, and that the army should keep to the nobler task, better adapted to its specialty, of reducing armed bands in the field.

This is a grave error into which our adversaries would certainly like to lead us. The job of the police is only to ensure the protection of the people in time of peace against ordinary offenders or criminals. But the police do not have the means of conducting combat operations against a powerful enemy organization whose aim is not to attack individuals protected by the police, but rather to conquer the nation and to overthrow its regime.

The protection of the national territory and regime is quite clearly the essential role of the army. By and large it has the means necessary for victory; there is only the question of will and method.

III
"THE SPECTACLE OF INSTABILITY"

Introduction

In the following readings we plot the preliminary stages of the Thirteenth of May: French bombing of a Tunisian border village, an Anglo-American offer of "good offices" to settle the Franco-Tunisian dispute, the fall of the Gaillard government following its acceptance of proposals submitted through the "good offices." "You are going to open up a crisis. How long will it last?" Gaillard asked the National Assembly moments before it overthrew his government. It lasted longer than any cabinet crisis of the Fourth Republic before it; and one of the chief problems of this section is to see why the problems which led to Gaillard's fall were so difficult to resolve. The answers are rooted in the Algerian problem. As a refuge for FLN forces operating in Algeria, the bombed village, Sakiet-Sidi-Youssef, represented one obstacle to concluding the war: the ability of the enemy to escape French jurisdiction. As an intervention into affairs France considered her own business, the "good offices" represented a second obstacle: the failure of France's allies in NATO to support her course in Algeria. Debate over Sakiet and the "good offices" inevitably led to a wider debate about the more basic question of how to win the war. Could France stop the FLN without a "reconquest" of newly independent Tunisia? Was action against Tunisia possible against the opposition of the United States and Britain? Could there be a middle-way combination of force and negotiation which could neutralize

Tunisia and bring the FLN to the conference table? Was France sacrificing her friendships with African and Asian peoples for the sake of the European population of Algeria?

This discussion culminated in the fall of Gaillard. But could it lead to the formulation of a generally accepted positive Algerian policy? The unsuccessful attempts of Georges Bidault and René Pleven to form a new government showed what policies were probably out of bounds given the divisions of the Assembly. They also revealed that now the demands of the North African military commanders and the French Algerian population became a factor to be considered in governmental combinations, alongside the wishes of the four major party blocs. Given the new pressures from across the Mediterranean, could the parties maintain the delicate structure of compromise which had permitted governments their majorities since 1956? This question was especially pertinent for the Independents, the group that was closest in outlook to the army and the French Algerians.

The altered situation of late April and early May provides some clue to the apparent paradox of Pierre Pflimlin's attempt to form a government. Ostensibly, in terms of the parliamentary support he might command, Pflimlin's candidacy seemed to be weaker than the position of now-defeated Gaillard. Yet his bid aroused deep fears among the partisans of *Algérie française* and ultimately led to the protest demonstrations in Algiers that opened the crisis. There were many predictions in Paris on May 12 that Pflimlin could not receive a vote of confidence from the Assembly: whence then the anxiety in Algiers? Was it perhaps fear that even if Pflimlin were defeated the parliamentary regime would produce another middle-of-the-roader to succeed him, that the "system" itself was fatal for French Algeria? Or was there a crisis over the policy question, a feeling by enough people that they were at a turning point, that the situation demanded a "yes" or "no" on Algeria, but not the middle way the Pflimlins proposed?

To neutralize the machine guns of the FLN, which periodically attack French planes flying over the frontier, the Algiers headquarters has had the Tunisian village of Sakiet-Sidi-Youssef bombarded.

Bourguiba has recalled his ambassador from Paris and forbidden all French troop movements in Tunisia.

(*Le Figaro*, February 10, 1958, p. 1)

AFTER THE BOMBARDMENT OF SAKIET-SIDI-YOUSSEF

DIPLOMATIC MOVES AND UNFAVORABLE COMMENTS ABROAD

As was easy to foresee, the air bombardment of the village of Sakiet-Sidi-Youssef—an operation whose results have been confirmed as seventy-five dead and eighty-three wounded—has had immediate international repercussions.

In Tunisia, where M. Habib Bourguiba has declared he will demand the immediate evacuation of French troops, including those at Bizerte, and will appeal to the UN, the heads of diplomatic missions have been invited to come to Sakiet-Sidi-Youssef this Monday morning to verify the destruction. The situation remains calm, but various strikes and protest demonstrations are planned.

At Paris an inter-ministerial council will meet under M. Gaillard's chairmanship as soon as he has received the report requested from General Salan. . . . In the United States Mr. Foster Dulles summoned M. Alphand, the French Ambassador, to request clarification and has not concealed his uneasiness.

(*Le Monde*, February 11, 1958, p. 1)

Statement Issued by the Department of State, February 9, 1958

The United States Government is profoundly disturbed by reports received of the incident at Sakiet Sidi Youssef, Tunisia, on the morning of February 8. We are concerned at the effect that this occurrence may have on the relations between two nations, both friends of the

U.S. Department of State, *American Foreign Policy, Current Documents* 1958 (Washington, D.C., 1962), 1086.

United States, who we continue to hope will find a means of reconciling their differences in the interests of the peaceful progress of the North African area.

The Secretary of State asked the French Ambassador to call on Sunday afternoon [February 9] in order to express our concern and to seek further information, which has been promised.

Assemblée Nationale, Second Session of February 11, 1958

M. PIERRE COT (*Progressive*)*: . . . General Salan has published reassuring statements according to which the military objectives have been reached. But you know that these reassuring statements are in contradiction to detailed and concurrent reports which can no longer simply be shrugged off. I refer especially to the joint statement of six French journalists, among whom are M. Chauvel of the *Figaro* and M. Delame of *France-Soir*, who I do not think can be suspect in your eyes.

On the extreme right: Yes they are! (*Shouts and laughter on the extreme left.*)

M. PIERRE COT: I add that these reports have been confirmed by Colonel Heyman, a Swedish citizen and legate of the International Red Cross, and by M. Helbling, representative of the International Red Cross, who attest—and they were on the scene during the bombings —that women, old men, and children were killed and that trucks bearing the emblem of the Red Cross were destroyed.

Therefore, I demand that the President of the Council tell us this evening what he thinks of these contradictions. Is he going to say that the reporters for *Figaro* and *France-Soir* are liars?

M. ALBERT PRIVAT (*Poujadist*): This wouldn't be the first time they've been lying. (*Shouts on the extreme left.*)

M. PIERRE CHARLES (*Poujadist*): They're brain washers.

M. JEAN-MARIE LE PEN (*Unaffiliated*): You don't have a monopoly on treason, Monsieur Duclos! (*Protests on the extreme left.*)

M. PIERRE COT: . . . And so he's going to have them prosecuted for damaging the morale of the army and the nation?

Journal Officiel, Débats Parlementaires, Assemblée Nationale, 1957–58, 663–74, 679–81, 695–6.

*[Deputies are here identified by party. The *Journal Officiel* actually identifies them by *département*—Eds.]

M. JEAN-MARIE LE PEN: No one testifies against his mother, against his country!

On the extreme left: Fascist!

M. PIERRE COT: My dear colleague, in a debate so serious and so unfortunate for all of us, I will not interrupt you if you speak. I ask that you please not interrupt me any more.

M. ROGER ROUCAUTE (*Communist*): Oh, he's only a torture addict!

M. PIERRE COT: I ask the President of the Council if he is going to treat Colonel Heyman and M. Helbling as impostors.

Several cries on the right and on the extreme right: Why not?

M. PIERRE COT: My next question resumes the inquiry published yesterday evening in *Le Monde* in an article entitled: "Who is responsible?" Who *is* responsible? Civil authority or military authority?

I don't think anyone is going to cover up for subordinates—as they did with the grounding of the plane carrying Ben Bella and in the case of the *Slovenia*—while simultaneously implying and repeating that they had been presented with a fait accompli and that sailors, pilots, and soldiers were really a little too hasty and exceeded the instructions they were given.

Who commands in Algeria? (*Applause on the extreme left and on some benches of the left.*) Who commands in this war which no one dares call by name? Civil authorities or military authorities? Then who has supreme power?

Ladies and gentlemen, this is an important question. For even if we can admit—and I don't say approve—that in the heat of action in a country where the frontier is indefinite a commander can get carried away into acts which are perhaps irregular but perhaps can be excused, in the case of the bombing of Sakiet-Sidi-Youssef things are very different.

We're talking about twenty-five airplanes. An operation undertaken by twenty-five airplanes has to be prepared minutely; it presupposes staff conferences and precise preparations. Then who gave the orders? What authority is it that takes responsibility for this bombing? This is the question I ask you. (*Applause on the extreme left and on some benches of the left.*)

My next question will be an extension of the one I have just presented to the Assembly. It may appear secondary, but it is important for international public opinion.

During the course of recent debates in the United Nations on the Algerian affair it was said and repeated, especially in the American press, that the French government had promised not to use materials furnished by the Americans in operations against the rebels in Algeria.

Today we know that of the twenty-five airplanes used to bomb this village (and, as was just stated, on a market day), seventeen were American.

The question I am asking is whether there was such a promise. If so, wasn't it violated?

Now I come, ladies and gentlemen, to political questions.

The first is to know what the government will do tomorrow to deal with an incident which, because of its effect on international public opinion, has acquired and continues to acquire an importance that perhaps, indeed doubtless, its authors did not foresee.

Mr. President of the Council, will you accept, or more precisely will your government accept, the authority of the United Nations?

Or instead will you use the right of veto* which is denounced when other [countries] use it?

Or will you accept the jurisdiction of the International Court of Justice, which, as you know, is empowered by Article 36 of its charter, approved by us, to investigate the facts of any event that might constitute a violation of an international agreement?

If you don't agree to submit to these procedures, then what kind of position will the Foreign Minister and his Socialist friends be in? They certainly can't have forgotten the words of Jaurès: "In international affairs, he who refuses to submit to arbitration marks himself in the general conscience as the aggressor. . . ."

Several voices on the extreme right and the right: Hungary! Budapest!

M. PIERRE COT: My second question on politics is, what will you do tomorrow to prevent unfortunate events, such as this one which the Tunisian and Algerian people have undergone, from ever happening again?

Proposals have already been made, notably by M. Maurice Schumann. These have already been referred to. In the new climate created by exploding bombs I'm afraid these proposals have been superseded, and now the question is whether you will consider the surveillance of the frontiers by an international force, which will perhaps be effective but will lead to an internationalization of the conflict, which, as you know, would be contrary to our interests.

Therefore I ask if the wisest course wouldn't be to admit the truth at last: that is that there is a state of war in Algeria which obliges you to treat the FLN as belligerents, but which also allows you to demand that other states respect the laws of war.

My question here is exact and I hope that your answer will be.

*[In the UN Security Council—Eds.]

Finally, ladies and gentlemen, what will you do tomorrow to re-establish the climate that is necessary, not only to resume negotiations with the Tunisian government but to put our whole policy in North Africa on the only solid base which it can have, namely on friendship between France and the peoples of North Africa. . . .

. . . From this platform where in the past men have spoken—men for whom "justice, liberty and the rights of man" were not empty words—I want to appeal to the peoples of North Africa not to condemn all Frenchmen. (*Murmurs and protests on the right and the extreme right. Applause on the left.*) And in this chamber I want to raise at least one voice in the defense of the victims of the bombings. (*Protests on the right and the extreme right.*)

M. JEAN CHAMANT (*Independent*): And our soldiers? They're the first victims, M. Pierre Cot. Maybe it's time to talk about them now! (*Interruptions from the extreme left.*)

M. PIERRE COT: You seem to forget that the subject of the debate is the bombing of the village of Sakiet-Sidi-Youssef by French aircraft. (*Interruptions from the right and the extreme right.*)

I wanted to raise my voice to declare that not only in this Assembly but in the whole country there are men who are trying their best to re-establish the confidence of the Arab world which is, as you know, the basis of our policy in Africa and which is doubtless—and the Minister of Foreign Affairs can be my witness—one of the best aspects of our foreign policy.

I wanted to say that we will work so that France shall again become in their eyes what she was before and what I am confident will be again tomorrow, the champion of the independence of all peoples, of their rights and their liberties, for this is—and, ladies and gentlemen, I beg the pardon of the President of the Council if he doesn't agree with me—the raison d'être and the mission of our country. (*Applause on the extreme left and some of the benches of the left.*) . . .

M. JEAN DE LIPKOWSKI (*UDSR*): We can't just resign ourselves to watching a trend, fatal not only for us but for all of the West, toward fanatic, antiwestern nationalism.

France ought to remain the center of attraction, and not Cairo or Damascus. This is still possible. Between the French Maghreb* and us, co-operation is still possible. Let us not compromise this future, which is *our* future, by moves that are based not on firmness but on disorganized action (*Applause on several benches of the left*), moves

*[Arab name for the region of Algeria, Tunisia, and Morocco—Eds.]

which in psychoanalytic terms could be called overcompensation for weakness.

Briefly, either we choose a policy of reconquest—a consistent policy: but then no one had better talk any more about the liberal mission of France, or her Moslem mission, nor even of her mission in the world, for I am convinced that we will end by creating against us a continuous front of opposition stretching from Agadir to Jakarta, until finally we are confined within the hexagon of France—or, on the other hand, we choose to make a demonstration of solidarity with overseas peoples. And in this case we recover our élan, we reverse the thesis of Lenin that the way to Paris passes through Peking and Calcutta. We have to realize that for us the route of our influence in the Middle East and Southeast Asia passes first through the French African community.

If we have faith in our world mission, if we know how to revise the contours of French greatness to fit the century, then, whether you like it or not, Franco-Maghreb and Franco-Tunisian solidarity is, as General de Gaulle has said, more desirable than ever. (*Applause on some benches of the left and the center.*)

THE PRESIDENT*: M. Deixonne, the last speaker, has the floor. (*Applause on the left.*)

M. MAURICE DEIXONNE (*Socialist*): Ladies and gentlemen, as the representative of the Socialist group I would like to express to this Assembly a sentiment of sadness and bewilderment at the unfortunate incident at Sakiet-Sidi-Youssef. . . .

Oh, certainly we are not equally affected by all of the condemnations which we receive. The accusations which come from Hungary or the Soviet Union cannot be considered free of hypocrisy! Even our British friends ought to know that we would be more receptive to their advice if they had taken ours during the unfortunate affairs of Cyprus and the Mau-Mau.

Likewise we don't want to join the chorus of certain segments of the press which seem to welcome the events of Sakiet as the fulfillment of their predictions.

For there are some Frenchmen who are never happier than when their country is in the wrong. (*Applause on the left.*) . . .

I would consider it a crime to say anything that could be taken either directly or indirectly as a reproach to the army, which I admire unconditionally for the varied tasks to which it has consecrated its

*[The President of the National Assembly was André Le Troquer, SFIO deputy—Eds.]

young forces on African soil. (*Applause on the left and on several benches of the center and the right.*) . . .

As regards the affair of Sakiet, I ask that it be placed in the proper context: first that of the arms traffic across the Tunisian frontier, so incessant that in three days our troops have captured eight machine guns; then, of the long list of attacks, which the government ought to have brought before this Assembly, and which have been directed against our airplanes almost daily from Tunisia since last September; then, of the ambush of January 11, which was the occasion of a particularly cruel massacre of several of our soldiers; then, of the equally important fact that with the floods now raging the mud is so deep our ground forces cannot move at present.

Not to place the affair of Sakiet in its terrible context would be to ignore the most elementary rules of justice and objectivity. The Assembly itself wouldn't be doing its duty if it didn't do everything it could to give a little more security to the young people we have sent there to defend French positions. (*Applause on the left, the right, the extreme right, and several benches of the center.*)

M. ROGER ROUCAUTE: Le Pen is applauding.

M. JEAN-MARIE LE PEN: Le Pen is a Frenchman. . . .

M. MAURICE DEIXONNE: The essential problem for us is to take measures to avoid the recurrence of similar incidents, for we have an imperative duty to protect our troops against hazardous initiatives and not to let them get involved in anything without very precise instructions.

Without any doubt, here, it is a question concerning the reform of governmental structures as well as of the apparatus of command.

We want to declare in an unqualified manner our support, Mr. President, not only for the primacy of civil power over military, but for the primacy of the government pure and simple (*Applause on the left*); for it is impossible to concede that in a situation so serious and so fateful, one minister,* even in the national defence, can by himself commit the government at the risk of destroying the efforts of his colleague in foreign affairs. (*Applause on the left. Shouts on the extreme left and on various benches.*) . . .

M. PIERRE MONTEL (*Independent*): To do justice to the army and to France, I would like to put what we are calling today the affair of Sakiet-Sidi-Youssef back in its context.

Will you please try for a few minutes to put yourselves—and it is

---

*[Jacques Chaban-Delmas, Minister of National Defense—Eds.]

easy for some of you because of the letters you are receiving from your own children—in the place of our young soldiers and our officers who are carrying on in Algeria a harsh and sometimes murderous struggle, and who often find themselves facing rebels who, after attacking a French post, cross the frontier to take refuge in Tunisian territory.

Do you really think anyone could expect these men constantly to stay calm and to reject any impulse toward their legitimate right of self-defense against those who attack them and then run for cover? It is in this context that we have to see the affair of Sakiet-Sidi-Youssef.

I have not heard a single speaker condemn the Tunisian government. We are told that France has violated international law and thereby is putting herself in a bad position in international public opinion. But I have not heard the slightest condemnation of the Tunisian government. . . .

It is in this context that we have to see French opinion and international opinion. In other words, the question is the following: will we tolerate the continued interference of Tunisia in the affairs of Algeria, interference going so far as belligerence?

The questions we are asking the government are very simple. If perhaps the affair of Sakiet is to be regarded as an error, as an ill-considered move on the part of the military authorities or even of the government or one of its ministers, and if it definitely does not represent the things *we* are demanding, then it was an error to have engaged in this operation.

We ask the government to tell us in the first place whether or not it takes responsibility . . .

M. PIERRE COT: Very good!

M. PIERRE MONTEL: . . . for it ought to. The army ought to obey, and it does obey; and in what a way and with what courage! The government ought to say that it is responsible, that it was really the government which ordered this action in the interests of the entire operation in Algeria.

In the second place, the government ought to tell us whether or not this affair of Sakiet means a political decision on its part to take a firm stand regarding the Tunisian government. I didn't say violence; I didn't say force; I am not talking about a policy of reconquest; I am talking about a firm stand.

The first firm stand—I refer to several among you and I regret that I have to say it—should be that our adversaries, in North Africa or elsewhere, no longer find their best defenders and their best support on the benches of our Assembly. . . .

In any case, the first duty of the government—and I congratulate the government for doing its duty, if it agrees with the analysis I have just presented—is to keep our army from being stabbed in the back as it was in Indochina, in Tunisia, and in Morocco. (*Applause on the right and several benches of the extreme right.*) . . .

M. JEAN-MARIE LE PEN: Ladies and gentlemen, only a week ago the National Assembly was asking itself what were the real causes of the disaffection in the army. I think that from this rostrum I can answer a number of people who, in questions of internal affairs, are always talking about impartiality. The disaffection of the army and of the nation stems from the fact that although Parliament is responsible for their mutual interest, a number of important news media, in any national or international event concerning France, place the first assumption of guilt on their own country. This is, I believe, the root of the problem. Thus, even before all the facts of the affair of Sakiet-Sidi-Youssef were known, even before anyone had studied the reactions of foreign governments or of the French army staff, a great part of the press opened fire and immediately used all the evidence against France.

Interrupting M. Pierre Cot, who alluded to the five French journalists who offered themselves as witnesses of the events at Sakiet-Sidi-Youssef, I said that both natural law and civil and criminal law excuse children from bearing witness against their parents.

What should we think of these men, who, by chance may have witnessed—which I deny—an act where France might have been guilty? Their duty as respectful sons, whatever errors their mother may have committed, was to keep quiet, sadly perhaps, but to keep quiet.

A man doesn't bear witness against his mother, a man doesn't bear witness against his country. (*Applause on the right and the extreme right.*)

M. MARC DUPUY (*Communist*): That's the ethic of the Hitler Youth!

M. JEAN-MARIE LE PEN: It is supposed to be difficult to be perfectly impartial. If this is true, if I am partial, permit me, ladies and gentlemen, to claim the honor of being partial toward my country. (*Applause on the right and the extreme right.*)

Many Frenchmen have been soldiers, and many of you, as non-commissioned officers and officers, have commanded your fellow countrymen. Those who have fought know that one can command men only if they are inspired with a respect which arises first of all from the sentiment that their lives are in good hands. There too, a commander or a captain is partial; first of all he is for his men.

I regret the civilian victims of the conflict as much as anyone else does, and I remember—at that time I was in a city of which 98 per cent was destroyed by Allied bombings—that not so long ago, during the last world war, the Allied bombings also claimed a considerable number of victims.

I am not making an accusation against our allies. At the most it is an accusation against war; but these memories ought to remind several of those countries' press or parliament representatives that, before passing judgment, they ought to take a good look at themselves. (Very good! very good! *from the right.*)

Have you asked yourselves, ladies and gentlemen, what the army may think?

What do you expect it to think when it knows beyond doubt or debate that in the Algerian war Tunisia is playing a role that M. Bourguiba himself is the first to admit is one of giving moral, material, and financial aid; when it knows that many consider with justice, as is corroborated by the testimony of the Arab radio stations and Radio Tunis, that Tunisia is playing the role of a cobelligerent? . . .

What do you expect it to think when simply by reading the papers it sees that people automatically put its country and the army in the wrong?

You ask, ladies and gentlemen, where the disaffection of the army comes from? Well, it comes simply from that! (*Applause on the right, the extreme right, the center, and some benches on the left.*)

It has long been said that the "drama" of the war in Indochina—the word is used often in this assembly—lay in the fact that the army did not have the support of the nation. But the great body of the population and of Parliament which subscribes to the thesis of *Algérie française* ought to make for total correspondence between the army and the nation; for, as everyone knows, almost 90 per cent of all Frenchmen support this idea as well as three-quarters of the French Parliament.

What do you expect the army to think of those who are driving a wedge between the army and the nation, who perhaps command the news media and powerful financial forces, but who certainly don't represent real popular forces?

You well know, M. Mendès-France, what your real power in the country is. You are well aware that you personally are the target for many of a patriotic, almost physical repulsion! (*Applause on the right and the extreme right. Interruptions from some benches of the left.*)

   Several benches of the extreme left: Racist! Racist!

   M. JEAN-MARIE LE PEN: It's not a question of racism!

   M. ANDRE PIERRARD (*Communist*): That's what's in your head, all right!

   M. JEAN-MARIE LE PEN: And here is the reason why, M. Mendès-France: it is because in the eyes of a country for whom pride is as necessary as bread and water, you are the symbol of a flood of setbacks and a series of failures worse than any France has known in the worst moments of her history. That's what you symbolize!

   Whether you like it or not, even if the responsibility was not undivided in the affair—and I grant you that—it was you who consented to be the man of defeat in Indochina. (*Shouts on several benches of the left and the center.*) . . .

   M. PIERRE MENDÈS-FRANCE (*Radical*): M. Le Pen, may I interrupt?

   M. JEAN-MARIE LE PEN: Gladly.

   THE PRESIDENT: M. Mendès-France has the floor with the permission of the speaker.

   M. PIERRE MENDÈS-FRANCE: Mr. President, if I have asked permission to question the speaker—and I thank him for it—it is not for any personal reason, for my colleagues know that I am not in the habit of answering attacks, which I disdain if they are only directed against my person. But I belong to a generation which has lived through a certain period in the history of France and which has had to make important decisions in an hour that was one of our most cruel and frightful; I am thinking above all of 1940.

   I am not throwing stones or accusing anyone at this point for the events and the attitudes of 1940. But I have the right to say that a certain number of men then showed that they were at one with the fate of our mortally threatened nation. The men who acted thus have the right to give their opinion when again so many terrible problems are set before the nation. . . .

   After the Liberation we wanted to learn a great lesson from all that had happened. It was then that General de Gaulle raised his voice at Brazzaville. It was then that we promised to the countries of Indochina the generous emancipation which they sought; it was then that ten successive governments promised them internal autonomy. It was then that the preamble of the Constitution was written, which, as you know, we all drew up.

   Let us be honest: none of these promises was kept. And the enthusiasm with which all these countries greeted these declarations of liberated France that was showing her gratitude to those who had helped to free her soil, was replaced, little by little, by disillusionment, impatience, and soon by anger, resentment, and finally rebellion.

This is the explanation of all our troubles, both here and over there.

First it was Indochina.

I had the opportunity in this Assembly, at a time when French public opinion was not yet prepared, to demand a revision of our policy in Indochina. Why? To tighten the bonds which everyone at the time knew could hold Indochina in the French Union, to link the destiny of our peoples in liberty and the promotion of men of merit, that is, to take steps toward greater autonomy.

If the pleas of some of the men in this Assembly—some of them sitting on the right—had been heeded, we would not have known eight years of war and the final catastophe of Dien-Bien-Phu.

And finally after the disaster, when there was a kind of reawakening, however late, how unhappy were those who now regretted that they had not spoken out and made themselves heard earlier, when there had still been time, now that they were asked to draw the cruel consequences of an impossible military situation. (*Lively shouts from the center, the right, and the extreme right. Applause on several benches of the left.*) . . .

The conditions of the armistice were cruel. I said this in the Assembly at that time. I never considered them a success. I have always considered them a great misfortune for France: as a misfortune that at that time we couldn't avoid.

And among the men who criticize me so often from these benches (*indicating the center and the right*), I remember there were many who spoke to me in this Assembly in the following words: "You are liquidating the errors of those who preceded you."

It was not I who used these words; it was one of our colleagues whose name, if I mentioned it, would perhaps surprise you.

The Assembly was so well informed that a majority of about 470 votes—I don't remember the figure any more and I apologize because I did not intend to speak today—adopted a resolution requesting me— listen to this—to continue—that was the word—the policy which I had proposed to the Assembly. I repeat, the resolution was adopted by 450 or 470 votes.

M. JACQUES ISORNI (*Independent*): Against fourteen!

M. JEAN LEGENDRE (*Independent*): Against fourteen exactly.

M. PIERRE MENDÈS-FRANCE: Perhaps. And in another ballot there may have been a difference of twenty-five or thirty votes, for other considerations may have been present and it was then a question of confidence.

But in any case I have the right to say that the Assembly agreed almost unanimously and in good conscience that we pull out of a situation under conditions which had become unavoidable and which no one had the right to criticize. . . .

M. ROBERT BRUYNEEL (*Independent*): Like Munich!

M. PIERRE MENDÈS-FRANCE: The conditions of the armistice were judged by French and foreign experts and again by our military leaders as the least bad that could be obtained at the time. . . .

M. JEAN LEGENDRE:The revolt in Algeria broke out under your regime, M. Mendès-France.

On November 1, 1954, you were in power. What did you do against the revolt?

M. PIERRE MENDÈS-FRANCE: You have asked a question, M. Legendre. Rest assured that it will receive an answer.

But what I am saying, what I attest to here, is that if in 1955 we had followed the policy that the Assembly had approved in 1954 on several votes, we would have moved progressively toward a sort of healthy federation—which even today I do not despair of—but by a more direct and peaceful and less unhappy path. We would have moved toward a sort of federation in which all the members of the French family of nations would have found places, and which they would have perceived as the advance and the emancipation that had long been refused them.

And here, I will answer the question which I was asked a moment ago.

The rebellion broke out on November 1, 1954. It was a small rebellion and at first it was localized. . . . (*Shouts on the right and the center.*)

I say that a small rebellion, local at first, broke out in the Aurès mountains.

What was the reaction of the government at the moment?

The reaction was extremely clear and here again I can say that it was approved by the great majority of this Assembly. It was twofold. First the government showed, as it had in other territories, that it did not intend to let things get out of control or to yield concessions contrary to the doctrine and the principles of French policy, that it did not intend to leave in danger men whose safety was menaced.

At that time we sent to Algeria . . .

M.PIERRE MONTEL: Three batallions!

M. PIERRE MENDÈS-FRANCE: . . . more men than the military authorities asked for.

We exceeded the requests. Why? Because the military authorities were reckoning by military needs, but for my part I always considered that to send troops to certain territories, Algeria, for example, was a move even more political than military. And this is the reason that I participated in the decisions taken at the beginning of 1956 when the delayed reinforcements were sent to Algeria. I believed that the presence of troops would show the determination of the government to control all events, would show its resolution not to let the situation get out of control; but at the same time this presence was to give the government the means to pursue a constructive policy; for to rely solely on force and violence—as I said a hundred times—would have been to resign oneself to failure.

Never in history has a military operation of this sort succeeded . . .

M. JEAN-LOUIS TIXIER-VIGNANCOUR (*Unaffiliated*): In Hungary!

M. PIERRE MENDÈS-FRANCE: . . . when it was not based on the support and the will of part of the population.

It was to arouse this support in the Moslem population that, at the very moment when we sent to Algeria reinforcements larger than those that had been requested, we announced a number of reforms, notably the application of the statute of 1947 which had been passed by a sovereign parliament, yet seven years later had not been put into effect.

If at that moment, this policy could have been carried out, I am sure for my part that we would have reached very quickly what today is called "pacification," but in the true sense of this word, that is, a reconciliation and an understanding with men who could collaborate loyally on the road to progress and liberty, and a bestowing upon the native populations that justice and equality they had so long been denied.

M. GUY PETIT (*Independent*): Let us not exaggerate.

M. PIERRE MENDÈS-FRANCE: Yes. I repeat that in 1955 this was possible and if it had been done the rebellion would not have grown to the magnitude it later reached.

However, we lost a lot of time. Later, in the middle of 1955, M. Soustelle proposed a program of reforms which, doubtless, is no longer adapted to today's needs; but which, at that time, if it had been carried out, would have had the same effect of reconciliation on the psychological level. Each time we let the opportunity slip by; each time we missed our chance. And each time—M. Naudet protested with a great deal of justification just now against these campaigns—the men who proposed this policy in the interests of the lasting permanence and the solidarity of the French Union were painted as enemies of their country or as tools of foreign interests.

I say that those who led these campaigns of hate and division did a disservice to their country.

You talk about the morale of the army? After all, it's those people who tell the army day after day: "While you are doing your duty, while every one of you is risking his life for his country, there are men back there in Paris in political circles, in the Assembly, who are trying to destroy. . . . (*Interrupted by the extreme right and the right.*)

Several cries on the right: It's in *L'Express!* Read *L'Express!*

M. JEAN-LOUIS TIXIER-VIGNANCOUR: Some people are embracing Masmoudi, who has the blood of our soldiers on his hands. It's the kiss of Judas! That's the truth! (*Protests on the left and the extreme left.*)

Several cries on the extreme left: Back to Vichy! Militiaman!*

M. FERNAND GRENIER (*Communist*): We wonder whom M. Tixier-Vignancour embraced when he was Minister of Information for Vichy!

M. PIERRE MENDÈS-FRANCE: I haven't forgotten the question asked by M. Le Pen concerning my former policy, and I will come to it now. I apologize for the length of my answer, but my colleague will certainly agree that this subject is worth the trouble. (*Applause on the left.*)

M. JEAN-MARIE LE PEN: I must say I agree.

M. PIERRE MENDÈS-FRANCE: I repeat—because every day people talk about the morale of the army and the state of mind of our boys over there—that people are playing a despicable game with the morale of the army when they instill in it a poison which leads it to think that while young Frenchmen are risking their lives, somewhere there are politicians who, for God knows what reason, are working against the interests of their country and who by their actions are somehow prolonging a murderous war which otherwise would have been terminated more rapidly.

I say that these hate campaigns are really campaigns of defeatism. (*Shouts on the right and the extreme right. Applause on the left and extreme left.*)

*[The reference is to the hated *Milice*, a terroristic security organization affiliated with the Vichy regime—Eds.]

M. JEAN LEGENDRE (*pointing to the extreme left*): M. Mendès-France, look who it is that applauds you!

There they are: your patriots! (*Lively protests on the extreme left.*)

M. PIERRE MENDÈS-FRANCE: I say that these campaigns are contrary to the national interest, that they divide the nation, that they are turning patriotic Frenchmen against one another. And I maintain that it is despicable to have fostered this division and this opposition instead of loyally searching together, even if there is disagreement, for the best way to put an end to this drama in which our country is caught.

I am one of those who has been implicated in these attacks. Therefore I thought it my duty to continue to say what I think, in the interest of our country. . . .

M. JEAN-MARIE LE PEN: M. Mendès-France, I have listened to you with a great deal of attention, for I think that just as a ray of light pierces into a dark room, we have put our finger right on the evil. On the subject of the bombings of Sakiet and the terrible division of the French national spirit, you have been a talented spokesman of *"Mendésisme"*; you have also been a terrible spokesman for the regime.

You have just outlined, M. Mendès-France, the story of ten years of the Fourth Republic.

Maybe there's a conflict of generations between us. I was one of those who was sixteen years old in 1944 and who thought that the men who had brought victory were bringing the national revolution . . . (*Shouts on the extreme left.*)

On the extreme left: Pétain's revolution?

M. JEAN-MARIE LE PEN: . . . which would make our country great; and the papers read: "from resistance to revolution." (*Interruptions from the extreme left.*)

I was of that generation which believed that with the Liberation would come the construction of a better world.

If this hope which moved us is over with, if it is dead now, it's because you have spoiled this revolution. (*Interruptions from the extreme left.*)

This wonderful hope which was born in our youth was ignominiously betrayed, and in place of the vision of grandeur which we expected, we have seen arise mediocrity, defeat, party struggles, the division of the nation, and perhaps even its end.

I believe, M. Mendès-France, that today you have hit the nail on the head. You have said how, after our disastrous policy in Indochina, we had to pay the price of six years of war carried on in such a sorry manner. As you said, you had to be the one who liquidated the situation, and I recognize that you weren't the only one responsible for this state of affairs.

But then you seem to have gotten carried away by your taste for sacrifices, and you seem to have thrived in the climate of hate which surrounded your position. That is why you were led to espouse the solutions you did. And if a policy can be judged by its results, then you ought to admit now that you were wrong.

On the other hand, if you believe that it was not you who was responsible, then tell us the underlying reasons for these setbacks. Tell the country—it is waiting —who is really responsible. (*Applause on the extreme right and on some benches of the right.*)

If there are men who are responsible, let them be brought before a high court of justice! If it is the institutions, then let them be abolished! I believe this is the real problem for our country. . . .

THE PRESIDENT: I have two resolutions on the agenda.

Resolution number one, submitted with a demand for priority by M. Brocas, reads: "The National Assembly, having heard the statements of the government, declares its confidence, and without any additions, passes on to the day's agenda."

Resolution number two, submitted with a demand for priority by Messieurs Jacques Duclos, Waldeck-Rochet, and Pronteau, in the name of the Communist group, reads: "The National Assembly, in view of the fact that it has been unable to obtain from the government, if not the actual acceptance of responsibility for the massive bombing of the Tunisian village of Sakiet, in any case not even a renunciation of this crime, inseparable from a policy contrary to the interests of France,

Condemns this policy, which, if followed, might lead to a general war in Africa; and declares itself in favor of a negotiated peace in Algeria, which is the only thing that can win France back her friends and her place in the world,

And without any additions, passes on to the agenda of the day."

From several benches: Adjournment!

THE PRESIDENT: I have heard a request for adjournment.

Is there any opposition?

The session is adjourned.

(*The session, adjourned at 10:30 p.m., is reconvened at 11:55 p.m.*)

THE PRESIDENT: The session is convened.

During the adjournment I received a third resolution from M. Berthommier, with a request for priority, which reads:

"The National Assembly, in view of the declarations of the President of the Council, renews its confidence in the French forces in Algeria and, without any additions, passes on to the agenda of the day."

I will consult the Assembly concerning the priority requested for resolution number one. . . .

I ask the Assembly to decide on the priority.

M. PIERRE MONTEL: I request the session be adjourned.

THE PRESIDENT OF THE COUNCIL: I demand the floor.

THE PRESIDENT: The President of the Council has the floor.

THE PRESIDENT OF THE COUNCIL: I would like to say that the government accepts resolution number one of M. Brocas.

THE PRESIDENT: It has been moved that the session be adjourned. Is there any opposition?

The session is adjourned.

(*The session, adjourned at 12:05, February 12, is reconvened at 12:50.*)

The session is in order.

I would like to inform the Assembly that resolution number one has been amended by its author. I will read this resolution in its new form:

"The National Assembly, having heard the statements of the President of the Council, and deploring the civilian losses,

Declares its confidence in the government,

And, without any additions, passes on to the day's agenda. . . ."

We will now vote on resolution number one moved by M. Brocas as amended.

A vote has been moved. (*The votes are collected.*)

No one else wants to vote? . . . The ballot is closed. (*The secretaries count the votes.*)

Here is the result of the ballot:

Number voting	518
Absolute majority	260
For	335
Against	179

The resolution is passed.

Analysis of the vote

335 deputies voted for:

95 Socialists (of 96) and 3 MSA (of 4); 21 Radicals (of 43); 13 UDSR-RDA (of 21); 10 RGR (of 14); 13 Democratic Left (of 14);

1 African Convention (of 7); 67 MRP (of 75); 19 Social Republicans (of 20); 80 Independents (of 91) and the 8 Peasants for Social Action; 3 Peasants (of 11); 2 unaffiliated.

179 deputies voted against:

The 142 Communists; the 6 Progressives; 19 Radicals, including M. Mendès-France; 4 UDSR-RDA, including M. Mitterand; 2 African Convention; 1 MRP; 3 Independents; 2 unaffiliated.

49 deputies abstained voluntarily:

2 Radicals; 3 RGR; 1 Democratic Left; 6 MRP; 6 Independents, including M. Montel; the 31 UFF [Poujadists].

24 deputies did not vote; 5 deputies had permission to be absent.

(Adapted from *Le Monde*, February 13, 1958, p. 6)

Letter dated 13 February 1958 from the Representative of Tunisia to the United Nations to the President of the Security Council

United Nations Document S/3952

Upon instructions from my Government, I have the honour to request you to convene the Security Council for the purpose of considering the following question:

> "Complaint by Tunisia in respect of an act of aggression committed against it by France on 8 February 1958 at Sakiet-Sidi-Youssef."

An explanatory memorandum on this question is attached.

Under Article 31 of the Charter, I have the honour to request you to permit me to participate in the discussion of this question and, accordingly, to inform me of the date on which the Security Council will meet for that purpose.

[signed]   Mongi Slim
Ambassador, Permanent Representative of
Tunisia to the United Nations

EXPLANATORY MEMORANDUM

On 8 February 1958, at 10 a.m., the small Tunisian village of Sakiet-Sidi-Youssef, near the Algerian border, was subjected to a sudden act of aggression.

United Nations, Security Council, *Official Records*, Thirteenth Year, Supplement for January, February and March 1958, 13–16.

Twenty-five bomber and fighter aircraft, in successive waves, subjected the village and area immediately surrounding it to a massive bombardment with bombs and rockets and continuous strafing by machine-guns.

Many persons had gathered in the village, for it was a market day and, in addition, the International Red Cross, assisted by the Tunisian Red Crescent, was scheduled to distribute relief supplies to the children of Algerian refugees in the area. The attack lasted for one hour and twenty minutes. Seventy-nine persons were killed, including eleven women and twenty children, and 130 were wounded, among them a large number of women and children.

Most of the village was destroyed, including homes, civilian buildings and the school.

Three Red Cross or Red Crescent trucks, clearly marked with their distinctive insignia, were destroyed or damaged.

This attack, which constitutes an act of armed aggression by France against Tunisia, is one of a series of deliberate violations of the integrity of Tunisian soil committed since May 1957 by French troops coming from Algeria which have on each occasion resulted in material damage, loss of life and, at times, the abduction of Tunisians.

On each violation of its territory, the Government of the Republic of Tunisia made strong protests to the French Government.

Each time these acts of aggression have been deemed to be serious, either because of their frequency over a specific period or because of the size of the losses sustained by Tunisia, the Government of the Republic of Tunisia has not failed to inform the Secretary-General of the United Nations and to draw his attention to the danger they constituted and the fact that they were a violation of the Principles of the Charter and the obligations devolving therefrom upon Member States, particularly under Article 2, paragraph 4 (letters MTP 278 of 31 May 1957, MTP 280 of 3 June 1957, MTP 281 of 4 June 1957, MTP 429 of 11 September 1957, MTP 430 of 12 September 1957, MTP 437 of 16 September 1957 and MTP 470 of 8 October 1957).

The permanent representative of Tunisia wishes to point out in particular that, when the constant threat to Tunisian sovereignty resulting from such violations of Tunisia's territory was deemed to be sufficiently serious, he informed the Secretary-General of the United Nations, by letter dated 11 September 1957 (MTP 429), that, in accordance with Article 51 of the Charter, the Tunisian Government proposed to exercise its right of self-defence.

Accordingly, the act of aggression committed on 8 February is of a particularly serious nature, not only because of the number of lives lost and the extent of the damage caused, but also because of the earlier acts of a similar kind committed since May 1957.

The permanent representative of Tunisia draws particular attention to the fact that the intentions expressed by the French Government do not appear to hold out any prospect that these deliberate attacks on Tunisia's sovereignty and flagrant violations of Article 2, paragraph 4, of the United Nations Charter, will cease.

Every effort made by the Government of the Republic of Tunisia, through friendly discussion, to end these numerous and deliberate violations, has proved fruitless.

Accordingly, upon instructions from my Government, I have the honour to seize the Security Council of the situation created by the deliberate act of aggression committed on 8 February 1958 and to request it to take whatever decision it may deem appropriate to put an end to a situation which threatens Tunisia's security and endangers international peace and security in that part of the world.

[signed]   Mongi Slim

Ambassador, Permanent Representative of

Tunisia to the United Nations

Letter dated 14 February 1958 from the Representative of France to the United Nations to the President of the Security Council

United Nations Document S/3954

Upon instructions from my Government, I have the honour to request that the Security Council should, at its next meeting, consider the following complaint brought by France against Tunisia:

> 'Situation resulting from the aid furnished by Tunisia to rebels enabling them to conduct operations from Tunisian territory directed against the integrity of French territory and the safety of the persons and property of French nationals.'

[signed]   G. Georges-Picot

Ambassador, Permanent Representative of

France to the United Nations

EXPLANATORY MEMORANDUM

In bringing a complaint before the Security Council, it is the purpose of the French Government to make it clear that the Tunisian Government has not shown itself capable of maintaining order on the Franco-Tunisian frontier, or disposed to do so. Tunisia thus stands in violation of the obligations assumed by it under Article 4 of the Charter upon its admission to the United Nations and is taking a position contrary to the good-neighbourly spirit which Member States must observe if they wish to live at peace with the other States of the international community.

It is in these circumstances that the Algerian rebels, aided and abetted by the Tunisian authorities, have been able in recent months to establish in Tunisia a complete organization enabling them to carry out numerous border violations and incursions into French territory where they commit particularly heinous crimes.

The 'Front de libération nationale' (FLN) has set up a veritable military infrastructure based in Tunis which, from the military point of view, has now become the main centre of rebel activity in view of the fact that, since last July, a general staff, responsible for the conduct of operations carried out in eastern Algeria, has been set up in the city with the Tunisian Government's permission.

Among the facilities available to the FLN in Tunisia are rest camps, bases, and quartering and training centers where the rebel bands receive training and weapons and are quartered for the purpose of military operations.

In addition to the asylum given by the Tunisian Government, Tunisian armed forces and the national guard provide the FLN with direct logistical support (organization of transport, the supplying of arms and equipment, and medical facilities). Tunisia is in fact the chief base for moving supplies to the FLN in the form of military weapons delivered in Tunisia to the FLN which then sends them into Algeria. The Tunisian authorities take part in this traffic and in the movement and delivery of weapons. The latter are generally stored in the premises of the Tunisian national guard which is also responsible for their transport.

The Tunisian authorities tolerate, and sometimes even facilitate, the movement of armed bands on Tunisian territory and incursions effected from Tunisian soil against French territory. Finally, Tunisian radio broadcasts constantly furnish moral support to the rebellion.

In these circumstances, it is not surprising that, in recent months, incidents in the vicinity of the border, resulting in the death of many members of the French armed forces and French civilians often in atrocious circumstances, have steadily increased in number and intensity. On many occasions, French patrols have encountered rebel groups operating from Tunisian territory, to which they returned when pursued; similarly, French aircraft have on several occasions, been fired on by automatic weapons in Tunisian territory.

A particularly serious incident occurred on 11 January last in the vicinity of Sakiet-Sidi-Youssef. In the course of an engagement with a rebel band which came from Tunisia, sixteen French soldiers were killed and four were taken prisoner. In addition, aircraft flying over French territory have on several occasions sustained damage caused by automatic weapons, including weapons fired from the building in this village occupied by the Tunisian national guard.

The French Government had warned the Tunisian Government of the heavy responsibility it was assuming by lending its assistance to the rebels. It had suggested measures to prevent the recurrence of such incidents. These warnings have unfortunately been without effect and no positive response has been made to our suggestions.

The reaction of the French Air Force at the time of the incident to which the Tunisian complaint refers was thus the outcome of the many acts of provocation to which our forces have been subjected. While the French Government deplores the losses suffered by the civilian population, and has the question of compensation for those losses under consideration, it cannot isolate this incident from the incidents which were its cause.

For these reasons, the French Government considers that Tunisia has seriously failed in its obligations as a Member State of the United Nations and has directly and indirectly caused very grave injury to the legitimate interests of France. The French Government accordingly asks that the assistance furnished by Tunisia to the Algerian rebels should be condemned by the Council.

[signed]   G. Georges-Picot
Ambassador, Permanent Representative of
France to the United Nations

Department of State Press Release No. 71 Dated 17 February 1958

After receiving indications from both the Tunisian and French Governments that good offices would be acceptable, the United States Government has decided to extend its good offices, in conjunction with the United Kingdom, in order to assist the Governments of France and Tunisia to settle outstanding problems between them.

Statement Made by the Deputy U.S. Representative (Wadsworth) Before the U.N. Security Council. February 18, 1958

The Government of the United States wishes to confirm its decision, as announced yesterday, to extend its good offices in conjunction with the Government of the United Kingdom in order to assist the Governments of France and Tunisia to settle outstanding problems between them.

I wish also to state, Mr. President, that my delegation wishes to express gratification that this offer has been accepted by both parties. In the first instance, the responsibility for a peaceful solution to the differences which are outstanding between France and Tunisia lies with those two countries under Article 33 of the United Nations Charter. The fact that the Governments of these two countries have elected to accept the good offices of two mutual friends is taken by my Government as an indication of their sincere desire to reach such a solution.

To a large extent, Mr. President, the precise manner in which these good offices are to be implemented will have to be worked out by the four powers involved, and, as one of the two powers which are extending their good offices, the United States hopes to be able to offer affirmative suggestions to advance the objective of a peaceful and equitable solution of these problems.

It is, we believe, a good augury for the future that the parties to the proceedings now before this Council are endeavoring, as suggested by Article 33, to settle peacefully the differences noted in their cross-submissions to the Council and the other outstanding problems between them by means of their own choice.

U.S. Department of State, American Foreign Policy, Current Documents 1958 (Washington, D.C., 1962), 1089–90.

Reply Made by the Secretary of State (Dulles) to a Question Asked at a News Conference, March 25, 1958

Mr. Murphy and Mr. Beeley of the United Kingdom, after having spent some days in Tunis in talking with the Tunisian Government and with President Bourguiba, have returned to Paris with a formulation

U.S. Department of State, *American Foreign Policy, Current Documents* 1958 (Washington D.C., 1962), 1091.

which has been agreed to by President Bourguiba and which we think takes considerable account of the preoccupations of both sides on this situation. It has been presented to the French Cabinet and is being discussed and considered. We do not know yet what the final official reaction of the French Government will be. Perhaps that will be forthcoming within a matter of hours or days. We hope that it will lead to a solution there of the immediate problem, although of course the major problems will take some time to resolve.

I want to take this occasion to say that I think Deputy Under Secretary Murphy and his British colleague have done a very fine job to date. I don't know whether their mission will be crowned with success or not. But whether or not it is crowned with success, they have already dealt with many problems that looked as though they were totally insoluble and have brought them into a compass which at least offers some reasonable hope. They have done a superb diplomatic job.

FOUR LEADERS OF THE RIGHT ADVOCATE A GOVERNMENT OF PUBLIC SAFETY

The theme of a "government of public safety" is to reappear in the round of Sunday speeches. MM. Jacques Soustelle and Roger Duchet have developed it. MM. Georges Bidault and André Morice have paraphrased it. These four leaders, who do not spare themselves in making speeches, have spearheaded the fight for French Algeria. Moreover, a number of members of Parliament of the right and the right center see in them the four pillars of a future government.

Yet if there is any policy that has been carried out with continuity for the last two years in Algeria, it is indeed the one which these individuals have not ceased to advocate. Their opponents are truly justified in ascribing entirely to them the results to which this policy has led, that is to say, a tragic impasse. But all four seek to escape the contradiction by charging the successive governments—and above all the present one—with not having applied this policy with enough strength.

A "government of public safety" of the kind desired by the right and sometimes by the center would not easily find a majority in the Assembly, even if it was presided over by a member of the MRP. The Socialists indeed could not support it, not even by abstaining. Has not their general secretary [Guy Mollet] just renewed his attacks against the right, its "resignation from responsibility," and its "blindness before the problems to be solved"?

M. Soustelle and doubtless also M. Bidault do not discount an appeal to General de Gaulle. But is the same true of M. André Morice and above all of M. Roger Duchet? The Independents include the greatest number of "anti-Gaullists" among the deputies, and according to a member, more than one anti-Gaullist would be found among the "80" [Independents] if one day the Assembly was summoned to entrust a "temporary magistracy" to Charles de Gaulle.

Finally, the sudden return to a "policy of force" in Parliament, militarily or even diplomatically, occurs at a moment when the country is indicating by various signs that it is beginning to worry, in any case to examine itself. . . . In the Nièvre as at Marseilles, the majority of voters have chosen neither the men nor the parties who have established a sort of monopoly over defense of the official Algerian policy.

The protagonists of a new regime and of a government of public safety, it can be seen, will run up against objections: the policy which they advocate has been put to the test for a long time; the "Gaullist" solution is not desired by all their partisans; public opinion is less devoted to them than it might have been in the past.

The contradictions and the weaknesses of the opposition, which in a certain manner counterbalance those of the men in power, are of use to the regime and the government in office. The latter is nevertheless injured by the reserve being manifested on the left and by the attacks which are multiplying on the right. The hypothesis that a crisis exists is not to be discounted. It is not possible today to foresee its outcome.

Jacques Fauvet
(*Le Monde*, March 4, 1958, p. 1)

DIFFICULT SEARCH FOR A COMPROMISE ON
TUNISIA IN THE COUNCIL OF MINISTERS

THE MODERATES AND THE PRIME MINISTER DO NOT VIEW A
RETURN TO THE SECURITY COUNCIL IN THE SAME WAY

The Council of Ministers has been sitting since 9:30 a.m., and after an interruption at 2 p.m. will resume discussions later in the afternoon. It is trying to find a way out of the Franco-Tunisian crisis and the breakdown of the "good offices." The meeting was preceded by a day filled with reverses and surprises. The postponement of the government's deliberations following a move by Mr. Murphy, the appeal by Mr. Eisenhower sent to M. Félix Gaillard, the unusual audience of the moderate [i.e., the Independents—Eds.] ministers with the President of the Republic have all shown ever more clearly from hour to hour the dual political and diplomatic aspects of the problem that the President of the Council must resolve.

The dilemma confronting the head of government, all considered, is quite clear: if he cedes to the primarily negative intransigence of the "moderates," he can no longer count on the understanding and thus the support of our allies; if he completely takes into account the reasoning of the allies and excessively modifies the position of the French government as hitherto defined, he risks being abandoned by one of the most important parties of his majority.

The moderate ministers have clearly revealed that the way the situation was evolving was not satisfactory to them. Three hours of conversation with the President of the Council were of so little success in convincing them that right after they left the Hôtel Matignon [the premier's official residence—Eds.] they set off for the Élysée. This visit to the President apparently was for receiving counsels of moderation, thus shielding themselves behind the wishes of that very highly placed guarantor in order to protect themselves from the stormy reaction of the rank and file. The five ministers' alarm is understandable given that the demands they formulated over the past weeks in their party's name have all in all hardly been satisfied. They have had to admit that the matter of airfields was only a "minor aspect" of the question and to be satisfied with promises about control of the frontiers.

Thereafter, if only for an instant, a control exercised unilaterally on Algerian territory was envisioned. In the present state of affairs, M. Félix Gaillard is seeking to resurrect the "good offices" while the moderates no longer believe that this new start will bring anything good for France.

The essential debate bears on the following point: is France returning to the Security Council to accuse Tunisia or to speak with conciliatory language?

The second concept is substantially that of Messrs. Eisenhower, Murphy, and Gaillard. The double objective must be that of avoiding any enlargement of the debate, i.e. any internationalization of the Algerian affair, but without compromising the partial results which the "good offices" have let us achieve.

The first view—that of the moderates—consists of restating the

French accusations against M. Bourguiba and winning a condemnation of and a halt to Tunisian interference. But there are contradictions in the degree to which such an attitude includes a risk of internationalization of the Algerian affair—an internationalization that M. Pinay's colleagues reject as much as does the President of the Council. . . .

Raymond Barrillon
(*Le Monde*, April 14, 1958, pp. 1, 3)

BEFORE THE DEBATE ON THE
RESULT OF THE "GOOD OFFICES"

THE SOCIALISTS: NO OTHER SOLUTION POSSIBLE
THE MODERATES: NO NEW SURRENDERS

The dual decision taken by the French government to resume the dialogue with Tunis on the basis of the positive results registered by the mission of "good offices," and to postpone until later the appeal to international bodies concerning control of the Algerian-Tunisian frontier—a decision the government will submit Tuesday for the approval of the Assembly—has provoked numerous reactions, summarized here:

—*Algiers*: Profound malaise and anxiety.
—*Tunis*: Prudent reserve, but satisfaction.
—*Washington and London*: Relief to the degree that the government will prevail in the Assembly.
—*Paris*: Rejection by Messrs. Soustelle and Bidault and several Independent leaders, including M. Duchet.

Since it is assured of support from the Socialists, the majority of Radicals, and the MRP, the Assembly's vote will depend upon the attitude of M. Pinay's colleagues.

The nearness of the district elections is not holding back the most intransigent moderates from running the risk of a ministerial crisis as of now. . . .

The government is back in the situation it was in on the eve of the parliamentary recess three weeks ago, but its room for maneuver is narrower:

—The substance of the "good offices" has not changed since then: evacuation of the French forces [from Tunisian airbases] and the opening of negotiations over the control of Bizerte.

—The position of the moderates has not been modified: refusal to abandon the airfields until the end of the Algerian war.

The decisions taken by the Council of Ministers Saturday and the very circumstances that preceded them have apparently only been able to reinforce the moderates' intransigence.

(a) The moderates have the impression that the government was ceding to American pressure; . . .

(b) The moderates feel that they have been tricked. Despite their rejection [of the good offices] they would have been resigned to the loss of the airfields had they been compensated by bilateral control of the frontiers;

(c) The moderates, finally, feel that they have had to give way to the exhortations of the head of state [President of the Republic Coty], and that the precipitous convening of Parliament, even if it was called for by their ministers, places them in a delicate situation; for with the debate taking place a few days before the local elections they will be less inclined to provoke a government crisis.

To these arguments, which are more emotional than political, can be opposed others of equal value:

(1) The moderates fear above all the internationalization of the Algerian affair. This fear is in opposition to the desire to take the Tunisian affair to the UN. No one would know what the outcome would be. . . .

(2) The moderates are demanding the end of the "good offices." However, although the two diplomats remain at the disposition of the two governments to facilitate a resumption of dialogue, their mission is in reality concluded. As for the surrender of the airfields, this was accepted by the French government from the first stage of the "good offices" and was not subordinated by it to control of the frontier.

(3) The moderates did not want to be set before a fait accompli. The anticipated convening of Parliament should give them satisfaction.

These arguments balance out. But the core of the argument lies elsewhere; it is in the conviction of several leaders of the right according to whom there are only two possible policies: negotiations or force. Not only in Algeria but also in regard to Tunisia. But according to them the government is practicing a third policy which borrows elements from the preceding two but is not understood by public opinion and is leading to negotiations, opened directly with Tunisia today and by devious routes with Algeria tomorrow. The majority of Independents do not want to share responsibility for this policy. . . .

What then do the adversaries of negotiation, either indirect or direct, want?

—To keep the guarantees France has in Tunisia until the end of the war;

—To assure "dignity and security" for the French forces by giving them freedom to leave their camps and counter wherever they are attacked.

If it is objected that this would at one blow endanger the security of the French living in Tunisia and definitely compromise our entire international position, the partisans of this thesis answer that it would not be necessary to proceed to action, but would suffice to affirm our will in order to make M. Bourguiba cede. His rejection of a controlling of the frontier, they add, is a "calculated risk" based on our weakness.

This somewhat backward thesis has at least the virtue of distinctness. It has the drawback of being unrealistic, externally as well as domestically. Nowhere is there a majority to approve it. Neither in the government, nor in Parliament, and certainly not in any international body. It is logical only for those who would go so far as to jeopardize the regime and the Atlantic Alliance. . . .

For now the moderates and their allies have only one choice to make: whether or not to provoke another ministerial crisis. Several of their leaders accept this risk, notably M. Roger Duchet. From their perspective they envisage only two hypotheses: either a team resolved on maintaining demands deemed essential no matter what the cost (and the Poujadists, their leader in the fore, are offering to enter such a cabinet), or a ministry resuming the "third way" chosen by the present government (from which the Independents would have to leave).

The Socialist attitude makes the second hypothesis more probable. The support of the SFIO is a trump for M. Gaillard. The division of the other parties is another. The abstention of the Communists would be a final one. But it is improbable. Joining the extreme right, the extreme left denounces "American pressures" (*L'Humanité*). It is not the custom of this party to abstain: certainly it would not do so if the question of confidence were posed.

There is no other possible policy—this will be M. Gaillard's theme. To any parliamentarian who comes to contest it, he will ask in return "But what policy are you defining for yourself?" And in his mind it can only be a question of a policy that takes account of the fact that France has given independence to Tunisia.

Jacques Fauvet
(*Le Monde*, April 15, 1958, p. 1)

Assemblée Nationale, Session of April 15, 1958

THE PRESIDENT: I have received several requests to question the government.

First from M. Jacques Duclos on the repercussions of the Algerian war on Franco-Tunisian relations and on the circumstances under which the governments of the United States and Great Britain have been led to extend their "good offices." I believe that, at the request of the government, M. Duclos has presented his questions in advance.

Second from M. Le Pen on the message from the government to the National Assembly, the results of the mission of "good offices," the problems of Franco-Tunisian relations, and more generally on all questions concerning the situation in North Africa.

Third from M. Pierre André, on the policy of the government in North Africa.

Fourth from M. Pierre Montel on the policy of the government regarding Tunisia, and what the procedure regarding the "good offices" should be.

When does the government propose to discuss these questions?

M. FELIX GAILLARD, PRESIDENT OF THE COUNCIL: The government asks that they be postponed, and it will interpret this postponement as a vote of confidence. . . .

M. PIERRE ANDRÉ (*Independent*): Mr. President of the Council, you have accepted the English and American good offices in order to facilitate the resolution of the Franco-Tunisian conflict. I have always judged that it was dangerous to accept the pretended good offices of two countries who have insulted us by delivering arms to Tunisia; but you thought in accepting these good offices that you could obtain supervision of the Franco-Tunisian border and hence Tunisian neutrality in the Algerian affair.

But you came up against bad faith on the part of Bourguiba, and England and America did not make your job any easier. Today, ladies and gentlemen, it is clear that the good offices have become bad offices, and, Mr. President of the Council, you should have refused to go any further with them. . . .

The French position was perfectly defensible. Tunisia was a French protectorate; France gave Tunisia independence, but not without certain conditions. When a revolt broke out in nearby Algeria, Tunisia not only let the rebels cross into its territory, but welcomed them,

Journal Officiel, Débats Parlementaires, Assemblée Nationale, 1957–58, 2136, 2138–41, 2144–5, 2147, 2152–4.

permitting them to rest, to rearm, to gather reinforcements and then to set out again against the French forces and against the Moslem populations faithful to France.

Thus Tunisia is the ally of the enemies of our country. . . .

Authority . . . is based on a unity of will between those who command and those who obey. A crisis of authority is inevitable if the army sees that those who nominate its leaders have no will to win and to gain the rapid victory which the existence of the army depends on. (*Applause on the right and the extreme right.*)

The affair of Sakiet shows the bankruptcy of politics in our country. I will explain myself.

Mr. President of the Council, no one in France maintained that the aerial bombing of a village where there was a fellagha* camp, but also civilians, was a praiseworthy act. It is enough to read the world press to see that. And it was not much comfort to remember that the sternest critics of France were journalists whose countries had drowned the Hungarian revolt in blood, had pitilessly suppressed the Mau-Mau uprising, had burned the village of Oradour with its inhabitants, had invented the "carpet of bombs" technique, had massacred innocent people at Oued Zem, at Meknes, and at Melouza. For the world knows very well that it is to the honor of France to be humane in all her actions, even in war (*Applause on the right, on several benches of the extreme right and some benches of the left.*), and those who saw with their own eyes the reports from Sakiet-Sidi-Youssef know that I am telling the truth.

To understand Sakiet-Sidi-Youssef, which is at the root of all that has gone on here for quite a while, we have to remember that for eighteen months Tunisia has served as a base of operations for the FLN as well as a place to retreat to and gather its forces after it has been attacked.

Faced with this critical situation, what policy did the French government follow? What measures did it take? Well, for months none at all.

Even the right to pursuit was denied to the army. Our soldiers were wounded and fell. Algerians were attacked and carried off to camps in Tunisia, while we stopped powerless at the frontier.

Finally, one day, thanks to the energy and will of M. André Morice, an electric barbed-wire barrier was set up for hundreds of kilometers. But this barrier, ladies and gentlemen, does not strike at the heart of the problem, that is, the de facto belligerence of Tunisia.

*[Algerian word used for the FLN rebels—Eds.]

Why did the French government tolerate this for eighteen months? Why did you never enter a complaint against this systematic and repeated violation of international law? Why didn't you do like the Israelis who retaliated, before the battle of Sinai, against the attacks and infiltration of the Fedayeen, by procedures which we could have taken for a model. . . .

The problem of the presence of our forces in Southern Tunisia— which we improperly call the problem of the airfields—does not affect solely the surveillance of air traffic. It is quite obvious that the day that neutral forces occupy our place, they will hardly concern themselves with the surveillance of air traffic.

By reason of the losses sustained before the Morice Line, the forces of the FLN have for some weeks been shifting toward Southern Tunisia, from which they could outflank this line on the south and directly menace our installations in the Sahara. Now, the mere presence of French forces at Gafsa, at Gabès, and elsewhere in the South thwarts the implantation of new bases for fellagha aggression. That is why Bourguiba seeks by every means to secure their departure. (*Applause on the right, the extreme right, and some benches in the center.*) . . .

If you refuse the necessary effort today, my dear colleagues, you'll never carry it through tomorrow. If this is so, then say it frankly, as the President of the Council just asked us to do. There has to be an end to the lying in our country today (*Applause on the right and the extreme right.*) and to dying for nothing.

I say that a French government that had faith in its own country would have known how to unite the people around it and how to make the American people understand the great drama of French Algeria. In any case if you had fully accepted your great responsibility, you never would have accepted what the good offices proposed to you. (*Lively applause on numerous benches of the right. Applause on the extreme right.*) . . .

THE PRESIDENT: M. Soustelle has the floor. (*Applause on some benches of the center.*)

M. JACQUES SOUSTELLE (*Social Republican*): My dear colleagues, in his address the President of the Council reproached some of us— me included, I imagine—for wanting to keep some kind of monopoly on patriotism.

I hasten to say that no one here has such pretensions, in any case not the present speaker, no more, I think, than the President of the Council has a monopoly on intelligence. (*Laughter on the extreme left, the extreme right, and various benches.*)

Most virtues and abilities are more or less well divided among us. Nevertheless I will try to present the problem that faces us, not, as Mr. President of the Council has reproached us, in a simplistic and haphazard manner, but with the greatest precision, which obliges me to retrace a few steps to remind you what the nature of this problem is.

The sole, the true, the unique problem we face at this moment is Tunisian belligerence. There is no other problem. . . .

The prolongation of the conflict has its roots in the attitude of Tunisia. There isn't a military commander or a civilian leader in Algeria, especially in the east, who hasn't testified, either in writing or verbally, that without Tunisian aid to the FLN, the Algerian conflict would have been over by now. (*Applause on the right, the extreme right, and some benches of the center.*)

This conflict goes on solely because of Tunisian support. The men who are dying in Algeria today, the assassinated Moslems, the French soldiers who fall in ambush, are the victims of Bourguiba and his tactics.

But it must be said, the French government has refused for months to bring the problem of Tunisian belligerence before world opinion, to accuse Bourguiba before the world, to bring a dossier that months ago was already overwhelming.

The acceptance, or, according to certain versions, the solicitation of good offices by the French government was a grave error whose consequences we are still paying.

The partiality of those who exercised these good offices was already known and couldn't really have surprised anyone. The arms deliveries to Tunisia* had already proved what the apparent impartiality of those who have given their good offices really meant. But above all, we knew well just by reading the American press, for example the statements of our American correspondents, that their whole policy is dominated by a fiction, that of "Bourguiba, the great friend of the West. . . ."

The American policy which I have spoken of has been a perpetual Munich, and we now find ourselves faced with this Munich.

Aren't the "good offices" of M. Murphy and M. Beeley strangely reminiscent of the mission of Runciman to Czechoslovakia, which was the first step toward the dismemberment of that unfortunate country?

We read in the press or we hear in the Assembly the same argument: we have to choose between bad and worse; we have to preserve

*[By the United States—Eds.]

the peace; we have to maintain the Allied front; we have to choose between a solution which perhaps isn't very honorable, and the risk of war.

Do I have to remind you that the result of Munich was both dishonor and war too? (*Applause on several benches of the center and numerous benches of the right and the extreme right.*)

M. RAYMOND TRIBOULET (*Social Republican*): Very good! (*Laughter on the extreme left.*)

M. JEAN PRONTEAU (*Communist*): The ones who applaud are the ones who voted for Munich.

M. JACQUES DUCLOS (*Communist*): We were the only ones to vote against Munich.

M. JACQUES SOUSTELLE: Then I am surprised that those who voted against Munich in 1938 have become such Munichers today.

In any case, I did not vote and for a good reason.

The good offices were only justified if they dealt with the question of Tunisian neutrality. But from the beginning the partiality of MM. Murphy and Beeley toward Bourguiba's Tunisia was evident. The good offices were rapidly transformed into mediation, and then, it must be said, into arbitration exercised against us. The problem of belligerence was completely left aside. If M. Murphy had exercised on M. Bourguiba a hundredth of the pressure he put on the French government, M. Bourguiba would have been obliged to renounce his belligerence against France. (Very good! Very good! *from several benches of the center, the right, and the extreme right.*) But far from proceeding in this manner (as the latest issue of the *Sunday Times* reveals) the assistants of the ambassador of the United States in Tunis immediately tried to make contact with the FLN terrorists, whom they considered as rightful representatives and as the successors to France in North Africa.

Thus we have arrived at a situation where no one talks about Tunisian belligerence any more, but only about the concessions which France ought to make. . . .

In any case no one has the right *not* to try a new policy.

When we talk like this people answer: What about peace? Oh, but I know! We are all human and at certain times we feel what Léon Blum called "flaccid weariness" after a day- and week-long tension has been resolved.

If you abandon Algeria—and unfortunately the good offices in their present form are the first step toward abandoning Algeria—you won't have peace in North Africa. You will have war, a war infinitely larger, more extensive, bloodier, and more inhuman than the one we are fighting today.

Remember the lessons of the Third Republic. It tolerated the loss of the Rhineland, then the *Anschluss*,* then Munich. And this ended with the destruction of the regime and the defeat of the country.

I am telling you my whole opinion, my dear colleagues. If the situation is not corrected today, it will be too late tomorrow. And to those who nourish the hope that perhaps a France deprived or relieved of its overseas possessions would be happy and calm like Switzerland or Sweden, I would like to say that this just isn't possible, and that at the most we would be like Spain in decline, which tore itself apart for years, perhaps for centuries.

That is why, Mr. President of the Council, I want to avoid in my conclusion any statements that might provoke hostility toward me. I want to talk with serenity about a problem which is infinitely beyond all of us, about something which began before us and will last after us and which is called "France."

I believe that if we follow you today we will put France in danger. That is why we are not following you. (*Applause on several benches of the center, and numerous benches of the right and the extreme right.*) . . .

THE PRESIDENT OF THE COUNCIL: Ladies and gentlemen. At this late hour and at the end of a debate which, if I may say so, has displayed so much passion—more than necessary—I address this Assembly in the concern that I have for my duty and for the responsibility which this evening is mine, and which tomorrow morning may be yours. . . .

For months and for years, France has been confronted from the four corners of the globe with enormous problems; and our present forces have not always been as equal to them as our ambitions and our hopes.

Ladies and gentlemen, will you please consider the number of times when, due to our inconsistency—this is the proper word—we have thrown away the cards we held in our hand? (*Applause on the left, the center, and a few benches of the right.*)

A few months ago, when after continuous effort we had for an instant brought the rebellion in Algeria to its knees militarily, and when the preceding government begged you to give it the political means to profit from this success, then a coalition, an unnatural mar-

*[The incorporation of Austria into Germany in March 1938, accomplished by Hitler through the threat of force—Eds.]

riage took place here to deprive the government of the means it asked you for. (*Applause on the same benches.*). . .

If today, after long deliberation, the present government assures you that it is in the interests of France to accept the decision that the government has taken, then, in what concerns Tunisia, Algeria, and perhaps other African territories, it has reasons for telling you this.

You reject this decision; or at least it appears that the majority of you are going to reject it. Then you are going to open up a crisis. How long will it last? Where will you find a majority for a new government tomorrow? What will happen meanwhile, to the economy, to our finances, and to society? What will happen in Algeria? What will be the reactions in Tunisia and throughout the world?

If this is true, it has to be said this evening.

Are you sure that tomorrow morning a new government can be formed?

This isn't my problem; it's yours. But if I speak out, you will understand that it is not to defend the government which you have entrusted to me, it is simply because I would be reproached tomorrow for not having said in so grave a moment what I have just said. (*Applause on the left and the center.*) . . .

THE PRESIDENT: The ballot is open. (*The votes are gathered.*)

No one else wants to vote? . . . The ballot is closed.

(*The secretaries count the votes.*) . . .

Here are the results as verified of the ballot:

Number voting	576
Absolute majority	289
For	255
Against	321

The National Assembly rejects the motion.

(*The President of the Council, followed by the members of the government, leaves the Assembly.*)

Analysis of the vote of the Assembly
255 deputies voted for:

95 Socialists (of 96) and 3 MSA (of 4); 29 Radicals (of 43); 14 UDSR-RDA (of 22), including M. Pleven; 6 RGR (of 14); 5 Democratic Left (of 14); 6 African Convention (of 7); 70 MRP (of 75); 1 Social Republican (of 20), M. Chaban-Delmas; 24 Independents (of 91); 2 Peasants for Social Action (of 9).

321 deputies voted against:

The 142 Communists; the 6 Progressives; 1 MSA; 14 Radicals, including M. Mendès-France; 7 UDSR, including M. Mitterand; 7 RGR; 9 Democratic Left, including M. Morice; 3 MRP, including M. Bidault; 17 Social Republicans; 61 Independents; 6 Peasants for Social Action; 10 Peasants (of 11); 30 UFF [Poujadists] (of 31); 8 unaffiliated (of 11).

8 deputies did not vote; 11 deputies had permission to be absent.

(Adapted from *Le Monde*, April 17, 1958, p. 6)

AFTER THE REJECTION OF
AN "AFRICAN MUNICH"

BE SAVED TOGETHER OR PERISH TOGETHER

The national deputies who, Tuesday night, defeated the government were not acting for the fun of it. They did not yield, as some members of the Parisian press would have us believe, to some kind of nihilist vertigo. Quite on the contrary, they were trying to hold France back at the brink of the chasm suddenly opened beneath her feet by Anglo-Saxon diplomacy, the docile instrument of Bourguiba's blackmail.

To fasten the same reproach upon the 61 moderates, the 30 Poujadists, the 17 Social Republicans, the 9 Morice Radicals, the 7 members of the RGR, the 6 Peasants, the 3 Popular Republicans, the 8 unaffiliated who voted against the Gaillard government, and the 148 Communists who voted against this government as they vote against all other governments, is as easy as it is dishonest. This would amount to claiming that on Tuesday MM. Thorez and Duclos were thinking the same thoughts and pursuing the same goals as, for example, MM. Antoine Pinay and Joseph Laniel, MM. André Morice and Jean-Paul David, MM. Georges Bidault and Jacques Soustelle.

It is self-evident: the feelings which motivated the former were as different as they could possibly be from those which motivated the latter. The extreme left, official ally of the FLN, the forces behind all campaigns of subversion, feared that the government might deliver Algeria to the Americans instead of the Russians.

The other side of the Assembly, on the other hand, thought that it was time at last to halt the fatal drift of events to which the government seemed resigned. Those who are accused today of having begun a ministerial crisis really were representing the will of a country tired of being duped by its worst enemies and being betrayed by its best friends. Someone had to say "no" to Tunis, London, and Washington. It was said. The ballot of Tuesday has no other meaning.

But look how the tearful chorus steps out on the apron and rends the air with its lament. "The system has been stalled." "The country has been thrown to adventurism." This is what the *Figaro* has been saying, whose editorialist also deplores the "entirely negative action" of the "adversaries of M. Gaillard."

First of all: there are no "adversaries of M. Gaillard": there are only adversaries of a policy which, doubtless in good faith, M. Gaillard has judged compatible with French interests, but which the analysis of MM. Pierre André, Jacques Soustelle, Marcel Rogier—among others—has showed to be terribly dangerous. The President of the Council, M. Christian Pineau, all of the ministers, and what is more, all the parties of the government coalition had proclaimed, in the course of these last weeks, the absolute and primary necessity of forcing neutrality and strict frontier controls on Tunisia.

This very reasonable demand was the moving force of French policy toward Tunisia. "The increasing number of incidents on the frontier," said M. Félix Gaillard on March 27, on the eve of the parliamentary recess, "is the basic cause of our difficulties with Tunisia." THEREFORE THIS PROBLEM HAS TO BE RESOLVED FIRST OF ALL. . . .

In reality, only one thing emerged for certain from the debate: American diplomacy, in collusion with Bourguiba whom it considered "its man," was trying to corner France into a capitulation which would soon have been followed by a second one. If it put off indefinitely dealing with the central problem of the frontier, American diplomacy begged to inform us that in exchange Bourguiba renounced, provisionally, any internationalization of the Algerian affair. But MM. Murphy and Beeley knew very well—and we know it too—that Bourguiba had publicly boasted, without drawing the least comment from his British or American mediators, that he would seek new "good offices" on this question when he wanted to.

It was obvious after this that MM. Murphy, Beeley, and Bourguiba could not get the best of the French at a single blow. It thus became more suitable to nibble away at the French position, and in the last analysis, the Gaillard government consented to this nibbling and all its tragic consequences.

One more time: why these cries of despair from some of our Parisian colleagues? Have they learned nothing from Munich? And nothing from the exercises in whitewashing defeat we have had to witness since Indochina? Or do they think that by saying "yes" to all the suggestions from abroad they are following the straight line of our national tradition?

IF THERE ARE ANY WHO, LIKE M. ARON, BELIEVE SANCTIMONIOUSLY THAT ALGERIA CAN BE LOST WHILE METROPOLITAN FRANCE IS SAVED, THEY ARE VERY MISTAKEN.

EITHER WE WILL ALL BE SAVED TOGETHER, OR WE WILL ALL PERISH TOGETHER.

HAVE THEY FORGOTTEN THE STATEMENT M. GUY MOLLET MADE ON RADIO ALGIERS ON FEBRUARY 9, 1956?: "IF ALGERIA IS LOST TO FRANCE, THERE WILL BE NO MORE OF ALGERIA, BUT THERE WILL BE NO MORE FRANCE."

Thus, for us, the governments and the men who lead them don't make much difference. We are interested only in the policies they pursue. If Algeria is a new Alsace-Lorraine—as M. Félix Gaillard recently said at Doullens—then, consequently, measures must be taken not to lose it, for if it is lost, this time we will not have any hope of liberating it. The fall of the Gaillard government is the normal consequence of an error committed by this government. It will be useful if it arouses all of the parties and all of our statesmen—including those who at this time may feel bitter—to become aware of the national "imperatives."

WE SHALL NOT TIRE OF REPEATING THAT THERE IS ONLY ONE SOLUTION: POLITICAL TRUCE AND A CABINET OF PUBLIC SAFETY, ONE THAT WILL TELL THE TRUTH TO THE COUNTRY AND DEMAND FROM IT THE NECESSARY SACRIFICES, WHICH ARE WELL WITHIN OUR CAPABILITIES.

IF NOT, THE SACRIFICE OF OUR SOLDIERS WILL HAVE BEEN IN VAIN, AND ALGERIA IN TIME WILL BE FOREVER LOST.

Alain de Sérigny
(*L'Écho d'Alger*, April 17, 1958, pp. 1, 10)

WILL A BIDAULT OR SOUSTELLE GOVERNMENT OF THE RIGHT HAVE A MAJORITY IN THE NATIONAL ASSEMBLY?

1. The causes of the check.

They are of various categories.

Logically, first, the government was unguarded through the fact that it had accepted the evacuation of the airfields without furnishing the counterpart of a control of the frontiers. This is the argument which weighed strongest among the moderates. . . . The information of M. Pierre André concerning the airfields of the South, borrowed from a good military source, impressed the Assembly, which could see its confirmation in the silence, surprising in such a debate, of M. Lacoste and M. Chaban-Delmas.

Politically, the Independents could hardly take a different attitude without being run over by the nationalist current, and, from that point of view, the fact that the debate took place in the middle of an electoral campaign* harmed the government. To associate oneself with a policy in contradiction to the position of the *Centre national des Indépendants* would have been to weaken it, to compromise it, and only to leave the extreme left and the extreme right face to face. This is the thesis successfully maintained by M. Roger Duchet.

Psychologically, finally and above all, anti-Americanism, even xenophobia, animated and dominated the factions of the right. It is less the result of the "good offices" than the very fact of the mission of the two Anglo-Saxon diplomats which worked against the government. If a different procedure had been adopted, the same results, namely the same bases for resuming the Franco-Tunisian dialogue would not have run up against the same objections.

Xenophobia is only an aspect of a pervasive nationalism, and the latter, which is spread through all the groups, is the consequence of the retreat of the French throughout the world, of the decisions taken during the course of these past years in Indochina, in the Indies, or in Africa. All are indiscriminately interpreted as defeats and then resented as humiliations. This sentiment generously nourished the Poujadist wave in the last elections; it has now reached the neighboring groups. Indeed the deputies only reflect the state of mind of one part of public opinion. But even when they deplore it, they encourage it by giving in to it.

2. The union of the extremes. . . .

The conditions in which the government fell are at once classic and paradoxical. For the third time since the elections of 1956, the moderates have provoked the crisis by mingling their votes with those of the extreme left. They will continue nevertheless to judge harshly the men or the groups that would associate themselves with the extreme left to form the next ministry. . . .

3. The development of the crisis.

The logic of the parliamentary system will require that the personal-

*[The first round of cantonal (district) elections was to take place the following Sunday, April 20—Eds.]

ity entrusted with forming the new cabinet be one of the leaders of the majority which overthrew the government. In the present case those responsible are numerous: they are M. Duclos and M. Mendès-France just as much as M. Pierre André and M. Jacques Soustelle.

This same logic therefore recommends a development of the crisis in three stages:

(1) It is first necessary to know whether or not a "government of the right," in favor of a policy of force or at the very least of a refusal of all concessions, disposes of a majority and by what methods and with what means the partisans of such an attitude think they will best assure the defense of French interests.

But does the policy of M. Soustelle or of M. Bidault have a chance to unite a majority of the Assembly? This will become known by calling one or the other.

(2) It will be then necessary to know whether or not a policy oriented not more to the right but more to the left disposes of a majority. Is a government still possible that does not include the moderates or the Communists but has the support of one or the other? An experiment to answer these questions could be the duty of M. François Mitterrand. If the results of this experiment are judged inadmissible, the question might still remain: could not the Socialists, the Radicals, the UDSR, and the MRP, if they really want it, together find a new solution for the Algerian problem?

(3) If these attempts turn out negatively it will be necessary to return to the formula of the preceding governments and therefore to the same policy, with freedom to present it a little differently. But if it falls to the moderates or the Socialists, the new cabinet must include only the men who can really pledge their party, namely the leaders. The so-called "majority" governments of MM. Bourgès-Maunoury and Félix Gaillard proved to be more precarious, because they were more divided, than the so-called "minority" government of M. Guy Mollet. In the absence of the socialist leader, could it be presided over by M. Mitterrand or by M. Pleven? The former President of the Council [Pleven] has been importuned after each crisis.

But, whoever it will be, the next minister must bring the Franco-Tunisian dispute back to the area of North African, or simply African, policy.

Jacques Fauvet
(*Le Monde*, April 17, 1958, pp. 1–2)

Lyon (ACP): M. Jacques Soustelle arrived at Lyon this afternoon in order to participate in the campaign meetings for the cantonal elections. When he was asked what he foresaw as the development of the crisis, the Social Republican leader replied:

"I believe that it is a little early to ask me this but I would like to say two things: first, that this crisis was inevitable from the time they persisted in their desire to accept this unacceptable basis of discussion for the Tunisian affair.

"This was a point of such capital importance that deputies belonging to many parties could not resolve it. And that rendered the crisis inevitable. . . .

"This crisis could now develop in an unexpected manner.

"I am not a prophet, but what I hope is that it will permit a step, as great a step as possible, toward what to me seems indispensable, a government of public safety, a government of union with a truce among the parties.

"Indeed a truce among the parties seems to me altogether indispensable if we want to get out of our difficulty."

An allusion having been made to an appeal to General de Gaulle, M. Soustelle replied:

"How was this crisis started? On a question which brings up North Africa and which is also an international question, that of our relations with our Atlantic allies.

"Now, I believe I am making a sensible statement in saying that among the men now living who enjoy a name, prestige, and authority in France, General de Gaulle is among the most qualified to attack problems of this nature."

(*L'Écho d'Alger*, April 17, 1958, p. 1)

STATEMENT BY PREMIER-DESIGNATE GEORGES BIDAULT, APRIL 20, 1958, 7:40 P.M.

The President of the Republic has asked me to form a government. In an hour of grave national anxiety I could not refuse this appeal. I hope that the aid necessary for confronting my task will not be refused me.

Today Algeria, where our youth is fighting, which has been French for generations and for which a new organization has just been sovereignly fixed by the representatives of the nation, is for our country the problem that surpasses all others.

In a world which professes to proscribe racism, Algeria, the fruit of our long efforts, must provide the exemplary proof that a community can exist where French Moslems and French of European origin live together in strict justice.

Algeria is our heritage and our mission. No intrusion, no concession to the spirit of abandonment, can be tolerated in its regard. Algeria is not only the work of our ancestors. As the indispensable channel for Sahara oil, it is also the guaranty of a better future for France and for all the peoples associated with its destiny.

To lose Algeria would be to lose the nation's economic independence, the realization of which is now possible in a short time. Such a disaster must be averted at all costs.

France is faithful to the treaties which she has signed, and particularly to the Atlantic Pact. She expects from her allies only the same fidelity and the same respect of these treaties.

France has no plan to make war on anyone, but she intends clearly that no one do the same to her.

(*Le Monde*, April 22, 1958, p. 2)

STATEMENT OF THE MRP AFTER THE MEETING OF ITS PARLIAMENTARY DELEGATION, APRIL 22, 1958.

The MRP, while asserting its affection for M. Georges Bidault, has not declared itself in favor of the constitution of the government he proposes to form.

Proclaiming its will to avert any solution of abandonment, it remains convinced that a reinforced effort to seal off the frontiers and the pursuit of a generous policy of reforms are the conditions of reconciliation and peace in a new French Algeria.

(*Le Monde*, April 24, 1958, p. 2)

PIERRE PFLIMLIN: "WHY THE MRP DID NOT FOLLOW GEORGES BIDAULT"

It was not a spirit of abandonment that motivated the majority of the MRP. But we refuse to allow ourselves to be caught in the dilemma: rigidity or abandonment.

We believe that there exists a third policy, no doubt more difficult to define, and still more difficult to carry out, especially in a state of opinion where passion too often gets the better of reason, but which is nevertheless the only policy capable of saving the French positions in North Africa.

This policy, which requires at once firmness as well as self-control, generosity as well as lucid realism, will use force as much as is necessary against rebel forces and terrorism, while avoiding unjustifiable excesses. But inspired by the conviction that force alone cannot solve the Algerian problem, it will secure a loyal and liberal application of the *loi-cadre*, appealing to all the representative elements of the Algerian population, even some of those who have opposed us, to participate in the construction of a truly new Algeria. It does not repudiate, on the contrary, it is ready to renew the offer contained in the declaration of January 9, 1957, to engage in negotiations with the representatives of those who are fighting, in order to determine the terms of a cease-fire and the guarantees surrounding the elections which can be organized when calm is sufficiently re-established.

In order to block the aid supplied to the rebellion across the Algerian-Tunisian and Algerian-Moroccan frontiers, this policy will strive more to assure physically the sealing off of the frontiers than to demand assurances and guarantees that the fragile authorities established at Tunis and Rabat could not easily give and still less easily respect. . . .

Quite obviously the government of Georges Bidault would have been constituted and sustained by those who, from the Social Republicans through the majority of the Independents to the Poujadists, have endeavored for a year to prevent the vote of the *loi-cadre* and to empty it of its substance. Certain of them, for example M. Jacques Soustelle, still rejected it at the time of the final vote. On the subject of Tunisia and Morocco as in regard to our allies, these men have not ceased to advocate rigorous and hard positions which would one day place us before the alternatives of capitulating in humiliation or taking the risk of a general conflagration in North Africa, while the world powers form a coalition against France.

We are confident that the best among the partisans of rigidity want to defend the national interest, maintain peace and preserve our alliances as sincerely as we do. No one will dare deny the patriotism of Georges Bidault and his attachment to peace. But we believe that the methods which they prefer would inevitably lead to the opposite of what they desire.

Such a conviction could not bend to the exigencies of friendship or to counsels of political prudence.

(from *Le Nouvel Alsacien*, April 23, 1958; quoted in
(*Le Monde*, April 25, 1958, p. 5)

TO THE PRINCES WHO GOVERN US

It is certain that if in spite of the opposition of the majority of the MRP membership (28 to 25), M. G. Bidault had appeared before the National Assembly, he would have crucified not only his party colleagues but also a good number of deputies belonging to other political groups.

Our readers will understand that we are talking about neopatriots who would gladly give away Algeria so long as no one saw them doing it, and about those who, to be sure, declare without batting an eyelash that there can never, never be any question of losing this province, but who at the same time refuse to support the only means which can save it.

The brief statement made by M. Bidault as he left the Élysée is explicit enough for us to imagine the cold sweat which must have broken out on the foreheads of many of his friends before the votes were counted.

It is symptomatic but no less curious that the leaders of the "party of fidelity" were quite eager to give M. Bidault their agreement in principle for his program while they rejected the men most qualified to put it into effect, M. André Morice and even more especially Jacques Soustelle. In short, the President-Designate would have had to give the nod to men who, after approving his program, would very neatly have sabotaged it. . . . No more, no less.

After this there is nothing to guarantee, as M. Bidault announced after his withdrawal, that "there will soon be a majority for the cause he has defended and will continue to defend." A parliamentary majority is what he means. For, as M. Bidault has already correctly said, "in any case this majority exists in a nation which has remained healthy despite so many bad advisers, as the quiet courage of the young men bearing arms shows."

In any case, the courageous attempt of the deputy from the Loire will have its impact on the course of events. "The principal merit of M. Georges Bidault," our colleague Paul Le Gall observes very

justly in the *Parisien Libéré* (one of the few Parisian newspapers that
has constantly backed the national position), "will be to have helped
put an end to dangerous equivocation. . . ."

But if the choices are clearer now, those who, after M. Gaillard,
will bear the responsibilities of power ought to realize that they will
not decide the fate of Algeria without Algeria itself taking part in
their decision. The candidates for the Presidency of the Council are
perhaps unaware of this, and, if so, we have the duty to inform them:
no one in the world, not even a chief of state, can make the Algerians
—the Moslems no more than the "Europeans"—consider themselves
as cattle to be disposed of as circumstances dictate in international
deals. In other words, they are aware of the impossibility of a military
Dien-Bien-Phu and they will never allow themselves to be victims of
a political Dien-Bien-Phu.

Advice to the "princes who govern us. . . ."

(*L'Écho d'Alger*, April 24, 1958, p. 1)

STATEMENT BY PREMIER-DESIGNATE RENÉ PLEVEN, APRIL 24,
1958, EVENING

I have studied only one question with those with whom I conferred:
that of Algeria. My objective is to fix a certain number of fundamental
points that would be the subject of a solemn declaration by the national legislature and would determine the orientation of our Algerian
policy through all the vicissitudes of politics.

The reception I met with from the principal political leaders consulted today has been encouraging.

In this regard, I read somewhere that it is said I am seeking an
Algerian policy for a majority. No. I am seeking to find out whether
the Algerian policy that I believe is indispensable can unite a large
national majority.

In reality I am moved by the conviction that save among those who
would accept a secession in Algeria, the divisions on Algerian policy
result from many misunderstandings, prejudices, sometimes even criticisms of intentions.

I am endeavoring to remove them.

I know that this manner of proceeding demands patience, and I
ask public opinion to understand that it would be better to spend two
or three days trying to resolve the crisis at its base than to build upon

an equivocation a government which would fall again in a few months precisely on the Algerian question.

How can France then make her adversaries, her allies, the world understand that she is following a policy in Algeria if her governments come apart every few months precisely over this very question?

How can she continue to have any policy at all, if this question, which is at the heart of all the others, is subject to continual fluctuation?

I am sure that all Frenchmen understand the difficulties of my task.

(*Le Monde*, April 26, 1958, p. 2)

EXCLUSIVE INTERVIEW WITH M. JACQUES SOUSTELLE

. . . QUESTION—M. Pflimlin wrote yesterday in the *Nouvel Alsacien*: "We refuse to allow ourselves to be caught in the dilemma, rigidity or abandonment. We believe that there exists a third policy. . . ." Do you believe this too?

ANSWER—A war is being fought against us in Algeria. A war can only be won or lost: there is no "third policy." Either France stays in Algeria, or the FLN takes power. People are only fooling themselves when they say there are intermediate solutions. I read with interest in the *Nouvel Alsacien* that the policy desired by M. Pflimlin, which he rightly called "hard to define," refuses "to start out on a path which leads to reconquest," or "to be trapped into systematic xenophobia."

Since no one advocates reconquest and no one is a systematic xenophobe, I wonder whom M. Pflimlin could have been thinking of when he wrote these lines. A man so well informed as the president of the MRP certainly can't have been influenced by the slander campaigns against the honorary president of his party [Bidault] and several other parliamentarians. Is the conclusion, then, that the defense of Algeria and the French positions in North Africa seems to some people to be tainted with a dangerous extremism? But what could anyone propose which would not be either the salvation of Algeria or its abandonment?

QUESTION—M. Pleven is looking for a formula which can achieve national unanimity on Algeria. Do you believe this is desirable? Do you believe it is possible? And if so, on what basis?

ANSWER—Everyone knows perfectly well which Algerian policy, with the support of the majority of Parliament and the country, can bring a happy end to this agonizing drama. From M. Guy Mollet to M. Bidault the lines of this policy have not changed. Several votes of confidence, numerous policy declarations by successive governments and the first article of the *loi-cadre* have gained overwhelming majorities.

What is important is less agreement on formulas than unanimity of will in action. To pursue the destruction of rebel bands, to block off the frontiers, to accelerate and extend the implementation of reforms, to halt foreign interference, and lastly to combat on the home front the efforts at demoralization and defeatism that are trying to render vain the sacrifices of the country—these are not political positions or doctrines, but simply the statement of actions which ought to be carried out with perseverance.

Why, in this situation, are accusations being thrown back and forth? This is a grave symptom of the present moment, for it leads to suspicions that underneath words that have stayed the same, some people are contemplating some kind of "shift" toward adventure and secession.

I don't see anything wrong with M. Pleven trying to formulate one more time what has already been said by several governments and by Parliament itself. But this new declaration of intent will remain a dead letter if people, on behalf of some false illusion of symmetry, try at the same time to fight the terrorists who want to tear Algeria from France and the patriots whose only goal is her salvation.

Furthermore, we can't forget that the crisis of April 15 was not provoked by Algerian policy but by the "good offices." Let's not get off the track. What is important today is less the Algerian policy of the next government—for it is to be expected that it will continue that of its predecessors and we are only asking for energy and coherence in its application—than the attitude which it plans to adopt toward Tunisian belligerence and the mistakes of the Anglo-Saxons. This is the problem over which the last government fell, and it is the one which has to be resolved first of all and without equivocation.

And I mean "without equivocation." At the point we have now reached there has to be an end to ambiguities. In Parliament and in the country those who are resigned to pulling out have to stand up and be counted and likewise those who refuse. Everything else is insignificant.

I am convinced that ONLY A GOVERNMENT OF PUBLIC SAFETY CAN IMPLEMENT A POLICY IN ACCORD WITH THE WILL OF THE COUNTRY. It has been said that the present crisis isn't a crisis like all the others.

If it ends only in equivocation and the formation of a government of half-measures and tergiversations, it will only have marked one more step in the acceleration of decadence. It can, on the other hand prove to be healthy if it permits what so far we have too often lacked: a choice, a clear choice, a commitment without reticence, action without afterthought.

(L'Écho d'Alger, April 26, 1958, p. 3)

A REPORT ON PREMIER-DESIGNATE RENÉ PLEVEN'S MEETINGS OF APRIL 25, 1958 [excerpt]

M. René Pleven, who had an hour-long conversation with Marshal Juin before seeing M. Paul Reynaud, then received M. Chaban-Delmas, who acquainted him with everything concerning the military situation.

In the presence of M. Robert Lacoste, a "technical conference" was then held with the participation of General Ely, Chief of the General Staff, General of the Army; Admiral Nomy, Chief of the General Staff of the Navy; General Salan, Commander of the Armed Forces in Algeria; and General Jouhaud, Commander of the Air Forces in Algeria.

These military conversations lasted from 6:50 p.m. to 8:40 p.m. At 9:45 p.m. M. René Pleven made the following brief statement: The military leaders have informed me among other things that the question of the control of the frontiers, which so rightly disquieted public and parliamentary opinion in these last weeks, has made great progress, thanks to the admirable effort carried out by our army.

(Le Monde, April 27–28, 1958, p. 2)

DEMONSTRATIONS ON THE PUBLIC THOROUGHFARES REMAIN PROHIBITED [Algiers, April 26, 1958]

The office of the Minister for Algeria stated yesterday evening:

"M. Robert Lacoste wishes it remembered that all demonstrations on the public thoroughfares are prohibited."

It was learned shortly afterward that M. Robert Lacoste left Paris this morning to return to Algiers. . . .

(L'Écho d'Alger, April 26, 1958, p. 1)

I want to make known to you the reasons why I regard a demonstration planned for the public thoroughfares to be needless and inopportune, especially since this initiative has no important justification.

The visit I made yesterday in Paris has confirmed me in this opinion. Indeed I had a long discussion concerning the situation of Algeria with President-Designate Pleven, who also received our military chiefs: General Salan, chief commander of the armed forces in Algeria, and the deputy commander, General Jouhaud. In these conversations the military chiefs and I indicated to M. Pleven the nature and extent of the supplementary means which would permit an acceleration of the purification of Algeria, once our frontiers are well tightened up. Moreover, we laid stress on certain fundamental facts of the Algerian problem, the disregard of which could lead us to chimerical and fatal solutions that would have us throw away all our forces. Foremost among these facts is our unbending will to remain French and our absolute condemnation of all foreign interference.

In addition, I strongly insisted to President Pleven, as I did to the head of the former government and other political figures, that France must assert a clear and unmistakable determination in the Algerian affair, as the sole means to swing the balance in our favor.

I can say that at the present moment French opinion and the men in responsible positions are examining the Algerian situation with a new burst of patriotic feeling and good will.

You must take this into consideration, await what will emerge from it, and summon confidence through confidence, which in no way debars vigilance.

After having given a great example of patriotic wisdom, good sense, and heroism by so long resisting a provocative and barbarous terrorism, Algiers must henceforth give the example of a calm and united will and compel destiny to order, calm, and cohesion.

We must take care not to confuse agitation and action, not to allow grand and noble sentiments to be exploited by political factions in quest of followers.

Do not forget that mobilization of the populace in the streets, if one wants it to be of advantage, must be reserved for solemn moments or times of great danger. That is not the case today.

(*Le Monde*, April 27–28, 1958, p. 3)

—NO FOREIGN INTERFERENCE IN ALGERIAN AFFAIRS
—FORMATION OF A GOVERNMENT OF NATIONAL SAFETY
—FORMAL OPPOSITION TO ANY GOVERNMENT OF ABANDONMENT

More than fifteen thousand residents of Algiers answered the call of the veterans' associations and the patriotic movements Saturday afternoon. With a calm and silence appropriate to the gravity of the occasion, they expressed the unshakeable will of Algeria to remain French, to reject any sentiment for pulling out, to oppose all foreign interference in French problems, and, finally, to demand the formation of a government of national safety.

The apprehensions which this peaceful demonstration might have aroused were unfounded. There was not a single incident as the processions converged upon the monument to the dead. Order was maintained by the veterans. The police force, discreetly placed on the scene, had orders to intervene only in case of a disturbance. There was none.

Although reinforcements of soldiers, mobile guards, and CRS* were placed on alert, the guardians of the peace watched those responsible for order, with tricolor armbands on their sleeves, manage the processions and repeat the instructions for calm to the men and women of all classes and origins who participated in this stirring patriotic demonstration. . . .

With moving silence the demonstrators, in ranks of ten or twelve across, advanced through the streets lined with closed shops. Their numbers kept growing all the way to the monument to the dead. No disorder. No hostile cries. The demonstration maintained a perfect and significant dignity. Cascades of applause fell from the balconies. "Join us! You're not watching a show!"—the loud speakers exhorted.

At four o'clock the three processions joined at Laferrière Square. The delegations, grouped according to their branch of service, gathered around the monument. The crowd, estimated at more than fifteen thousand persons, observed a minute of silence, disturbed only by the motors of two helicopters, which since the beginning of the afternoon had outlined their gray shadows against the blue sky. . . .

Standing on an automobile, a leader of the veterans invited the

[*Compagnies républicaines de sécurité—riot police—Eds.]

crowd to swear fidelity to French Algeria and to the mother country. There followed a new and extended ovation. The motion, to be delivered later to the prefect of Algiers, was read aloud. It was acclaimed with enthusiasm. The demonstrators then separated peacefully. One segment with flags at its head accompanied the delegates of the movement to the prefecture. There at five o'clock, in good order and in silence, the impressive demonstration by the French citizens of Algiers was terminated.

M. Serge Baret, the Prefect, thereupon received a delegation that had come to transmit to him a petition addressed to the President of the Republic.

This petition stated: "In the hours when their destiny is at stake in the National Assembly, in which they have no representatives, all French Algerians of all origins, gathered together in a silence and calm that signify the measure of their discipline and their determination, proclaim their unshakeable will not to tolerate the least foreign interference in national problems.

"They swear on the tombs of their dead to oppose by all means the formation of any government of capitulation.

"They demand the formation of a government of national safety, the only one capable of restoring the greatness of their fatherland.

"The veterans' associations and the patriotic movement of Algeria, Algiers, April 26, 1958."

M. Serge Baret answered the representatives of the veterans and the patriotic associations in these words:

"You have showed your will to preserve French Algeria. It is inscribed in the spirit of all those here who devote their efforts, day after day to fulfill this national demand.

"The Minister for Algeria has just expressed the same wish, which has been affirmed once again in the highest councils of government.

"The approval he has gained for nearly three years in this country should earn him the thanks of all of you.

"Do not complicate his heavy task. The world is watching us. . . ."

(*L'Écho d'Alger*, April 27–28, 1958, pp. 12, 8)

When I was summoned to the Élysée, I said to you that before responding to the offer of the President of the Republic to form a government I would insist on ascertaining whether there existed a large national majority for the Algerian policy I want to follow.

I have therefore discussed various points of this policy most searchingly with the individuals I consulted.

The care with which they examined them underscores the value and the importance of the accord which they have nearly all given me.

Confident in this accord, I was able today to give a positive reply to the President of the Republic. He has confirmed my nomination, which I have accepted.

I am now therefore undertaking a second step, whose difficulties I do not overlook. Urgent economic, financial, and social problems, just to mention these, await the new government. I will be examining them in the coming hours.

They can only be overcome by a resolute and united team of ministers, whatever their political labels. This debars bargaining for office among the groups. I am therefore asking the parties on this basis if they agree to participate in the government.

I am also asking for a truce among the parties that would constitute the governmental majority.

Those associated with the same policy must no longer denounce each other before public opinion each Sunday evening.

Certain circumstances will not permit me to obtain the replies I need as quickly as I should now wish. The law calls for all general councils [elected in the district balloting of April 20 and 27] to meet next Wednesday, April 30. For this reason a great many members of Parliament will be away from Paris.

Moreover, because of May 1, one of the major parties [the SFIO] has informed me that it can give its decision about possible participation only next Friday.

In these circumstances I cannot consider a debate on investiture before the beginning of next week.

I wanted to explain to you this schedule, which my own wishes could not change.

(*Le Monde*, April 30, 1958, p. 3)

IN ORDER TO REACH NEGOTIATIONS IN ALGERIA—NO PRELIMINARY CONDITIONS

After three and a half hours of discussion, the executive of the Socialist International has adopted a draft declaration on Algeria which will be forwarded as the recommendation by the executive of the International to the council of the Socialist International that will meet at Brussels in June. The text, "which constitutes a compromise," as M. Guy Mollet emphasized at the end of the deliberations, declares among other things that "the problem of Algeria constitutes a menace to peace."

The executive of the Socialist International then declares itself "in favor of peaceful negotiations to put an end to the conflict on the basis of a guarantee of democratic liberties permitting all Algerians to have an equal part in the future of the country." Then it declares:

"The détente required for negotiations can be gained only if all involved parties abandon the preliminary conditions which they now insist upon. One cannot expect either the French authorities or the various organizations representing Algerian opinion to open negotiations on conditions which imply a capitulation in advance. Accordingly, the International considers that the conditions for negotiation must not exclude either of the two grand conceptions, namely: integration of Algeria with France or independence on the basis of democratic rules, accompanied by guarantees of the rights of minorities."

(*Le Figaro*, April 30, 1958, p. 13)

RESOLUTION ADOPTED BY THE NATIONAL COUNCIL OF THE SFIO, MAY 2, 1958, AT PUTEAUX

After having assumed the heaviest responsibilities for sixteen months, the Socialist Party consented to participate in two governments of a wider coalition. But this agreement did not assure governmental stability.

Today the party is called upon to consider an offer of a coalition similar to the preceding one. It thanks M. Pleven and assures him that its answer is not dictated by differences relating to the principles that he expounded to its delegates in regard to Algeria. But in the present circumstances the National Council cannot consider participation in such a government.

The latter would in fact include representatives of those groups that, with the help of the Communists' votes, have in less than a year taken the weighty responsibility of overthrowing the Guy Mollet and Bourgès-Maunoury governments, then of refusing the investiture of Guy Mollet, finally of opening the present crisis by supporting excessive and adventurous views.

The National Council assures President Pleven of the vote of its parliamentary group in favor of his investiture and of its firm will to furnish him its support.

It affirms finally that its decision is in no way aimed at M. Pleven. In the present situation it would make the same response to any other offer of participation or direction of the government.

(*Le Monde,* May 4–5, 1958, p. 3)

SPEECH OF GUY MOLLET AT PUTEAUX, AT A BANQUET OF THE SFIO FEDERATION OF THE SEINE, MAY 3, 1958.

The Communist Party seeks at any price to break the isolation in which it finds itself, but Budapest has not yet been forgotten by the French workers. (*Applause.*) On overseas problems like those of North Africa its policy is not understood by the public and especially not by young people. The Communists well know that young people are no longer voting for them, but they follow orders and will not change so long as the order is not given them to change.

As for the right, which is becoming the precursor of Bolshevism in France, it has just waged the most demagogic electoral campaign seen in thirty years. The *Indépendant du Pas-de-Calais* explained the policy we propose for North Africa by our concern for preserving our interests, and it alluded to property that Lacoste and I are supposed to own there. (*Laughter and protests.*) Our comrades from the Pas-de-Calais told me, "This time there are things you can no longer demand of us."

The right is 110 deputies, 140 with the Poujadists, who mean to lay down the law to 250 democrats. That is the principle of active minorities. We answered no.

(*The speaker then explains the possibilities which are open to the party in view of the proposals of M. Pleven.*)

There was an entering into opposition. But this catastrophic view was not carried. The temptation of a "majority of the left" miscarried. I myself indulged for a moment in the idea of a retreat to the Aventine.* But that would not be possible without leading the country to calamity. One cannot consent to expose the unconcern of others at the cost of a republican catastrophe.

From that point the choice was limited: support, participation, or leadership.

As the district elections have shown, there is a yearning in the country for Socialist leadership. But it is not possible to consider that. We no longer want to take responsibility if we are no longer to be accorded the means to carry out our designs in full. (*Lively applause.*)

They have discovered that we are a national party, but when we have tried to make it clear that nothing is possible if the workers are not conscious that this nation is theirs, that they must share the benefits as well as the sacrifices, then we have not been understood.

Anxious reporters have come to see me five or six times to ask, "Are you sure that that is what your motion demands?" That is, however, perfectly clear.

There remain participation and support. I admit that I was deeply hesitant, for it is a short step between the two.

Participation has the advantage of allowing us to influence domestic governmental action, but our participation is a participation that no longer really exists, since we have been asked to join with men who never cease to proclaim that they have nothing in common with us. We recognize the risks; we have taken them. As to this government and as to any other, there is no longer a possibility of participation. (*Lively applause.*)

We will not allow every government to exist. We have said no to the dangerous policy of the right. But we must say yes if there is no risk of injury to the Republic. We will accord support only when governments are involved whose composition and line of action are not dangerous for peace and republican institutions. We will refrain from interfering with a policy different from our own, but public opinion must understand that if we can give our votes, we cannot give our men.

*[In June 1924 some 140 deputies from the Socialist, Liberal, Republican, and Catholic Popular parties walked out of the Italian Chamber in protest against the murder of one of their moderate Socialist colleagues, Matteotti, by a group of Fascists close to Mussolini, who was already Premier but not yet dictator. This abandonment of Parliament was called the Aventine secession, after the hill to which the Roman plebs had withdrawn from the city in the time of Caius Gracchus. After Mussolini declared his ultimate responsibility for Matteotti's death on January 3, 1925, the Aventine deputies attempted to return to the Chamber. They were prevented from doing so, and in 1926 they were declared to have forfeited their seats—Eds.]

The right does not see the interest of the country, but only its own. A certain number of politicians are involved only for themselves, and not merely the minimum number. (*Applause.*) Those men are surprised, because they do not know us. They do not understand that we are giving up ministries, because they look only for advantages. Yet remember we were in power for sixteen months, but our *Populaire* [the Socialist newspaper in Paris—Eds.] is still threatened daily with extinction.

We have just assumed a heavy responsibility. You must consider yourselves mobilized from now on. I have carried on one campaign of truth across the country. I am going to carry on another. This time there must be a tour by many, and all the members of Parliament must be included. If I find the same reception in the country that I have found here, then there will again be grand victories for the Socialist Party.

(*Le Monde*, May 6, 1958, p. 2)

OPEN LETTER TO M. GUY MOLLET, SECRETARY-GENERAL OF THE SFIO

Mister President:

On February 9, 1956, in Algiers, after commenting on the open letter that I had deemed it necessary to write you, a letter by which I informed you of the Algerians' desperation at feeling themselves abandoned, you asked me to publish immediately the declaration you then made to me: "If Algeria is lost to France there would be no more of Algeria, but there would be no more of France."

That evening at the microphone of Radio Algiers, addressing yourself first to the Europeans, you expressed yourself in these terms: "You, Europeans, some people have sought to give you the reputation of colonialists. I do not share this view. Doubtless there is a small egotistical minority among you who bitterly defend their own interests and political positions. They have taken their precautions and willingly choose the most outrageous political alternatives.

"Alas, they are behind the extremist organizations and the shock troops some hope to mount against the government of the Republic. It is they who are abusing the good sense of patriotic men for interests that are in no ways French.

"There is also the immense mass of the European population: farmers, workers, employees, shopkeepers, teachers, doctors, the men who have settled in Algeria for several generations, who have their families, their homes, their dead. I HAVE HEARD THEIR VOICE AS ONE FROM THE TIME OF MY ARRIVAL AND I HAVE BEEN TRANSFORMED BY IT. For them Algeria is the most beautiful country in the world, it is their little country, that which is held most dear. Outside Algeria they cannot live. They see France only through Algeria.

"These men, you who listen to me, believed that France would abandon them. I have understood their despair, that profound despair which has stifled their whole being. That is why I tell you calmly that, even if I suffered from them, Monday's unhappy demonstrations contained a healthy aspect. For many they were the means of affirming their attachment to France and their anguish at being abandoned by France. If that is what the great majority wished to make understood, let them know that they have been heard. FRANCE WILL REMAIN PRESENT IN ALGERIA. THE BONDS BETWEEN THE MAINLAND AND ALGERIA ARE INDISSOLUBLE.

"The French-Moslem community is and will remain a community without rifts. Such is the will of the government. Such is the will of the overwhelming majority of the parliament. Such is the will of France."

To the Moslems you then said:

"You too have your extremists. Among you there is a handful of FANATICS AND CRIMINALS WHO TAKE THEIR ORDERS FROM OUTSIDE ALGERIA AND SERVE INTERESTS THAT ARE IN NO WAYS ALGERIAN. There are also those whom poverty has made susceptible to these extremists' propaganda, who have been misled. I do not recognize you among them. I turn toward you, the immense mass of the Moslem people who are hesitant, who are anxious, who are suffering. You hesitate, my Moslem friends, because you doubt French intentions. You have feared that you will be abandoned. I tell you clearly that there has never been any question of it. THERE NEVER SHALL BE ANY QUESTION OF IT. The government is fighting; France is fighting to stay in Algeria and it will stay. There is a future for Algeria only with France. What would France be without Algeria? What would become of Algeria without France? Are you anxious? You fear all extremists. I declare to you simply that order and justice shall be maintained. French power is not a vain term. Justice will be applied rigorously, rapidly, and calmly, equally for all."

And you ended your address with these words:

"Tomorrow I will greet the Resident Minister in Algiers, my friend Robert Lacoste. I know him. He is a loyal and courageous man who has shown his mettle. I WILL BE TOTALLY ANSWERABLE FOR HIM. YOU CAN DEPEND ON HIM AS ON MYSELF."

In these very days, on the morrow of M. Gaillard's fall, after informing you of the anguish with which I was filled by the growing international attention paid to the Algerian question I recalled to you your declaration of Algiers and did not fail to tell you what the man on the street is thinking, the man who incarnates real French good sense —that the salvation of Algeria and France demands a truce among the parties in order to form a government of public safety.

You answered me that this truce among the parties seemed impossible to realize because of the attitude of the moderates. They claim, you said, that they want to keep Algeria French but refuse to agree to the taxes that her salvation requires; and in this regard you expressed regrets in my presence that the Algerian war "has been financed by the Ramadier loan and not by taxes." I then observed to you how unjust it was to discredit the moderates with this charge.

It is unfortunately true, I added, that some among you, as in every party including yours, are ready to abandon our African province on condition that their sacrifice is not too visible, but most are ready to ask the necessary sacrifices of the taxpayers. You will recall, I think, that I made clear to you that if financial reasons alone were really those that made a party truce impossible my friends and I would not hesitate to participate actively in sweeping away the sand that keeps the machine from turning.

Alas, I realize once again the extent of my illusions. The accusations raised against the moderates have only one pretext—to throw up a smokescreen that will cover your party's retreat.

It is no secret to anyone, however, that this strategic withdrawal has as its objective only the elimination of Robert Lacoste from Algeria. This man, it is true, is becoming intolerable to the SFIO. Did he not announce his fears of a diplomatic Dien-Bien-Phu before the last Socialist national council at Puteaux? And for troubling on this occasion, as at others, the serenity of the party members, who dream of goodness knows what miraculous solution, did he not merit the implicit disavowal with which you have associated yourself? "I will be totally answerable for him," you proclaimed in Algiers two years ago. Well, it would be more loyal to confess now that you are so no longer; and that under your party's pressures—made even more acute by the decisions of the London conference of the Socialist International—you have deliberately opted for socialist "doctrine" to the detriment of the preservation of Algeria.

For, finally, given the subversive war waged against us, have you measured the psychological consequences of your decision? Do you believe that in adopting this attitude you are strengthening the confidence of the Europeans and Moslems in Algeria to whom you in fact took an oath that France would never abandon them?

Quite to the contrary, we hear from all sides that once again the European and the Moslem populations are beginning to doubt French will. As in February 1956, their disarray is expressed by the painful question you know well, since you answered it then better than you are answering it today: Is France going to abandon us? And yet barely a few days ago, as Robert Lacoste left the office of M. Pleven he indirectly gave you this advice: "France needs only a clear and unfailing determination in order to swing the balance in our favor." Did you shut your ears to this sort of warning?

Had you already condemned M. Robert Lacoste secretly—as might be further suggested by the silence you were confined to before the fall of M. Gaillard, that is, at the moment when you would have had to arbitrate between the diplomatic theses of M. Pineau and exactly the opposite ones of the Minister for Algeria? I do not know. Whatever the case, you would agree that if a party truce is impossible at least a truce on hypocrisy is required. At least have the courage, Mr. President, to say outright that your party no longer rejects a diplomatic Dien-Bien-Phu, which the Algerians fear along with M. Lacoste but which they shall never accept. Never, I assure you, and no more than the soldiers would accept it to whom you have entrusted the protection of a national territory, and who listening to you believe in the sacred character of their mission.

Let us resume, M. President. No one is deceived either in Algeria or in metropolitan France: the Algerian war would long be over if the diplomacy of M. Pineau had aligned with the policy of M. Lacoste. But neither you nor your successors could proceed or wanted to proceed to this union, however indispensable. And quite, quite gently you have gone far enough to view as really beneficial those false "good offices" that are leading us directly—you have read, I imagine, the American press, and the disclosures of Mr. Robert Murphy have not escaped you—to the internationalization of the Algerian problem, in other words to a discreet whitewash of defeat.

But if you've gone so far, better not to hide it. Pierre Charpy reports in *Paris-Presse* that M. Robert Lacoste suggested to a private Socialist meeting: "If today the Socialist Party wants to change its Algerian policy, say so, say it clearly, say it quickly; do not shed the blood of our soldiers for nothing a day longer." There is honest language.

You must hear it, Mr. President, and echo it. For every Frenchman who has followed you for two years has the right to know why, given circumstances graver than ever before, the Guy Mollet of May '58 does not become again the Guy Mollet of February '56.

Alain de Sérigny
(*L'Écho d'Alger*, May 6, 1958, pp. 1, 12)

STATEMENT BY PREMIER-DESIGNATE RENÉ PLEVEN, MAY 6, 1958, 1:20 A.M.

The President of the Republic has summoned me in order to inform me that after having consulted a certain number of political personalities in regard to the new situation created by the Socialist Party's decision against further participation in any government, he has taken the decision to designate me again to form a government, despite my earlier declining.

I declared to the President of the Republic that even if I were disposed to set aside all personal preoccupations, I could not compromise on what seems to me indispensable in order for the new government to have the means to act efficaciously and to survive. I also informed the President of the Republic that I would return to see him tomorrow [May 6] at 6 p.m. and that I would give him a positive answer if the discussions I have scheduled with various individuals furnish me the necessary assurances.

(*Le Figaro*, May 6, 1958, p. 15)

STATEMENT BY GUY MOLLET AFTER A ONE-HOUR CONVERSATION WITH PREMIER-DESIGNATE RENÉ PLEVEN, MAY 6, 1958

As he declared previously, President Pleven wants to demand of the Assembly—if it comes to an investiture—special powers relating to the economy and, naturally, Algeria, as well as a guarantee of duration, without so far specifying their importance in other respects. This morning he wanted to know the extent to which the Socialist group, after the recent declarations of Puteaux, could furnish its support in this matter. I could only confirm to M. René Pleven the SFIO's will to support him. I see nothing in the proposals made to me this morning which would be in contradiction with our readiness to offer support.

(*Le Monde*, May 7, 1958, p. 1)

By Frank Kelley

Pierre Pflimlin, fifty-one-year-old lawyer from Alsace who is outgoing Finance Minister and prominent in the Catholic (MRP) Party, accepted last night from President René Coty a mandate to try to form a new government for France. . . .

M. Pleven, with a prospective Cabinet lined up and ready to go before the National Assembly today to seek the customary vote into office after outlining his program, gave up in obvious disgust when the Radical-Socialist Party decided to pull three members out of the Pleven line-up because a fourth and "rebel" Radical, André Morice, advocate of a tough policy in Algeria, was to be named Defense Minister once more.

President René Coty, watching the clock tick toward the fourth week of his nation's political void, received M. Pleven's final rejection with displeasure but understanding. . . .

(New York *Herald Tribune*, European Edition, May 9, 1958)

STATEMENT OF PREMIER-DESIGNATE PIERRE PFLIMLIN,
MAY 8, 1958, 11:40 P.M.

The President of the Republic has entrusted me with the task of forming a government. I shall be investigating the possibility of uniting a team of Frenchmen and a majority around a specific program of action. All of us are taking part in the search for a formula calculated to realize a union of the parties. At present I think it is no longer an hour for compromises. I think that what matters is that with a clear view of the realities, France be able to choose her destiny. It is therefore important to seek a program of action on the basis of the concrete facts in the domestic area, in Africa, and in the world. From tomorrow I will be working toward that program, and I will then convey my answer to the President of the Republic.

(*Le Monde*, May 10, 1958, p. 2)

The present crisis shows that the political parties are profoundly divided over the Algerian question. The press implies that the abandonment of Algeria will be considered in the course of a diplomatic process which will begin in negotiations with a view toward a "cease-fire." I allow myself to recall to you my conversation with M. Pleven, in the course of which I pointed out explicitly that the clauses of a "cease-fire" could be only these: "In conformity with her appeal for a 'cease-fire' France invites the rebels in Algeria to deliver up their arms and guarantees them, under a generous amnesty, their return to the embrace of the renewed French-Moslem community."

The army in Algeria is troubled by its feeling of responsibility:

in regard to the men who are fighting and risking a worthless sacrifice if the national legislature has not resolved to preserve a French Algeria, as the preamble of the *loi-cadre* stipulates;

in regard to the French population inland, which feels itself abandoned, and to the Moslem Frenchmen, more numerous with each day, who have again given their trust to France, confident in our repeated promises never to abandon them.

The French army would unanimously feel the abandonment of this national patrimony to be an outrage. It would be impossible to foretell its despairing reaction.

I ask you kindly to call the attention of the President of the Republic to our anguish, which only a government firmly resolved to maintain our flag in Algeria could blot out.

(*L'Anneé Politique*, 1958, 529–30)

Transcript of the Trial of General Raoul Salan, May 1962 (Excerpts)*

HEARING OF MAY 17, 1962. TESTIMONY OF GENERAL JACQUES ALLARD, GENERAL IN ACTIVE SERVICE.

M. TIXIER-VIGNANCOUR (*lawyer for the defense*): I would like to ask General Allard whether he took part, with General Salan, in the drawing up of a telegram which the latter sent to President Coty on May 7. . . .

I would like to ask General Allard whether he remembers which persons were present when this telegram was written, what the substance of the telegram was, and whether he can tell us about the conversation between General Salan and M. Robert Lacoste.

GENERAL ALLARD: I would like to say first of all that the telegram in question was drawn up on May 9, not on May 7. On May 9, the information we received on the situation—that is, the exhaustion of the civilian population and also the fears that had arisen in the army —was disquieting.

We were in the middle of a ministerial crisis; I went to see General Salan and said to him, "We have to do something." He agreed and said: "We have to report this to someone, but to whom? To the highest authority of the state, that is the President of the Republic, the only one in the right position because the others preside only over current business." Thus the telegram was written under the direction of General Salan in his office with General Jouhaud on his right and myself on his left. All three of us participated in writing this telegram whose content is known to everyone.

It was General Salan who judged it necessary to repeat in the first part of the telegram what he had told M. Pleven a few days before in Paris about the only acceptable conditions in his mind for a cease-fire. Concerning the meeting of General Salan and M. Lacoste on the evening of the ninth, I was not there in person. I knew that M. Lacoste had given his full agreement to General Salan that the telegram would be sent by the fastest route, using General Ely as an intermediary, to be delivered to M. Coty that very night.

Le Procès de Raoul Salan, Compte Rendu Stenographique (Paris, 1962), 187–9. From the series "Les Grands Procès Contemporains," under the direction of Maître Maurice Garçon of the Académie Française, reprinted by permission of the publisher, Éditions Albin Michel, Paris.

*[General Salan was being tried on charges connected with the generals' revolt in Algiers in April 1961 (See below, pp. 390ff.) and with the terrorist activities of the underground Secret Army Organization (OAS)—Eds.]

M. TIXIER-VIGNANCOUR: On May 11, General, there was a meeting at the office of M. Maisonneuve with M. Mairey* who was sent by M. Pflimlin. Could you tell the High Court the tenor of this conversation?

GENERAL ALLARD: I was, in fact, called by General Salan to the office of M. Maisonneuve. M. Lacoste was in Paris; M. Mairey was there. He was, I believe, the personal secretary of M. Pflimlin and was instructed to come and see how the declaration of investiture which M. Pflimlin proposed would sit, so to speak, with people in Algeria.

I believe he came especially to see the reaction of the responsible leaders, especially to the article dealing with Algeria.

The text was read by M. Mairey, and I ought to say that we immediately raised objections of the most serious nature. The passage of the ministerial declaration more or less basically reproduced the one which appeared in a newspaper, I believe an Alsatian one, and had been reprinted in the Algerian papers a few days before, arousing a great surge of emotion not only among the civilian population but in the army as well. It was a question of the good offices of Tunisia and Morocco; at bottom it was a question of negotiations, and we told M. Mairey that this truly was not acceptable and that if this passage were left in he could expect grave and very harsh reactions from the civilian population.

General Salan outlined the situation in Algeria to him. M. Mairey took no notice. The meeting lasted about an hour. M. Maisonneuve was there just about all the time; General Jouhaud, Admiral Auboyneau, General Salan, and myself were also present.

M. TIXIER-VIGNANCOUR: And General Dulac?

GENERAL ALLARD: General Dulac must have been there.

M. TIXIER-VIGNANCOUR: Thank you, General. I would like to ask you the same question I asked General Valluy: do you understand, in light of the accusations against your former commander before the High Military Court, the motivation and intentions of General Salan? . . .

GENERAL ALLARD: I believe that to answer this question one has to think of all that has been demanded of the French army for the last twenty years. When one thinks of the amount of self-denial, of sacrifice, of devotion, of responsibilities which have been demanded of us throughout the world for the honor of France and the French flag, and that the tombs of our sons, of our troops, and of our comrades, and of the victories we have won—that all that has been for nought, that we have been deprived of all that.

*[Pflimlin's envoy was actually M. René Paira.—Eds.]

SOLEMN APPEAL OF THE VIGILANCE COMMITTEE TO THE ALGERIAN POPULATION, MAY 10, 1958

Faced with the imminent constitution of an incontestable government of abandonment, the Vigilance Committee representing the veterans' associations, patriotic groups, and political parties which organized the demonstration of April 26, 1958, demands that the entire population of Algiers consider itself in a state of mobilization in the service of Algeria.

Frenchmen of Algeria, Europeans and Moslems, the national recovery must come from Algeria and for the second time in fifteen years Algeria will save France.

On Tuesday, May 13, at 1 p.m. all activity will cease in the city. The entire population of our communities will assemble en masse on the Plateau des Glières at 3 p.m. to demonstrate its opposition to an unacceptable government, at the same hour that the National Assembly will be meeting.

(L'Écho d'Alger, May 11–12, 1958, p. 3)

WE MUST FIND A WAY OUT

As I wrote yesterday in *Dimanche Matin*, the deterioration of our policies cannot be tolerated a minute longer.

We must find a way out. There is not a day, not an hour to lose. It is no longer possible for a system of government to be preserved in which "doses" of one party and another have been administered in search of a utopian equilibrium, but only to produce, since that bloody All Saint's Day of 1954, ministerial teams fated to impotence—ministerial teams where contradictory tendencies confront one another, as even yesterday in the Gaillard cabinet, a foreign policy à la Christian Pineau was in constant opposition to the French policy in Algeria of M. Robert Lacoste; ministerial teams in which the national defense is constantly stabbed from behind, from the home front, by the horde of sell-outs, defeatists, and demagogues of negotiation and capitulation—more murderous than thousands of fellagha and terrorists.

We must find a way out. . . . It is no longer possible to preserve this monstrously absurd paradox: to entrust the formation of a government to M. Pierre Pflimlin, who advocates a program that borders

216

on the *Mendésiste* views of pulling out of Algeria—and this after the ministry of M. Félix Gaillard was brought down by a massive majority of men like Lacoste, Bidault, Soustelle, Duchet, and Morice, determined to preserve Algeria forever from the menace of foreign interference acting in more or less open collusion with the FLN or its allies.

We must find a way out. We can prolong no longer such a deteriorating situation, in which the rebels can boast with audacity of a new crime: the assassination of three French soldiers kidnapped from French territory in Algeria with the aid of Tunisia.

For weeks, even for months, with all of French Algeria deprived of representation in the National Assembly, we have tried to make the voice of reason heard. For weeks and for months we have tried to make Parliament understand that this is no longer the time for Byzantine party struggles, for petty disputes, for personal ostracisms; that the time has come to form a government of public safety above the parties and their miserable quarrels, the only one which today can save the nation from the disaster that the loss of French Algeria would mean for it and for the West.

For weeks and for months we have cried in vain. All of France has been exhausted by the political formulas of a system powerless to reform itself. It has been proven and verified that despite all the fine declarations of prime ministers, the successive governments have been incapable of uniting or acting effectively enough to resolve the Algerian question.

This is why I appealed yesterday to General de Gaulle to break his silence.

I turn to him because he embodies passionate devotion solely to his homeland, to the grandeur of France. Because I am convinced that if he speaks, he will speak with an authority that no one can contest and will finally set the deputies in line with the country, which does not want to lose Algeria. Because I am convinced that he can lead our political figures, united around him in a party truce, in order to restore a policy worthy of France. Because I am convinced that this soldier will never permit the sacrifices of our soldiers in Algeria to have been in vain.

It is all the more necessary for General de Gaulle to speak, since certain politicians who would not hesitate to "liquidate" Algeria if they were in power, are taking advantage of his silence to be the interpreters of his thought.

This is not the time to bring up old responsibilities or personal grudges from the time of the Committee for the Liberation of Algeria and from which I myself am not exempt.

We must find "a way out." We must save our nation in danger.

Before this imperative, nothing else can matter. I see only one solution. I have stated it, ready to consider another if I am sure it will be better.

Alain de Sérigny

(*L'Écho d'Alger*, May 11–12, 1958, p. 1)

TELEGRAM FROM THE UNION FOR THE PRESERVATION AND RENEWAL OF FRENCH ALGERIA (USRAF-ALGÉRIE) TO ANTOINE PINAY, PRESIDENT OF THE INDEPENDENTS IN THE NATIONAL ASSEMBLY, MAY 10, 1958

At no price could we accept a Pflimlin government; authorship of newspaper articles, notably in the *Nouvel Alsacien*, leaves no doubt of his intentions Stop We implore you to dissociate yourself from policy of abandonment that he embodies. Respectfully yours.

TELEGRAM FROM THE UNIVERSITY MOVEMENT FOR THE MAIN-TENANCE OF FRENCH SOVEREIGNTY IN ALGERIA TO ANTOINE PINAY

French Algerians fiercely opposed to Pflimlin government Stop Pflimlin newspaper articles and declarations leave no doubt on intentions of liquidation for French Algeria Stop We implore you to oppose policy of President-Designate. Respectfully yours.

(*L'Écho d'Alger*, May 11–12, 1958, p. 3)

LIST OF MINISTERS IN THE PROPOSED PFLIMLIN GOVERNMENT, MAY 12, 1958

President of the Council   Pierre Pflimlin, MRP*
Minister of State   Houphouet-Boigny, UDSR-RDA*
Foreign Affairs   René Pleven, UDSR
Justice   Robert Lecourt, MRP**
Interior   Maurice Faure, Radical Socialist*

Finance and Economic Affairs   Edgar Faure, RGR
Algeria   André Mutter, Independent
Sahara   Corniglion-Molinier, RGR
National Defense   De Chevigné, MRP
National Education   Senator Jacques Bordeneuve, Radical
Overseas France   André Colin, MRP
Industry and Commerce   Ribeyre, Independent**
Public Works   Edouard Bonnefous, UDSR**
Labor   Bacon, MRP**
Agriculture   Boscary-Monsservin, Independent**
Housing   Garet, Independent**
Public Health   André Maroselli, Radical
Veterans' Affairs   Vincent Badie, Democratic Left
* Held office in the Gaillard cabinet in a different position.
**Held office in the Gaillard cabinet in the same position.

(*Le Monde*, May 13, 1958, p. 2)

PIOUS HOMAGE TO THE MEMORY OF THE THREE YOUNG FRENCH
SOLDIERS COWARDLY ASSASSINATED IN TUNISIA BY THE FLN

MASS ASSEMBLY IN ALGIERS. . . .

From all points of the horizon in France and abroad, the indignation
of the civilized world is mounting against the new crime perpetrated
in Tunisia by the FLN: the assassination of three military prisoners,
Sergeant Richomme and soldiers Decourteix and Feuillebois.

Throughout Algeria, as on the mainland, under the auspices of the
Action and Unity Committee of the veterans and Algerian reserve
cadres, mass public ceremonies will take place this evening at 6 p.m.
in a calm and dignity appropriate to the gravity of the event.

In Algiers, as everywhere on the mainland and in Algeria, this pious
homage to the memory of the three martyrs will be expressed before
the monument to the dead at 6 p.m. At the same hour at Bône (in
a ceremony we will cover) the French army will posthumously confer
the military medal and the cross of military valor with palms on the
three victims of FLN barbarism.

Furthermore, a mass demonstration will take place as announced
on the Plateau des Glières in order to express Algeria's French will
that a government of public safety be constituted. But the hour originally planned has been changed. . . .

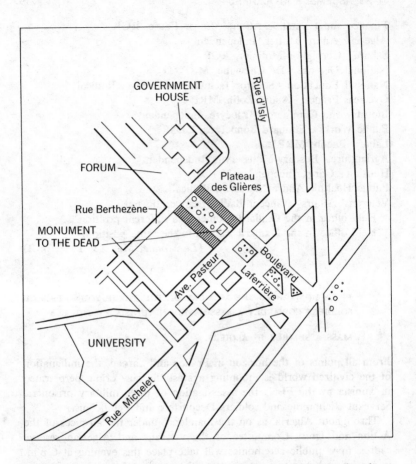

The demonstration planned for this afternoon at 1 p.m. has been moved to 5 p.m. for practical considerations. The orders for the strike are still to be maintained from 1 to 8 p.m., and the populace is invited to make arrangements that will enable them to be present at 5 p.m. on the Plateau des Glières (below the Laferrière Gardens).

It is understood that the strike order will be rigorously applied to all public establishments (offices, restaurants, cafés, cinemas, industries, commercial establishments, public and private transport, etc. . . .).

It goes without saying that the security services will be assured for every sector of activity.

All Frenchmen concerned with keeping Algeria French will make it an imperious duty to answer the appeal of the Vigilance Committee. . . .

(*L'Écho d'Alger*, May 13, 1958, p. 12)

A HISTORIC DAY YESTERDAY AT ALGIERS

THE DEMONSTRATORS OCCUPY THE MINISTRY FOR ALGERIA

A CIVILIAN AND MILITARY COMMITTEE OF PUBLIC SAFETY IS CONSTITUTED UNDER THE PRESIDENCY OF GENERAL MASSU

From 1:30 p.m. the physiognomy of the streets of Algiers had taken on a strange appearance. Traffic was light, secondary arteries practically deserted.

Following the order issued by the Vigilance Committee, all stores, offices, workshops, warehouses were closed. Toward 1:30 employees began to gather on the sidewalks in front of some establishments before making for the center of town.

At Chemin Yusuf: the gates of the Transit Authority depot are locked, the sheds crammed with streetcars, buses, trolley-buses. Groups of transit workers in front of the gates, many wearing tri-color ribbons on their jackets or shirts. Everywhere in the city are encountered many young men wearing cockades.

In the upper town the majority of stores and shops are likewise closed. . . .

At 2:30 a great many young men, young women, and boys collect in front of the stores on the Rue Michelet. A little later they have the opportunity to applaud a first procession of a few hundred persons, climbing the Rue Michelet from the direction of Bresson Square. The first *Marseillaise* is then struck up and the slogan "Algérie française" rings out.

This procession, making for the Place Hoche and passing the American cultural center, across from the Notre Dame library, answers "Algérie française," and marks time on the pavement. At this instant some groups rush at the display windows, shatter them with rocks, while others enter the premises.

Immediately the library is rushed and sacked, and its books are strewn over the surface of the Rue Michelet.

At 3:25, emerging from the Chasseriau slope and entering the Rue

Richelieu, there arrive delegations carrying flags and standards on which one may read Fort-de-l'Eau, Maison-Blanche, etc.

At the same moment pamphlets are thrown from automobiles at the Carrefour de l'Agha.

3:35. Coming from Rue Hoche via Boulevard Victor-Hugo and issuing forth onto the Rue Michelet, thousands of men and women of all ages follow a flag reading "Algérie française, against the whole world." It is the procession of the high schools.

From the Rue Drouillet the Rue Michelet offers the vista of a colorful human stream, from which flags and banners emerge. It is nearly impossible to move forward from the Place Foch. The road is completely obstructed by young men sitting on the pavement, while the crowd peacefully enters the gardens of the university, where the gates have been reopened, to await 5:00.

Actually it is only 3:50. For the first time there appear four truck-loads of republican guards and "paras" of the Third Colonial Parachute Regiment, who alight in front of the American cultural center where a cordon of police is already stationed.

It is now 4:00, and the terraced grounds of the monument to the dead are covered with people, as are the stairways surrounding them.

Several thousand persons sing the *Marseillaise* while the delegations from Coléa, from Rivet—carrying a sign on which is written "Rivet wants to remain French"—and from the Blida USRAF move forward.

At 4:10 some young men leave the grounds around the monument, cross the Rue Berthezène and station themselves on the steps of the Forum. Little by little they collect together and reach the second landing of the monumental stairway. On the esplanade in front of the entrance of the Ministry for Algeria are assembled fifteen cars and five jeeps full of CRS.

At one point government employees appear at the windows and are hissed by the demonstrators. A detachment of CRS, helmeted and carrying weapons, then takes up position at the top of the steps.

But the young men immediately mass again on the Rue Berthezène and move in procession toward the Avenue Pasteur. The arrival of a delegation of Moslem war veterans has fortunately created a diversion. The crowd massed on the sidewalks has discovered the Moslem color guard, which is wildly acclaimed. . . .

At 4:30 three hundred veterans representing more than twenty associations assemble behind their flags at Bastion XV. . . .

A veritable human tide submerges the Plateau des Glières. How can one estimate this roaring mass—they are more than one hundred thousand—which has taken up position on the grounds and on public buildings and which blocks every line of entry to the monument to the dead?

A loudspeaker from the newspaper *Bled* emits patriotic slogans. The crowd repeats, "Algérie française," and hoots at the names of Mauriac, Coty, Pflimlin, Mendès, Chevallier. . . .

It acclaims the watchwords issued by the leaders: "Any decisions which do not originate in a government of public safety will be considered to be null. . . . The people will only obey a government which achieves the unity of all the peoples of the French Union. . . ."

But the veterans clear a way for themselves. Young men have volunteered spontaneously to see that order is kept. Joining hands they open the way for the procession, at the head of which is marching a prominent disabled veteran: M. Mouchan.

Two automobiles equipped with amplifiers precede the flags. A microphone sounds: "European and Moslem veterans, side by side as at the front, desire to render honors to the three assassinated soldiers: Sergeant Richomme, Privates Decourteix and Feuillebois. . . ."

Slowly the flags climb as far as the flame of remembrance. The crowd is everywhere, even on the monument to the dead. Clusters of human beings cling to the iron railings. A thousand flags are waved from the balconies. At the monument to the dead, where Moslem *harkis* stand guard, MM. Burckhardt, Laquière, Gazagne, de Sérigny, and others have preceded the delegations. Two wreaths are laid, one by the veterans, the other by the railway workers "in homage to three martyrs," of whom one is the son of a railwayman of France.

The flags are then lowered. A minute of silence is observed on the Plateau des Glières. It is impressive, this immense crowd which suddenly becomes silent.

But then the *Marseillaise* is taken up again. Amid the noise of the cries of "Algérie française!" and "The army to power" one hears the strains of military music. Now the government authorities are arriving in their turn. Only with great difficulty do the air force band, a detachment from the cavalry school and the color guard of the 45th Communications get to take their places on the Avenue Pasteur.

It is 5:55. The confusion is indescribable. The crowd is roaring, "The army to power." At this moment waves of tear gas reach the foot of the avenue, blinding everyone. From the stairways of the Forum behind the monument to the dead the CRS have stepped into action.

On the Avenue Pasteur during this time sirens from traffic jeeps have opened a passage through the crowd. They precede the black sedan of General Salan, who is accompanied by General Jouhaud, Admiral Auboyneau, Generals Allard and Massu, and Prefect Serge Baret.

An immense outcry is raised, drowning out the ordinary sounds. With great difficulty and only with the help of military police, the official cortege passes through the entrance of the square and moves to the base of the monument, where a simple wreath of roses is placed.

The sound of "*Aux Champs*" and of the *Marseillaise* is hardly audible, so strongly has the enthusiasm of the crowd burst forth.

New cries are heard as the cortege descends: "Massu to power! Massu to power!"

The first clashes occur around 6:15, as General Salan and the official cortege descend, amidst the acclamation of the crowd, from the monument to the dead to rejoin the district general staff on foot. A sudden cry bursts forth from the multitude and is immediately taken up by a loudspeaker: "The CRS have provoked us without any violence on our part. Everyone to Government House. We'll overtake them up there." A succession of major collisions was to be the consequence of this first engagement between CRS and demonstrators, which appeared mild, all considered. What exactly happened to start with? It seems that the young demonstrators wanted to "march" on Government House. They ran into the CRS who were screened from view on the stairways of the Forum. The demonstrators say a tear gas grenade burst, wounding a young man.

From 6:15 on compact groups of young men moved off for the assault on Government House. The first clash set them against the CRS, few enough in number, who were attacked with stones. The CRS were driven back to the entrance gates. The gates were shut. They soon had to give way under the ramming of a truck transformed into a bulldozer. While the CRS were pursued into the court of honor by the increasing number of demonstrators, the guards, quickly outflanked, left the way free. The demonstrators first invaded the library, where windows were smashed and books thrown to the ground and torn up. The demonstrators, mostly very young and now numbering a hundred, spread through the floors of the building and attacked the archives. The first appearance of flames brought on the firemen. For more than an hour the papers hurled through the windows floated at the mercy of the wind and fell to the Forum.

There, some sixty cars had already been seriously damaged. Windows were smashed, tires punctured, fenders dented. Toward 6:45

the demonstrators, brandishing their flag, reached the top floors of Government House, from which they called to the densely massed crowd on the Forum, which acclaimed them. They lowered the tri-color flag of Government House, then ran up the flags they were carrying. In the hall of Government House the statue of the Republic was pulled from its base and carried away.

Colonel Ducourneau, chief of the military cabinet of the Minister for Algeria, vainly tried to calm spirits from the balcony of the second floor. He could not make his voice heard. Then seizing a blackboard which he brandished above the crowd, he wrote in chalk: "I have just telephoned Paris. We have demanded a government of public safety." Then on the other side of the blackboard: "The army is the guarantee of a French Algeria."

The colonel was applauded, but the demonstrators did not stop. Toward 7:35, amid the cries and roars of the excited crowd, Generals Salan, Allard, and Massu arrived in a car.

At 7:00 the crowd filled the Forum in front of Government House. Scarcely contained, it may be imagined, by the cordons of parachute troops of the 3rd CPR, some wearing the famous Bigeard caps, close to thirty thousand persons, packed tightly together, having come from all sides, from the monument to the dead and the adjacent streets, force the barriers and the cries start again: "Algérie française!," "The army to power," "Soustelle with us." The first lines of demonstrators had just reached the gates of Government House when tear gas gre-nades, thrown by guards from inside Government House, exploded.

After a short retreat there was a new charge. Colonel Ducourneau's appeals for calm remained without effect, and the gates were broken open by a truck taken by storm by the young men and driven up to the front steps. Nothing more could dam this tidal wave.

Invading the great hall of Government House they unbolted the statue of the Republic from its base; borne aloft by four men it was shown to the crowd, carried around, and acclaimed.

The Government House officials who had not complied with the call for a strike witnessed the invasion of their offices.

Chairs were sent immediately flying and bundles of papers were thrown out the windows. Telephone wires were cut, corridors flooded, windows smashed.

Nothing more resisted this immense fit of wrath, which only the presence of a chief and the constitution of a Committee of Public Safety could calm.

The latter was formed on the spot, in order to avoid bloodshed and to prevent this demonstration of the entire populace from turning into a riot.

This committee, which yesterday evening at 8:45 took the name of the Combined Civil and Military Committee of Public Safety, was presided over by General Massu, seconded by Colonel Trinquier of the 3rd CPR, Colonel Thomazo, deputy to the commanding general of the army corps of Algiers, and Colonel Ducasse. Twelve civilians formed the liaison between the military authorities and the people of Algiers. General Massu came out onto the balcony and urged calm to the crowd, which acclaimed him to the point of delirium.

He read the first proclamation of the committee, which was to stay in charge in Algiers while awaiting the formation of a government of public safety in Paris.

The demonstrators then withdrew from Government House, but not from the Forum, where they settled down to pass the night waiting for the formation of a government of public safety in Paris. Already it was rumored that Jacques Soustelle was returning to Algiers, and when a plane passed over the city around 11:30 the crowd, convinced that it was Jacques Soustelle who was arriving, got ready to give him a reception to equal the one accorded him two years previously at his departure.

(*L'Écho d'Alger*, May 14, 1958, pp. 6, 12)

TELEGRAM FROM GENERAL MASSU TO PRESIDENT OF THE REPUBLIC COTY, MAY 13, 1958

We inform you of the creation of a civilian and military committee of public safety at Algiers, presided over by General Massu, in consideration of the seriousness of the situation and the absolute necessity of maintaining order and avoiding all bloodshed. This committee vigilantly awaits the creation of a government of public safety, alone capable of preserving Algeria as an integral part of metropolitan France.

(*L'Écho d'Alger*, May 14, 1958, p. 12)

Assemblée Nationale, Session of May 13, 1958

M. PIERRE PFLIMLIN, PRESIDENT-DESIGNATE OF THE COUNCIL: Ladies and gentlemen, once again, while our army is fighting, while an acute crisis of the franc threatens to suffocate our economy, and while hostile forces crystallize against us throughout the world without our being able to rely on our friends, a lapse of authority has paralyzed the state.

Three times in less than a year, the efforts of the nation have been counteracted by three ministerial crises. Out of twelve months, the Republic has spent three without leadership and without policy, during a time when the rhythm of history is accelerating, and in a world which no longer waits for our decisions to go its way.

The spectacle of this instability is unworthy of a people whose energies are still intact and which remains capable of sacrifices for the grandeur of the country. It has destroyed the attachment of Frenchmen to the regime to a really dangerous degree of disaffection. The degradation of our institutions menaces the very existence of the Republic. It is becoming clear that our liberties will only be safe when authority, force and prestige again become permanent attributes of power. (*Applause in the center.*)

This demand is a prerequisite for the success of any policy. Action without duration, however correct the intent may be, remains an impulse without a future, a passing fancy. Governments begin to die at the moment they are born, and too often the energies which they should use to propel the nation toward its destiny, are wasted in staving off the fall of the regime.

I have no illusions that the government which has been formed today can escape the precariousness of those which have preceded it. In the context of institutions as they are, it is vain for a new government to expect to last very long. Therefore this government doesn't want a long life for its own sake, but it wants to create conditions for the future by reforming institutions so that governments can last. (*Applause from the center and some benches of the left.*)

The first step has been taken in this direction. The National Assembly has passed a bill revising several articles of the Constitution. This reform, as important as it may be, is not sufficient. The government will request that the revision be extended to other articles of the Constitution, to create a coherent body of provisions reinforcing the

Journal Officiel, Débats Parlementairés, Assemblée Nationale, 1957–58, 2253–5, 2258, 2271–3.

executive power. To this effect it will present a proposed resolution and demand its adoption as soon as possible.

I have in mind especially the revision of Article 13 of the Constitution. On numerous occasions already, Parliament has given the government a more or less extensive delegation of powers. It has become common to vote emergency legislation which is limited to establishing principles, leaving a margin of interpretation to the governments for their implementation.

I propose that we make the law correspond to the fact, by permitting Parliament to give the government long-term powers to implement a definite program. (Very good! Very good! *from several benches of the center.*) Thereby a real compact of the majority could be concluded which could even become a permanent basis for legislation.

One of the essential causes of the instability of ministries is the fact that a government can be brought down by a momentary alliance of minorities which are opposed to one another and cannot unite to produce a positive majority. To remedy this situation, the government will ask that a system of constructive censure motions be introduced into the Constitution, which will oblige the authors of a censure motion to propose a program of government and to nominate a President of the Council. This reform will permit a correct functioning of the parliamentary regime and will restore to the concept of the majority, which is the cornerstone of every democracy, its real meaning.

Just as urgent is the reform of the provisions in the Constitution concerning the French Union. We have to put our Constitution in accord with developments set in motion in the overseas territories by emergency legislation. These developments prove that, thanks to the wisdom and the moderation of their elites, our overseas territories can achieve their legitimate aspirations peacefully and build modern, democratic states. The reform of Title VIII will be preceded by a consultation of the representatives of the populations. The new provisions will strive to permit the territories to take new steps toward democratic control of their own affairs by creating, in accord with them, the Franco-African Community, composed of organs which will safeguard and foster common interest. . . .

In Algeria, the government of France can have no other objective than to re-establish peace. But to attain this objective there is no other path than through effort.

This is why the government holds that its first duty is to ask the nation for new sacrifices. The means at the disposition of the command will be increased by providing the army with the necessary men and supplies. I know that in many families this decision will be felt harshly. But I am sure that Frenchmen will understand that it is better to bring the hour of peace nearer by a supreme effort than to prolong indefinitely a drama which weighs heavily on the conscience of France.

The rebellion would long ago have been without means and without hope if it had not received external aid whose source we know all too well. We have to continue and complete the program which has been undertaken with success, to block off the Algerian-Tunisian frontier. If it becomes necessary, we will have to do the same on the Algerian-Moroccan frontier. To hinder the arms shipments we will rely more on the effectiveness of our barricades and the action of our troops than on international control. We will not spare the necessary means to realize this objective.

Although the use of force is necessary, we are convinced that it is not enough. The war which is going on on African soil, as well as throughout the world, is also a psychological war. We will not have won definitely so long as we have not conquered or reconquered the minds and the hearts of men. We don't want to establish a fragile truce which will be broken in a few months or years, but a real peace, founded on the free consent of the men and women who live in Algeria.

That is why we will implement the broadest and most liberal interpretation of the *loi-cadre*. The installation of new institutions has already permitted some Moslem Frenchmen to show their desire to participate with us in the construction of a new Algeria. Those who have been the first to show their trust in us in this way can rest assured of our thanks and our loyalty. . . .

The day when it becomes obvious that the rebellion has lost every hope of success and is ready to give up, then the government will choose—if it seems to be in the interests of our country—the most favorable moment to offer talks for a cease-fire.

Let there be no doubts about the nature of these talks or their object. The government will hold to the principles of the declaration of January 9, 1957, which were endorsed several times by the Parliament. . . .

In speaking of the eventuality of a cease-fire, even though the idea isn't new, I have aroused actions whose gravity I do not underestimate. But it was my duty to state clearly at a moment when the government prepares to demand new sacrifices from the nation, that it is not resigned to a permanent war, but will be alert to seize any possibility which might arise to restore peace.

I say these words in the interests of clarity and loyalty. With the same sharpness and the same resolution I declare right now that the government will never permit the bonds which unite Algeria to France to be broken. (*Applause on the center and several benches of the right and the left.*) . . .

The government has made its decision on all the essential questions. It considers itself justified in asking your confidence because it is profoundly convinced that its decisions represent the interests of the country. If you endorse them, the government will set out on its narrow path, buoyed by the conviction that the Republic can still be saved if it succeeds in uniting, enlightening, and guiding our indestructible national energy. (*Lively applause on the center and several benches of the left and the right.*) . . .

(*The session, adjourned at 4:15 p.m., is reconvened at 6:05 p.m.*)

M. PIERRE ANDRÉ (*Independent*): . . . The first duty of the government is thus to convince our allies that in Algeria we are fighting a war in the interests of the whole free world; to remind them that the Atlantic alliance applies to Algeria just as well as to France.

If the rebellion in Algeria is our business, external aid against us is the business of our allies as well as ours. But, not only have they not put a stop to it, they encourage it. Such an attitude is intolerable for us.

Furthermore, as Marshal Montgomery has shown, to be anticommunist in Paris or on the Elbe, while fostering direct and indirect dealings with the Russians elsewhere is a completely insane policy. As regards internal affairs the duty of the government is to put an end to treason and defeatism. It is also to proclaim solemnly, not just here, but in Algiers where it will have a profound effect (*Interruptions from the left and the extreme left*), that France will never let herself be thrown out of Algeria or the Sahara or the overseas territories.

Ladies and gentlemen, for months I have been outlining the conditions for a swift return to peace in Algeria. They are quickly said: we have to give the army the materials and the period of service it demands and nothing more. We have to maintain and extend the work of military pacification; but most of all we have to replace with civil functionaries soldiers, who are doing tasks which aren't theirs . . .

From the extreme left: Massu!

M. PIERRE ANDRÉ: . . . professors, teachers, doctors, civil engineers, administrators, municipal officials, policemen.

Policy for French Algeria has to be unified by creating a ministerial committee which has this special responsibility.

Essentially we have to convince the world and the Moslems of Algeria that France will never leave, and especially that all those who throw in their lot with French Algeria and fight with us, will never know the miserable and tragic fate of our Moroccan and Tunisian friends.

I propose that, if these conditions are filled, we can be done in a few months with the rebellion and the guerrillas.

From the extreme left: In a quarter of an hour!

M. PIERRE ANDRÉ: The achievement of the work we have begun is not beyond our forces. If Algeria is going to be lost, it will not be in Algiers, in Oran, or in Constantine, but in Paris. And to yield to foreign pressure, today as before, when victory is within reach, would be absolutely inexcusable. (*Applause on the right and the extreme right.*)

M. PIERRE PFLIMLIN: Mr. President, I request adjournment.

M. WALDECK ROCHET (*Communist*): I request the floor.

THE PRESIDENT: M. Waldeck Rochet has the floor.

M. WALDECK ROCHET: Ladies and gentlemen, at the request for adjournment . . . (*Protests on the center and the right.*)

M. FERNAND BOUXOM (*MRP*): Adjournment first!

THE PRESIDENT: M. Waldeck Rochet wants to speak on the request for adjournment. (*Protests on the center and the right.*)

M. WALDECK ROCHET: Until now the Communist group hasn't said a word in this debate. I would like to answer a few words to the President of the Council's request for adjournment. (*Protests on the center and the right.—Noise. M. Waldeck Rochet mounts to the rostrum. Lively applause on the extreme left.*)

From the center and the right: Adjournment!

M. WALDECK ROCHET: Ladies and gentlemen. At the moment when we are discussing the installation of the government, very grave events are taking place in Algiers. According to the latest reports, General Massu . . .

M. HENRI DORGÈRES D'HALLUIN (*Peasant Group*): Has saved France! (*Shouts from the extreme left.*)

From the extreme left: Fascist!

M. WALDECK ROCHET: . . . has occupied the government buildings and has established a committee which has just addressed an ultimatum to the President of the Republic. This means, in fact, the creation

of an illegal and insurrectionary government against the Republic and
for Algerian secession. (*Lively applause on the extreme left. Shouts
on the right and the extreme right.*)

From the center: Adjournment!

From the right and the extreme right: Algérie française! Algérie
française!

From the extreme left: Fascists!

M. WALDECK ROCHET: We believe that the first measure to take in
order to assure the authority of the republican state . . .

M. HENRI DORGÈRES D'HALLUIN: Is to send Russian tanks to Algiers!

M. WALDECK ROCHET: . . . is first of all the immediate dismissal and
outlawing of the dissident General Massu. (*Applause on the extreme
left. Protests on the right and the extreme right.*)

We believe that this demands—and these will be my last words—
the union of all republicans . . . (*Shouts on the center and the right.*)

M. FERNAND BOUXOM: Adjournment!

M. WALDECK ROCHET: . . . the union of all those who want to save
our liberties and stop the dissidents and the adventurers. (*Shouts on
the center, the right, and the extreme right. Applause on the extreme
left.*)

From the center and the right: Budapest!

M. WALDECK ROCHET: This is why, a few moments ago, the Communist group proposed to the representatives of all the republican
groups in the National Assembly (*Shouts from the center and the
right.*) to unite immediately and take measures to stop this coup and
guarantee respect for the law. (*Shouts on the center and the right.
Applause on the extreme left.*)

Our party calls the working class and the people to unite in action
to bar the way against the dissidents. We believe, in fact, that the
situation is grave enough that the session ought to be adjourned, so
that the groups can deliberate immediately in order to take measures
to save the Republic. (*Lively applause on the extreme left. Shouts on
the center, the right, and the extreme right.*)

M. LAURENT CASANOVA (*Communist*): *Vive la République!* Down
with the dissidents! (*On the extreme left the deputies chant*: Fascism
will not pass!)

(*On the right and the extreme right the deputies chant*: Algérie
française!)

THE PRESIDENT-DESIGNATE OF THE COUNCIL: I request the floor.

THE PRESIDENT: The President-Designate of the Council has the
floor.

THE PRESIDENT-DESIGNATE OF THE COUNCIL: Ladies and gentlemen, it is true that grave events are going on in Algiers, but it is not the Communist Party which will save the Republic and save liberty. (*Lively applause on the center. Applause on the left and the right. Shouts on the extreme left.*)

M. WALDECK ROCHET: These men are the accomplices of the rebels!

THE PRESIDENT-DESIGNATE OF THE COUNCIL: I requested an adjournment so that those who are responsible for preserving the republican order can combat the situation.

M. ROBERT CHAMBEIRON (*Progressive*): What are you going to do?

THE PRESIDENT-DESIGNATE OF THE COUNCIL: In the shortest possible space of time, the National Assembly will be called, this very night, to assume its responsibilities. (*Applause on the center.*)

For my part, I am ready to assume mine. (*The deputies of the center stand up and applaud. Applause on the left and several benches of the right.*)

THE PRESIDENT: The session is adjourned.

(*The session, adjourned at 10:40 p.m., is reconvened on Wednesday, May 14, at 1:15 a.m.*)

THE PRESIDENT: The session is in order. There are still seven speakers on the list. The President-Designate of the Council has the floor.

THE PRESIDENT-DESIGNATE OF THE COUNCIL: Ladies and gentlemen, it is my duty to say that in the exceptionally grave circumstances we are living through, it would be in the interests of our country that this debate be cut off.

In the hours to come, France must have a government. (Very good! Very good! *on the left, the center, and a few benches on the right.*)

Of course you will make your decision in full liberty, and in full consciousness of your responsibilities.

I ask that the speakers give up their time so that a vote can immediately be taken. (*Applause on the left, the center, and a few benches on the right.*)

THE PRESIDENT: Do the speakers give up their time?

From several benches: Yes. . . .

THE PRESIDENT-DESIGNATE OF THE COUNCIL: Ladies and gentlemen, I have outlined the government's program to you. I think it is clear.

The problem, in our mind, is to save Algeria. When France has established herself undeniably in a position of strength, then we must seize the occasion to restore the peace which will be the fruit of victory.

To reach this goal it will be necessary to avoid taking initiatives, however justified they might be, which would risk an explosion in all North Africa and might internationalize the conflict.

This is, in brief, the policy I want to carry out.

It may be that some patriots may differ with me on the choice of means. I respect their opinion. But I ask them do do me the honor of believing that the men who surround me and I myself cannot have the slightest desire or temptation to abandon Algeria. (*Applause on numerous benches of the center, the left, and some benches of the right.*)

But right now there is another problem.

In Algiers, Frenchmen, whose agony I understand and whose restlessness I appreciate, have let themselves be carried away to grave actions; and there are also military leaders who have taken—and I say this with profound regret—an attitude of insurrection against republican law. (*Lively and prolonged applause on the center, the left, the extreme left, and some benches of the right.*)

M. HENRI DORGÈRES D'HALLUIN: You are defending the system. (*Lively shouts on the center and the left.*)

THE PRESIDENT: M. Dorgères d'Halluin, you are out of order.

THE PRESIDENT-DESIGNATE OF THE COUNCIL: It would be tragic if a wedge were driven between the Frenchmen of Algeria and the Frenchmen of metropolitan France, for there is only one way to save Algeria, and this is to preserve national unity, and it can only be preserved in the Republic. (*Applause on the center, the left, and some benches of the right.*)

This is why I ask the National Assembly to assume its responsibilities.

My dear colleagues, you have to recognize that we are perhaps on the brink of civil war.

But without doubt the beneficiaries of this civil war will be these men here (*pointing to the extreme left*) with whom nothing could reconcile me.

M. RAYMOND LAINÉ (*Poujadist*): They just applauded you. As for us, you have thrown us out of the community of the nation.

THE PRESIDENT-DESIGNATE OF THE COUNCIL: Therefore I ask the National Assembly, without further delay, to rise to the level of its responsibilities, which oblige it, in this historic hour and before the nation to make its decision. (*Applause on the center, the left and several benches of the right.*) . . .

[*The vote is taken and the votes counted.*]

THE PRESIDENT: The session is in order.

Here are the verified results of the vote of confidence:

Number voting	403
For	274
Against	129

The assembly has given its confidence. (*Applause on the center and the left.*)

The President of the Republic will be informed of the results.

Details of the voting

274 deputies voted for:

4 Progressives (of 6); 87 Socialists (of 95) and the 2 MSA; 40 Radicals (of 42); 15 UDSR-RDA (of 20); 13 RGR (of 14); 7 Democratic Left (of 14); 7 African Union; 71 MRP (of 74); 25 Independents (of 91); 3 Peasants for Social Action (of 9).

129 deputies voted against:

1 Radical; 1 UDSR; 1 RGR; 7 Democratic Left, including M. Morice; 1 MRP, M. Bidault; 13 Social Republicans (of 19); 58 Independents; 4 Peasants for Social Action; 9 Peasants (of 11); 29 UFF [Poujadists] (of 30); 5 unaffiliated (of 10).

137 deputies abstained voluntarily:

135 Communists (of 142); 1 Progressive; 1 unaffiliated.

42 deputies did not vote; 11 deputies had permission to be absent.

(Adapted from *Le Monde*, May 15, 1958, p. 5)

IV

"A SORT OF RESURRECTION"

Introduction

At the outset of the crisis, Pierre Pflimlin called the events of Algiers a "dramatic misunderstanding." By May 19 the drama remained high, but there was little room left for misunderstanding; during the six days following May 13 uncertainties and ambiguities of position gave way to firmness and commitment. As the readings of this section show, there was a desire on all sides to maintain legality. But could this wish prevent a conflict?

"Republican defense" became a much-used phrase in the days following May 13. But what could Pflimlin and his Council of Ministers do to counter the threat from Algiers? Legally, by investing General Salan with extraordinary powers, the government retained control in Algeria. By maintaining this thread of authority, which left the generals a foot in both camps, it avoided an outright confrontation by force. Nevertheless, if not legally in mutiny, the army in Algeria continued to tolerate a revolutionary claimant against the legitimate power in Paris. How long could the government hold off condemning the generals, particularly after Salan's *"Vive de Gaulle!"* on May 15? What forces could it summon in its defense? If it did proscribe the military leaders, could it defend itself without seeking the aid of the Communists and their great following?

Across the Mediterranean, soldiers and the Committee of Public Safety faced the anomalies of a revolution halted halfway in its course. Like the President of the Council, the army leaders had a stake in preserving legality. However, using only legal means, could they influence the government any more than it could influence them? What did the men in Algiers propose to do if Pflimlin refused to bow out? In answering these questions, we must, as Paris did, look for signals in their words and actions. How much threat lay in their speeches and broadcasts, and how much bluff? Were the demonstrations of French-Moslem integration a justification through the *vox populi* or a stage-managed sham?

While this fencing for position went on, the Gaullists tried to exploit their opportunity. But the situation also held its perplexities for de Gaulle. The General was a professed believer in legality and legitimacy; if he now declared himself ready to assume power, he did not wish it to be against the will of the nation. If, however, as spokesmen of the government urged, he was to renew his attachment to legality by condemning the movement of Algiers, would he not in the same breath lose his chief trump—the pressure that the soldiers and civilians on the other shore of the Mediterranean were exerting for his return? In speaking to the nation, de Gaulle had to choose his words carefully. To what policies did he commit himself in his statements? How much did he leave for others to guess? And how truly did the Gaullists in Algiers, Delbecque and then Soustelle, represent the ideas of the man they wished to restore to power?

THE RUBICON

And so certain elements of the army of Algeria have crossed the Rubicon. United with groups of the extreme right, they have formed this local Committee of Public Safety, whose name, during Robespierre's second centennial, acquires a flavor of bitter derision: for the real Committee of Public Safety did not trifle with the subordination of the military to civil authority and knew how to maintain discipline among the generals by the most energetic means.

One day it will be necessary to draw up a balance sheet of responsibilities. Some are diffuse and distant. The dissolution of the state for the last two and a half years, which has already disgusted those who have been living peacefully in metropolitan France, has been more strongly resented by the soldiers who were fighting. Nothing could be more natural. When authority is seized by force, it is always because it has in a way been unoccupied. The tolerance of the cabinets and the Parliament in the face of a long series of initiatives taken by several military leaders gave them the impression that they alone could act and, in short, that they could act freely.

Other responsibilities are closer and more direct. A coup d'état is not something that can be improvised. The scenario for this one is too well arranged on many sides to be the effect of chance. The investigation of Parisian collusion in what must be called a plot against the security of the state should spare no one. Notably, receiving the Cross of Military Valor does not entitle a minister to abandon his post and to abandon it in extremely disturbing circumstances. Moreover, in this domain the civilian authorities must not hide their own responsibility behind that of the army.

For the moment, it is not yet a matter of punishing those who have flung the nation into this insane escapade. The high courts will sit tomorrow. Today, if there is still time the essential is to stop the evolution of events which can get out of hand. Paris is not Algiers. It is useless to occupy the Palais d'Été so long as you do not occupy the Palais-Bourbon. If the first act was ridiculously easy, the second will meet other obstacles. Let the right have no illusions. It has never succeeded in imposing its will on Parliament: the Sixth of February, 1934, only served as a cloak for a change in the majority which was, in any case, inevitable. The right, moreover, has never had control of the streets; in Paris its cohorts do not amount to much if the mass of the people are set in motion. And can they believe that the people will remain passive on the day when the Republic is really threatened?

Until yesterday the country did not believe in the fascist danger. It considered the Communists to be more disturbing than the agitators of the extreme right, who did not seem serious: this was clearly seen in the district elections. But if the threat of dictatorship becomes tangible, close, and immediate, everything will change. The atmosphere of 1936 and 1944 will return. This is what the act of May 13, 1958, is leading to: the Algerian extremists are presently assisting at the birth of what they feared above all—a left-wing majority. In normal circumstances M. Pflimlin would never have obtained the abstention of the Communists.

Yesterday's rebellion also runs the risk of ending in secession or civil war. The installation of a fascist regime in Algiers is reinforcing democratic sentiment in Paris. The slide toward the left on the mainland is hardening the North African extremists. And so on. The superpatriots of the pseudo–Committee of Public Safety have managed to break the fundamental bond on which rests the idea of the Nation: that all parties and groups of the country must submit to the exigencies imposed by our common life. The majority of Frenchmen in Algiers, but not perhaps of all of Algeria, are ready to overthrow the Republic. But the majority of Frenchmen in France remain profoundly attached to it. The former must yield to the will of the latter: to be French is, first of all, to accept France.

Let the leaders of the army look reality in the face. Because of its social and economic structure, its degree of political evolution, our country has advanced beyond the era of *pronunciamentos*. The Algiers coup cannot succeed. It can only plunge the nation into an atrocious struggle which will surely lead to the complete loss of Algeria and the French Union and doubtless to the arrival of a people's democracy in Paris. There is still time for all to submit to the principle of the subordination of the military to the civilian power, the cornerstone of the state.

There is still time for the government to help this return to reality by giving proof of the most extreme energy. Any sign of weakness that might lead the insurgents of May 13 to believe that they were going to succeed in making M. Pflimlin submit to them, as they made M. Guy Mollet submit on February 6, 1956, will lead to a result contrary to the desired one of re-establishing the country's unity and legality. We have entered into a revolutionary phase in which events are very swift and logic, implacable. If the Republic gives way before the rebellion, in a few days civil war will replace republican order.

Maurice Duverger
(*Le Monde*, May 15, 1958, p. 1)

COMMUNIQUÉ NO. 1 OF THE ALGIERS COMMITTEE OF PUBLIC SAFETY, MAY 13, 1958.

We announce to the populace of Algiers that Pflimlin's government of abandonment has just been invested by 273 votes against 124, with the aid of Communist votes.

We express our gratitude to the populace which has stayed up to welcome M. Jacques Soustelle.

M. Jacques Soustelle has twice been prevented from coming to rejoin us.

The third time he succeeded in gaining safety, and we hope that he will be with us before the day is over.

The Committee entreats General de Gaulle to consent to break his silence and address the country, with a view toward formation of a government of public safety, which alone can save Algeria from abandonment and thus from a "diplomatic Dien-Bien-Phu," against which M. Robert Lacoste has warned many times.

In any case the Committee of Public Safety which represents you will continue to assure liaison between the populace and the army, which is assuming power until the final victory.

Until Jacques Soustelle appears, the directorate of the Committee is composed of General Massu, M. Delbecque, delegated by M. Jacques Soustelle, M. Madani, M. Lagaillarde.

We decree the mobilization henceforward of all French strength in the service of the country and ask you to be ready to respond at the first call issued by the Committee of Public Safety.

We are proud to show the world that the populace of Algiers has known how to devise a perfect demonstration of the absolute fraternity of the French population—Europeans and Moslems—united under the banner of France.

The Committee of Public Safety
(*L'Écho d'Alger*, May 14, 1958, p. 12)

COMMUNIQUÉ OF GENERAL SALAN, CHIEF COMMANDER IN ALGERIA, BROADCAST OVER RADIO ALGIERS, NIGHT OF MAY 13–14, 1958

Having the mission to protect you I provisionally take in my hands the destiny of French Algeria.

I ask you to have confidence in the army and its chiefs and to show this through your calm and your determination.

(New York *Herald Tribune*, European Edition, May 14, 1958)

1. Beginning today, May 14, General Salan, chief commander of the armed forces and commander of the Tenth Military District, is provisionally assuming civil and military power in order to assure the maintenance of order, the protection of persons and property, and the conduct of military operations.

2. The Committee of Public Safety, which has been constituted at Algiers under the pressure of events in order to affirm the will of the Franco-Moslem population to remain French, will assure liaison between the populace and the military command, which will pass on its orders to the Committee.

3. It is important that the full machinery of administration be reactivated as quickly as possible in order that there be no disturbance in the life of the country and the conduct of military operations.

4. The populace is requested to remain calm, with dignity and discipline. The military authorities ask each individual to have confidence in them and to resume work.

General and Chief Commander of the Armed Forces.

[signed] General Salan

(*L'Écho d'Alger*, May 15, 1958, p. 12)

"WE'VE HAD IT," SAID SEVERAL COLONELS AS THEY LEFT THE OFFICE OF THE COMMITTEE OF PUBLIC SAFETY:

THEY HAD JUST LEARNED OF M. PFLIMLIN'S INVESTITURE

The French Broadcasting System transmitted a real documentary Wednesday evening at 7:15 in the program "Paris Speaking" on the France I network: a complete report on the situation in Algiers by four of its staff while paratroopers guarded the Radio Algiers building and some even stood guard in the studios.

Here are the main parts of their conversation:

Hello! Paris. Hello! Paris. . . .

There are four of us in this studio which is guarded by troops, by the paratroopers—four journalists.

PARIS: What is the situation?

ALGIERS: The general impression is that of great confusion. When the one o'clock news bulletin was released, different appeals for calm were made, notably by General Salan who requested the people to open their stores and to resume normal activity.

But at the same time, on the other hand, sound trucks were going through the city, leaflets were being distributed urging the inhabitants to gather at the Forum, the great square that is in front of the Ministry for Algeria, and to demonstrate throughout the afternoon.

During the course of the day the inhabitants have already received two, three, and even four sets of special orders. There is the case of a businessman near the radio station who was told to close his store at the beginning of the morning, then to reopen it during the morning, and, finally, to close it once again at the end of the morning. . . .

PARIS: Have you been able to broadcast the appeal of President Coty?

ALGIERS: No. They didn't let us. Demonstrations against the studios were feared.

PARIS: What were the reactions to the news of M. Pflimlin's investiture?

ALGIERS: The reactions, on a psychological plane, were enormous for the military officers who had been in a closed meeting with the Committee of Public Safety since five o'clock.

At two in the morning, they had reached the ninetieth motion or resolution of the Committee of Public Safety.

I saw several colonels coming out of the doors of the office where the Committee of Public Safety was sitting. Their reaction was unanimous: "We've had it."

The reaction of those anonymous men—the fifty or so plotters who were also waiting behind me at the doors of the office of the Committee of Public Safety—their reaction was very brutal.

Sensing that they were lost, literally lost, they had one last card available, and they played it. They said: "We are going to arm the civilian population and if you run us out, you'll leave with us and you'll lose out as much as we. The game will be lost for you as well as for us."

As for the crowd's reaction, it should be realized that yesterday evening, at the precise moment that we've been talking about, the crowd in large part—all of Algiers in large part—was gathered on the Place du Forum which is situated in front of the Ministry for Algeria.

People, for the most part young men and young women, were literally camping there amid the debris of automobiles that had been overturned during the course of the day, amid the debris of broken windows of all sorts and heaps of paper from the archives that had been thrown from the windows during the course of the demonstrations. This was an absolutely passionate crowd, absolutely uncontrollable, in the middle of which no news item could have gotten a serious hearing or any meaningful reaction. This was a crowd that yelled slogans, that from time to time sang the *Marseillaise*, a crowd incapable of any considered reaction or of the least cool judgment.

(*France-Soir*, May 16, 1958, p. 5)

MOVING DIALOGUE BETWEEN PARIS-INTER AND RADIO ALGIERS

"WE HAVE ALL DECIDED TO STAY WITHIN THE REPUBLICAN LEGAL FRAMEWORK," DECLARE THE JOURNALISTS OF THE ALGERIAN STATION

PARIS: What is the Committee of Public Safety doing?

ALGIERS: It is in permanent session, but orders are being issued just about everywhere. There is so much confusion that one hundred and four resolutions have been moved by different committees.

Colonel Trinquier has decided to send home the men of the territorial units that were set up among the population of Algeria. These men are to change to civilian dress and lay down their arms. . . .

PARIS: Are you free to broadcast news?

ALGIERS: There is someone here, a former member of M. Chaban-Delmas's staff who was assigned to serve with M. Lacoste. He censors the news. . . .

PARIS: Can you tell us what role General Salan is playing?

ALGIERS: We can discuss it only in veiled language.

General Salan is not doing what he would have liked to be able to do.

The word from the leaders of the agitators is: "Salan has left us in the lurch."

There is a clear vacillation among the military, even with Massu. . . .

It is known that the second phase of the operation set in motion here—the blocking of M. Pflimlin's investiture in Paris—has failed.

PARIS: And in other Algerian cities?

ALGIERS: The interior, which always reacts twenty-four hours behind Algiers, has gotten as far as constituting committees of public safety.

PARIS: *Au revoir. Bon courage.* There are moments when one is proud to have a newsman's pass in one's pocket.

(*Le Figaro*, May 15, 1958, p. 4)

The Committee of Public Safety was founded by the following persons:

General Massu, president; Colonel Trinquier, Colonel Thomazo, Colonel Ducasse; MM. Armand Perrou, sales representative; André Baudier, accountant; Rodolphe Parachini, clerk; Gabriel Montigny, business agent; Joseph Jolivet, works manager; Paul Moreau, company director; Doctor Lefèvre; MM. Robert Martel, farmer; Morieau; Pierre Lagaillarde, lawyer; Delbecque; Dumont; Arnold.

After its establishment the Committee of Public Safety resolved to add the following members:

M. Chikh; Commandant of the Reserve Mahdi; M. Mohammed Said Madani, foreman; Berkani, Merlo, Froment, Coulondre, Cosso, Martin, Muller, Régard, Mouchan, de Sérigny, L'Hostis; Armand Vacher, business chief; René Vinciguerra, Government House official; Marcel Schambill, office manager.

(*L'Écho d'Alger*, May 15, 1958, p. 12)

GENERAL MASSU DEFINES THE OBJECTIVES OF THE COMMITTEE OF PUBLIC SAFETY

Yesterday at 6 p.m., in the offices of the Tenth Military District headquarters, General Massu held a press conference, which was attended as well by officers of General Salan's staff and press officers from the armed forces command.

General Massu gave an account of the events of the thirteenth, and more particularly of those which led to the formation of the Committee of Public Safety, whose presidency he assumed.

"After General Salan placed the wreath at the monument to the dead, I returned to my quarters at Hydra.

"I was informed there was trouble at Government House and set out as fast as possible, only to find the building in fact damaged and people all over the place. That didn't please me very much.

"I was caught," General Massu continued, "by a group of young men in M. Maisonneuve's office. The crowd was roaring. We didn't have a mike to make ourselves heard and to explain to all these people that this demonstration was out of place.

"General Salan then arrived, obviously unhappy. The crowd didn't let him speak and gave him an unfriendly and absolutely unjustified reception.

"There in that office, there were a dozen men, ages thirty to thirty-five, and some young men, of whom the most eloquent was a tall fellow wearing glasses. He told us that a representative organ had to be created, capable of channeling the demonstration, and that it was indispensable that we be on it.

"I looked at General Salan, who was listening to these words. He said nothing. I had only thirty or forty seconds to think. I decided to accept in order to control the actions of this committee, taking into account only the patriotic sentiments that inspired these young men and which correspond to our own, we who are fighting in Algeria.

"My civilian comrades wanted me to fill out the committee through the entry of other military men. So I designated my chief of staff, Colonel Ducasse, and Colonel Trinquier, whose action in delicate situations had been advantageous at Algiers. Finally, and without asking his opinion, Colonel Thomazo, to assure liaison between the committee and the army corps, where he works. Besides, he is known among the veterans."

General Massu then specified the three goals the Committee of Public Safety had set for itself:

(1) "Restore order at Algiers. It has been attained without bloodshed, which for me constitutes an important result.

(2) "Obtain the creation of a government of public safety in metropolitan France. A great hope stirs the civilian members of the Committee: Soustelle in Algiers. And if General de Gaulle takes a position, perhaps even presides over a government of public safety, 'Inch' Allah!' [Allah willing]

"The news from Paris, particularly the investiture of M. Pflimlin in office, arrived late at night. There was disappointment among the crowd which was camping in the Forum.

"It is certain that neither the previous statements of the new head of government nor the interview given by M. Lacoste to M. Daniel of *L'Express*, which even mentioned a 'diplomatic Dien-Bien-Phu,' were likely to make M. Pflimlin popular here."

After recalling the various messages sent by the Committee of Public Safety to President Coty and several other individuals, General Massu stated the third goal of the committee.

"To explain to the civilians there that the war against the fellagha would continue, that it was important not to inconvenience the field command, that it was necessary to maintain the unity of the army by upholding the chain of command.

"It was therefore urgent not to prolong the insurrectional atmosphere so as not to risk severance from metropolitan France, which could have enormous disadvantages for us.

"This viewpoint," General Massu stressed, "was accepted by all."

General Massu then described his conference with General Salan yesterday morning and his insistence upon Salan's taking a position. Salan then did so.

"Therefore the subordination of the committee to General Salan is clear and the unity of the army's hierarchy upheld. That is, moreover, why this press conference is taking place at the Tenth Military District headquarters and not at Government House."

General Massu also stated that M. Chaussade, general secretary of Government House, had agreed to work with General Salan.

"So I endeavored to return the administrative machine to working order and assembled the directors and heads of services. I told them I would help them get started at work."

Concerning the gatherings of the populace at the Forum, General Massu declared that it was mostly a question of the delegations from Mitidja. "I spoke to them and advised them to return to work."

General Massu then affirmed that he did not know who instigated the march on Government House or who was behind the pamphlets of yesterday urging that the strike be carried on and the soldiers of the territorial army be mobilized.

"It is certain that there are people here who do not wish us well. Who threw the first tear gas grenade? That justifiably angered the demonstrators. The devil could tell me!

"This Committee of Public Safety overseen by General Salan is a good thing. As for me, I'll continue my mission, to channel the aspirations of the people of Algiers within the framework of public order."

(*L'Écho d'Alger*, May 15, 1958, p. 12)

FIVE MONTHS AGO, MASSU SAID TO ME . . .

Five months ago, as special correspondent for *La Croix* in Algeria and anxious to get information from every source, I asked General Massu for an interview which he was kind enough to give me. He asked me, however, not to speak of this conversation (it is forbidden for a superior officer to grant the press an interview without authorization from the Ministry of National Defense). I kept that promise. After the part that the General took in the events in Algiers, this formal reservation no longer holds and it is possible to relate what was nothing but a simple conversation and not—I wish to make clear once more—an interview.

General Massu received me in his staff office of the Tenth Paratroop Division, installed in an old villa in the moorish style. An extremely simple room, almost bare. On the walls some maps and photographs. The General, in battle dress, was seated at his work table. He never stopped toying with a horn-handled knife. On the table, a single book: *Counter-Revolution, Strategy and Tactics*. This book, written by an unknown author, is forbidden in France. It was published in Belgium and it will perhaps be remembered that last January a businessman from Lyons who tried to bring copies of it into France was arrested for that reason. *Counter-Revolution, Strategy and Tactics* has been, I was to establish later, widely circulated among the military cadres in Algeria, even in the highest echelons. This book preaches the seizure of power by the army in Algeria and, drawing from the Spanish example of 1936, its return to France in order to establish a fascist regime there. The General, in the course of our conversation, was to read me several excerpts from the book which he judged particularly well "put."

His first words were directed against the press in metropolitan France.

"You can't know," he told me, "the evil that the press is doing here. It is paralyzing us. . . . Torture, torture, that's the only word you know—but I am forced to practice it. How could I do otherwise? I'd really like to see Billotte here. . . . It's easy when you're in Paris. (It will be remembered that at that time a lively controversy had developed between General Massu and General Billotte on the subject of procedures for repression.)

"All of that," the General suddenly went on, "is Pétain's fault."

And, as I displayed quite a bit of surprise, not immediately grasping the relationship:

"Yes, it's Pétain's fault. It was he who taught masochism to Frenchmen. He taught Frenchmen to beat their breasts, crying *mea culpa*. Now you, the press, are continuing that. But we, here, we're working. Here, look!"

The General took out some personal photograph albums with pictures taken in the Djurdjura region where his division was at that time. His men had proceeded to regroup villages and had constructed a few schools. The photographs were of these schools and one could see young Arabs seated at their desks, like all the school children of the world. Under the photos, several naïve captions, written, I think, by the General himself: "We are educating ourselves." "We are learning French."

"Look at those kids, how they've got good heads," the General said to me.

I questioned him on the state of the army's morale.

"We are here to win," he told me. "We have not come here to defend the privileges of the Europeans in Algeria. You know, there are those here known as 'ultras.' "

And the General explained to me at length, as though I were perfectly ignorant of Algerian affairs, who these "ultras" were.

"Well," he said, "these 'ultras' of the Vigilance Committee came to see me last September when they wanted to organize a general strike against the *loi-cadre*. They wanted me to support them. I told them this: 'I, Massu, I obey the orders that I've received. If you start trouble, I'm going to hit you as I've hit the FLN. If necessary, I'll have you shot.' They didn't budge."

That was how General Massu talked December 17, 1957. He seems to have evolved a great deal since then. I must say that he didn't appear to me—at that moment—as a man to attempt an adventure for his own ends. He did not seem to nurse any personal ambition. On the contrary, he gave the impression of a simple and naïve military man, only a freebooter who could be used by the extremists (and even then they were already trying) and who read very bad things.

Jacques Duquesne
(*La Croix*, May 15–16, 1958, p. 4)

Transcript of the Trial of General Raoul Salan, May 1962 (Excerpts)

HEARING OF MAY 19, 1962. TESTIMONY OF M. ROBERT LACOSTE.

M. ROBERT LACOSTE: What was the situation when he [Salan] arrived? General Lorillot, his predecessor, who was a man of high moral worth, of great conscience and high professional merit, had been up against a really hard situation and had obtained definite results. Among other things, he had restored the situation in all the regions of Algeria, he

Le Procès de Raoul Salan, Compte Rendu Stenographique, 312–15. From the series "Les Grands Procès Contemporains," under direction of Maître Maurice Garçon of the Académie Française, reprinted by permission of the publisher, Éditions Albin Michel, Paris.

had defended the entire collective patrimony of Algeria, and he had tried to cut the routes by which arms entered the country.

And at this moment in the Algerian affair there had been some miscalculations. First the recruits left; that was a large number of fighting men who departed. Since January we had been deprived of our spearhead, that is the best troops, those who were always on the march and who had been immobilized by the Suez affair.

Furthermore, the fellagha were organizing into well-formed and well-armed units.

Morale was not particularly good either because the departure of the recruits and the inconvenience of Suez had naturally discouraged the Algerians. Furthermore, they were terrified of what the government might do before the coming session of the United Nations.

Terrorism was spreading, not only the terrorism against Moslems— for let us not forget that when Salan arrived the FLN was killing four hundred Moslems per month. The statistics are there at the headquarters of the Gendarmerie and anyone can consult them. Not only was there that terrorism, but there was also urban terrorism which was already blindly directed against Europeans.

The first thing Salan did was to send out a general directive. He said he was eager to see the whole army in motion: no immobility, he said, no winter quarters. He wanted an active campaign. Furthermore, he gave orders to support with good faith the reform policies which I had undertaken at the request of the French government and parliament.

Good results were obtained quite rapidly. And despite the fatigue of the troops, Salan continued at this pace, so that by the end of 1957*—three months after he had taken command—we had gained a decisively improved position.

The number of reprisals of every nature had diminished very markedly, at least 50 per cent in the cities, and particularly in Algiers; in November and December 1956 in this city of seven hundred thousand inhabitants, only one person was killed.

The communal reform which was the keystone of the pacification policy was carried on successfully, thanks to the army and thousands of Moslems who, at the peril of their lives, proudly accepted municipal office and the tricolor sash. These were the first results.

A few weeks before the end of 1957, the arms which the FLN had been able to procure throughout the world arrived in the countries

*[Lacoste must have meant the end of 1956 or the beginning of 1957; Salan took over the North African command in November 1956—Eds.]

bordering on Algeria and began to cross the frontiers. We had to fight what we called the battle of the frontiers which, after the battle of Algiers, was the great feat that saved the situation. Our best troops fought this battle of the frontiers, inspired, of course, by Salan.

It was then the month of May. I departed. What was the situation I left after having worked for eighteen months together with Salan?

First, the general decline of terrorism. Then a serious breakdown of the secret organization of the FLN. The frontiers had been shut off after the meritorious battle of which I just spoke, one whose history, I believe, the French army would be interested in seeing written someday.

The frontiers were shut off; fourteen hundred Moslem communes had been effectively created. The Saharan front which our adversaries wanted to establish had not been established, and it could not be after February 1957.

Oil started to flow at Hassi-Messaoud, it went to Touggourt, to Biskra, then to Philippeville. Thanks to the army, from January 1958 oil could be shipped in special boats which carried it to France.

This was the total. Now a judgment on Salan. . . . He was a very good soldier; he was really a soldier at heart. He loved his troops; he had the kind of plebian sense for the troops that officers have who are self-made. He knew his soldiers one by one. My colleagues and I were always impressed by the knowledge he had of terrain and of men. He could tell you instantly the worth of this company or that man in the most distant corner of Algeria and, if something happened somewhere, which man should be sent there to restore the situation.

Thus, incontestable professional merit. He was so much the friend of his troops, so much the soldier, that I often thought he only felt at home in this military environment. Elsewhere he was shy.

He had a kind of reserve which could have been taken for a love of secrecy but which was basically a sort of inability to move in other milieux than his original one, which he loved profoundly, almost savagely. I never saw him lose his temper except on very rare occasions. But always for the same reason. That was when he felt the need to say, with a startling tension in his face and raising his voice: "They're going to play the same trick on us as in Indochina; but I'll defend the army and my comrades to the very end." This is the only time I ever saw this man lose his temper, and I speak of it because it is very significant.

Politically I can say he was republican, not only by conviction but, I believe, by family tradition. We never talked about politics. I don't think he was very well acquainted with the party struggles, if he understood politics at all. He obeyed the authorities. He never criticized the policies of the government. And he obeyed in circumstances which I would like to emphasize.

First, on September 17, 1957, those who are called for convenience the "ultras" wanted to organize a great protest demonstration against the *loi-cadre*, which granted a single electoral college. I said to Salan and Massu: these people are completely crazy. Why demonstrate against a law which is, in my opinion, the only means of bringing enough calm to Algeria to allow it to approach a real solution.

Salan and Massu understood perfectly: they said the necessary things and gave the right orders; there was no demonstration against the *loi-cadre*, unpopular as it was.

A little before May 13, the Algerian crowd was in a terrible uproar because people talked only of good offices, because the party of immediate negotiation kept growing, and in Tunis M. Bourguiba was talking big and French prisoners had been executed in his territory.

All the parties and all the groups had planned a huge demonstration for April 26. We were in the middle of a ministerial crisis, and I believe it was at this moment that M. Pleven, having been nominated, asked Salan and me for our advice. Salan had great influence over certain veterans' associations and especially with the veterans of the French Union. He spoke to them and finally the idea of this demonstration was abandoned.

But on April 25 M. Delbecque arrived, who was at that time on the staff of M. Chaban-Delmas. He arrived in a military airplane, landed on military territory; he was protected by military security. All the groups and all the associations met again, their plans were revived, and the project of the demonstration was taken up again.

I arrived the next day from Paris and learned from the responsible authorities, whom I found in M. Maisonneuve's office, that there was no chance and that my interdiction would not do any good. I went on the radio, I talked to the people of Algiers, and in the end the demonstration was not a great success.

I believe that the policy we followed, Salan and I, could have been continued. There was the *loi-cadre* which I mentioned to you, and which Salan had accepted so fully that he had ordered Judge-Advocate Colonel Gardon to write a juridical analysis of it to send to all the units. This law created the single electoral college for all the Moslems. It divided Algeria into territories, each one with an autonomous government and parliament, leaving them the possibility of making a federal Algeria. It created procedures for, or more precisely, possibilities of conciliation between the two communities, attempting to realize

what ought to have been realized sooner: peaceful co-existence between
the communities of Algeria. This law, in Article 16, paragraph 2, left
room to revise the provisional institutions of Algeria by agreement
of the Algerian parliaments and the French Parliament.

This was the policy Salan and I followed. He followed it loyally.
If I didn't state this I would be a liar. We passed through these trials
together, we took decisions together, and we arrived together at positive results.

I am very sad to be here.

RADIO BROADCAST TO THE ARMED FORCES BY PRESIDENT OF THE
REPUBLIC RENÉ COTY, MAY 14, 1958, 6:30 A.M.

Guardian of national unity, I appeal to your patriotism and your good
sense not to add to the country's trials that of a division of Frenchmen in the face of the enemy.

Every breach of discipline can only profit those we are fighting.

Chief of the army by virtue of Article 33 of the Constitution, I order
you to remain on duty under the authority of the government of the
French Republic.

(*Le Monde*, May 15, 1958, p. 1)

THE FIRST DAY OF THE PFLIMLIN GOVERNMENT

Shortly after the official announcement of its investiture, the Pflimlin
government held an extraordinary meeting of the Council of Ministers
at the Élysée. At its end M. Pflimlin made the following statement:

"In this first meeting the government has examined the situation
in Algeria. It is convinced that the events which have occurred there
are the result of a dramatic misunderstanding. The will of the government is to defend Algeria. The first measures it has decreed aim to
augment the nation's endeavor to keep Algeria French.

"It is necessary that our compatriots in Algeria and our army, which
evokes the admiration of the country, be fully persuaded of this. And
I am convinced that once confidence is restored in the resolution of the
legitimate government of France, national discipline will be respected
by all."

Yesterday morning [May 14] M. Pierre Pflimlin, President of the
Council, addressed the following radio appeal to Algeria:

"The government invested last night by the National Assembly has immediately taken steps to deal with the situation created by the events in Algiers.

"The starting point of these events will be brought to light. Responsibility will be established. It appears that the intentions of the government have been systematically distorted in the minds of the Frenchmen of Algeria. It is falsely accused of wanting to carry out a policy of abandonment in Algeria.

"In reality, its program of action, approved by the National Assembly, anticipates that new sacrifices will be demanded of the nation in order that as soon as possible, a victorious peace will reward the effort of our army.

"Once more I solemnly affirm that the government will never allow the ties which unite Algeria to France to be broken. But Algeria can be saved only by national effort, prosecuted in unity and discipline under the direction of legitimate authority. The government will not fail in its task. It will enforce the laws of the Republic and the demands of public safety.

"It asks those who represent it on Algerian soil to do their duty.

"It asks the French of Algeria as well as those of metropolitan France to give it their trust."

The deliberations of the inner Council, in which MM. Pflimlin, Mutter, Pleven, Corniglion-Molinier, Lecourt, and de Chevigné participated, began at 11 a.m. and ended shortly before 1 p.m.

The following official communiqué was published:

"The ministerial committee meeting at the Hôtel Matignon has surveyed the situation. At noon it appears to be the following:

(1) "At Paris: during the night it proceeded to arrest some fifty persons for subversive activities. A judicial inquiry has begun.

"Contrary to certain rumors, there is only one officer among the persons arrested.

"The government has decided to prohibit all demonstrations on the public thoroughfares in Paris and across the country.

(2) "In Algeria: the situation is as follows. The normal functioning of authority has been opposed only in Algiers.

"The government has commissioned General Salan, chief commander of the forces, to maintain order at Algiers and to assure the protection of persons and property. General Salan has taken over this mission beginning May 14.

"In all other principal towns the civil and military authorities report no important incidents. The government has determined that until new orders are given, the inspectors-general of administration on extra-ordinary mission of Constantine and Oran will be directly subordinate to the Minister for Algeria, along with the three prefects of Tizi-Ouzou, Orléansville, and Médéa, which form part of the region of Algiers.

"The government cautions the Algerian and metropolitan populations against false information spread with the aim of agitating spirits and creating confusion."

(*Combat*, May 15, 1958, p. 4)

APPEAL OF THE POLITICAL BUREAU OF THE FRENCH COMMUNIST PARTY

A fascist coup de force has occurred in Algiers. General Massu and the ultra-colonialists have occupied the official buildings. They have hurled an ultimatum at the President of the Republic. They demand that a government of their choice be formed in Paris.

This is the result of the policy of retreat adopted in the face of the colonialists' demands and of the worst kind of reaction, a policy that has developed continuously since the capitulation of February 6, 1956.

In Paris itself, seditious gangs today tried to take part in the plot hatched in Algiers against the Republic. The fascists have been able to demonstrate freely in the streets. A few hours previously *l'Humanité* was confiscated once again because it was telling the truth about the events in Algeria.

The Political Bureau of the French Communist Party emphasizes the gravity of the fascist danger, of the official connivance which is benefiting the seditious, and of the repeated attacks against democratic liberties.

It calls on the workers to deliver without delay the massive reply which is necessary to nip seditious intrigues in the bud. It calls on them to gather together immediately in every factory and to express in every possible way (delegations, work-stoppages, street demonstrations) their determination to defend the Republic.

It requests that all of the federations, sections, and cells of the party make the necessary contacts with the organizations of the Socialist Party and of all the republican parties and groups for the purpose of initiating common antifascist and workers' action to impose respect for legality on the seditious generals.

It invites Parisians to make the meeting organized for the fourteenth of May at the Cirque d'Hiver a powerful, popular antifascist demonstration.

For the immediate removal and outlawing of Massu and his accomplices!

For the dissolution of the fascist groups!

For a government of democratic union and defense of republican institutions!

Gather together in all the factories, cities, and towns of France! Act together, all forces united to defend the Republic and liberty!

Fascism shall not pass!

The Political Bureau of the French Communist Party

May 13, 1958

(*L'Humanité*, May 14, 1958, p. 1)

DECLARATION BY GEORGES BIDAULT, ROGER DUCHET, ANDRÉ MORICE, AND JACQUES SOUSTELLE, MAY 14, 1958

In the name of the endeavor upon which we have ventured in common to establish a government of protection for a French Algeria, we the undersigned, certain of expressing the passionate conviction of innumerable Frenchmen, proclaim:

(1) Algeria is and will remain French;

(2) No "cease-fire" is admissible which keeps arms in the hands of those who use them for slaughter;

(3) The army of Algeria is the shield and the honor of the nation; It is attached to republican liberties;

It is defending them, together with integrity of the territory, at the cost of its blood;

(4) Its action and that of the Frenchmen there are the expression of a patriotic renewal, an additional proof of their will to remain French;

(5) It is not by arresting patriots and veterans that Frenchmen will be reconciled;

The tragic misunderstanding of which M. Pierre Pflimlin has spoken must be repaired as soon as possible, the unity of the nation restored and the authority of the Republic re-established;

(6) These objectives of salvation require in all urgency the establishment of a government of union and national safety;

(7) Last night all of the national deputies were in accord on these objectives: no consideration of any order is admissible which delays their realization for a single instant.

(*Le Monde*, May 15, 1958, p. 6)

SO HE CANNOT GET TO ALGERIA—

M. J. SOUSTELLE IS THE TARGET OF REINFORCED SURVEILLANCE

M. ROBERT LACOSTE TELLS THE ASSEMBLY: 'WHAT IS HAPPENING CANNOT SURPRISE ME'

Paris (AFP)—While in the corridors of the Palais-Bourbon before this afternoon's public session, M. Robert Lacoste conversed familiarly with reporters who asked him about the Algerian situation:

"What is happening cannot surprise me. I warned this might occur. At present it concerns me no longer."

M. Lacoste indicated further that he had had contact yesterday evening, while he was still Minister for Algeria, with Generals Salan and Massu.

"General Massu assured me," he said, "that the Committee of Public Safety would take no decision of a political or administrative nature. It is above all a vigilance committee that shall remain vigilant until there is formed in Paris a government that will maintain France's presence in Algeria."

For his own part, M. Jacques Soustelle, who passed by a few minutes later in the Hall of the Four Columns, expressed surprise to the reporters at the announcement that he had been "placed under police protection following threats of death that the FLN made to him."

"I have been watched for six months," he said, "that's nothing new. Why say anything about it today? It is true that it has been intensified since last night. . . .

"Furthermore, I have protested at the police prefect's against certain methods: for instance I was awakened this morning shortly after my return from the Assembly to ascertain that I was indeed at my residence. Moreover, they are taking note of the comings and goings of those persons who are visiting me. These methods don't have very much in common with democracy. . . ."

When a reporter asked him the question: "And supposing it is to prevent you from going to Algeria?" M. Soustelle answered:

"It is indeed an efficient method for preventing me. But I am not sure that others who might wish to get there could go so easily. . . ."

(*L'Écho d'Alger*, May 15, 1958, p. 1)

M. PFLIMLIN PLANS AN ENLARGEMENT OF HIS CABINET [MAY 14]

There was a great deal of political activity yesterday afternoon at the Hôtel Matignon and the Palais-Bourbon, after M. Pierre Pflimlin decided to rearrange his government and enlarge its national base by persuading the Socialists and, if possible, M. Antoine Pinay, to enter his cabinet. Numerous political meetings marked this activity at the Prime Minister's office: at the beginning of the afternoon one with M. Guy Mollet, then with the Independent ministers of the new government and M. René Pleven, Minister of Foreign affairs, Maurice Faure, Minister of the Interior, Robert Lecourt, Minister of Justice, Pierre de Chevigné, Minister of National Defense, and André Colin, Minister for Overseas France. The development of the situation in Algeria was another of the ministers' preoccupations and was debated at length because it dominates all new political decisions that must be considered in respect to the structure of the government.

The first positive decision emerging from these discussions became known about six in the afternoon when the three Independent ministers of the new government—MM. Ribeyre, Garet, and Boscary-Mons-servin—who until now had not known whether they would remain in the Cabinet, announced after a new interview with M. Pflimlin:

"Given the vote by our group during the polling last evening, we came to deliver our resignation to the Prime Minister. However, the Prime Minister underlined the exceptional gravity of the present situation and the risks that our country is running today. For this reason we have decided that it is our duty to delay the execution of our plan."

The executive committee of the Independents and Peasants had, a short time earlier, demanded the withdrawal of its ministers from the government. Around 6:30 p.m., however, M. Pinay was called to the Hôtel Matignon and was offered the vice presidency of the Cabinet.

"Personally, I am not hostile," confided the Independent leader as he left the Prime Minister's office, "but how can I fight the tide in my group?"

This was the objective of a meeting that M. Pflimlin had during the evening with M. Roger Duchet, but nothing was revealed about the interview. Nevertheless, it was agreed that M. Pinay, like M. Guy Mollet, was to see the Prime Minister again today.

At the National Assembly meetings of the groups followed. This is how the story unfolded:

257

4:00 p.m. Caucus of the Valois Radicals [i.e. that faction of the
Radical Socialists named after the party HQ on the Place de Valois—
Eds.].

After an examination of the situation in Algeria, confidence in M.
Pflimlin and his government was renewed.

5:00 p.m. Executive committee of the Independents-Peasants:

Very large majority for the withdrawal of the Independent ministers.

Should M. Pinay agree to enter the government? Deputies were
very divided—some of them were ready to accept this offer on the
condition that the widening of the cabinet would completely guarantee them that the government would in fact adopt the Algerian
policy that the Independents have always called for; the others demanded the withdrawal of the Independent ministers and opposed
the entry of M. Antoine Pinay. The latter did not think that a government of national union could be led by M. Pflimlin. As for those of
the moderates ready to accept the entry of M. Pinay into the cabinet,
they made it a condition that men like MM. Guy Mollet and Georges
Bidault as well as M. Robert Lacoste (who they hoped would return
to Algeria) would also be members.

6:30 p.m. The Socialists, for their part having met since 5:15, suspended their deliberations in order to take "time for reflection."

They would, however, be disposed to enter the government on the
condition that they retain a certain number of portfolios which would
permit them to defend the institutions of the Republic.

7:15 p.m. The Independent-Peasant group heard the account given by
M. Antoine Pinay who had met with M. Pflimlin at the office of the
Prime Minister:

The Independent leader stated that he had transmitted the conditions
of his participation in the government as they had been defined by
the executive committee: the entry of M. Robert Lacoste (as Minister
for Algeria) and of M. Georges Bidault into the government.

M. Pflimlin asked for time to reflect on this proposition. The group
had thereupon decided to have another meeting at 5:00 p.m.

Some of the participants at the meeting emphasized that M. Pflimlin
"had not said no" to M. Pinay's suggestion. On the other hand, the
impression was that the essential condition of the Independents was
M. Robert Lacoste's return to Algeria.

Other conditions would have been formulated: a non-partisan
cabinet of limited duration and legislative elections within six months.

9:00 p.m. The Socialists decided to support the Pflimlin government by
61 votes in favor and 6 against (11 abstaining):

"We are ready," declared M. Mérigonde, the group's spokesman, "to collaborate with all those who have accepted either the platform of M. Pleven or that of M. Pflimlin.

"Which, practically speaking, excludes nobody.

"No condition concerning persons or portfolios is set. M. Pflimlin is perfectly free to place whom he wishes where he wishes. . . ."

The names that most continuously circulated in the corridors were those of MM. Guy Mollet, Jules Moch, who would be offered the Ministry of the Interior, and Robert Lacoste, who could either return to Algeria or take the Ministry of National Defense.

And to explain the attitude of his group, M. Mérigonde repeated the formula of one of his colleagues: "The Republic is threatened and we answer: 'Present.' "

The Socialist group will meet once again this afternoon at four o'clock.

(*L'Information*, May 16, 1958, p. 2)

THE THIRTEENTH OF MAY 1958

The Thirteenth of May 1958 is a date that will remain engraved in the history of Algeria, in the history of the French nation. One hundred thousand patriots—European and Moslem Frenchmen—massed around the monument erected to the memory of their people, whose common sacrifice contributed so much to the glory and grandeur of the mother country.

One hundred thousand patriots come to render homage to the memory of three martyrs to barbarism: three soldiers kidnapped from French territory with the aid of Tunisia and assassinated in Tunisia by the FLN. . . . One hundred thousand patriots, aware of the political shabbiness that made such a crime possible, have responded with a categorical NO to a "diplomatic Dien-Bien-Phu. . . ." A diplomatic Dien-Bien-Phu that along with Robert Lacoste we dreaded from a Pleven government and that we continue to dread from a Pflimlin ministry which installs the same Pleven at the Foreign Office.

This day will prove to the world the living reality of the Franco-Moslem community, which was cemented on the battlefield and which nothing can destroy.

It will express above all the unanimous determination of Algeria's peoples and of our admirable army no longer to allow defeatism and treason, favored for more than four years by the blindness of successive governments, to continue to stab our soldiers in the back and support the growing cancer of demoralization in the heart of the country.

The bankruptcy of the government and powerlessness of parliament, illustrated by endless crises, could not in the long run but surrender Algeria and Algiers, and soon all that counts of France for clear-thinking patriots.

The dispatches from Paris bear witness that Algiers will once again be the catalyst of a recovery of national consciousness.

Such is the primordial meaning of the Thirteenth of May 1958, of the constitution of the Committee of Public Safety—spokesman for the Algerian peoples alongside the army in order to demand the formation of a government of public safety, of national safety, alone capable of assuring the revival of the country and the rescue of French Algeria.

During the previous days in Algiers, then at Oran, M. Robert Lacoste passionately reaffirmed that an unfailing determination, expressed unequivocally, would assure the salvation of French Algeria in a struggle already more than half won. I was among those who urged him to remain here so long as no party-truce government was formed. He said, "I shall remain until the transfer of power." And certainly he had this intention. But in the meantime—after the meeting in London of the Socialist International at which M. Guy Mollet was present—the policy of the SFIO had evolved further. I imagine that having decided no longer to participate in a government, the party insisted on removing M. Robert Lacoste from Algeria . . . to keep him from any deviation from its new orthodoxy. . . . (Thus there was no minister at the May 13 patriotic demonstration with its prodigious scope. . . . M. Robert Lacoste's presence would perhaps have prevented a part of the crowd from committing certain excesses.)

It was in the light of this party control exerted at such a grave moment over one of the most energetic ministers whom we have known these past years that, while in the plane taking me to Paris last Saturday, I decided to prepare hastily the public appeal published in *Dimanche Matin* which asked General de Gaulle to break his silence.

Last Monday I was received by M. Mutter, an hour before the party meeting that was to decide whether or not the Independents would participate in the Pflimlin government. In the course of an interview whose moving nature I will never forget, I pleaded with the former Minister of Veterans' Affairs not to accept the Algiers position offered by a President-Designate of the Council whose views bordered on the prospects of a "diplomatic Dien-Bien-Phu."

Efforts and emotions expended in vain. . . . This brave Trojan, doubtless dizzy with the happiness of soon holding a key portfolio, delivered a paper to me at the end of the conversation . . . his "curriculum vitae" intended for publication in the *Écho d'Alger* . . . !

We are very grieved not to have Jacques Soustelle here. . . .

We can be at least assured that Soustelle is present in spirit at our side. The same for Georges Bidault, André Morice, Roger Duchet. Their common message will be read elsewhere in witness.

But enough said about this imminent past, especially since without requiring further commentary it illuminates a part of the drama that we are traversing.

How far have we come at present? That is what matters.

General Salan's communiqué broadcast yesterday tells us clearly.

One cannot overemphasize the last lines—the appeal to calm, dignity, discipline, confidence, work.

Calm, dignity, discipline.

Let us follow with one heart alone, one spirit alone, the directives of the chief, who while waiting for this triumph has taken the destiny of our French Algeria into his hands.

More than ever we must give an example of union in this discipline. We owe it first to our brothers, to our Moslem compatriots whose resolution to remain French despite so many threats, despite the painful spectacle of politicians' discussions that for so long tore them between hope and despair, we can never greet too warmly.

It is through ordeals, transcending hollow and sonorous formulae, that are forged Franco-Moslem fraternity and the indissoluble bonds between mainland France and Algeria.

We owe to our country this union in discipline.

We owe it to the world that is watching.

In the hours we are now living through it is this union, which, despite the game-playing of a worn-out Parliament, must permit the advent of that national government we summon with all our prayers and which today can be formed only by General de Gaulle.

Alain de Sérigny

(*L'Écho d'Alger*, May 15, 1958, p. 1)

A magnificent day of patriotic enthusiasm and Franco-Moslem enthusiasm in Algiers yesterday! Popular fervor burst forth at the Forum when in the name of the Committee of Public Safety M. Delbecque announced from the balcony of the Ministry of Algeria to the crowd below that General de Gaulle had finally spoken.

That he had responded to the anxious question of the Frenchmen of Algeria: "I hold myself ready to assume the powers of the Republic."

At the end of that hot day there was an instant of intense emotion; then the crowd struck up the *Marseillaise* before the soldiers standing at attention.

The Algerians had waited in the Forum all day, without concern for the sun or fatigue.

In the morning there had already been one impressive demonstration of popular enthusiasm when General Salan spoke. The General had appeared at the balcony at 10:30, surrounded by Generals Jouhaud, Allard, and Massu, and some committee members. At the moment when General Salan's car, preceded by his escort of jeeps, had started to penetrate the crowd to reach the entrance one cry burst forth: "Vive Salan!"

"No," answered the general. "Not 'Vive Salan!' Today only 'Algérie française' is to be shouted."

Shortly thereafter M. Delbecque presented General Salan. In a strong voice Delbecque spoke out:

"Men of Algiers, and through you to all the people of Algeria and mainland France, we are announcing and we confirm that the Committee of Public Safety has just renewed its expression of unfailing confidence in the army and in General Salan."

"In the name of the army of the Algerian people General Salan is going to say a few words to us. Honor and Country, Algérie française, I give you General Salan."

In a voice that was both grave and emotion-filled Salan spoke out:

"Men and women of Algeria, my friends: First of all, know that I am one of you since my son is buried in the cemetery of Clos-Salembier. I could never forget him; for he is in this earth that is yours. . . ."

An immense shout then drowned out the General's voice: "Vive Salan." "Salan is with us." The General continued:

"For eighteen months I have been waging war on the fellagha; I shall continue to, and we shall win it.

"What you have just done by showing to France your determination to remain French by any means will prove to the whole world that through all ages Algeria will save France.

"*Every Moslem is following us.* The day before yesterday at Biskra, seven thousand Moslems went to carry wreaths to the monument to the dead in order to honor the memory of our three men shot on Tunisian territory.

"My friends, the action taken today has brought close to us all the Moslems of this country. Now, for us, for everyone here, the only conclusion can be victory with this army, which you have never ceased supporting, which you love, and which loves you.

"With the generals around me, General Jouhaud, General Allard, and General Massu who has protected you from the fellaghas, we will win because we have deserved to win and because it is the sacred path to France's greatness.

"My friends, I cry 'Vive la France, vive l'Algérie française, vive de Gaulle.' "

The peroration of General Salan's address was applauded a long time. The crowd sang the *Marseillaise* and shouted "Algérie française."

When the general returned to his car he greeted the applauding crowd with his two arms raised. . . .

At 6 p.m. finally M. Arnould announced:

"M. Delbecque is going to inform you of an important communiqué."

In a voice marked with emotion M. Delbecque read the declaration of General de Gaulle.

There was an outburst of joy. An immense ovation exploded. The *Marseillaise* was sung together by ten to fifteen thousand people. "Vive de Gaulle," "Vive l'Algérie française," the population shouted. Enthusiasm doubled when Commandant Mahdi appeared at the balcony.

A living symbol of the French-Moslem brotherhood that no incident had been able to destroy even when it was most in question, the Commandant too was very moved.

He spoke in an impressive silence:

"My dear brothers, my dear sisters, I ask of you a minute of silence in the memory of our sons and brothers fallen for French greatness and for French Algeria. We are going to fight to the end against the fellaghas in the pay of the foreigner . . .

"We are going to cry with all our strength: 'Vive la France, vive l'Algérie française, vive de Gaulle.'"

The crowd shouted its joy. The news had already begun spreading through the city. After months of suffering Algeria is recovering hope.

(*L'Écho d'Alger*, May 16, 1958, p. 3)

DECLARATION OF GENERAL DE GAULLE, RELEASED TO THE PRESS AT 5 P.M., MAY 15, 1958

The degradation of the state inevitably leads to the estrangement of the associated peoples, to uneasiness in the fighting forces, to national dislocation, and to the loss of independence. For twelve years France, at grips with problems too difficult for the regime of the parties, has been entangled in this disastrous process.

In the past the country, from its very depths, trusted me to lead it in unity to its salvation.

Today, in the face of the ordeals which mount anew before it, let the country know that I hold myself ready to assume the powers of the Republic.

(*Le Monde*, May 17, 1958, p. 4)

ENLARGEMENT OF THE PFLIMLIN MINISTRY LIMITED TO THE ENTRY OF M. GUY MOLLET

M. ANTOINE PINAY DECLINES

Another feverish and at times dramatic day yesterday, at the Matignon as well as at the Palais-Bourbon. It was dominated by two events: first, enlargement of the ministry; second, a declaration by General de Gaulle.

The enlargement of the ministry had been partially secured the previous evening insofar as the Socialists were concerned. It remained in doubt with respect to the Independents. The repercussions it would have on the original structure of the cabinet also were not known.

Late in the morning a communiqué stated the intentions of M. Pflimlin:

"The President of the Council has asked M. Guy Mollet and M. Antoine Pinay to join the government with the title of Vice President, in order to show clearly that at the moment when grave threats hang over the country, the republican and national forces unite around the government of the Republic."

Shortly afterward it was learned that M. Guy Mollet had accepted the offer of M. Pflimlin. . . .

What would M. Pinay do? The rightist ministers did not lose hope of convincing him. And M. Pflimlin, with good reason, did not intend to enter into endless negotiations for a larger change at a moment when the situation demanded his attention at every instant.

But the Independent group intended to secure the return of M. Robert Lacoste to Algeria, without considering, however, that after the proclamation of General Salan, this return would have no meaning. M. Pflimlin having refused to yield to such a request, M. Pinay declined the post offered to him. . . .

M. G.

(*Le Figaro*, May 16, 1958, pp. 1, 6)

Assemblée Nationale, Second Session of May 16, 1958

THE PRESIDENT: On the agenda is a discussion of the proposed law number 7163 declaring a state of emergency in metropolitan France.

As the committee has agreed there is an emergency, the discussion will take priority according to the emergency procedure.

M. Gagnaire, secretary of the Interior Committee, has the floor.

M. ETIENNE GAGNAIRE (*Socialist*): Ladies and gentlemen, your Interior Committee has just met and recommends that you adopt the bill on the ι.genda, reading as follows:

"Sole article.—The state of emergency, instituted by Law number 55–385 of April 3, 1955, amended by Law number 55–1080 of August 7, 1955, is extended over all of metropolitan France for a period of three months after the promulgation of the present law. . . ."

M. JACQUES ISORNI (*Independent*): Ladies and gentlemen, it is possible that we are living through the last days of the Fourth Republic. (*Protests and laughter on the left, the extreme left, and several benches of the center.*)

M. PIERRE DREYFUS-SCHMIDT (*Progressive*): You are taking your desires for reality.

M. JACQUES ISORNI: And I would like to express my conviction, at

Journal Officiel, Débats Parlementaires, Assemblée Nationale, 1957–58, 2366–71, 2374–8, 2381, 2385.

the moment when General de Gaulle has addressed the nation. . . . (*Interruptions from several benches.*)

M. PAUL COSTE-FLORET (*MRP*): You're quite the one to talk.

M. JACQUES ISORNI: General de Gaulle has addressed the nation over the heads of the authorities of the Republic by demanding the "powers of the Republic."

If these words still make sense, they mean that he demands executive power and legislative power, that is, dictatorship. (Very good! Very good! *on the left and the extreme left.*)

He demands them at the moment when part of our people, desperate and in peril, seem to appeal to him.

I am speaking to you, my dear colleagues, but—perhaps I have some illusions—with the idea and the desire that my words will be heard across the Mediterranean. While most of us have written "Algérie française" in our hearts, as have thousands of soldiers who are fighting, and as all Algeria is crying, General de Gaulle has never spoken these words. While so many Europeans and Moslems turn toward him anxiously, he does not turn to them. He answers only: "I, de Gaulle!"

While we are convinced that Algeria is a French land and that the bonds which unite us to Algeria are indissoluble bonds of flesh, General de Gaulle talks about "associated peoples."

How well I understand that certain men here have wished for his return, and how well I understand why Bourguiba has sometimes echoed his words!

Into what adventure does General de Gaulle want to lead us . . .?

Mr. President of the Council, you said the day before yesterday that we were on the brink of civil war. Today this may be true.

We are faced on one hand with this threat and on the other with the national uprising in Algeria. This threat has to be laid to rest, and simultaneously the uprising has to be reintegrated into the unity of the homeland. . . .

But today, Mr. President of the Council, you have asked the National Assembly to vote a legislative provision on the state of emergency and you know who voted for it in committee and who is going to vote for it now.

Do you believe that a political maneuver like this can enable you to change the situation in Algeria and, as I just said, to reintegrate the uprising into the unity of the country?

Because I don't think that you are the man for this mission I will vote against the state of emergency which you have requested.

But—and I speak to you with feeling and remembering certain

words which you have spoken—don't you believe that by altering [the composition of] your government immediately, by trying to preserve the narrow bond which perhaps is becoming narrower hour by hour, which will allow you to avoid simultaneously the "Popular Front," civil war, and the secession of Algeria, yes, don't you believe that if you alter your government, with the support of the men of good will in this Assembly, you will save the situation, you will save France, and, if you hold to it, the Fourth Republic? (*Applause on several benches of the right and the extreme right.*) . . .

M. RAYMOND TRIBOULET (*Social Republican*): I remember the position taken formerly by the largest party in the Assembly, the party which yesterday, standing courageously at the head of this new majority, demanded an emergency meeting of Parliament and emergency measures—I mean the Communist Party. I remember a time when a Socialist minister proposed laws in which the Communist Party was called "scoundrels"—and these laws didn't go nearly so far as the law of April 3, 1955, wanted to take us—and then the Communists demonstrated in this Assembly until the Republican Guard had to enter this assembly hall.

Then the Communists were defending public liberty—so they said. Today they propose that you suppress it, and you follow them! (*Applause on some benches of the center and many benches of the right and the extreme right.*)

Why? Because of the events in Algiers, you say.

M. MARCEL-EDMOND NAEGELEN (*Socialist*): And General de Gaulle's statement!

M. RAYMOND TRIBOULET: How is this law declaring a state of emergency going to help in Algeria, and how are you going to make it help . . . ?

How could it be said, after reading this declaration, that General de Gaulle, who with all his comrades—of which you were one, M. Naegelen—re-established the Republic, and who says that he wants to put himself at the service of this same Republic . . . is a menace to republican institutions? How could such a threat be found in this declaration, which answers only the insistent demand of all the parties in the Assembly (*Protests on the extreme left and the left.*)—I am talking about the national parties (*Shouts from the same benches.*)—who said to General de Gaulle: "Is it possible that today you are no longer interested in public affairs and the fate of your native land?" The General gave the only noble, dignified, and short answer he could. He wrote—and I appeal to your good faith to confirm this—"Let the country know that I hold myself ready. . . ." (*Protests on the extreme left and the left.*)

He is only notifying the country; he is at the disposal of the nation. But it has never crossed General de Gaulle's mind—and you, who have been his comrade, you cannot deny this—to attack in any way either the Republic or liberty. (*Shouts on the left and the extreme left. Applause on some benches of the center.*)

It is a different story with the resolution which you want us to enact on the pretext of your false indignation, of this theatrical suspense which is not really heartfelt—for you know the man perfectly well. (*Applause on some benches of the center.*) Is it possible to say, my dear colleagues, on such pretexts, when you have before you the man who liberated our country. . . .

M. RAYMOND GUYOT (*Communist*): No! the people liberated our country.

M. RAYMOND TRIBOULET: . . . and who has served the Republic and served it well, how can you say. . . .

M. GUY MOLLET, VICE PRESIDENT OF THE COUNCIL: M. Triboulet, will you allow me to interrupt?

M. RAYMOND TRIBOULET: Please do. . . .

THE VICE PRESIDENT OF THE COUNCIL: I hope that the Assembly listened to what M. Triboulet was saying with the greatest attention. This is perhaps an important event.

If emotion—which I understand and share, and which justifies my presence in this assembly—does not blind us, we may perhaps draw important conclusions from what M. Triboulet has just said, in case it turns out to be true.

After the part of his speech where he recalled what we all owe to General de Gaulle, I wished that we all could have applauded. Personally I refrained from doing so myself.

In the part of your speech where you stated, M. Triboulet, that General de Gaulle did not want a dictatorship, I wanted to applaud you again. In the hours that followed the Liberation, because he had become aware that the efforts he had put forth abroad to save our country could not be carried on in metropolitan France without the unity of all classes of the nation and the support of the common people—republicans, democrats, and even revolutionaries—General de Gaulle, it is true, restored the Republic to our country.

This is true, and I wish that all of us together could applaud this memory. (*Applause on the left, the center, and numerous benches of the right.*)

But then I stop, unless you are right, M. Triboulet.

You tell us: "There is nothing to fear in General de Gaulle's statement. He isn't calling people out on the streets and he doesn't ask that institutions be overthrown."

M. Triboulet, if what you have said makes any sense, if General de Gaulle declared this afternoon that you have been a faithful interpreter of his thought, then how relieved people would be in this country. (*Lively applause on the left, the center, and numerous benches of the right.*)

If my friends and myself, who were Gaullists in the days when we could have been nothing else, were distressed upon reading his statement, we were distressed not at what it said but at what it did not say. (*Applause on the left and the center.*)

There is an astonishing sort of confusion in this statement, between today and the days of 1940. Already in 1940 we—I was going to say all, but that would be too much—a number of us took a stand against the illegitimate government. . . .

M. JEAN-LOUIS TIXIER-VIGNANCOUR (*Unaffiliated*): Legitimate.

THE VICE PRESIDENT OF THE COUNCIL: I said illegitimate.

M. JEAN-LOUIS TIXIER-VIGNANCOUR: Legitimate!

THE VICE PRESIDENT OF THE COUNCIL: I understand your position, M. Tixier-Vignancour. We will never agree on this point (*Applause on the left and the center.*) but the speaker on the rostrum certainly agrees with me.

M. RAYMOND TRIBOULET: And he applauds you.

THE VICE PRESIDENT OF THE COUNCIL: Today, on the other hand, no one can say that the government approved by this assembly is an illegitimate government.

M. MICHEL MAURICE-BOKANOWSKI (*Social Republican*): No one is saying that.

THE VICE PRESIDENT OF THE COUNCIL: Then why not say that it is legitimate? (*Applause on the left, the center, and several benches of the right.*)

There is another omission which is particularly serious in the days we are living through: all of us advocate varied and different positions on the means of saving Algeria and of preserving the bonds that unite Algeria and France, but we have all said that we want these bonds preserved. We may have differed on the means, but we never differed on the end. But—and I am talking less about the military authorities, with whom I am not yet acquainted enough to make a statement, than about the civilians—civilians over there are beginning to ask whether

Algeria should belong to our community at all. Is there a single word in his statement to condemn that? It is terribly lacking in this statement! (*Applause on the left and numerous benches of the center.*)

Yes, M. Triboulet, there are many of us here who would like to continue to regard General de Gaulle with the great esteem and the profound admiration which so many memories have planted in our hearts. But nevertheless, General de Gaulle's statement is too clearly insufficient for us. (*Lively applause on the left, the center, and numerous benches of the right.*)

M. RAYMOND TRIBOULET: I thank the Vice President of the Council, who, scarcely invested in his high office, has just intervened in the debate to give, in the greater part of his speech, what I found a moving response to the statement of General de Gaulle. (*Stirs on the left.*)

M. Guy Mollet has recalled the time when all classes, all opinions, all the convictions of the French populace were gathered in the Resistance, with General de Gaulle as their leader.

Haven't you noticed in the General's statement this same reference: "In the past the country, from its very depths, trusted me. . . .

From the left: In the past!

M. RAYMOND TRIBOULET: . . . to lead it in unity to its salvation."

This statement seems insufficient to you; but, my dear colleagues, can any of you say: "That should have been deleted" or "This should have been added"? (*Shouts on the left and the extreme left.*) . . . Isn't the main point here this answer to the wishes of the greater part of the nation, which is disturbed at this division between Algeria and France, which we deplore as much as you, M. Guy Mollet, and which we would like to see ended?

And we think, without doubt, that we can give our confidence to the president of the present government to defend the Republic . . .

M. ROBERT COUTANT (*Socialist*): With Delbecque!

M. RAYMOND TRIBOULET: . . . but, alas, we cannot think or hope that his personal action will be enough to end this unhappy division of our country.

Therefore, at the moment when this schism in the nation makes its appearance, General de Gaulle answers simply: "I am letting the country know that if it calls me, I will answer." There's nothing else to it. (*Shouts on the left and the extreme left.*)

From the left: "If it calls me. . . ." Who's calling?

M. RAYMOND TRIBOULET: Because you think that this statement is too short, you doubt the republican loyalties of a man whose whole past—didn't one of his best comrades, who is not in our group, just say, "but that's self-evident"—allows you to complete his statement in the sense of service to the Republic and service to liberty.

On the other hand the bill which you are proposing is contrary to all civil liberties.

At a time so difficult and unhappy, when national reconciliation is the first necessity, we cannot allow an abusive intervention of the administration or the police to divide the country still further. We will not vote for the bill which is before us. (*Applause on some benches of the center and several benches of the right and the extreme right.*) . . .

M. MARCEL-EDMOND NAEGELEN: I have been delegated by the Socialist group to state very calmly, but very resolutely its intention to defend national unity and republican institutions against any attack (*Applause on the left.*) . . .

And national unity and republican law and order are incontestably in danger.

M. LOUIS JACQUINOT (*Independent*): Not yet! That isn't what M. Guy Mollet said. If I understood right, his intervention was an appeal to General de Gaulle to complete or comment on his statement.

M. MARCEL-EDMOND NAEGELEN: M. Jacquinot, I don't think you are qualified to interpret the words of our friend Guy Mollet. . . .

It has just been said that this statement is perhaps more disturbing because of what it doesn't say than what it says. In the statement which the General felt obligated to make yesterday, there is not one word recalling these military leaders to the respect of the law and civil authorities. They have abused the authority conferred on them by civil power in order to revolt against this power and its institutions.

The higher the position of a leader, the more it is imperative for him to give an example of civic loyalty and discipline. Other distinguished generals, at least as distinguished as the generals of Algeria to whom I am referring, did this during the Great War of 1914–18 and after this war, the most costly of all that France has borne.

I am telling you, I assure you with emotion: we must attest with great sadness and indignation that General de Gaulle has not added his voice to that of the perfectly honest man in the Élysée whom the Constitution makes chief of the army, to recall the generals to the discipline which they ought to exemplify to their troops. (*Applause on the left and the extreme left and several benches of the center.*) . . .

THE PRESIDENT: M. Bidault has the floor. (*MM. Moisan, Schumann, and Teitgen [leaders of the MRP] leave the room—various gestures and shouts on the right.*)

M. GEORGES BIDAULT (*MRP*): Ladies and gentlemen. I say to those who would like to stay and listen to me. . . . (*Applause and laughter on the right and the extreme right.*)

M. FERNAND BONE (*Poujadist*): Wait a few minutes and the whole MRP will have left. . . .

M. GEORGES BIDAULT: Mr. President of the Council, the state of emergency allows the government to decree house arrest for suspected persons; it authorizes searches by day and by night; it authorizes control of the press, radio, cinema, and even the theater. . . .

We have not forgotten the severe criticism and express reservations that were stated in this Assembly, even by my friends, when a similar bill was proposed and finally passed for the defense of Algeria. That bill concerned exclusively the French *départements* in Algeria. It has never been proposed before to extend its application to metropolitan France. I am thus compelled to state that what was never requested for the defense of the nation is now being requested for the defense of the regime. . . .

Today it is proposed; you have spoken for it with eloquence and emotion largely shared by the Assembly in order to defend the regime.

Tell us clearly. What you hope to defend, I hope and believe, is not the weakness, the disorganization or the abuses of which you yourself have been one of the sternest critics. What you must have in mind is the Republic, the real Republic, the Republic which guarantees the liberty of its citizens, the basic rights and, do not forget, the defense of its territory. . . .

The coalition you preside over, the measures you propose, the support which M. Jacques Duclos is going to assure you in a few moments (doubtless in the most moderate terms)—this support whose claims and influence I fear your upright intentions will not long be able to avoid—do not correspond to these necessities of public safety.

The Republic you want to save is in danger. You find supporters you do not want, while among those whom you will need, some cannot, at least not yet, come to you.

This is why—with regret, with sadness, with distress, but in the conviction that even in my solitude it is better to obey God than men (*Applause on the right and the extreme right.*) and, as you yourself have written, better to obey one's conscience than political prudence— I cannot, at least in the present circumstances, vote for the bill you have placed before us. (*Applause on the right, the extreme right, and some benches of the center.*)

THE PRESIDENT: M. Jacques Duclos has the floor. (*Applause on the extreme left.*)

M. PIERRE MONTEL (*Independent*): There's Kerensky on the rostrum.

M. JACQUES DUCLOS (*Communist*): Ladies and gentlemen, in these particularly grave hours for the future of our country, for us Communists, as for all republicans, one thing is more important than all others: to defend the Republic . . . (*Shouts on the right and the extreme right. Applause on the extreme left.*) against the dangers which threaten it. . . .

We do not want this; we do not want France to undergo the shame of a military, fascist dictatorship. (*Applause on the extreme left.*) . . .

We also approve of the other measures of protection that have been taken. As for the emergency law, the Communist group has unanimously decided, considering the present situation, to vote for it.

M. ANTOINE GUITTON (*Independent*): That figures!

M. JACQUES DUCLOS: But this vote calls for a few observations.

The state of emergency law restricts everyone's liberties. Still, when we are obliged, as is the case, to count on the working class and on the people to defend the Republic, is it not illogical, ladies and gentlemen, to deprive these defenders of their democratic liberties and of the right to exercise this defense: Is this not really weakening the defenses of the Republic instead of saving it? (*Applause on the extreme left.*)

In the great moments of the French Revolution, Saint-Just said: "No liberty for the enemies of liberty," which meant in substance: liberty for the defenders of liberty. (*Applause on the extreme left. Shouts on the right and the extreme right.*) . . .

THE PRESIDENT: No one else wants to speak?

The balloting is open on the single article of the proposed law.

No one else wants to vote? The ballot is closed.

(*The secretaries count the votes.*)

THE PRESIDENT: Here are the results of the balloting.

Number voting	575
Absolute majority	288
For	462
Against	112

The National Assembly has confirmed.

The Vote
462 deputies voted for:

The 142 Communists; the 6 Progressives; 94 Socialists (of 95) and the 2 MSA; 41 Radicals (of 42); 18 UDSR-RDA (of 20); 12 RGR (of 14); the 14 Democratic Left deputies; 14 African Union (of 15); 73 MRP (of 74); 38 Independents (of 91); 5 Peasants for Social Action; 2 Peasants (of 11); 1 unaffiliated.

112 deputies voted against:

1 Radical; 1 UDSR; 2 RGR; 1 MRP, M. Bidault; 16 Social Republicans; 48 Independents; including MM. André, Montel, and Pinay; 2 Peasants for Social Action; 8 Peasants; 29 UFF (of 30); 4 unaffiliated.

7 deputies did not vote; 12 deputies had permission to be absent.

(Adapted from *Le Monde*, May 18–19, 1958, p. 5)

GUY MOLLET WOULD LIKE TO OBTAIN THREE SPECIFIC ANSWERS
FROM GENERAL DE GAULLE [MAY 16, 1958]

In the lobby of the Assembly, M. Guy Mollet stated that he would like to have an answer from General de Gaulle to three questions:

(1) Do you recognize the present government as alone legitimate?

(2) Do you disown the promoters of the committees of public safety in Algeria?

(3) Are you ready, if you were eventually summoned to form a government, to appear before the National Assembly with a program and, if you were defeated, to withdraw?

He added a little later that these three questions did not constitute an appeal on his part, but a formal demand.

(*Le Monde*, May 17, 1958, p. 2)

TESTIMONY OF CONFIDENCE:

MOSLEMS JOIN LOCAL COMMITTEES SPONTANEOUSLY AND IN
GREAT NUMBER

During a conference held yesterday evening at Government House a press officer announced that Algeria was virtually covered with committees of public safety. In hundreds of communes, villages, and *douars* local committees of public safety have been created—a list of which is published elsewhere.

Delegates are arriving from every point in Algeria; the last ones will probably arrive in Algiers today, in order to install a committee for all of French Algeria.

Massive rallies of the Moslem population, to act in parallel, have been announced. A very distinct easing of tension, moreover, has been registered in the Moslem quarters of Algiers and the interior.

This evening a representative of the Moslem population will attend a press conference at Government House and make a declaration.

The distress of Tunisia before the events in Algiers has been stressed with satisfaction: Bourguiba is silent and the bands of the FLN at the Tunisian frontier line are retreating into the interior of the country.

There is another element of satisfaction, we are told further. M. Picard, chief secretary to M. Soustelle has arrived in Algiers. The declaration of General de Gaulle, greeted in Algiers with enthusiasm, opens the way for President Coty to create the government of public safety that has been demanded so strongly in Algiers.

Residents of Algiers will be able to resume work in calm and happiness.

At the Committee of Public Safety itself the decision of General de Gaulle was received with satisfaction and deep emotion.

There has been equal attention paid to the vibrant homage that Algiers yesterday morning gave to General Salan, who embodies the definitive stance assumed by the army for a renovated French Algeria.

Also stressed was the critical importance of the rallies among the Moslems who are joining local committees spontaneously and happily, thus expressing their confidence and the great hope born of the recent events.

In answer to a question asked by a reporter about the present position of General Salan in regard to the French government, the press officer recommended to the questioner the General's speech in Algiers this morning.

In regard to military operations there is nothing particular to note anywhere in Algeria.

                                        (*L'Écho d'Alger*, May 16, 1958, p. 3)

"ALGERIA WILL BE SAVED—WE HAVE SWORN IT—AND FRANCE WITH HER," M. DELBECQUE DECLARES ON RADIO ALGERIA, SPEAKING IN THE NAME OF THE COMMITTEE OF PUBLIC SAFETY

At the beginning of yesterday afternoon and during the evening broadcasting schedule of Radio Algeria, M. Delbecque, a delegate of the Algiers Committee of Public Safety to General Salan, presented the stirring speech we are publishing below. M. Delbecque was presented at the microphone by M. Alain de Sérigny, a member of the Committee and a delegate to the Supreme Command, with the the following words: "Listeners in Algeria and metropolitan France! Delbecque is going to speak to you. It is an honor and pleasure for me to present him to you.

"Delbecque is one of our own. He is one of the purest of us, one of the most attached to this Algeria we wish to save together with France, of which she is one of the dearest and most beloved provinces, and the most tested. To this Algeria which as of today arises and looks forward to her destiny with calm and confidence while at the same time she announces the restoration of France and the return to peace.

"Delbecque is also the trusted associate of Jacques Soustelle and the intimate repository of his thought, and that guarantees the value of what he will tell us.

"In speaking about Algeria Delbecque knows what is at question; for this former commando chief was recalled as an officer and for six months he covered the *djebel* in the area of Sakamady—not exactly a bed of roses.

"Like Soustelle, Delbecque has sworn to make himself the apostle of French Algeria. He is my colleague on the directing committee of the USRAF in Paris and I meet him again in Algiers where together we sit on the Algerian Committee of Public Safety. Together we have been accredited by the Committee to the headquarters of General Salan in order to assure a permanent liaison between the former organ and the chief commander of the armed forces.

"But Delbecque is above all my friend, and it is with all the warmth of my friendship that I invite you to hear him. A man tempered as he is, with his energy, his dynamism, can never speak without saying something important.

"Delbecque, the microphone is yours."

DELBECQUE'S ADDRESS

"Three days that can henceforth be called 'the three glorious days' of Algiers, are the point of departure, I am sure, of the French renaissance, of her restoration of greatness, of her re-establishment in the dignity and esteem of nations.

"It is appropriate today to stop and tell you, French Algerians of all origins who have been the artisans of this recovery, and you, French of the mainland who have been its spectators, how far we have come, what are the fruits of our action and the reasons for our unshakeable confidence.

"In three days, responding to the call of the Algiers Committee of Public Safety, similar local committees have formed spontaneously and with enthusiasm in every city and village of Algeria and among numerous professional or corporative associations. What the *loi-cadre* sought to obtain in way of a popular representation you have achieved in a surge of brotherhood without any external pressure, like an action having its origins in an instinct to preserve, not only property and persons, but above all the friendship of the union of the communities you represent. . . .

"Is this, I ask you, an organization in opposition to the republican regime? To our attachment to democracy? Under the leadership of our army chiefs you, Algerians, have given a splendid example of your political maturity, of your worthiness to live under the rule of liberty, trusting to the authorities that you have freely chosen. . . .

"What months of bargaining could only sketch out you have brought forth from your fervor, your wisdom, your sense of humanity, your certitude in the destiny of the French nation. No one could be deceived, and our Moslem compatriots have felt this by instinct. They are rediscovering the true face of beloved France, of fraternal France; and it is for that reason that they are joining our committees en masse. After so many months of suffering, the specter of doubt is finally dissipating in the clarity of a regenerated friendship. Never since the tragic All Saints' Day of November 1954 has it been given to us to take note of a similar calm, or equal spirit. . . .

"For let us be certain, we are today at the point of departure of a renewal, and that is quite another thing from what we are accused of: fomenting a plot against the Republic. Ridiculous! On the contrary, we are in process of saving this French Republic with all its values and all its territories by regranting it confidence in itself. We are reconstructing the shaky residence in which the French overseas territories felt so ill at ease because they had lost confidence.

"They were told of a French Union that hitherto was no more than a social necessity; they are going to rediscover that it is a reality and that in this union they will find the place of beloved children and family.

"We have halted our fall on that dizzy slope down which the politicians' aberrations had precipitated us. Let it suffice for me to recall that cascade of surrenders, which after Tunisia and Morocco led us via the ministry of "good offices" to that diplomatic Dien-Bien-Phu that along with Robert Lacoste we had reason to dread.

"We know that this had led us to and then kept us in a war all the more cruel for being fratricidal. We know too, and we cannot forget it, that before the bankruptcy of what remained of the public powers the voices of clairvoyant Frenchmen did not cease to be raised. In the first rank of these it is appropriate to cite Jacques SOUSTELLE, who having been a great governor-general, has become the passionate defender of this country which he loves with all his soul and which returns that love in full. We greet at his side the BIDAULTS, the MORICES, the DUCHETS, the MONTELS, the ROGIERS, and so many others that I cannot cite them all, but whose names will remain graven in the heart of Algerians.

"And thus I ask this question of all Frenchmen who hear me: 'Will not what some among them call the Algerian insurrection, but which is only an insurrection against dishonor and not against our beloved country, provoke the recovery of the French nation? Will my appeal to national pride find no echo among the witting or un-witting defeatists who take pleasure in prostrating themselves before what they believe to be the irreversible sense of history and who refuse to be the artisans of their own destiny, the sons of their own works?' Do they forget that we are above all heirs, and that we do not have the right to throw on the auction block that which our fathers bequeathed us. . . .

"I appeal to the families of our soldiers, to the fathers and to the mothers among whom many mourn. These women are one with us, a pact is sealed between us. I plead with them to solidify the hesitant ones around them, the weak, to forge their energies, to give the example of greatness of soul—they who through their children are united in every fiber of their heart to this beloved and suffering Algeria that we want to save, and France with her.

"I call and beseech finally the National Assembly, the chief of gov-ernment, the national parties of that Assembly who must prove even today that they are 'national' by forging French unity through their votes.

"We will save this France; already since May 13, in front of the monument to the dead in Algiers, she has given signs of her revival. Today she ceases to be the sick man of Europe. Against her the law of the jungle is no longer invoked; she retakes her place of dignity, a peaceful but self-conscious dignity. Her friends will be happy to watch her resume her traditional mission. Her adversaries and her scorners will cease talking of her agony. Her vocation in the construction of the Europe of tomorrow will be able to be affirmed with all the more energy, since she will carry with her these African lands that her genius has been able to wake from torpor and send to the community of civilization.

"The France of Joan of Arc, of Foch, of Clemenceau, a peaceful France but jealous of her liberties—this is the true France, and not that caricature that the parties, electoral interests, and local city-hall ambitions have made of her; and it is because they sense that the true France can support them no longer that the parties, electoral interests, and ambitions want to oppose her, embodied today in DE GAULLE, whom we have chosen as leader.

"And that is why we, Frenchmen of Algeria, European and Moslem, assembled in our committees of public safety, why we appeal to de Gaulle, above the parties and for the salvation of France. . . ."

(*L'Écho d'Alger*, May 17, 1958, pp. 1, 3)

MM. JULES MOCH, ALBERT GAZIER AND MAX LEJEUNE JOIN THE GOVERNMENT

Friday evening May 17 M. Pflimlin altered his government through the following appointments:

M. Max Lejeune [SFIO], Minister of State.

M. Jules Moch [SFIO], Minister of Interior.

M. Albert Gazier [SFIO], Minister of Information.

M. Maurice Faure, who was Minister of the Interior, was appointed Minister for European Institutions.

(*Le Monde*, May 18–19, 1958, p. 3)

GENERAL SALAN CALLS AGAIN UPON M. PFLIMLIN TO OFFER HIS
RESIGNATION TO M. COTY

THE PRESIDENT OF THE COUNCIL ANSWERS WITH AN ABSOLUTE
"NO" THUS ASSUMING TERRIBLE RESPONSIBILITIES BEFORE
HISTORY

At Algiers yesterday a new page of history was written! The arrival
of M. Jacques Soustelle unleashed enthusiasm, catalyzed energy. For
several days M. Jacques Soustelle sought to get to Algiers. He has
finally succeeded after many vicissitudes.

M. Alain de Sérigny lived through the events of that arrival with
an emotion one can well imagine. He has given us this hasty report.

At 1:30 p.m. he left Generals Petit and Jouhaud to go to the military club. At that moment even General Salan did not know of the
imminent arrival of M. Jacques Soustelle. M. de Sérigny telephoned
M. Delbecque who was absent. But M. Mamy informed him that
"everyone has left for Maison-Blanche [the military airport]."

M. de Sérigny thought it was to greet M. Sid Cara whose arrival
was expected. He telephoned immediately to the general headquarters
of the Tenth District and learned that General Salan and Generals
Allard, Massu, Jouhaud, and Petit had left for the airport.

M. de Sérigny now went there himself. What surprise and what
emotion reigned! He found M. Jacques Soustelle, who had just landed
from his plane, in the disembarkation hall. And around him his traveling companions for the trip: General de Bénouville, M. René Dumont,
M. Geoffroy de la Tour du Pin, and M. Charles Béraudier, assistant
to the mayor of the city of Lyon.

A conference was underway at that moment between M. Jacques
Soustelle and the generals. It was important. . . .

M. de Sérigny participated in it after embracing his friend
[Soustelle], the admirable defender of Algeria.

First of all, M. Jacques Soustelle had to be told about the development of events—for in metropolitan France, naturally, news is ab-
breviated if not distorted, and censorship has already been imposed
on the press—and then about the plan for leading M. Pflimlin toward a
more exact comprehension of the situation. . . .

Since the beginning of these memorable days, General Salan has
not ceased deploying all his efforts, trying everything that is humanly

possible, to get the President of the Council to accede to delivering his resignation to President Coty.

Yesterday morning, too, an envoy of M. Pflimlin conferred first with General Salan, then with M. de Sérigny.

In the course of this latter conversation, and understanding that perhaps it was a question of self-esteem that prevented M. Pflimlin from resigning, M. de Sérigny proposed giving a speech that evening over Radio Algiers; he would appeal to the patriotism of the President of the Council and recall the conversation he had had with with him at the prefecture in Strasbourg, when with Marshal Juin he was the guest of the prefect Tremeaud, the former prefect of Algiers whose deepest sentiments had been so cruelly hurt.

M. de Sérigny wanted to make clear, that at that time (September 3, 1956) M. Pflimlin had been badly informed about the true meaning of the Algerian events and about the solutions to bring to Algerian problems.

M. de Sérigny intended yesterday to repeat to him that having been led into error by certain politicians and by certain high ecclesiastic authorities, who were themselves probably deceived, he was viewing the situation in a false light.

These politicians, these high church authorities, had to become conscious, in turn, of their own awesome responsibilities, recognize their errors in the light of present events and intervene with the President of the Council to tell him the truth, nothing but the truth, but the whole truth.

M. de Sérigny had decided, with the complete agreement of General Salan, to give this address with the goal of inducing M. Pflimlin to resign voluntarily, on the grounds that he now understood the historic events of Algiers and their true significance.

Thus everything had been prepared in order clearly and objectively to inform the government about the gravity of the situation. And General Salan had given all the instructions necessary to put a halt to a tragic misunderstanding.

On his arrival at Algiers M. Jacques Soustelle agreed to remain in the shadow until a new intervention with M. Pflimlin was attempted by General Salan.

M. de Sérigny, who experienced these moving moments completes the account:

—I still hear Jacques Soustelle saying to General Salan: "General, I have come here to place myself in the service of French Algeria and thus of the country. Everything must be subordinated to that goal.

I do not want to do anything that might hurt the moves you propose to make. . . ."

Greater abnegation cannot be conceived, nor a more complete disinterestedness on the part of a man who for years has defended French Algeria with so much faith and intelligence.

M. Jacques Soustelle agreed to efface himself if the situation demanded it, in order to allow M. Pflimlin to reflect one more time and make the wise decision and the only one that could reintroduce harmony among all Frenchmen, on both shores of the Mediterranean, without distinction of origin.

At 2:30 p.m. Jacques Soustelle took a private automobile and returned to Algiers incognito, by the Femme Sauvage Ravine.

But the people have a sixth sense. They already knew that Jacques Soustelle had arrived. They proclaimed their joy in the streets with an extraordinary enthusiasm and exaltation. Automobiles flowered with tricolored flags and banners. Loud shouts of "Vive Soustelle!" "Vive l'Algérie française!" could be heard.

Once more the crowd chose the Forum as a rallying place, the focal point of their patriotic fervor.

At the residence of M. Alain de Sérigny, M. Jacques Soustelle awaited the result of General Salan's intervention with M. Pflimlin. At 3:45 p.m. the General, who had already furnished M. Pflimlin with every possible explanation, intervened once again to try and win consent for his resignation.

Alas! the President of the Council categorically refused and answered simply that he intended to convene the Council of Ministers for that very evening.

M. Pflimlin had not comprehended! M. Pflimlin persists in his error. By his absolute "no" he takes on his shoulders the most awesome of responsibilities.

From his balcony overhanging the Bay of Algiers M. Soustelle viewed this city of depths from which arose the clamor and cries of enthusiasm; and then he rode in triumph at the side of General Massu down the Avenue Fourreau-Lamy and the Boulevard du Tlemly and arrived at the Forum, darkened by the crowd. . . .

The crowd was vibrant with the strongest emotion.

(*L'Écho d'Alger*, May 18, 1958, pp. 1, 4)

M. JACQUES SOUSTELLE AT THE MONUMENT TO THE DEAD. . . .
THOUSANDS OF MOSLEM WOMEN PROCLAIM THEIR DESIRE TO
JOIN THE WORK OF RENOVATION THAT HAS BEEN UNDERTAKEN

The Plateau des Glières was far too confined to welcome the thousands and thousands of Algiers citizens who came to applaud Jacques Soustelle.

On Saturday evening the spokesman for the Committee of Public Safety had announced to the crowd that the former governor would place a wreath at the monument to the dead Sunday morning.

From 9 a.m. on, the steps and Laferièrre Square, the Avenue Pasteur and even the Viviani Gardens were filled with a vibrant and impatient crowd. All the balconies were festooned with tricolored flags many of which bore the cross of Lorraine. A cordon of military police barely succeeded in containing the crowd, and police kept traffic moving while the drivers sounded "Algérie française" on their horns. . . .

Precisely at 11 a.m., preceded by General Massu's Peugeot 403, the 15 CV in which M. Soustelle was seated beside General Salan burst from Rue Pasteur. . . .

Generals Allard and Jouhaud, Prefect Baret, and the members of the Committee of Public Safety got out of the cars in turn. While they saluted the flags of the veterans' demonstrations, cries of "Algérie française," "Vive Soustelle," "Vive de Gaulle," "Vive Massu," were gloriously resumed. . . .

After the Minister had rekindled the flame of remembrance a minute of silence was observed. No music, but in an impressive unity everyone was silent and the flags were dipped.

Soustelle sang the *Marseillaise* and thousands of voices took up the national anthem.

The drive toward the Avenue Pasteur was difficult: everyone wanted to touch Soustelle! The people applauded him, threw him kisses. General Salan and the civilian and military personalities were also applauded.

The Plateau des Glières was literally invaded. What enthusiasm! What patriotic faith . . . !

General Salan spoke first.

"M. Soustelle for whom all of you were waiting, has just laid a wreath at the monument to the dead. With him at my side are Generals Massu, Allard, and Jouhaud. This gesture symbolizes the homage of all those who left this land to fight in 1914–18, to those who left in 1940 on the 'Allette,' those who took the 'Ile d'Elbe' and disembarked in Italy, those who, having left here, liberated mainland France.

"By remaining solidly united—by blood, the French with the Moslem French—we shall win the contest and France will understand us."

Then M. Jacques Soustelle addressed the microphone while the crowd greeted each of his sentences with warm applause.

"My friends, you see us here before you: General Salan and General Massu who represent the army, Prefect Baret who represents the administration, all our friends on the Committee of Public Safety who will soon be united in a single committee covering all Algeria. Among us there is only one idea and one passion: the nation.

"It is for her that you have assembled today, as we have ourselves. It is our thought in common."

M. Soustelle had to add specially:

"France, the French Union, the whole world have fixed their eyes on Algeria where they see the will of a united people manifest itself to save its country.

"But there is yet more: after so many years of hesitation and suffering something has been unchained in people's hearts and souls, and that proud motto engraved on the arms of the Republic, 'Liberty, Equality, Fraternity,' has become a living reality in Algiers. There exists no longer a community of diverse origins and different religions, there are only Frenchmen.

"Ah, my friends, what a spectacle you give to the world today— not by proclaiming a principle, but by realizing it. We may have different first names but only one family name: France!"

Then M. Jacques Soustelle recalled the lying propaganda that seeks to make people believe that the movement born in Algeria is no more than an artificial organization of fanatics and rebels.

"This movement" Soustelle declared, "in which all of Algeria is in upheaval, has an equivalent only in the greatest periods of our national history. It is directed neither against our institutions nor against the country; it is a spontaneous movement by a province that intends to remain attached to liberty and to France.

"It shows the solidarity of the army and the people, cemented together indestructibly.

"Yes, tomorrow history shall say that Algeria saved France. Our will shall become neither discouraged nor wearied. It will assert itself in the eyes of the entire world and above all in the eyes of our mainland brothers. Soon unity will be recovered on the other side of the Mediterranean and one will be able to say that Algeria has rendered to France one of those services that can be rendered only once a century."

After inviting the population to calm, determination and dignity, M. Soustelle concluded amid the wild acclaim of thousands of voices, "Vive la République!," "Vive la France!," "Vive l'Algérie française!," "Vive de Gaulle . . . !"

Yesterday residents of the city's suburbs and the countryside utilized their Sunday to join city residents at the Forum. In the unending clamor, among the antennae of the loud-speakers and the stirring of thousands and thousands of faces, there were banners awave from Chiffalo, Ménerville, Maréchal-Foch, Bou-Haroun . . . sometimes inscribed only with the motto, "Vive la France!"

The Moslem women came to the Forum yesterday. The previous evening one dared not believe this could occur, or at least dared not hope for so many. Were they in their own turn going to break with their strict customs? Would they make such a departure? Their arrival, planned for 6 p.m. was ahead of schedule. At 5:15: the first banners, first delegations, first *haïkas*. Here were the women from Chiffalo, then from Castiglione and Bou-Haroun. They had been accompanied on their historic trip by the people of these coastal towns. What a greeting! The clamor, ovations, applause, the waving hands did not stop. . . .

It was now 5:50 p.m. The delegations continued to grow, the loud-speakers to ask that space be cleared, and the crowd remained vibrant. It was really true: the Moslem women were arriving in larger and larger groups. The first ones to come greeted the others with great gestures, laughter, *youyous*.

6:05 p.m. On the balcony now made famous through the will of the people, Generals Salan, Massu, Gracieux, Allard, Jouhaud, and Gilles, and Colonel Thomazo surrounded M. Jacques Soustelle, Dr. Sid Cara, M. Lopez, and members of the Committee of Public Safety. . . . M. Soustelle turned to the Forum and made this declaration:

". . . Perhaps never in the history of Algeria has there been seen such a meeting with Moslems and Europeans fraternally united.

"If tomorrow—Inch'Allah—those who write history tell of these days, they will say that for the first time in Algeria Moslem women assembled—our sisters, who have come to attest by their presence that every barrier has been lowered and that nothing more divides those who live here: that there are only ten million Frenchmen.

"My friends, it can be said that here we have only the sons and daughters of one and the same mother, perhaps bearing different first names but having the same family name: that of our common country.

"My friends, how we have awaited this day!

"If anywhere in the world there are still people who are sufficiently ill-informed not to understand these historic facts, let them come here or look at the photos, let them listen to the airwaves.

"Let them know that this is no angry crowd that is tearing itself apart, but only Frenchmen who have decided once and for all to remain French.

"And if there still exist skeptics or men misled by propaganda who believe that the great national movement born here is directed against progress and liberty, let them see our Moslem brothers and understand that a great human and French emancipation is in progress.

"We claim the three words of the motto of the Republic, 'Liberty, equality, fraternity!'. . ."

Some Moslem women made the great gesture of tearing off their veils and showing their faces. Not all followed. But the fact that they had come itself marked a great step. The spokesman for the women of the Cité Mahieddine—a beautiful dark girl—climbed to the balcony and harangued her sisters:

"For many months we have become aware of the efforts of the army and its officers to improve our administration, and we want to participate equally in this administrative effort.

"We, the Moslem women, have become especially aware of the necessity of change, the essential condition for progress.

"We understand how greatly our traditional garments and our existence as recluses are elements separating us from our French sisters of different religion.

"We strongly desire to start down the road of modernization and profit by the lofty period through which Algeria is now passing to accentuate our advancement.

"We also reaffirm to the military authorities and to the Committee of Public Safety our confidence and our total support for the successful conclusion of the patriotic undertaking which has resurrected in us the immense hope for renewal of brotherhood, joy, and peace under the auspices of mutual confidence between our communities." A young, affianced Moslem man and woman, clad in European clothes, arrived at the balcony to proclaim their joy without constraint and their pride at embodying here the face of the new Algeria.

And this Sunday on the Forum comes to an end with patriotic songs.

Night falls. The windows of the Ministry of Algeria remain lit, for behind these walls men work without interruption for new tomorrows.

(*L'Écho d'Alger*, May 19, 1958, p. 4)

Press Conference of General de Gaulle Held in Paris at the Palais D'Orsay on the Conditions of His Return to Power on May 19, 1958

It is almost three years since I have had the pleasure of seeing you. You will remember that, at our last meeting, I told you of my anticipations and anxieties with regard to the probable development of events and also of my determination to remain silent until such time as I could serve the country by speaking.

And indeed, since that time, events have taken a more and more serious turn. What has happened in North Africa during the past four years has been a harsh ordeal. What is now happening in Algeria in relation to metropolitan France and in metropolitan France in relation to Algeria may lead to a new and extremely grave national crisis.

But this may also be the beginning of a sort of resurrection. That is why it seems to me that the time may have come when it would be possible for me to be directly useful to France once again.

Useful for what reason? Because some while ago certain things happened, certain things were accomplished, things which the nations associated with ours have not forgotten and which foreign countries have remembered. Perhaps this sort of moral capital, in the face of the difficulties that assail us, the misfortunes that threaten us—perhaps this capital might have a certain weight in political life at a time of serious confusion.

Useful also because it is a fact of which we must all take note—whoever we may be—it is a fact that the exclusive party system has not solved, is not solving and will not solve the mighty problems which confront us, especially that of the association of France with the peoples of Africa, and also that of the coexistence of the various communities living in Algeria, and even that of internal harmony within each of these communities.

The fact is there. I repeat that everyone must recognize it. The battles that are taking place in Algeria and the fever raging there are but the consequences of this lack.

And if things continue in the way they have started, we all know perfectly well that the system of government, as it now exists, will be unable to find a solution. It may make plans, it may express intentions, it may even take action and make efforts in various directions. I repeat that it will not reach a solution, and consequently we run

French Embassy, Press and Information Division, *Major Addresses, Statements and Press Conferences of General Charles de Gaulle May 19, 1958-January 31, 1964* (New York, 1964), 1–6.

the risk that one day these solutions will be imposed from without, which undoubtedly would be the most disastrous outcome possible.

Useful, finally, because I stand alone, because I associate myself with no party or organization whatsoever, because for the last six years I have not been politically active and for the last three years I have not issued any statement; in short, because I am a man who belongs to no one and who belongs to everyone.

How can I be useful? Well—if the people wish it—just as I was in the previous great national crisis: at the head of the government of the French Republic. Having said this, I am now prepared, gentlemen, to answer the questions you wish to ask.

QUESTION: General, you said that you were prepared to assume the powers of the Republic. What exactly do you mean by that?

ANSWER: When you assume the powers of the Republic, this can only mean those powers that the Republic itself has delegated to you. That seems to me like a perfectly clear statement. Now about the man who made that statement.

The Republic? There was a time when it was denied, betrayed by the parties themselves. And it was I who rebuilt its armies, its laws, its name. I fought the war in order to obtain victory for France, but I did it in such a way that it also was a victory for the Republic. I did this along with all those who, without a single exception, wanted to join me, and as their leader I re-established the Republic at home. In its name, on its behalf, in accordance with its guiding spirit, my government accomplished a tremendous task of regeneration. Political regeneration: the vote granted to women, citizenship given to the Moslems of Algeria, the beginning of associating within the French Union peoples who formerly were dependent on us. Economic and social regeneration: the nationalization of the mines, of the gas industry, of the electric industry, of the Bank of France, of the principal credit establishments, of the Renault works; the establishment of labor-management committees, organization of social security on such a scale and in such a manner that the workers would be protected from centuries-old scourges, family allowances granted in such a way that families would be helped and also that the birth rate would rise . . . which it did; the establishment of certain organs for the development, the modernization and the prosperity of the country; for instance, the investment plan which would draw from the resources of the present the means of ensuring the wealth of the future; the Petroleum Bureau, so that exploration could be carried on in metropolitan France and in the Overseas Territories for this source of energy which we absolutely must have; a start in the development of atomic energy through the establishment of the commission for that purpose.

When all this was done, I gave the people the chance to speak as I had promised to do. And when it had elected its representatives, I passed on to them—without any reservation, without any condition—the powers I was charged with. When I saw that the parties had reacted like the *émigrés* of old, that is to say that they had forgotten nothing and learned nothing, and that consequently, for me as for the others, any genuine government was impossible, I withdrew. I did not try to force their hand. Subsequently they drew up a poor constitution. They did this in spite of me, against me. I did not attempt to violate it in any way.

Then, in order to try to put an end to the confusion and to create a just and strong state, I instituted the Rally of the French People, inviting everybody to join it, regardless of origin, ideas or sentiments, or even of party labels; I did this only to obtain, through legal means, the institutions that seemed necessary to me. It so happened that the old system succeeded in leading astray, little by little, the elected representatives of the RPF, so that I no longer had any means of action within the law. So I went back home.

Now when there are—and it is not the first time that it has happened in eighteen years—when there are professional saviors of the Republic, who furthermore would not have restored the Republic if they had been alone; when there are professional saviors of the Republic, who impute evil purposes to me, such as violating public liberties, destroying republican institutions, uprooting the rights of the labor unions, I let it go . . . and pass on; which does not prevent me, as well as many others, from asking them what they are doing, these professional saviors, with liberated France and the restored Republic.

QUESTION: How do you judge the current events in Algeria, the revolt of the population, the attitude of the army?

ANSWER: In Algeria there is a population of French extraction, as well as Moslem, which for years has been living in the midst of war, murders, and violence. And this population has realized, ever since this situation has been going on, that the present system established in Paris cannot solve its problems. Even more important, it has seen this system recently turn toward [good] offices from abroad. This population has heard a man—a man who, by the way, is my friend and who was at the time the Minister for Algeria—declare publicly, on the spot, "We are headed for a diplomatic Dien-Bien-Phu." How could this population, being in such a fever, not revolt in the long

run? They see, in Paris, one crisis succeed another indefinitely, and
the same representatives of the same parties distribute amongst themselves the same ministerial posts and mingle together, without anything
either definite or effective coming out of it. Once more, how could
such a population fail to revolt in the long run? Then, this population
has sought, it is now seeking a remedy for its misfortunes outside
parliamentary coalitions. It is absolutely normal and natural; and, then,
it cries "Vive de Gaulle," as all Frenchmen do, in anguish and in
hope.

And besides, this population now offers the magnificent spectacle of
an immense fraternization which may afford a psychological and moral
foundation for tomorrow's agreements and arrangements—which is
infinitely better, of course, than combats and ambushes. Moreover, the
best proof that the French of Algeria do not want at any price to
break away from metropolitan France is precisely the fact that they
say "Vive de Gaulle." One does not shout "Vive de Gaulle" when one
is not on the side of the nation.

The behavior of the army—in these circumstances, the army noted
this tremendous popular emotion. The army considered it its duty to
prevent this emotion from turning into disorder. This it did and it was
right to do so. Furthermore, the army, as you well know, is also profoundly affected by the tragedy through which the country is passing
—that country which it serves very well and often at great sacrifice,
sometimes despite a good deal of misunderstanding. The army, I say,
feels in the depth of its being all the disadvantages and the mediocrity
which are characteristic of the deficiency [in the system of government]
that I stressed earlier. And then, finally, this army in Algeria is in close
contact with the population and consequently cannot escape or prevent
itself from experiencing the same feelings as these people, and the
same overwhelming desire as they to see Paris at last solving its problems.

I understand full well the attitude and the action of the military
command in Algeria and, in my opinion, it would be absurd and deplorable just because there was no authority left in Algeria except a
de facto authority—it would be absurd, under this pretext, to cut all
forms of communication between metropolitan France and Algeria.
It would be absurd because it would be to the detriment of the Frenchmen who are there, whether they are of French extraction or Moslem,
civilians or soldiers, and even to the detriment of many Frenchmen on
this side of the sea. It would seriously compromise France's position
and it would create a state of affairs, the outcome of which cannot be

known. Therefore, I believe that the best thing to do—and even the only thing to do—would be to prevent Algeria from drawing away from France; Algeria must remain with us. As for the army, it is normally an instrument of the state, providing, of course, that there is a state.

I need not stress the urgency of finding a solution; a decision must be made quickly because events and people's thinking are moving fast.

QUESTION: M. Guy Mollet, after his recent speech in the National Assembly, listed certain questions concerning the procedure for your eventual return to power. Would you like to comment on them?

ANSWER: I have the highest regard for Guy Mollet. I don't hesitate to say so. During the war he fought for France and for liberty, risking everything. He was one of my companions and I recall that after the liberation I went to Arras on my way back from visiting our mines which were in a pitiful state. After greeting and expressing our confidence in the miners whom the country so sorely needed, I spoke to the people of Arras from the balcony of the town hall on the main square, and I shall always remember that Guy Mollet was there at my side. Those are things that one never forgets. Afterward, I did not see him again. Why? I do not know. But I have followed his political career from a distance. I will not say that I have always agreed with what he has said and done or tried to do. Moreover, in the regime in its present form, no man of merit can succeed, but what he has done has never altered my esteem for him.

So much for my feelings. And now there are Guy Mollet's questions. . . . I have been told and I have read in the newspapers that he raised a certain number of questions: first, second, third, fourth. . . .

My answer is that if de Gaulle were led to assume—or if he should have delegated to him—exceptional powers for an exceptional task, in an exceptional time, it is obvious that this could not be done according to the rites and procedure that are so habitual that everyone is tired of them . . . and a procedure would have to be adopted—also an exceptional one—for investiture from the National Assembly, for example.

You know that events speak very strongly for themselves, and when there is basic agreement procedures can have considerable flexibility. All my public actions are there to prove this.

Should the occasion arise, I would undoubtedly make it known to an authorized person what sort of procedure seemed adequate to me.

In case I should be asked by the French people to arbitrate, that would be all the more reason for me not to specify at the present time

what the conclusions of my arbitration would be: indeed, the parties
concerned must be heard, a decision must be rendered and we must
be in a position to carry it out—all these are factors that do not at
present exist. I know of no judge who hands down his decision before
hearing the case.

QUESTION: Don't you think that the statement you made on May
15 had the effect of reviving the movement in Algiers which was on
the point of dying out?

ANSWER: I wish to give courage and strength to those French people
who want to remake the national unity, whether they are on one side
of the Mediterranean or the other. There is no other question. The
rest is so much talk—talk from a world that is not mine. Later on
we will understand the attitude of those responsible; there is another
fact, moreover, and it is that at present generals are being treated
as seditious persons, while up to now, as far as I know, no penalty
has been inflicted on them by the public authorities, which have even
delegated more authority to them. In that case, I who have no public
authority—why do you want me to treat them as seditious persons?

You see, in this tragedy, one has to be calm and collected. One has
to be serious. It is absolutely necessary. I am endeavoring to be so.

QUESTION: What would be your policy regarding relations with
Morocco and Tunisia?

ANSWER: I have just said that the great problem to be solved is
the very question of the association of France with the peoples of
Africa, and especially with those whom you have just mentioned.
Everybody knows my feelings and purposes in this respect.

QUESTION: What would your attitude be toward basic public liberties?

ANSWER: Did I ever make any attempt on basic public liberties?
On the contrary, I restored them. . . . Why should I, at the age of
sixty-seven, begin a career as a dictator . . . ?

It is not possible to solve the serious national crisis of the present
time within the limits of everyday routine. As a matter of fact, one of
the politicians recently charged with untangling the famous crisis,
which has really been going on for twelve years, this politician himself
admitted that it was necessary to form a government but a government which would be different from the others.

I find that our country has been extremely weakened and that it
is struggling against great difficulties, and even great threats, in a
disturbed world. I find that France holds some good cards for the
future: the birth rate; an economy that has gone beyond the stage of

routine; French technology, which is constantly developing; the oil which has been discovered in large quantities, and so on.

These cards which we hold may lead, in the near future, to the resurgence of France, to great prosperity in which all Frenchmen must share and in which the people who need and ask for our assistance may also be associated. But it is true that, for the moment, we are in a sad plight, and that is why my last word will be: "I thought it would be useful for the country to say what I have said. Now I shall return to my village and I shall remain there at the disposal of the country."

V

"A VOTE EXTORTED BY INSURRECTION"

Introduction

To paraphrase a venerable proclamation: "The Republic is dead. Long live the Republic!" The readings in this section lead us over this threshold, but not without our wondering in what measure de Gaulle himself aided in the mercy killing. The demonstration of "integration" that was designed to reinforce the moral position of the Algiers Committee of Public Safety yields to the final stages of the crisis, in which the occupation of Corsica by paratroopers introduces a more direct military pressure. Among the readings here are later recollections and testimonies as to how far the orders for the Corsican occupation and even a possible air drop on Paris can be traced back to Colombey-les-Deux-Églises. The reader must ask not only to what extent he believes de Gaulle himself knew and approved specific orders, but also how concrete or delphic the General could be in encouraging his supporters.

Another major series of questions is provoked by the defenders of the Republic, the men in Paris. The speeches of Pierre Mendès-France provide the most memorable evaluation of the expiring regime, the most poignant condemnation of its demise under the possible threat of violence. The statements of the Communist leader Jacques Duclos raised hard and embarrassing questions to the government and rudely exposed its velleities of preserving legal forms for what had become an insurrection. But we must also ponder the growing gap between republican rhetoric and the discreet disengagement of individuals from the regime; the subtle indications that crucial republican leaders were willing to accept a de Gaulle solution. Guy Mollet's letter of May 25, the sudden resignation of Pflimlin on the morning of May 28, and the letter to the Assembly by President Coty are pivotal events—what considerations lay behind them? In seeking answers we reach the limitation imposed by contemporary history: the unavailability of documentation that might resolve questions of what men intended by their actions. There is no guarantee the documentation will ever be available, nor that what we learn will be unambiguous. In any case, for the present we must construct plausible explanations from disparate press reports and public statements. And beyond the specific questions of individual intentions, fears, and calculations, lie the wider puzzles, the great "ifs." Might more determined resistance have rallied supporters and discouraged the army? Would the conflict necessarily have degenerated into civil war? Would de Gaulle have continued to wait yet more years for the new summons to leadership?

Assemblée Nationale, Session of May 20, 1958

M. PIERRE MENDÈS-FRANCE (*Radical*): My dear colleagues, I must confess that since the beginning of this debate, I have received a surprise.

Only a few days ago, we had here a session devoted to the same problems—or I should say to the same agony. A great number of speakers here, while interpreting them very differently, referred to statements made the night before by a man who has played a great role in our history and has rendered his country distinguished service. The contradiction of interpretations had led to a sort of truce when new statements by General de Gaulle were announced.

Thus I thought I would hear the speakers follow up the dialogue that was begun the other day. But I have noted with surprise that, until now, as important as they are, yesterday's statements have not been mentioned.

I would like to end this hesitation and this silence by speaking with total frankness, but not without emotion.

Journal Officiel, Débats Parlementaires, Assemblée Nationale, 1957–58, 2400–404.

I am one of those in this Assembly who followed General de Gaulle during the war and who is still, if you will excuse me for saying so, proud of it.

I am also one of those who, even if they did not always approve entirely of his political position, thought that one day soon General de Gaulle could perhaps put at the service of our divided and torn homeland the immense stock of prestige, glory, and confidence he commands, not only in metropolitan France, not only abroad, but especially among the native populations in all the overseas territories making up the French Union, which is menaced today.

In the eyes of many Frenchmen, de Gaulle could best be the architect of national reconciliation. There are many who for years have turned to the liberator of the country to ask him insistently and anxiously to take a stand on the national drama we are involved in and to help the country escape from the sad crisis it is caught in.

General de Gaulle never answered these appeals. But then sedition broke out in Algiers . . .

From the extreme right: It isn't sedition.

M. PIERRE MENDÈS-FRANCE: . . . and soldiers or civilians invoking the name of General de Gaulle took the grave decisions of which you are aware. And immediately they obtained what so many others had long awaited for in vain: the voice of June 18 spoke out again, but alas—and it is the first sentence of his statement of last week, taken up and developed yesterday—to justify or to excuse their behavior, to condemn the parties, these parties whose weaknesses and past faults I know better than anyone, . . . but to say nothing about factions, perhaps even to cover for them at the moment they were leading an uprising; to revive, intentionally or not, a movement which was growing weaker before he spoke and to restore the courage of these men at the moment they were beginning to see the antinational folly of their endeavor. (*Applause on the left, the extreme left, and some benches of the center. Lively shouts on the right and some benches of the center.*)

This voice which we scarcely recognize—we who will never forget that of June 18—this voice offered the insurrection in Algiers a response in metropolitan France. And thus, de Gaulle, who might have been, who owed it to his past to be the arbiter and the symbol of unity, is advising, aiding, and supporting—I repeat, whether he wants to or not—those who have created the division between Algeria and metropolitan France . . . and the schism of hearts and minds, those who risk casting the country into civil war.

Yes, what a disappointment for those who in the unforgettable past gave him unreserved and unlimited confidence, and who today must see two parties set against one another, perhaps even more cruelly after his appeals than before: on one side the patriots, the soldiers, led astray both by the revival of the memories of setbacks, humiliations, and dangers and by the lies and violent acts by which they have been deceived and intoxicated for years; and on the other side, the democratic and progressive forces, without which or against which the national recovery would never have taken place. De Gaulle cannot be unaware of all this. (*Applause on the left and the extreme left.*) ...

Instead of turning against himself the people's emotion which now will remain vigilant in the hours of peril, General de Gaulle should have fostered it and appealed to it to reinforce the Republic, for which he now reserves his criticism after—it's true and we won't forget—having previously restored it.

General de Gaulle cannot have desired these new convulsions in our country, yet he has just aggravated an already critical situation by what he has said and also by what he has not said.

This is why the men who formerly joined, followed, listened to, admired, and loved him, repudiate him, if there is still time, in order to resolve any ambiguity and to prevent the prestige of a great past with which they were linked and a glorious name of which they too were proud from hindering opposition to insurrection and, perhaps tomorrow, to murderous civil war. (*Applause on numerous benches of the left and the extreme left.*) ...

We await now, anxiously and impatiently, firm action on the part of the government, which has been inhibited until now by scruples that are honorable and understandable, but which surprise, distress, and paralyze our country when they signify the weakness of a state mocked by insolent and aggressive sedition. (*Applause on numerous benches of the left and the extreme left. Stirs on the right.*)

Mr. President, in these difficult hours you have demonstrated your straightforwardness and coolness, but you also have at times retained a certain amount of equivocation in your attitude toward the events and the men in Algiers. In this way, you have perhaps played into the hands of the intriguers and troublemakers of Algiers (*Lively protests on the right and the extreme right. Lively applause on the extreme left.*) and those here who will seize on this pretext to avoid dissociating themselves from them. (*Shouts on the extreme right.*)

The men of the Convention never compromised on the supremacy of civil power or on the indivisibility of republican authority. Let us learn this lesson from them in order to assure the rule of law.

Your power, Mr. President of the Council, doubtless greater than you think, lies in your legitimacy which we are going to confirm by our vote. But this power and this legitimacy are only justified and maintained by action. Therefore we call you to action.

This action demands first of all that you finally condemn without reservation or compromise the agitators of all sorts, the carpetbag politicians over there and the spokesmen of minor interests (*Lively applause on some benches of the left and the extreme left.*) who are exploiting patriotic emotions for their own fraudulent schemes. . . .

Do not tell us that the means at your disposal are weak. Once before, in times past, the Republic was forced to suspect some of its representatives and some of its generals. But it based itself on the people, and the governments of republican defense themselves assumed the leadership of the republican struggle. They took all initiative upon themselves and by their courage and their energy suffused the whole nation with the unshakeable will to protect its rights, its liberties, and its independence against internal and external dangers.

My dear colleagues, a former Minister for Algeria, who is not among my friends, asked this morning in a southwestern newspaper: "Should Algeria be sacrificed to save the Republic, or the Republic be lost to save Algeria?"

Well? I answer that at this moment you risk losing both the Republic and Algeria together, but that, if in the name of the sovereign people, you sternly block off the path of adventure, your determination can keep open the great road of liberty and French union in this historic hour.

Mr. President, we have entrusted the Republic and the nation to you. Now their fate depends on your government. (*Applause on numerous benches of the left and the extreme left.*) . . .

M. RAYMOND TRIBOULET (*Social Republican*): Don't you understand that this man alone, precisely because he wanted to be of service to his country, decided, when the schism between Algeria and France began to arise (*Shouts on the left and the extreme left.*) that he had to come out of his isolation and his silence? . . .

It is absolutely false to think for a single moment that General de Gaulle intervened at the demand of people in Algiers or anywhere else. He intervened because, at a tragic moment in our national destiny, he thought in good conscience that he could serve his country in the role of an arbiter. (*Shouts on the extreme left.*) Ladies and gentlemen, he does not want to fill this role—even yesterday he said, and said with serenity (*Shouts on the extreme left.*) he does not want to fill it in a spirit of violence, with the spirit you called for, M. Mendès-

France, when you spoke of the Convention. Perhaps it could be said regarding the Convention, that you are only pint-sized men of the Convention (*Shouts on the left.*) and that when you call for vengeance against another part of the country, you in no way represent national sentiment, which calls for unity.

General de Gaulle has just said: If I can help my country restore this unity, by playing the role of a peaceful arbiter, I am ready. This is clearly the position that General de Gaulle takes, and I regret that you are raising a misunderstanding in this Assembly, which at the present hour seems criminal to me. (*Applause on some benches in the center and at the extreme right.*)

THE PRESIDENT: The President of the Council has the floor.

THE PRESIDENT OF THE COUNCIL: Ladies and gentlemen. I want to answer briefly the speakers who, in this debate, have raised factors important for understanding and decision. . . .

Some people have asked me the following question: who will exercise the special powers for the maintenance of order?

The answer is simple. Until now, by virtue of events previous to those which began on May 14, and previous to the formation of the present government, the special powers for the maintenance of order have been exercised in all the departments of Algeria by the military authorities.

The government has no intention of innovating on this point. This statement seems sufficient and unequivocal to me, and if you want it explained one more time, I will state here again that if, in the future, judgments can be rendered in calm and objectivity and on the basis of complete information on certain instances of individual behavior, the government, for its part, considers that in the face of a difficult and sometimes dramatic situation, the military commanders who exercise authority in Algeria have obeyed our wish to defend national unity, public order, and republican legality. (*Applause on numerous benches of the center and the right, and several benches of the extreme right.*) . . .

Let us not make the mistake, which would be fatal for the nation and the Republic, of forcing into the camp of the factious those whom we can still think acted in good faith, as good Frenchmen, and as good republicans. (*Applause on the center, the right, and several benches of the extreme right.*)

Perhaps there is another policy in the tradition of the Convention, which M. Mendès-France just spoke of. I remember that the great men of the Convention were as concerned with national unity as with the defense of the Republic. (Very good! very good! *from the center*.)

For its own part, the government will do its full duty. It does not think that national unity can be saved outside of the Republic. Nor does it think that the risk of civil war can be avoided, a civil war which could be the end of our liberties unless we succeed in the days to come in restoring the union between France and Algeria.

It is this passionate desire to hold fast to both ends of the chain, to defend both the Republic and the country, that inspires the resolution of the government. (*Applause on the center, the right, and some benches of the extreme right*.) . . .

SPEECH OF GENERAL SALAN AT ALGIERS, MAY 20, 1958

Citizens of Algiers and Algerians:

During the course of these days an intense outcry has risen to Paris from this Forum, which has become the stronghold of resistance to abandonment. In a unanimous surge of patriotic fervor you have cried out your fierce will to construct a new and fraternal French Algeria, marked by a life led in common by its diverse communities.

Yesterday evening at Paris, in the very heart of Île-de-France, one calm voice made itself heard: General de Gaulle exclaimed: "This may be the beginning of a sort of resurrection. A decision must be made quickly because events and people's thinking are moving fast."

Therefore, yesterday in Paris, he who in other times crucial for the nation was able to show the way of salvation affirmed publicly, forcefully, and without ambiguity that he understood our anguish and our enthusiasm.

Together with Algiers, Oran, Constantine, with the inhabitants of the towns and *douars*, with those of the plains and plateaus, with the mountaineers of the most remote *djebels*, and the nomads of the Sahara—all are gathering to affirm their pride and their will to be French, and to express their certainty of our victory.

From all of French Algeria surges an immense cry of patriotism and faith. Ten million French resolved to remain French, to remain really French, indissolubly tied to the army and to the Republic, say to you my General that your words have given birth in their hearts to vast hope for greatness and national unity.

(*L'Écho d'Alger*, May 21, 1958, p. 3)

M. PASCAL ARRIGHI, DEPUTY FOR CORSICA, HAS ARRIVED IN ALGIERS.

M. Pascal Arrighi, deputy for Corsica, member of the Radical and Radical Socialist group, succeeded in reaching Algiers yesterday evening, in order to put himself at the service of the Committee of Public Safety.

(L'Écho d'Alger, May 20, 1958, p. 1)

GENERAL SALAN ADDRESSING THE ALGIERS CROWD AT THE FORUM: INDIVISIBLY UNITED WE WILL GO UP THE CHAMPS-ÉLYSÉES TOGETHER . . . AND WE SHALL BE COVERED WITH FLOWERS.

Again yesterday evening the Forum welcomed several thousand Algiers citizens, animated by the same patriotic faith as on preceding days.

A long ovation surged from the enthusiastic crowd, which was waving flags and acclaiming its leaders, when Generals Salan, Allard, Massu, and M. Jacques Soustelle appeared on the balcony of Government House.

The crowd repeated "The army to power!" Then at 7:30 p.m. General Salan approached the microphone and spoke out in a strong voice:

"Thank you for that good word: The army to power! Be sure to say to yourself that now we are united and that thus we will go up the Champs-Élysées and we shall be covered with flowers."

A great roar drowned out the General's words.

M. Jacques Soustelle spoke in turn to affirm the patriotic and unfailing union of all.

"Our presence here," he said, "symbolizes the union of all the national forces which, starting from Algiers, have undertaken the salvation of our threatened nation. At the same time we save Algeria it is to France that we will bring salvation.

"Tell yourself often that in the decisive days we are now living through there is one way and only one to assure the triumph of our national cause: union. Union against all divisive maneuvers, union of the army and the Algerian people, united around the prestigious name of General de Gaulle, toward whom all Algeria is turning as supreme recourse of the nation's salvation.

"Vive la France! Vive de Gaulle!"

(L'Écho d'Alger, May 22, 1958, p. 10)

M. Antoine Pinay, who left Paris by automobile Thursday, May 22, shortly after 1 p.m. . . . arrived at Colombey-les-Deux-Églises at 4 p.m.

At 5:40 M. Pinay's vehicle left La Boisserie without even stopping in front of the newspapermen, who tried in vain to slow it down, and took the road for Paris. . . .

Back in Paris about 9 p.m. M. Antoine Pinay arrived at the Hôtel Matignon at 10:15 to meet M. Pierre Pflimlin, whom he informed of the results of his visit. At the end of this interview, which lasted three-quarters of an hour, M. Pinay declared simply that he found General de Gaulle "extremely frank, very friendly and very affable," and that his impression had been "very good."

He refused to comment on his visit to M. Pflimlin, emphasizing that only the President of the Council could, if he judged it proper, reveal the results of his journey to Colombey. A short while later an aide of the President of the Council reported that General de Gaulle reaffirmed to the Independent leader that he remained at the disposition of the country.

(*Le Monde*, May 24, 1958, p. 3)

THE CENTRAL COMMITTEE OF ALGERIA DEMANDS A GOVERNMENT OF PUBLIC SAFETY AND ISSUES AN APPEAL TO PUBLIC OPINION ON THE MAINLAND

After several days of sensitive discussions the Committee of Public Safety for Algeria and the Sahara was constituted Friday morning, May 23, at Algiers.

The tone of the declarations and appeals emanating from this committee show that it intends not only to exercise power in Algeria to the exclusion of the legal authorities but aspires also to affect public opinion and the government in metropolitan France. It was observed, nevertheless, that M. Jacques Soustelle is not a member of the committee. . . .

A statutory decree bearing the signature of General Salan defines the role of the committee, which provides a geographic representation for Algeria and the Sahara and which is the emanation of all the committees of public safety formed since the beginning of events. . . .

The executive of the Algerian Committee of Public Safety has been constituted as follows:

Presidents: General Massu and Dr. Sid Cara, former Secretary of State for Algeria.

Vice-presidents: General Jouhaud, commander of the Fifth Air District; M. Delbecque; and M. Azem Ouali, president of the mayors of Grande-Kabylie.

Secretaries: M. René Denis, Captain Renault, and Dr. Lefèvre.

Liaison attachés: MM. Abdesselam, former member of Dr. Sid Cara's staff, Arnoult, de Sérigny, Martel, Madani, and Captain Marion.

(*Le Monde*, May 24, 1958, p. 1)

IF A DE GAULLE SOLUTION DOES NOT COME SOON—"IT IS NOT OUT OF THE QUESTION THAT WE WILL AID OUR FRIENDS ON THE OTHER SIDE OF THE MEDITERRANEAN," DECLARED THE SPOKES-MAN FOR THE ALGERIA-SAHARA COMMITTEE OF PUBLIC SAFETY LAST NIGHT

. . . With the adoption by General Salan of the statutory resolution confirming the official existence of the Committee of Public Safety and the definitive constitution of the CPS for Algeria and the Sahara, we have completed phase one, declared Lieutenant Neuwirth, information officer for the Committee of Public Safety.

Our first action has been to launch a solemn appeal to all Frenchmen on the mainland, in the French Union and to those abroad as well. They too must create committees of public safety to support our action.

As far as Algeria is concerned, you know that the CPS will arise not only in the towns but also on professional and social levels. One matter of extreme importance is the appearance of the CPS's in trade-union circles.

M. Neuwirth then cited the political demonstration of last evening which had brought to the Forum the representatives of the Algerian Gas and Electric Workers and the railwaymen of the Algerian Railroads.

He next gave a list of those French trade unionists who had recently taken a stand in favor of the patriotic movement in Algiers. "Force Ouvrière," especially, has shown that it has not been duped by the maneuvers and propaganda intended to present the *élan* of the Thirteenth of May as just another meeting. The FO knows that it is not a question of some sort of South-American "pronunciamiento" but rather of a true French recovery.

The second stage, M. Neuwirth continued, is precisely to make metropolitan France take a stand. A number of encouraging signs give us hope that before long the Frenchmen on the other side of the Mediterranean will all understand our action. At Pau and Perpignan, they have created committees of public safety. . . .

Col. Lacheroy added: "We are trying above all to remain in touch with public opinion. Despite censorship, we will reach the public. And in bringing pressure to bear upon public opinion, we are acting indirectly upon those parliamentarians who, let us not forget, often spend their weekends in their districts."

. . . To a journalist asking if General Salan foresaw a solution without de Gaulle, he replied: "The statutory decision of the CPS is sufficiently explicit: to set up a government of public safety presided over by General de Gaulle. As regards the means of action: we have faced up to our responsibilities; let those living in metropolitan France do the same.

"But it is not out of the question that we will aid our friends on the other side of the Mediterranean."

(L'Écho d'Alger, May 24, 1958, p. 4)

MESSAGE FROM PASCAL ARRIGHI, DEPUTY FROM CORSICA,
TO M. JACQUES SOUSTELLE

"An enthusiastic populace has created a Committee of Public Safety, installed in the Prefecture of Ajaccio, and acclaims the name of General de Gaulle.

"The movement is spreading to all communes.

"The paratroops maintain order; there have been no incidents.

Faithfully yours, Pascal Arrighi."

THE DEMONSTRATORS WHO SATURDAY OCCUPIED THE PREFECTURE IN AJACCIO ACCLAIM THE NAMES OF GENERALS DE GAULLE, SALAN, AND MASSU

Ajaccio (ACP)—It was learned this morning that the government of Ajaccio had been prepared by a committee formed in Corsica immediately after the Algerian demonstrations of May 13. Ever since his arrival in Algiers, Pascal Arrighi, Corsican Radical deputy of the Queuille-Morice faction, has been addressing the Corsicans by means of Radio Algiers.

The final preparations for the demonstrations were made during a secret meeting of the committee held in the back room of the Café Ajaccio at 9:30 p.m. Friday, presided over by MM. Maillot and Serafini, the former Social Republican deputy of the *département*.

On Saturday morning, the news was transmitted by word of mouth that there would be a mass gathering at 5:30 p.m. in Place de Gaulle.

At the hour designated for the demonstration, small groups began to form on the Cours Napoleon and on the Place de Gaulle. Although everyone had known about the imminent arrival of parachutists, since early afternoon, the rumor that the CRS from Nice were also expected began to circulate. But at 6:30 p.m. it was the paratroopers who arrived at the Place de Gaulle.

Immediately afterwards it was rumored that the CRS had arrived. One of Air France's Brègues, usually providing the Marseilles-Ajaccio air connections, had landed at Campo de l'Oro at 12:45 p.m., and immediately took off empty in the direction of Nice, urgently called back for transport service by the Minister of the Interior. On its return to Corsica, it carried national guardsmen. With helmets and arms these were then stationed in front of the military hospital intended for Algerian soldiers.

Meanwhile, in Place de Gaulle, the trucks and jeeps of the paratroopers were surrounded by demonstrators, among whom were many young persons who greeted the soldiers with cries of "Vive Massu."

The demonstrators then proceeded up the Cours Napoleon. Easily pushing aside the guard, they opened the doors and gates of the prefecture and filled the Palace Nancini and the office of the prefect. Opening a window, M. Maillot addressed the crowd and had them applaud the names of Generals Massu, Salan, and de Gaulle.

Beside the speaker stood Pascal Arrighi, wearing his tricolored sash; Antoine Serafini, leader of the Ajaccio Bonapartist Party; members of the civil and military commission of Ajaccio; and members of the republican committee of Corsica.

In a few minutes the paratroopers occupied the prefecture, the Amatucci barracks, and the offices of the PTT [Postal, Telephone and Telegraph Services—Eds.] while the CRS moved into the City Hall.

Despite the appeal of Serafini and Arrighi, who asked the crowd to disperse so that the leaders might work and form the Committee of Public Safety, the crowd remained at an estimated size of eight to ten thousand.

At 7:15 p.m., the Committee of Public Safety was formed and the list of its members made public. MM. Maillot and Serafini were presidents, and M. Arrighi refused to take part. "I am here to serve," he said, "and I must continue to serve on a higher level in Algiers and Paris."

At the prefecture, the Secretary-General M. Mouret, replaced the prefect of Corsica, M. Marcel Savreux, who was confined to his quarters. Mr. Mouret also participated in the deliberations of the Committee of Public Safety and of the civil and military commission.

The commission, which had arrived from Algiers at 5 a.m. at Calvi's Sainte-Catherine airport, aboard a plane piloted by Captain Alata and Sergeant Paoletti, was composed of MM. Arrighi, Palvacai, Belgodère, and Renucci for the civilians and of soldiers led by Captain Boher, delegate of General Salan.

At 7:45 p.m., the members of the CPS and those of the civil and military mission appeared on the balcony of the prefecture.

After M. Maillot had read the names of the CPS, M. Serafini read a sympathetic telegram addressed to Algiers by the Committee, asking for the constitution of a government of public safety presided over by General de Gaulle.

At eight o'clock, the demonstrators, led by MM. Maillot and Serafini, marched through the city, stopping at the monument to the dead before invading the chambers of the city council, as well as the offices of the mayor and his deputies—all to the strains of *L'Ajaccienne*.

(*L'Écho d'Alger*, May 26, 1958, p. 4)

Transcript of the Trial of General Raoul Salan, May 1962 (Excerpts)

HEARING OF MAY 19, 1962. TESTIMONY OF M. PASCAL ARRIGHI, DEPUTY FROM CORSICA.

M. TIXIER-VIGNANCOUR: The witness played an important role in the events which lay behind General de Gaulle's return to power. I would like to ask him whether, to his knowledge, the events in Corsica in 1958 were brought about by General Salan, or by someone else?

M. ARRIGHI: The return to power of General de Gaulle took place, as is known, on June 1, 1958. This return began with the Thirteenth of May, by setting Operation "Resurrection" into motion—the opera-

Le Procès de Raoul Salan, Compte Rendu Stenographique, 317–20. From the series "Les Grand Procès Contemporains," under direction of Maître Maurice Garçon of the Académie Française, reprinted by permission of the publisher, Editions Albin Michel, Paris.

tion for which General Dulac had come to Colombey on May 28 to talk to General de Gaulle—and ended with the reform of the Constitution.

The events in Corsica—the only ones I will talk about, as I did not participate in any others—took place on May 24 and the night of May 24–25.

I always paid careful attention to the Algerian affair and expressed my fidelity to the cause of French Algeria, a fidelity which did not waver in the course of the years. As secretary for the Committee of the Interior of the National Assembly for Affairs concerning the Joint Organization of the Saharan Regions, I arrived in Algiers on May 19. Other members of Parliament were arriving or had already arrived there: M. Jacques Soustelle, M. Dronne, M. Hénault. It happened that I met them at lunch or at dinner along with M. Roger Frey, the present Minister of the Interior, who had come in secret from Spain to Algiers, and General Massu.

I ought to say, gentlemen, that from May 19 to May 21, the question of trying anything at all in Corsica was never brought up.

Things changed when a messenger from Paris arrived on May 21.

M. Jacques Soustelle and M. Roger Frey had an office at the Villa des Oliviers, which was the Algerian residence of General de Gaulle in 1943 and 1944. M. Roger Frey told me in the late afternoon of May 21 that a message had arrived from Paris. It said that on May 18 at Colombey, General de Gaulle had asked M. Olivier Guichard— who was one of his principal colleagues—to send instructions to Algiers to prepare the adhesion of Corsica to Algiers.

It was from this date on that the affair crystallized: preparations were set under way by the Gaullist group in Algiers, that is, essentially the colleagues of General de Gaulle: M. Jacques Soustelle, M. Roger Frey, and General Massu. The details were worked out not at the headquarters of the Tenth Military District nor at Government House, but at the Villa des Oliviers.

And Friday, May 23, General Massu said to me, "At last! We have been able to gain the agreement of General Salan, who has been opposed until now."

An executive order was signed by one of the colleagues of General Salan, bearing the names of three civilians and an officer whom I didn't know and whom I never saw. My name was added *in extremis* at the request of M. Roger Frey. As a deputy and general and municipal councillor of Ajaccio, there could be no question of my hiding when grave events might be occurring in my native country.

But when M. Guy Mollet declared that "criminals and fools were behind the operation in Corsica," when M. Claude Fuzier, the editorialist of the newspaper *Le Populaire*, wrote on May 26—I am quoting from memory, but I think that my memory is faithful—"Will the conspirator of Colombey, who refused to condemn the adventure of Algiers, condemn the adventure of Ajaccio?" And when M. Vincent Auriol wrote to General de Gaulle: "Disassociate yourself from a movement . . . [which he termed] seditious"! . . . General de Gaulle could not throw his weight against a movement which he had requested at Algiers as well as at Ajaccio!

When M. Pierre Pflimlin told the National Assembly that sanctions ought to be taken against the civilians and military personnel responsible for the affair of Corsica, he didn't know that if sanctions had been taken, the law could have struck the highest circles including the present Minister of the Interior.

Finally, by his statement on May 15, the General set the events of May 13 back in motion. Didn't he say in his press conference on May 19: "What the Army has done, it has done well! How could you expect this population not to rise up in its present condition?"

And finally he prompted the demand for Operation "Corsica."

I should add that I used all my authority and powers of persuasion in order that there should be no mistreatment or arrests. Documents and archives were neither destroyed nor taken away. The Communist representatives could take their places freely. There were no wounded or dead, as there often are at the time of elections. . . .

In conclusion, there were two generals in the Corsican affair and the events that I saw and knew of in May 1958.

One was circumspect, prudent, and reserved, and, to use the vocabulary of the left wing, he was the "most republican" general: he is before this tribunal today.

The other was demanding, hurried, exacting; and he was the "least republican" general; the Communists at that time called him a "dissident general": he is at the Élysée!

Letter from Guy Mollet to General de Gaulle, May 25, 1958

My General,

We do not know one another. Contrary to what you might have thought I was not at your side at Arras, as I was still a lieutenant in Normandy. As for me, I have certainly seen you, but from afar, like all those who followed and loved you, no more. We have thus never met, never spoken—and I doubt that events will ever allow us to do so.

Several times during the last two days I have received one of your assistants, M. Guichard. I have asked him to communicate to you my estimation of events. I do not doubt that he has done this. He has insisted that I tell you in person the motives which dictate my action. I considered the idea, but I think that the latest developments forbid me from following this suggestion.

Forty-eight hours ago I expressed to M. Guichard my fear that your return to power today would serve the interests of Bolshevism in a nearly irrevocable manner. It was then not only a question of your advent following the events of Algiers. Your silence after the event of Ajaccio transformed my fear into near certainty.

I have dedicated my life to the defense of liberty against whatever threatens it, against all those, Fascists or Bolsheviks—they are the same—who admit to themselves the right to create your happiness without your say and even against you through violence. That has merited me in turn the condemnations of the Nazis, the Bolsheviks, the FLN, and the ultra-antirepublicans.

But no more explanations of my intentions, that would be too long. Let us pass quickly to my analysis of the situation.

In Algeria the Algerians of European origin fear being abandoned. They have said this with sincerity and violence simultaneously. Having heard it already in February 1956 I know all that is worthwhile in this cry; I have understood it. And if everything were halted there it would be perhaps beneficial, since friends and foes in the world would be obliged to understand this fear and this time to recognize it.

The army—too long flouted—has prevented the worst; it too has recognized and even shared in what is valuable in this movement. I too understand it, just as you do.

The rallies then took place. That is normal, you have known others. We do not have the right to slight their meaning. But we must no

longer overestimate their importance. If integration is possible, bravo
from all my heart: the Socialist that I am could only thrill with all
his being when he is told that differences of race, of color, of religion
are giving way, and the patriot is happy to know that this is occurring
around France and in France.

But the structure of the world is not as simple, in my opinion, as
propaganda would have it. There is an Algerian personality; to deny
it can be a mistake.

I believe, moreover, that all I am telling you here is all but unnecessary; I dimly sense that you must think in this way.

Then why do I regard your coming to power as a mistake?

Because you have not said, you could not say either how or why
you are today demanding power. Because the deep instinctive fear of
the popular masses against personal government someday will raise
the people against you or your memory.

Is that to say that in my view you would be a candidate for dictatorship? Even in the quietest hours of this Republic which you gave us I
proclaimed my belief that you did not want dictatorship since you had
refused it when it was offered to you. But I admitted my fear that all
your will would not suffice to prevent you from becoming a dictator
in spite of yourself. It would take too long to attempt to tell you here
the reasons I had.

Is that to say, further, that I subscribe to the calumnies which make
you a neutralist, a foe of the Atlantic Pact, a virtual ally of Moscow?
No. I feel you want France great and independent, but not isolated and
handed over to the enemy.

Thus none of these reasons move me. But I understand the dreadful
game of the Bolsheviks—and I am speaking of those who direct the
action from Russia, not of the pawns which are moved in France and
which can be sacrificed if the need arises, even less of the hundreds
of thousands of honest men who follow them without belonging to
them. The essential difference between them and you is that you know
that you are transient and mortal and they believe themselves eternal,
that you want to act directly upon the present while they think only
of what they call history, the fatal march of time.

If, then, they could appear to have been the sole defenders of
liberty and of the Republic which they scorn, which you do not
threaten, but which your new supporters place in question; if, afterward, on the supposition that you succeed, they are able to wait for
the hour of disillusionment and difficulties which the situation makes
inevitable, they can well think of being your successors. When? In

ten weeks, ten months, ten years, it doesn't matter to them. And we, the socialist democrats, we are compelled to cry to you: think of the future of the liberties which you helped us so much to regain.

That is what I would have had to say to you. But everything is changing and getting worse. Madmen are venturing an attempt at a pronunciamento—and at this hour you have not disowned them. France remains the only country in Europe to experience a "putsch"; its authors intend to use your name and you are silent. I have not succeeded in understanding this, and I express my anguish to you.

Simply.

Guy Mollet

Letter of General de Gaulle to Guy Mollet, May 26, 1958

My dear President,

Your letter causes me to think that we are indeed nearly agreed on matters that are basic.

I regret only the more that you believed you could not carry out your intention of seeing me. It seems to me that for the sake of the unity of the country and, before long, of its independence, everything commands that a direct contact—as discreet as one wishes—should be established immediately between the government and myself, in order to prevent the situation from becoming still worse.

Be assured in any case, my dear President, of my most sincere regards.

Charles de Gaulle
(*Le Monde*, September 16, 1958, p. 5)

Assemblée Nationale, First Session of May 26, 1958

THE PRESIDENT: On the agenda is a report from the government. The President of the Council has the floor.

M. PIERRE PFLIMLIN, PRESIDENT OF THE COUNCIL: Ladies and gentlemen. The government considers it its duty to inform Parliament of the situation created by the events which have taken place in Corsica on May 24 and 25.

Here is a brief résumé of the important facts.

Journal Officiel, Débats Parlementaires, Assemblée Nationale, 1957–58, 2476–7, 2483–7, 2489, 2494.

On the morning of May 24 an airplane from Algiers brought M. Pascal Arrighi, deputy of Corsica, to Calvi. In the afternoon the prefect was informed that ten military trucks were headed toward Ajaccio while a demonstration was being organized around the prefecture. To assure the maintenance of order the prefect requested that reinforcements be sent as soon as possible. Two planes were requisitioned to transport a company of the CRS stationed at Nice, but this company arrived at Ajaccio too late and could not intervene.

Between six and seven o'clock the prefecture was seized by the rioters, led, according to the reports we have received, by M. Arrighi, who stripped the prefect of his powers and installed in his place a committee of public safety of twelve members, including in particular M. Maillot, municipal councillor, and M. Serafini, former mayor-deputy of Ajaccio.

Similar committees have been installed in other towns; they do not express the will of the populace, and I want in particular to note the fact that in conditions which required courage, the municipal council of Bastia affirmed its fidelity to republican institutions. (*Applause on the center, the left, and some benches of the extreme left.*)

These are the facts. It would be foolish to deny their gravity.

Several times, speaking of events in Algeria, I stated that the popular movements which have arisen in Algiers and other cities could to some extent be explained,—despite the excesses which accompanied them and the political capital which was made of them (Very good! Very good! *from the center*),—by the great emotion of our compatriots in Algeria who wanted to show their determination to remain French.

I also stated that to appreciate fairly the role played initially by the military commanders in Algeria, the necessity for them to maintain order while avoiding bloodshed had to be taken into account.

For the events in Corsica there is no justification, there is no excuse. (*Applause on the center, the left, and several benches of the right.*)

There can be no doubt that this is an attack against the legal order, an insurrection against the laws of the Republic. It was obviously premeditated; the operation was conceived, prepared, and carried out with the aim of overthrowing the legitimate authority and replacing it by a dissident power.

Judicial proceedings will be initiated against those who are guilty. For the present, sanctions have been declared by the responsible ministers, notably by the Minister of National Defense.

The role played by M. Arrighi leads the government to place a bill this very day before the National Assembly, providing for the possible impeachment of any member of Parliament who has undertaken an action tending to remove from the authority of the government of the Republic any part of the territories under this authority. (*Applause on the left.*)

If any Frenchmen doubted the existence of a plot against republican institutions, the events in Ajaccio ought to have opened their eyes. (*Shouts on the right and the extreme right.*)

Yes!

M. ROGER LÉGER (*Poujadist*): They were disarmed when they arrived!

M. CHARLES LAMARQUE-GANDE (*Socialist*): Shut up, rebels!

THE PRESIDENT OF THE COUNCIL: Until now, order has been maintained in metropolitan France owing to a number of precautionary and preventive measures, some of which were put in effect by the law of the state of emergency; and I would like to praise the effectiveness of the actions of the Minister of the Interior. (*Applause on the center and the left.*)

The events in Corsica have led the government to reinforce further the security measures. Dispositions have been taken to counter all attempts at subversion which might arise anywhere in the metropolitan territory.

To maintain public order, the government will utilize all the means at its disposal with inflexible vigor. It will utilize them against all those, whatever their political tendency or their designs, who rebel against the law.

But I want to say clearly that to save our endangered liberties, it is not enough to use the forces of order when needed. When the menace becomes this grave, it is not enough for the public powers just to do their duty. It becomes the business of the nation as a whole. (*Lively applause on the center, the left, a few benches of the extreme left, and several benches of the right.*)

I want to follow out the thread of my thought.

The danger which threatens us is civil war. To combat this peril, all those who believe in the Republic and national unity have to stand up against the dissidents. (*Applause on the center, the left, and a few benches of the right and the extreme left.*)

I am convinced that they will not try to persevere in their undertaking if they see all Frenchmen resolved to defend their fundamental liberties (*Applause on the center and the left.*), for it is really a question of our fundamental liberties, not of the defense of a political system whose weaknesses and faults many of us here recognize.

The government has proposed to you to institute, starting tomorrow, a thoroughgoing reform of our institutions . . .

M. ALBERT DE BAILLIENCOURT (*Radical*): Referendum!

THE PRESIDENT OF THE COUNCIL: This reform has to be completed in the next few days to belie those who claim that the republican regime is incapable of reforming itself and who try thus to justify arbitration and violence. (*Applause on the center and the left. Shouts on the extreme right.*)

This arbitration we ought to reject with all our concerted energies. I do not know who will win this test of strength in the end, but I know that civil war can only lead to the decline of the nation and will lay us open for a humiliating defeat in Africa.

As much as and more than attachment to the Republic, it is patriotism which must inspire the national revival that will bar the way to the dissidents.

In these decisive hours, Parliament ought to give an example of unity and discipline. Today, in this Assembly, there must be expressed gravely, resolutely, and unbendingly the will of the nation to defend its unity in respect of the laws of the Republic. (*Lively and prolonged applause on the center, the left, and some benches of the right and the extreme left.*)

Assemblée Nationale, Second Session May 26, 1958

M. JACQUES DUCLOS (*Communist*): I would like to say that the proposed resolution submitted to us ought not to apply only to M. Arrighi, but also to other deputies such as MM. Soustelle, Dronne, Le Pen, Demarquet and Berthommier.

It is an inadmissible fiction to try to separate arbitrarily the plot of Algiers from the coup in Ajaccio.

Let's be done with this fiction which the whole nation considers as a manifestation of benevolence toward the plotters of Algiers.

The truth is that the attack, aimed against republican institutions in Corsica by fascists and parachutists (*Stirs on the right and the extreme right*), throws the real character of the rebellion in Algiers into relief.

As for us, we Communists have emphasized since last May 13 that what was happening in Algiers was a plot against the Republic, which was going to be synchronized with a parallel movement in Paris and in all France.

The object of the dissidents, civilian and military, is to impose by force on the people of France a government of their own choice, a government at the service of the ultra-colonialists in Algeria who once were grouped around Pétain but have now found another leader. By their statements as much as by their actions, Massu, Soustelle, and other dissidents are showing that their plan is to impose by force the formation of a de Gaulle government. . . .

The interests of France demand that we stop sending soldiers to Algeria and that we be done with the fiction of considering as patriots —as men trying to "shepherd" the rioters of Algiers—the plotters who are moving into an attack against the Republic. (*Applause on the extreme left.*)

The fascist assault against Corsica was prepared in Algiers. . . .

It was from Algiers that the traitorous deputy Arrighi set out on board a military airplane, accompanied by an officer who brought "paras" from the garrison of Calvi to mount the attack on the prefecture of Corsica.

This fact underlines the direct responsibility of the triumvirate Massu-Soustelle-Sid Cara and that of General Salan who, when he talks about "walking up the Champs-Élysées" (*Shouts on the extreme left; stirs on the extreme right*), is making it very clear that he intends to use troops from Algeria to strangle public liberties in France. (*Applause on the extreme left.*)

There are the plotters whom it is the government's duty to accuse.

The situation is grave, but if it is, it is because the government has not wanted to face reality. . . .

The government has not acted. The President of the Council, instead of perceiving where the real danger lies, instead of acting as is his duty, always alludes to an imaginary peril on the extreme left. (*Shouts on the extreme right.*)

And without wanting to assign responsibilities for the course of events which has led to the present situation, I must point out with regret that by persistently raising obstacles against the unity of the working class and the democratic forces for the defense of our liberties, the Socialist leaders are in practice playing into the hands of those who count on our divisions to impose a military, fascist dictatorship upon France.

It is time for unity in action in order to guarantee, by the union of popular forces, the victorious defense of the Republic.

Furthermore, even with a great deal of good will, will the government be able to face the assault on the Republic with only the forces at its disposal, which are in part infiltrated by Gaullists? The way things have happened in Corsica cannot help but lead us to wonder. . . .

The chief of the generals in revolt, the inspirer of the plot against the Republic must be shown that the Republic will not let him get away with it. We do not want the kind of Franco who, using the army to personal ends, will do here what was done in Spain twenty years ago.

We don't want the military fascist dictatorship of de Gaulle, erected through the horrors of civil war and on the misfortunes of our country. (*Applause on the extreme left.*) . . .

Tomorrow the workers on the job will not hesitate to show their determination to fight, and this afternoon the CGT has published a communiqué from which I am going to read a few lines:

> The working class is the essential force of republican defense; it must show its determination to save the Republic and its desire that the plot be wiped out. Knowing that the working class awaits immediate directives for action from its central organs, the CGT assumes its responsibilities and asks all workers and all unions to unite and stop work, Tuesday, May 27, from two o'clock on.

(*Applause on the extreme left.*)

And the communiqué addressed to the working men and women of France continues as follows:

> Together and with all the republicans, we can make the afternoon of Tuesday, May 27, into a powerful demonstration of the unity of the French forces of antifascist action and republican defense against the dissident instigators of civil war, for that matter of all war.
>
> Assemble after you have stopped work; unite; elect or enlarge your committees of vigilance for the defense of liberties and the Republic. Demonstrate against the factions and demand of the government that it vigorously employ the exceptional powers which were granted to it to strike down the plotters without mercy.

M. GUY JARROSSON (*Independent*): This is a call for demonstrations!

M. JACQUES DUCLOS: "Reinforce your organizations and your forces to retaliate immediately and with determination against any demonstration or action of the plotters." (*Applause on the extreme left.*)

From the right: It's a call to the streets!

M. JACQUES DUCLOS: One thing is clear, ladies and gentlemen: the government is lagging behind the state of mind of the republican segment of the country, which is becoming more aware every day of the gravity of the situation and the necessity for action.

From this podium, in the name of the French Communist Party, I call workers and republicans to unity and action. The people must count above all on their own unity and action to bar the way to the dissidents.

As for the government, it ought not forget that the country has its eyes on it and that it will be judged by its acts. Those who compromise with an aspirant to dictatorial power cannot keep a republican country quiet.

But, whatever the circumstances, the elemental force of the people is stirring; they are now aware of the origin of the events and know who are the supporters and collaborators of the coup that the men of Algiers organized at Ajaccio. On this subject the question is what the government will do to rid Corsica of the dissidents. There too, it will be judged by its acts. . . .

The Republic cannot be lost unless indecision, fear and resignation penetrate the popular masses by a sort of contagion from above.

But among the people there is an enormous stock of courage, clear-sightedness, and confidence in the outcome of the combat. No, the dissidents will not impose their will on France. Thanks to the union and the action of the people, nothing can stop the great masses of our country from rising up with the firm resolution to shrink from nothing in order that France and the Republic may live. (*Lively applause on the extreme left.*) . . .

THE PRESIDENT: The session is reconvened. I will read the proposed resolution:

"Referring to Article 22 of the Constitution, the National Assembly may, when the suspension of the parliamentary immunity of one of its members has been declared, decide by a separate vote that until the decision of a court, this deputy will be deprived of the right to participate in the work and the votes of the National Assembly and will not have any of the benefits attached to his mandate."

No one else wants to speak. . . .

Here is the result of the ballot:

Number voting	545
Absolute majority	273
For	395
Against	150

I began yesterday the regular process necessary to the establishment of a republican government capable of assuring the unity and independence of the country. I am relying on this process to continue and on the country to show, through its calm and its dignity, that it wishes to see it end successfully.

In these conditions any action which puts public order into question, from whatever side it might come, carries the risk of serious consequences. Even in making allowances for circumstances I could not approve such actions.

I expect the ground, naval, and air forces now in Algeria to continue their exemplary conduct under the orders of their chiefs: General Salan, Admiral Auboyneau, and General Jouhaud. To these chiefs I express my confidence and my intention to establish contact with them immediately.

(*Le Monde*, May 28, 1958, p. 1)

SFIO "MANIFESTO," ADOPTED THE AFTERNOON OF MAY 27, 1958, BY THE SOCIALIST PARLIAMENTARY GROUP AND EXECUTIVE COMMITTEE BY 112 VOTES AGAINST 3 AND AN ABSTENTION

Called by the dissidents of Algiers and Corsica, General de Gaulle has just let it be known that he is beginning what he calls a "regular process" aimed at forming his government.

The Socialist members of Parliament declare:

(1) That the duty of the regularly invested, legal government is to remain at its post as long as it retains the confidence of the majority of the National Assembly.

(2) That in no case will they rally to the candidature of General de Gaulle, which in the form it is presented in and through the reasoning that accompanies it, is· and remains by any estimation a defiance of republican legality.

(*Le Monde*, May 29, 1958, p. 4)

Assemblée Nationale, Session of May 27, 1958

THE PRESIDENT: The President of the Council has the floor.

M. PIERRE PFLIMLIN, PRESIDENT OF THE COUNCIL: Ladies and gentlemen. Following a statement published today around noon by General de Gaulle, the National Assembly has expressed the desire to hear me. I have the duty to bring to its attention facts of which it ought to be aware.

Yesterday, May 26, around 4 p.m., a message reached me from General de Gaulle proposing a meeting which, according to the author of the message, had been rendered necessary by the exceptional gravity of the perils that menace the country.

I accepted this proposition and the meeting took place last night.

I took this course because I judged that it was my duty not to reject a possibility that was offered to spare our country from the trials of civil war. (*Applause on several benches of the center.*)

I asked General de Gaulle to make use of his moral authority to recall to the respect of the law those who had set out, or might be tempted to set out, on the path of insurrection against republican order.

I have to say that at the end of the conversation I had not obtained any assurance that General de Gaulle would publicly take a position in the near future in favor of the maintenance of public order. I had no knowledge of the noon statement until after its publication.

I can attest that General de Gaulle formally stated that, all things considered, he could not approve of an action, from whatever side it came, which threatened public order.

I am grateful to General de Gaulle for taking this position.

Last night's meeting also dealt with various aspects of the national crisis our country is going through.

Confirming his recent public statements, General de Gaulle affirmed to me that he did not see any other way of coming to power than by legal means. He said he was ready to talk with political leaders who were interested in examining with him the conditions in which a government could be formed under his direction.

The President of the Council, for his part, did not forget for one moment that he was invested only by the National Assembly and that he could place only in your hands the mandate you have given him. (*Applause on the center and the left.*)

The moment has come for every man to take his responsibilities.

Journal Officiel, Débats Parlementaires, Assemblée Nationale, 1957–58, 5325.

It is the task of the political groups in this Assembly and their leaders to choose in full conscience of their responsibilities to the nation and the Republic the path they want to follow.

For the government, the path of duty is clear: we will not create a lapse of power. (*Applause on the center, the left, and a few benches of the extreme left.*)

You have been called together this evening to decide on the proposed resolution regarding the revision of the constitution. I have told you this morning the importance and the significance that the government places on this vote. I appeal to the only [acceptable] majority: republican and national.

In deciding for or against you will decide the fate of the government and you will make what is doubtless a decisive choice for the future of the country. (*Applause on the center and the left.*) . . .

AFTER THE RESIGNATION OF M. PIERRE PFLIMLIN

M. COTY CONSULTS MM. GUY MOLLET, TEITGEN, AND PINAY BEFORE SUMMONING GENERAL DE GAULLE

In Paris, the President of the Republic spoke at noon with M. Gaston Monnerville, President of the Council of the Republic [the upper chamber—Eds.]. From 3:30 p.m. on he is to receive MM. Guy Mollet, Antoine Pinay, and Pierre-Henri Teitgen.

M. Coty, who already consulted M. Le Troquer at 4:45 this morning, had first to decide if he would immediately summon General de Gaulle. Once summoned, it would be up to General de Gaulle to calculate the chances he has to win investiture according to rule.

At Colombey-les-Deux-Églises this morning, General de Gaulle was visited by an important personality. According to certain reports it might have been General Catroux, Grand Chancellor of the Legion of Honor. The General had been about to go to Paris Tuesday afternoon [May 27] when the news received from Paris dissuaded him.

Throughout the country the demonstrations organized by Force Ouvrière [Socialist trade unions—Eds.], the CFTC [Catholic trade unions—Eds.], and the Action Committee for Republican Defense, including the non-Communist parties of left and center, took place this afternoon. They were supported by the Communist Party and the CGT.

The evolution of the crisis will be profoundly influenced by the conditions in which it was opened last night.

The decisive ballot concerned the resolution that must legally open the vote on a project for constitutional reform. To be adopted this proposition must receive the absolute majority of the deputies constituting the Assembly (i.e. yesterday 296 votes). It must then undergo the same test in the Council of the Republic. The revision that was envisaged concerned thirteen articles of the Constitution.

By receiving 408 votes against 165 the proposition has been and remains adopted. But by giving the ballot the significance of a vote of political confidence M. Pflimlin had made clear in the morning that he would not count the 142 Communist ballots. Even deducting these, there still remained a large majority of 266 against 165.

Under these conditions the government was led to give as its reason for dismissal not the support of the Communists but the withdrawal of the moderates' ministers and of their support. In fact, beyond the constitutional revision, beyond even the fate of the government, the Assembly had been indirectly invited to decide for or against a resignation of the cabinet that would potentially leave the field free for the appeal to General de Gaulle.

In terms of the decision, however, the crisis was not open at all since the government had won 408 votes and the constitutional revision was even initiated. That is why M. René Coty, applying the terms of the Constitution of which he is the guardian, could only refuse provisionally the collective resignation that M. Pflimlin presented to him.

After having consulted the presidents of the Assembly and the leaders of the three principal "national" parties of the Assembly, MM. Pinay, Mollet, and Teitgen, the Chief of State had to decide whether or not he would call General de Gaulle immediately.

Only a categorical opposition of one of the persons consulted would prevent him.

P. V.-P.

(Le Monde, May 29, 1958, p. 1)

THE SFIO INFORMATION CONFERENCE BROUGHT UP THE EVENTS OF MAY 13 AT LENGTH

. . . M. Jules Moch, who was the Minister of the Interior under M. Pierre Pflimlin, affirmed that from May 27 on he was able to confirm that a certain number of the generals commanding the military districts—four out of nine, he said—made no secret of their favorable feelings toward the men of Algiers. While the parachutists were intending to occupy prefectures and city halls, the gendarmerie was not trustworthy. As for the police, they had been infected since the scandalous demonstration at which they had given way in front of the Palais-Bourbon. The gendarmerie opened its ranks to let the demonstrators pass if the latter wore military decorations or parachutist berets. On the subject of Corsica, the former minister declared that only one sub-prefect, that of Sartène, remained loyal to the government.

If General de Gaulle published a communiqué saying that he had begun the regular process for succeeding to power, it was because he had received the same information on the situation as the Minister of the Interior. The services at Place Beauvau had been informed that on the evening of May 28 a landing from Algiers and an attempt by parachutists against Paris could take place.

De Gaulle alone could return the army to order. . . .

(*Le Monde*, July 8, 1958, p. 3)

GENERAL MIQUEL ADMITS HAVING DIRECTED A CLANDESTINE
RESISTANCE MOVEMENT IN METROPOLITAN FRANCE

Although a week old, a declaration of General Miquel, a beaten candidate at Oran, deserves to be reported insofar as it illuminates the events which occurred in the days following May 13 and constitutes a new element to be placed in the dossier of that period. . . .

"From May 14, in agreement with General Salan, I was the chief of a clandestine movement of resistance for all of France. I am thus the one who brought de Gaulle to power."

It has been confirmed elsewhere that on May 13 itself General Miquel, who then commanded the Fifth Military District at Toulouse, was in direct telephone communication with General Salan.

(*Le Monde*, December 6, 1958, p. 2)

Transcript of the Trial of General Raoul Salan, May 1962 (Excerpts)

HEARING OF MAY 18, 1962. TESTIMONY OF GENERAL ROGER MIQUEL

M. TIXIER-VIGNANCOUR: During the events of May 13 General Miquel was General Salan's chief agent for metropolitan France, and thus he was led to make contact, with one of his officers as the intermediary, with General de Gaulle and to discuss the problem of the landing of military forces in metropolitan France.

GENERAL MIQUEL: Yes, I was General Salan's deputy in metropolitan France. General Salan had made me responsible for determining, according to the situation, the day when the landing could take place. To make this decision, or more exactly to implement the decision of General Salan, I needed especially to know whether General de Gaulle, who had been called by the majority of the nation, gave his assent to this landing.

I sent an officer to Paris whose mission was to make contact with a member of General de Gaulle's entourage; I specified either M. Foccart or M. Guichard. The officer left and returned in one day; he gave me the following account: "I saw M. Guichard, who told me: General de Gaulle does not wish a landing in Paris, but he will accept whatever situation presents itself."

MORE THAN TWO HUNDRED THOUSAND PERSONS MARCH FROM NATION TO RÉPUBLIQUE

THE PARTISANS OF A "POPULAR FRONT" ARE IN THE MAJORITY AMONG THE "DEFENDERS OF THE REPUBLIC"

Tens and tens of thousands of Parisians—more than two hundred thousand according to some estimates, and five hundred thousand according to others—marched Wednesday from the [Place de la] Nation to the [Place de la] République to demonstrate their attachment to democracy and say what they think of a possible recourse to General de Gaulle. For several hours, from 5 p.m. to 9 p.m., an immense tide

Le Procès de Raoul Salan, Compte Rendu Stenographique, 216–17. From the series "Les Grands Procès Contemporains," under the direction of Maître Maurice Garçon of the Académie Française, reprinted by permission of the publisher, Éditions Albin Michel, Paris.

surged all along the 2800 meters which separate the two squares. The watchwords repeated by the crowd—"Stop fascism!" " 'No' to de Gaulle!" "Long live the Republic!"—watchwords taken up on innumerable banners, indicated beyond any possible misunderstanding the intent of the demonstration.

The calm in which the march proceeded, the earnestness of the demonstrators, who mixed joy with seriousness, gave this vast gathering an impressive character that all observers acknowledged. The capital never lost its sense of humor; some improvised shouts—"De Gaulle to the museum!" "The *paras* to the factory!"—were mingled with official slogans.

The "fraternization" of the Socialists and Communists brought back to memory scenes that had not been beheld since May 1, 1947. The participation of many Radicals in the demonstration allowed recollections of the great gatherings of 1936, even of the antifascist *journée* of February 9, 1934.

One might well wonder whether, in reaction to the events of Algiers, the demonstration of May 28, 1958, would not be the prelude to the birth of a new and long-lived Popular Front.

Starting at 4:30 p.m. groups of several thousand persons assembled around placards along the Cours de Vincennes and at the Place de la Nation. Near a banner larger than all the others, displaying the words "Long live the Republic!" across some ten meters, were the organizers of the demonstration.

It was they who began the march precisely at 5 p.m., moving in the direction of the Boulevard Voltaire. In front could be recognized M. Perrin, senator from the Ivory Coast, secretary-general of the UDSR; the Socialist deputy M. Deixonne; MM. Commin, Courrière, and Marius Moutet; many members of the RDA; M. Claude Bourdet and the trade union leaders of the CFTC and FO. Next, surrounded by a cordon of police wearing tricolor armbands, came a large number of non-Communist members of Parliament, the majority from the SFIO. Thus were united side by side MM. Pineau, Gazier, Minister of Information in the outgoing government, Jacquet, Savary, Ramadier, Naegelen, Depreux, Doutrellot. Among the Radical leaders were noted MM. Daladier, Mendès-France, Hernu, Chatelain, Leclerc, Souquez, Panier, Hovnanian, and not far from them M. Mitterrand of the UDSR. The MRP was represented by deputies Mme. Francine Lefebvre and M. Cayeux and many municipal councillors. Among the union delegations that had arrived from all points, organized in factory or neighborhood groups, the representatives of education were prominent, and included M. Francis Perrin, High Commissioner for Atomic Energy, many university professors, and members of student organizations.

The leaders of the CGT and the Communist Party, who answered the call of the organizing committee without being invited, marched behind. However, in some ranks significant reconciliations were occurring spontaneously: marching, for example, arm in arm were the Communists MM. Fajon, Ducollot, and Garaudy and the Socialists MM. Lussy, Gozard, and Titeux. Similarly, leaders of certain trade union organizations fraternized in many spots.

In the front ranks this "unity" was realized thanks to the discipline of the militants of the extreme left, who did not seek to interject slogans other than those calling for "defense of the institutions." Between two *Marseillaises* the participants repeated "Long live the Republic!" "We will defend the Republic!" or "Long live liberty!" trying to drown out the voices of those shouting other slogans. However, soon cries of "Fascism shall not pass!" "Unity of action!" and "Popular Front" rose from the sidewalks, the following lines [of marchers], and the cordons of police themselves. . . .

On the Boulevard Voltaire the march at first encountered only some passers-by ranged in one or two rows along the sidewalks: young children, curious but hesitant to applaud. But starting at Place Voltaire and above all from the Boulevard Beaumarchais several thousand persons coming from the other direction mingled with the demonstration, applauding the passing leaders and repeating the slogans. . . .

Until 9 p.m., nearly four hours after the start from Nation, delegations arrived [at the Place de la République] via the Boulevard Voltaire and blended into the mass of demonstrators, around which rather high-spirited young people wandered noisily in every direction. During this time the monitors of the organizing committee succeeded in preventing the formation of any sizable procession beyond the square. At nightfall, in the midst of strollers and returning automobiles, the last groups went home, still calling for the "unity of action" whose partisans constituted the largest troop in the march.

The disciplined dispersion of such an imposing procession provides evidence that the organizers, if not all the participants, desired to show their strength in calm and not to turn the district into a new "Forum." They were still counting on the National Assembly to serve as their speaking place. But it could be imagined what would happen if new street demonstrations were to intervene in the solution of the present crisis.   (*Le Monde*, May 30, 1958, p. 3)

Transcript of the Trial of General Raoul Salan, May 1962 (Excerpts)

HEARING OF MAY 21, 1962. TESTIMONY OF MAJOR GENERAL ANDRÉ DULAC, CHIEF OF STAFF TO THE COMMANDER-IN-CHIEF OF ALLIED FORCES IN CENTRAL EUROPE.

M. TIXIER-VIGNANCOUR: Mr. President, the first question relates to the mission which he carried out—May 28, 1958, if my memory is correct —to Colombey-les-Deux-Églises; and regarding this mission, since he was close to General Salan at that time, would he kindly tell us what the latter did, what was the meaning of his [Dulac's] mission, and what result could he report to General Salan?

GENERAL DULAC: On the evening of May 27 a telegram reached General Salan from Paris, requesting him to send one of his representatives to describe the military situation to General de Gaulle.

I departed under these conditions, accompanied by two air officers and an officer from my staff; the two air officers were included in order to be able to furnish a more complete range of information concerning the army than I myself could supply.

The interview itself took on the following character: General de Gaulle first asked about General Salan's health and physical condition after the time—which he understood was difficult—he had gone through, and also how fully he had carried out his duties, both civil and military, since he had had both. After that, bringing up the political situation in Paris that day, he gave me the impression of thinking that the process had been stopped from developing favorably, in a manner such as had long not been spoken of.

He asked me what projects were under way relating to the sending of airborne troops against Paris. I gave him an account of what I knew of this project.

After that, he expressed regret that it seemed necessary to consider such an action and told me to convey the following message to General Salan: "Tell General Salan that what he has done and what he will do is for the good of France."

I set out again, therefore, carrying this message, and I gave an account of this interview to General Salan, while also delivering to him a short written report that I composed on the way, thus complet-

Le Procès de Raoul Salan, Compte Rendu Stenographique, 375–6. From the series "Les Grands Procès Contemporains," under the direction of Maître Maurice Garçon of the Académie Française, reprinted by permission of the publisher, Éditions Albin Michel, Paris.

ing the mission. This is why I think I am able—and have the duty—to say that on that evening of the twenty-eighth and on that day of the twenty-ninth General Salan alone was in a position to decide whether or not there would be a military action against Paris.

Assemblée Nationale, Session of May 29, 1958

THE PRESIDENT: Ladies and Gentlemen, I beg the deputies kindly to rise. (*The deputies stand up.*)

I have received the following letter from the President of the Republic.

"The President of the Republic; Paris, May 29, 1958.

"Mr. President,

"I have the honor to forward to you herein, in duplicate, the message which I am addressing to Parliament by virtue of Article 37 of the Constitution. . . .

"I would be obliged to you for kindly reading the message and the present forwarding letter to the National Assembly.

"Yours very sincerely,

R. Coty."

This is the message of the President of the Republic:

"Mr. President, Ladies and Gentlemen, Members of the Parliament.

"The very day that the congress of both houses of Parliament, without my soliciting the honor, called me to the first magistracy of the Republic, I promised—and will hold that promise to the end—scrupulously to obey the Constitution. But I immediately insisted that we would be unable 'o defend properly our free institutions unless we contrived to reform them.

"I restated this to you in my inaugural message. In most of my public addresses since then I have repeated that among all true democracies the French Republic is, on the one hand, the one most assailed by fearsome problems and, on the other hand, the one whose governments are the most fragile and thus the most feeble.

"If thus I passed beyond the traditional limits established by my predecessors, I believed myself authorized to do so, not only by the assent of successive chiefs of government, but also, as is known, by the approval of your great majority.

Journal Officiel, Débats Parlementaires, Assemblée Nationale, 1957–58, 2556–7.

"Four and one-half years will soon have passed without my increasingly pressing appeals having any effect. And whatever may have been the valor and patriotism of the men who have succeeded each other in power, the state has not ceased to disintegrate.

"Now we are on the verge of civil war.

"After having fought so hard for forty years against the enemy, will Frenchmen tomorrow fight against Frenchmen?

"On either side men have the deep conviction of serving the country, which many on both sides have defended at the cost of such heavy sacrifice. On either side men seem to be preparing for a fratricidal struggle. Are we then a nation where force could supersede right? Whoever may be the temporary victors, what would remain after an inexpiable struggle? What would remain of our France?

"There have been throughout our history, after the most violent internecine discords, great days of French reconciliation in a surge of national unity.

"National unity cannot be achieved by anarchy, but only by respect for the law.

"When it is a question of forming a government, in the present state of our Constitution, it is the President of the Republic who proposes and the National Assembly which disposes.

"Obviously there is clearly no question of my multiplying designations [of candidates for Premier]. The choice that rests upon me is therefore heavy with consequences. It imposes upon me an exceptional responsibility.

"That is why I must explain things frankly to you.

"In the hour of peril for our country and the Republic I have turned to the most illustrious of Frenchmen, to him who, in the darkest hours of our history, was our leader for the reconquest of liberty and who, having created national unanimity around himself, refused dictatorship in order to establish the Republic.

"On what conditions would he agree to take over the crushing burden of power? Would these conditions assure the necessary parliamentary majority for his investiture?

"I asked the President of the National Assembly and the President of the Council of the Republic—whom I thank for their valuable assistance—to be good enough to confer urgently with General de Gaulle on this question. This interview showed me that in present circumstances there remained considerable difficulties to be overcome.

"Should I, then, abandon calling on the man whose incomparable moral authority would insure the salvation of the country and the Republic?

"At such a moment, sacred union is our supreme duty. It commands all of us to sacrifice, if necessary, a part of our preferences and even of our convictions.

"To you, the representatives of the nation, I say that there can no longer be a question of parties settling the destiny of our country behind closed doors. Only when the President of the Republic has taken the initiative given him by the Constitution will you make your sovereign and free decision.

"I ask General de Gaulle to agree to come and confer with the Chief of State and examine with him what, in the framework of republican legality, is necessary immediately for a government of national safety, and what might, in a longer or shorter period of time, be done afterward to bring about a profound reform of our institutions.

"I will then take upon my soul and conscience the decision which rests upon me.

"If a failure of the attempt which I have undertaken were to make it clear that at such a critical moment I have erred, I shall not fail to draw the inevitable conclusions immediately. Unable to preserve henceforward the moral authority that is more than ever necessary . . ." (*Exclamations on the left and the extreme left.*)

On the left: This is inadmissible!

(*The deputies sitting on the extreme left and some deputies sitting on the left sit down.—Exclamations from several benches on the right and the extreme right.*)

M. ANTOINE GUITTON (*Independent*): Boors!

THE PRESIDENT: I beg of you, listen! It seems to me indispensable that everyone keep his composure.

"If a failure of the attempt which I have undertaken were to make it clear that at such a critical moment I have erred, I shall not fail to draw the inevitable conclusions immediately. Unable to preserve henceforward the moral authority that is more than ever necessary for him who is commonly called the supreme arbiter, I could only hand over immediately the whole of my functions to the President of the National Assembly in accordance with Article 41 of the Constitution. (*Movement on the extreme left.*)

"Mr. President, Ladies and Gentlemen, Members of Parliament, let my last word be one of confidence, confidence in this admirable people which, after having suffered the most painful tests in its long history, offers to France the prospects of a most magnificent rebirth.

"Representatives of the nation, the destiny of this people is in your hands. Each one of you, with cool-headedness and with dignity, will at the appropriate moment make his decisions so that France may live and the Republic may live." (*Applause on the right, on the extreme right, and from many benches in the center.*)

M. ARTHUR NOTEBART (*Socialist*): Long live the true Republic!

THE PRESIDENT: I am finishing my reading:

"Paris, May 29, 1958.

R. Coty.

"By the President of the Republic:

"The President of the Council of Ministers, Pflimlin.

"The Keeper of the Seals, Minister of Justice, R. Lecourt."

(*On the extreme left and from many benches on the left the deputies cry:* "Vive la République" *and* "Fascism will not pass!" *Then they rise and sing the* Marseillaise.)

Many voices on the left and the extreme left: Vive la République!

On the extreme right: Vive la France!

(*The deputies sitting on the extreme right and some deputies sitting on the right rise and sing the* Marseillaise.)

Many voices on the extreme left and from many benches on the left: Fascists be seated! Fascism will not pass! Fascism will not pass!

The President of the Council and the members of the government leave the meeting chamber, followed by deputies sitting on the right and the center.)

COMMUNIQUÉ OF GENERAL DE GAULLE, MAY 29, 1958

I have had the honor to meet with M. René Coty. At the request of the President of the Republic I informed him of the conditions under which I could assume the duties of government in this decisive moment for the destiny of the country.

Once invested by the National Assembly, the government would receive for a fixed period of time the full powers necessary for action in the present, very grave situation.

In addition, a mandate would be given to the government, following a procedure provided for by the present constitution, to prepare and to submit to the country by means of a referendum, the changes which must be brought about, particularly in regard to the separation and balance of powers and to the relations of the French Republic with the peoples associated with it.

I would be able to undertake the task of leading the State and the Nation only if these indispensable conditions are granted to me with the lofty and ample confidence that the salvation of France, the State, and the Republic makes a necessity.

I could rely, I am sure, on the ardent and resolute assistance of the entire French people to fulfill this national mission.

The events which press upon us could, from one day to another, become tragic.

It is of the utmost urgency that national unity be restored, order in the State be re-established and the authority of government be elevated to the level of its duties.

(*Le Monde*, May 31, 1958, p. 3)

Assemblée Nationale, First Session of June 1, 1958

THE PRESIDENT: The President-Designate of the Council has the floor.

M. CHARLES DE GAULLE, PRESIDENT-DESIGNATE OF THE COUNCIL: The rapidly accelerating degradation of the state, the immediate danger to French unity, Algeria in the throes of trials and emotions, Corsica suffering from a feverish contagion, opposing movements in metro-politan France hourly whipping up their passions and, reinforcing their action, the army, long tried by sanguinary and praiseworthy tasks but shocked by the lack of any real authority, our international position disparaged even within our alliances—such is the situation of our country. At this very moment, when so many opportunities, in so many directions, are offered to France, she finds herself threatened by disruption and perhaps even civil war.

It is in these circumstances that I offered my services to try, once again, to lead the country, the state, and the Republic to safety; and that, designated by the Chief of State, I have been led to ask the National Assembly to invest me with a heavy task.

In order to perform this task, means are necessary.

If you invest this government, it will propose that you give it these means right away. It will ask you for full powers in order to be in a position to act with all the effectiveness, speed, and responsibility demanded by the circumstances. It will ask you for these powers for a period of six months, hoping that at the end of this time—order having been re-established in the state, hope regained in Algeria, unity restored in the nation—it will be possible for the public powers to resume their normal course.

Journal Officiel, Débats Parlementaires, Assemblée Nationale, 1957–58, 2576–9, 2581, 2585–6, 2592; *Major Addresses, Statements and Press Conferences of General Charles de Gaulle*, 7–8.

But what good would be a temporary remedy, a remedy of sorts, for a disastrous state of affairs unless we decided to eradicate the deep-seated cause of our troubles? This cause—the Assembly knows and the nation is convinced of it—is the confusion and, by the same token, the helplessness of constituted authority.

The government which I shall form, provided I obtain your vote of confidence, will submit to you without delay a bill reforming Article 90 of the Constitution, thus enabling the National Assembly to give a mandate to the government to formulate and then propose to the country, through a referendum, the indispensable changes. In the explanatory statement which will be submitted to you at the same time as the text, the government will specify the three principles which must be the basis of the republican regime in France and to which it pledges that its bill will conform: universal suffrage is the source of all power; the executive and the legislative branches must be separate and apart so that the government and the Parliament can, each for its own part and on its own responsibility, assume its full powers; the government must be responsible to the Parliament.

Through the same constitutional reform, the country will be given a formal opportunity to organize the relations between the French Republic and the peoples associated with it. The government will pledge itself to promote this new organization in the draft which it will put to the vote of the women and men of France.

Having received this double mandate, conferred on it by the National Assembly, the government will be able to undertake the immense task which will have thus been defined. If I am to assume this double mandate, I shall first and foremost need your confidence. Then the Parliament must without delay—for events do not permit of any delay—enact into law the bills which will be submitted to it. These laws once passed, the Assemblies will adjourn until the date set for the opening of their next regular session. Thus the government of the Republic, having been invested by the elected representatives of the nation and given, with extreme urgency, the means for action, can then be responsible for the unity, integrity, and independence of France.

(*The session, suspended at 3:15 p.m., is resumed at 4:10 p.m.*)

THE PRESIDENT: The session is resumed.

M. PIERRE MENDÈS-FRANCE (*Radical*): Ladies and my dear colleagues, in this crucial moment, when we are going to take together a heavy responsibility, our thoughts are borne both toward the past and toward the future. Toward the past, for this session will mark the end of a period of our history; toward the future, because a new chapter of this history is going to be written by a man who already holds a distinguished place there, and because each one of us—those who are going to vote for, and those who are going to vote against—ought to hope with all the force of his patriotism that under a new leadership, France will know tomorrow the recovery, here as overseas, which we have awaited for so long and for which some of us know we have fought without respite.

The past?

The Fourth Republic is dying of its own failings. This regime is disappearing because it could not resolve the problems it was confronted with. After the Liberation, its patrimony, almost wholly intact thanks largely to de Gaulle, allowed hope and success. France, glowing and optimistic, seemed destined for a future worthy of her traditions. She needed courage and faith. She had them. She also needed courageous and clear-sighted leaders.

The jobs to be done were hard, but they were within her means. Two especially were decisive for her future.

The reconstruction, or rather the construction of a country more modern, younger, more dynamic; economic recovery, financial and monetary; these were the measure of social progress within and independence without. This was the first series of questions to resolve.

But the transformation of our former colonial empire was our greater and more difficult responsibility. Only innovating policies, opening the way to progressive emancipation, could foster and even reinforce the bonds uniting peoples and territories which today, as much as and more than yesterday, need each other.

The colonial domination of the nineteenth century can no longer withstand the popular movements that have appeared everywhere in Asia and in Africa. An association ought to be substituted for this domination; and it ought to be carried out in complete good faith.

This transformation corresponds to the sentiments of the native populations, equally desirous of liberty and advancement, and of union and close and intimate co-operation with France.

There were a certain number of us who feared from the beginning that if France did not follow by herself an unavoidable evolution conforming to her best traditions, she would soon encounter acute and perhaps bloody antagonism from violently nationalistic movements. To try to contain them alone by more and more rigorous repression would lead to a sort of legal fascism in those territories, and this fascism would later tend, by the force of events, to extend itself to metropolitan France. Little by little, the most elementary rights of man, the progress we believed we had achieved once and for all thanks to the struggles of our forebears, and our institutions themselves would be endangered.

The regime would allow itself to be pervaded and encroached upon. Haven't we already seen the President of the League of the Rights of Man declare, without anyone really being surprised, that his functions had become incompatible with his functions as a deputy?

At the same time, our people, burdened with the weight of twenty years of continuous wars, obliged to devote a considerable part of the product of their labors to unproductive and ruinous expenses, saw themselves deprived of the progress and the improvement to which they thought they had a claim.

Finally, the very independence of our country found itself under fire.

Let us not be surprised, then, that so many Frenchmen turned away, little by little, from the regime which had given them so much cause for discouragement, for disillusionment, and even for anger.

Thus in a few years, the Fourth Republic squandered its moral capital overseas, in France itself, and finally in the world. Thus "the system," which General de Gaulle has so often criticized and which indeed deserves much criticism, failed.

But it is not democracy which has failed, for it is because we have not respected the principles of democracy that we are where we are today. (*Applause on the extreme left and several benches of the left.*)

To try to call our failure the failure of democracy would be to lie one more time, and this lie would be even worse than the ones which preceded it, because it would close to France one hope which ought to remain open for tomorrow. (*Shouts on the right.*)

M. EUGÈNE PÉBELLIER (*Independent*): No one said that.

M. PIERRE MENDÈS-FRANCE: No, it is not the Republic, nor even the parliamentary system which ought to be condemned. Only the bad use that has been made of them has reduced us to impotence and led us to so many dead ends. (*Applause on the extreme left and several benches of the left.*) . . .

The representatives of the nation were mistaken to follow feeble and uncertain ministries—always at the mercy of the intrigues and maneuvers of interest groups and then falling, in the supposedly skillful game of false promises, evasions, and equivocations of governments whose members thereupon turned up in the next cabinet. (*Laughter and applause from the same benches.*)

Often enough I made myself disliked in this Assembly by warning of the dangers we were going toward with this fantasy composed of grand illusions and petty tricks.

The sentiments I feel for the person and the past of General de Gaulle notwithstanding, I will not vote in favor of his investiture; and he will be neither surprised nor offended.

First of all, I could not ever give a vote extorted by insurrection and the threat of a military coup. (*Applause on the extreme left and on several benches of the left.*) For the decision that the Assembly is going to take, everyone here knows, is not a free decision; the consent which will be given is vitiated. (*Protests on the right. Applause on the extreme left and some benches of the left.*)

I am not alluding here to the individual and specific, almost official, threats against a certain number of us, which public censure will thwart. I am talking about blackmail by threat of civil war, the announcement that a coup would be organized against the representatives of the people if their decision was not the one dictated to them. (*Applause on the extreme left.*) . . .

The French people believe we are free; but we are free no longer. My self-respect forbids me to yield to this pressure from the factions and from the street. And General de Gaulle, who has always jealously preserved his pride and his independence, even more when he spoke in the name of the nation, cannot be surprised when I raise a protest here against the affront we are the object of, and which even our errors of the past do not justify; for our mandate forbids us to abdicate before force, our mandate makes it a duty for us to return to democracy if we have strayed from it, and not to stray even further from it. (*Applause on the extreme left and several benches of the left.*) . . .

There is still the political problem of the investiture of the new government which is being demanded of us.

Here it is for me—I don't hesitate to say it—a matter of conscience such as I have not known for the twenty-six years I have sat in this Assembly.

Certainly the confidence, the personal attachment and the memory of the past that the head of government inspires in us weigh heavily in the balance.

But the other side, alas, weighs even more heavily.

It is all too true that the enemies of the Republic, the dissidents, making use of General de Gaulle's name, from the beginning distorted and gravely altered the character of the appeal made today to his arbitration.

It is also true that in a time when days and hours count, too much equivocation persists concerning the conditions and the meaning of an intervention which should at no moment have allowed any suspicions of tolerance toward the enemies of the Republic and of liberty.

For in the end, who is imposing this government on us? Alas, it is the same men who in the past have destroyed all attempts at a reasonable and humane solution in North Africa (*Protests on the right. Applause on the extreme left and several benches of the left.*), who have made war inevitable, have turned this war into a repression without a way out politically, have played on the nerves of a distressed European populace, and now exult because they take the credit for bringing General de Gaulle to power. . . .

Let de Gaulle, starting tomorrow, guarantee immediately and without reservation the liberties endangered by fascism, respect of republican legality, and the rights of man and the citizen; let him restore as quickly as possible a renewed popular representation in the framework of a strict separation of powers, then—and then only—will we arrive at the conciliation which we have the right, the duty, and the mandate to demand.

I dare say that General de Gaulle needs popular representation, and he needs the living presence of democratic forces if he wants to set himself today against the clamors of fascism and tomorrow against the demand, at first insidious but soon pervasive, for a sort of single party which will usurp his reputation and with which we are already openly threatened by the decisions made public in Algiers by men who make use of his name.

It is an axiom of democracy and a lesson of history that it is not unanimity gained in silence or equivocation, in agreement imposed or accepted, or in the discipline of a single party, but it is the confrontation of sincere beliefs that is most favorable to the determination and implementation of good policies. It is the recognized virtue of parliamentary institutions, when they are functioning correctly, to assure this salutary confrontation.

Let General de Gaulle never forget that without democratic freedoms—freedom of the press, freedom of association, freedom of thought and expression—the country will be condemned tomorrow or the day after to pass from fascist dictatorship to communist dictatorship after a long period of disorders, after interminable civil war, the permanent subjugation of man to violence and threats of violence, and the loss of national independence. (*Applause on some benches of the left.*)

As for us, in the precise knowledge of our weaknesses and our mistakes of yesterday, there is no better wish, no more sacred wish which we could have for our divided country than that expressed in a cry which is traditional, but in which for me today the agony is heard above the hope: Vive la République! (*Applause on some benches of the left and of the extreme left.*)

THE PRESIDENT: M. Deixonne has the floor. (*Applause on several benches of the left.*)

M. MAURICE DEIXONNE (*Socialist*): Ladies and gentlemen, for the first time it is not in the name of the Socialist group that I speak to this Assembly. I don't even pretend to speak in the name of those of my friends who with me will soon vote confidence for the government.

But in an hour like this it seemed improper to me that a bridge not be built between what was done yesterday and what will be done today and tomorrow.

We are not the ones who began the division among the workers. Not those who in 1951 sacrificed a whole legislature to ends which could not be considered national. And finally not those who, since 1956, have invested governments only to bring them down a few months or a few days later by changing their votes or withdrawing their ministers. (*Applause on the left and some benches of the center.*) . . .

A man whom one of the factions wanted to keep to itself is agreeing to put his immense prestige in the service of the Republic to hold Algeria back from secession and, with the democrats and while respecting democracy, to accomplish the indispensable reform of our institutions. I declare simply that in today's dangers as in yesterday's, I am one of those who, always with vigilance, plan to remain faithful to the Republic and the country. (*Applause on numerous benches of the left and several benches of the center and the right.*) . . .

M. FRANÇOIS MITTERRAND (*UDSR*): I am among those who wanted to listen to the opinion of the President-Designate of the Council concerning the events which have determined the course of this crisis, that is, the events in Algeria. But today like yesterday, I can only judge by indications such as the following: "The army, shocked by the lack of any real public authority. . . ."

Thus we have to examine the context point by point, both favorable and unfavorable.

Favorable points: a man with unique prestige, incomparable glory, exceptional services rendered. The man of Brazzaville, who, more than any other, signifies by his presence alone a hope for the overseas peoples. Yes, this is a hope for many of our brothers.

Finally General de Gaulle embodies an authority indispensable for

338	"A VOTE EXTORTED BY INSURRECTION"

the conduct of public affairs, and this is not negligible, even if it already gets us into the disquieting points.

I do not doubt, in any case, that the favorable points will lead certain of our colleagues to drop a positive vote in the ballot box, I do not doubt that they are sincere and that in this great debate around the question: "Will de Gaulle save the Republic or will he destroy it?" the same patriotic concern motivates their response.

Disturbing points: the reform of the Constitution. The indications we have received give us no information. I only know the general outline. Do I have to go back over the memories of an itinerary which began at Bayeux? It doesn't make much difference.

We will not fight for the rituals, for the customs, for the defects of this system which has been so denounced. Besides, some of the men who surround General de Gaulle in his government are particularly qualified to dismantle it. They made this system, they ran it, and they have destroyed it. (*Applause on the extreme left and several benches of the left.*) . . .

Some of you who are going to vote "for" can expand upon the favorable points. For myself, I would like to state my principal objection.

When on September 10, 1944, General de Gaulle appeared before the Consultative Assembly which emerged from the external struggle and the Resistance, he had with him two companions named Honor and Country.

His companions of today, whom he doubtless did not choose but who have followed him until now, are named Coup and Sedition. (*Applause on the extreme left and several benches of the left.*)

The presence of General de Gaulle signifies, even despite himself, that from now on violent minorities can safely and victoriously set out to attack democracy. (*Applause on the same benches.*) . . .

These are the events which allow us to assert that it is intolerable that we find ourselves faced with this choice: either accept the President of the Council who is proposed to us today, or be attacked by those who threaten us, those who proclaim clearly, frankly, and without any possible doubt that this is the furthest limit of their co-operation.

But when there was still time to resist and to preserve respect for the law, the government of the Republic, which had been confirmed by a strong majority, disappeared.

This government has died as it lived: sadly. (*Smiles.*)

Rather than this sudden disappearance, I would rather have heard at this decisive moment in our history a voice like that of Abraham

Lincoln which would have repeated his famous words of March 15, 1861:

"In *your* hands, my dissatisfied fellow-countrymen, and not in *mine*, is the momentous issue of civil war. The government will not assail *you*. You can have no conflict without being yourselves the aggressors."*

Yes, I would like to have heard these words. Perhaps they would have prevented the advent of this day at which we have arrived, this day when General de Gaulle comes before us, this day when we are placed before an ultimatum.

Yes, ladies and gentlemen, that is what determines my vote. I judge that the National Assembly is presented with the question: either accept a President of the Council whose merits are immense and whose role will permit—it is presumed—national reconciliation, but who has already been elected by the committees of Algiers, or you—you, the national representatives—will be thrown out.

The same thing appears in a motion, which I have in my hand, of the Committee of Public Safety of Algiers.

In brief, ladies and gentlemen, we will not accept this ultimatum. . . .

THE PRESIDENT: No one else wishes to speak? . . .

Here is the verified result of the count of the vote of confidence.

Number voting	553
For	329
Against	224

The Assembly has granted its approval.

The President of the Republic will be informed.

Many voices on the extreme left: Vive la République!

M. ROGER ROUCAUTE (*Communist*): Down with dictatorship!

The Vote

329 deputies voted for:

42 Socialists (of 95), including MM. Deixonne, Lacoste, Lejeune, Moch, Mollet, and Naegelen, and the 2 MSA; 10 UDSR-RDA (of 20), including M. Pleven; 4 African Union (of 16); 24 Radicals (of 42), including M. Gaillard; 12 Democratic Left (of 13); the 14 RGR; 70 MRP (of 74), including MM. Bidault and Pflimlin; 15 Social Republicans (of 20); 86 Independents (of 89); 7 Peasants for Social Action (of 8); 10 Peasants (of 11); the 30 UFF; 3 unaffiliated, including M. Tixier-Vignancour.

*[From the First Inaugural Address, actually delivered on March 4, 1861—Eds.]

224 deputies voted against:

141 Communists (of 142); the 6 Progressives; 49 Socialists, including MM. Gazier and Mérigonde; 4 UDSR-RDA, including M. Mitterrand; 18 Radicals, including MM. Bourgès-Maunoury and Mendès-France; 1 Democratic Left; 3 MRP; 1 Independent, M. Isorni; 1 unaffiliated.

35 deputies did not vote; 4 deputies had permission to be absent.

(Adapted from *Le Monde*, June 3, 1958, p. 5)

ON THE REDISCOVERED PATH OF GREATNESS

Twenty days after Algiers' decisive, contagious patriotic upsurge . . . Twenty days after the saving explosion of national determination . . . Twenty days after the rallying cry "Algérie française" had here reunited ten million Frenchmen and the army to all that the nation reckons the most authentic loyalty to the republican ideal . . . Twenty days after "Algiers' Thirteenth of May," General de Gaulle has finally received the powers of the Republic.

A final week of hideous spectacles, epitomized by false witness, and the Parliament, suddenly aware of the abyss into which its "system" was carrying the country, has finally understood the anguished appeal and the unshakeable will of the patriots of Algeria and of the army: at the brink of the chasm, at the brink of civil war—which the Communists are still trying to incite—General de Gaulle's government is partially constituted and the National Assembly has invested him with his powers.

The destinies of France are in the hands of the prophetic man of the 18th of June, of the liberator of the country, of the politician who is above party, whose profession of faith is contained in a private statement: "All my life I have thought of France in a certain way: France cannot be France without greatness."

There is nothing in the past torments, nothing in the tempest of an unprecedented crisis, which will not be stamped with the spirit of greatness under de Gaulle.

Such, as one should have expected, was his declaration yesterday to the National Assembly: one would look in vain in those three incisive pages for the least concession to demagoguery. It is a report of undeterrable intentions, following a report of the bankruptcy of the "system."

History will doubtless write that it is a statement of the decease of the Fourth Republic, read, approved, and countersigned by the very ones who made it perish by means of a new kind of homicide: homicide by imprudent stubbornness. . . .

It will be no surprise to note that the intentions of the embryonic government with regard to Algeria have not been stated precisely. General de Gaulle should come to Algiers soon. The decisive events which took place here after May 13—and particularly the magnificent movement of patriotic unity on the part of ten million Frenchmen in support of aspirations for total integration—impose on the head of the government the responsibility for determining, on the spot, all the deep causes, the entire magnitude, the full bearing that they can have on the destinies of France.

Here we are on the rediscovered path of greatness with General de Gaulle.

It was time for the impassioned cry of *"Algérie française!"* uttered for the safety of France, to be heard. Mendès-France and Mitterrand would have gambled up to the last minute on a Popular Front. Another lapse and the country was ready for a "Prague take-over." The "legal apparatus" of the Communists was already in place. And their shock forces in the street with their picks, their axes, and their heavy wooden placards, which have a number of uses . . .

The country had a narrow escape!

Alain de Sérigny
(*L'Écho d'Alger*, June 1–2, 1958, pp. 1, 3)

VI
"THE ALGERIA OF TOMORROW"

Introduction

The Algerian dilemma helped liquidate the Fourth Republic, but did not disappear with it. The selections in this section reveal the anguish it caused in the first four years of the Fifth Republic as well. The constitutional provisions included here must, of course, be read against those of the charter they replaced; they permit an evaluation of what role the chief executive might fill in the new governmental structure and by what authority. The presidential addresses mark the stages of de Gaulle's own emergence in the movement to divest France of Algeria, but they leave us with profound inquiries. At what point and why did de Gaulle decide that Algeria must receive independence? Or indeed had he believed at the outset of his new regime that France could durably retain her rule? What was the process of disabusing the partisans of *Algérie française* of their belief that de Gaulle shared their goals? How did domestic and foreign considerations move de Gaulle to define a new view of France's mission that allowed for giving up Algeria? The newspaper accounts here allow no more than a glimpse of the turmoil within metropolitan France between de Gaulle's accession and the trials of Raoul Salan and the other insurgent generals of April 1961; nor is there space in a book on the advent of the Fifth Republic for the defiant petition of Jean-Paul Sartre and other French intellectuals condemning the war, or for coverage of the wave of "plastic bomb" explosions, or the reawakening of a quasi-fascist French right around the *Algérie française* forces. To the partisans of French Algeria, de Gaulle's course was betrayal; and it is their evaluation that the last document, a transcript of testimony sympathetic to General Salan, forces us to confront. De Gaulle's career in 1962 was open to the same charges of desertion and treason as in 1940. Was the justification any stronger or weaker in 1962? Who was loyal in the highest sense, who the betrayer? Where was loyalty due? To upholding the past promises that the French Algerians would never be deserted; or to the restoration of peace in a political community lacerated by violence?

List of Ministers in the de Gaulle Government Invested by the National Assembly on June 1, 1958

President of the Council, in charge of National Defense and Algerian Affairs   Charles de Gaulle

Minister of State Félix Houphouet-Boigny (RDA Deputy)

Minister of State Louis Jacquinot (Indep. Deputy)

Minister of State Pierre Pflimlin (MRP Deputy)

Minister of State Guy Mollet (Socialist Deputy)

Minister Delegate to the Presidency of the Council   André Malraux

Minister of Justice   Michel Debré (Soc. Rep. Senator)

Minister of Foreign Affairs   Maurice Couve de Murville (last post held: French Ambassador to Germany)

Minister of Interior   Emile Pelletier (last post held: Prefect of the Seine Dept.)

Minister of Armed Forces   Pierre Guillaumat (last post held: Administrator-General, Commissariat for Atomic Energy)

Minister of Sahara   Max Lejeune (Socialist Deputy)

Minister of Finance   Antoine Pinay (Indep. Deputy)

Minister of National Education   Jean Berthoin (Rad. Soc. Senator)

Minister of Public Works   Robert Buron (MRP Deputy)

Minister of Industry and Commerce   Edmond Ramonet (Rad. Soc. Deputy)

Minister of Agriculture   Roger Houdet (Indep. Senator)

French Embassy, New York, *French Affairs*, No. 59, June 1958.

Minister of France Overseas   Bernard Cornut-Gentille (last post held: French Ambassador to Argentina)

Minister of Labor   Paul Bacon (MRP Deputy)

Minister of Housing   Pierre Sudreau (last post held: Commissioner for Housing in Seine Dépt.)

Minister of War Veterans   Edmond Michelet (Soc. Rep. Senator)

Minister of Post Office, Telegraph & Telephone   Eugène Thomas (Socialist Deputy)

Transcript of the Trial of General Raoul Salan, May 1962 (Excerpts)

HEARING OF MAY 18, 1962. TESTIMONY OF GENERAL ROGER MIQUEL.

M. TIXIER-VIGNANCOUR: At that time [May 13] General Miquel commanded the Fifth Military District; that is, Toulouse. Could he describe to the Military Tribunal the conditions under which he was asked to make a journey to Algiers, between June 20 and 25, 1958, I believe.

GENERAL MIQUEL: The dates of June 20 to 25 are not correct. The journey must have taken place on June 2 and 3. I knew through my sources of information that metropolitan public opinion was discontented with the government which had just been formed. To use an expression which recurred in all the bulletins of information: "The same crew is chosen, and we start all over again."

I was very struck by this information and I decided to go to Algiers to pass it on to General Salan. I took an airplane to Algiers where I met General Salan and his colleagues; I passed on to them the information I had gathered. There was a discussion of how much this information ought to be taken into account. General Salan drew the following conclusion: "Public opinion has demanded General de Gaulle; we should give him our confidence. Nothing more."

M. TIXIER-VIGNANCOUR: Did this conversation take place only between you and General Salan, General?

GENERAL MIQUEL: No. Other general officers were present.

Le Procès de Raoul Salan, Compte Rendu Stenographique, 216–18. From the series "Les Grands Procès Contemporains," under the direction of Maître Maurice Garçon of the Académie Française, reprinted by permission of the publisher, Éditions Albin Michel, Paris.

M. TIXIER-VIGNANCOUR: And what measures did you envision if he approved of the advice you brought him?

GENERAL MIQUEL: We planned to resume the project of a landing at once.

THE PRESIDENT OF THE TRIBUNAL: Who envisaged this solution?

GENERAL MIQUEL: I absolutely cannot tell you. There were four or five generals present at this conference. I can't tell you who took the initiative to say that the plans for a landing could be resumed.

THE PRESIDENT: It is quite a serious matter.

GENERAL MIQUEL: The question was debated.

M. TIXIER-VIGNANCOUR: Do you remember the names of the participants?

THE PRESIDENT: Do you want to tell them?

GENERAL MIQUEL: Along with General Salan there were General Jouhaud, General Massu, General Dulac, and General Lennuyeux; I believe that's about all.

THE PRESIDENT: General Salan's decision was taken on a project which had been envisaged by someone whose name you no longer remember; what position did General Salan take?

GENERAL MIQUEL: He talked hardly at all, he listened.

THE PRESIDENT: He took no position.

GENERAL MIQUEL: He concluded with the idea which I just stated, that is very simply: this was not the time to follow up on this project; we had declared our confidence in General de Gaulle; there was nothing to do but to wait.

M. TIXIER-VIGNANCOUR: General Miquel, until his retirement, was in very intimate contact with the matters which General Salan is accused of; can he indicate what he thinks were the motives which could have moved General Salan?

GENERAL MIQUEL: I think that General Salan, who was the civil and military legate in Algeria, who acted on orders and instructions, and who gained General de Gaulle his acclamation, had no reason to go back on his word and that he intended to give his confidence to General de Gaulle. I have no reason whatsoever to suspect that he thought otherwise.

M. TIXIER-VIGNANCOUR: And when he became the leader of the OAS, what do you think were his motives?

GENERAL MIQUEL: One single motive: to preserve French Algeria.

One felt it yesterday, at first glance, from a certain rustling of the busy morning crowd. The relief, the joy, the feeling of triumph spread by the news that General de Gaulle had been invested with the powers of the Republic, were not unmixed feelings. This rustling was part of a certain uneasiness and disappointment. The irresistible patriotic upsurge in Algiers on May 13 had just—whether one wished it or not—brought the liberator of the homeland to power. With one or two exceptions, none of the men who showed the greatest clear faith in the destinies of French Algeria were on the government bench on Saturday: neither Bidault, nor Soustelle, nor any of their companions during the struggle. People were surprised, bitter, occasionally indignant.

General Salan, too, sensed this stirring, he who quite properly had the radio broadcasts interrupted at the beginning of the afternoon in order to announce a message from General de Gaulle who, through him, spoke to all of Algeria: "I shall be among you on Wednesday. Wait for me calmly and with confidence."

This word, "confidence," alone, caused a relaxation and brought back the serenity without which reflection cannot be sound.

It is indeed proper to consider carefully all of the circumstances which surround the end of the terrible nightmare that France has had for years.

General de Gaulle has repeatedly said that he intended to accept only those powers conferred by legality. There are of course a number of inconveniences involved in this respect for the laws. But how slight they are as against the advantages which such respect offers as compensation! Not the least of them is that of dispelling the hideous specter of civil war, of gagging the Gorgon's head of Communism which is always in search of false pretexts.

It is within legality that General de Gaulle has obtained his investiture, openly demanding full powers and [the freedom] to build a true constitution.

One must at this point yield to the evidence. Without mentioning the distorting censorship of M. Gazier, there is a time lag of at least a week between Algiers and the metropolis in the exact understanding of events which arise here. This gap is infinitely greater between the public, which early on discerned the national meaning of the *"Algérie française"* movement, and the fauna of the Palais-Bourbon, which is corrupted by the "system" and cut off from the nation.

Who would be ingenuous enough to imagine that General de Gaulle, twenty days after the explosion of May 13, would have obtained the investiture if, in the unhealthy atmosphere of the Chamber of the dying, he had from the start presented himself in the company of the most ardent defenders of the patriots of Algiers—dubbed "factious and rebellious"—who lifted him to the halls of power?

We should not forget that barely four days ago, the Socialist Party (to speak only of it), encouraged by its most eminent sectarians, misled by false evidence, and almost in its entirety shaken by demagogic fears, aligned itself in a bloc against a pretended "tyrant."

Let us reflect some more. The difference in wave lengths for the understanding of the facts, is enormous between Algiers and London, and Washington, and the other capitals. The presence of Algeria's most trustworthy friends at the President of the Council's side from the swearing-in ceremony onward (assuming that it could have taken place) would have been fatally misinterpreted. The whole world would have said: "De Gaulle is the prisoner of the people of the Thirteenth of May. Now you see him paying them ransom."

Instead of this degrading calumny, we see the world paying homage to his rectitude, his self-denial, his republican virtues. We see Washington saluting his advent to power in an immediate official document, and expressing wishes for the restoration of French greatness.

And then there is above all Algeria. She is in the very forefront of the preoccupations of the head of the government. He knows what an admirable kind of movement of fraternization it was which made her quiver with French impatience. Before completing and organizing his government, he intends to evaluate, in Algiers, all of the consequences which that desire for integration will have for the very destiny of the nation.

That is why, having obtained a vote from the "system" on the constitutional reform, after applying the whip, General de Gaulle must be among us tomorrow—rid, this time, of the "system."

The bright realities which await him here will determine an essential part of his policies.

Alain de Sérigny
(*L'Écho d'Alger*, June 3, 1958, pp. 1, 3)

SPEECH OF PREMIER DE GAULLE AT ALGIERS, JUNE 4, 1958

I have understood you. I know what has happened here. I see what you wanted to do. I see that the road you have opened in Algeria is one of renewal and fraternity.

I say "renewal" in all its aspects, but very rightly you wanted to begin at the beginning, that is, with our institutions, and that is why I am here.

And I say "fraternity," because you offer this magnificent spectacle of men who from one end to the other, whatever be their community, are united in the same ardor and go hand-in-hand.

Well, of all that, I take note in the name of France, and I declare that as of today France considers that in all Algeria there is only one category of inhabitants. There are only Frenchmen, wholly French, Frenchmen having the same rights and the same duties.

That means that ways must be opened which until now have been closed to many. That means that a livelihood must be given to those who have not had it. That means that dignity must be granted to those whose dignity was contested. That means that a nation must be given to those who doubted they had one.

The army, the coherent, ardent, and disciplined French army, under the orders of its chiefs; the army tested under so many circumstances and which nevertheless has accomplished here a magnificent work of comprehension and pacification, this French army has been on this soil the leaven and the witness and it is the guarantor of the movement which has developed. It succeeded in damming the torrent to capture the energy. I pay homage to it. I express my confidence in it and I rely upon it for today and for tomorrow.

That we are Frenchmen with all rights, voting in one single group, we shall show in not more than three months, on the solemn occasion when all Frenchmen, including the ten million Frenchmen of Algeria, will have to decide on their own destiny.

The votes of these ten million Frenchmen will count as much as the votes of all other Frenchmen. They will have to designate, to elect—I repeat, in a single college—their representatives for public administration as all other Frenchmen will do. Once these representatives are elected, we shall see how to do what remains.

May they take part together in this immense demonstration, all those from your cities, your *douars*, your plains, and your *djebels*. May even those take part who through despair have thought it right to carry out on this soil a fight—which I recognize myself as courageous, because courage is not lacking on the soil of Algeria— which is courageous but which is nevertheless cruel and fratricidal.

I, de Gaulle, open the door to reconciliation to them.

Never more than here and more than tonight have I felt that France is so noble, so great, and so generous. *Vive la République! Vive la France!*   (*Le Monde*, June 6, 1958, p. 3)

ORDER OF THE DAY NO. 4, ADDRESSED TO THE ARMED FORCES BY
GENERAL RAOUL SALAN

I have the honor to communicate to you the letter in which General de Gaulle, President of the Council of Ministers, has specified my powers, as well as the order of the day which he addresses to the ground, naval, and air forces of Algeria.

I feel a just pride in the homage which has been rendered to you.

You have never ceased to give proof of your faith and your enthusiasm in the mission which is incumbent on you, and you have shown your fine discipline.

The office of Delegate-General of the government in Algeria, which has devolved upon me, is for you as for me a proof of the total confidence General de Gaulle has placed in the army.

Be worthy and continue to serve with magnanimity.

It is by greatness of heart that we will win peace in Algeria.

General of the Army, Raoul Salan
(*L'Écho d'Alger*, June 8–9, 1958, p. 12)

MESSAGE FROM GENERAL SALAN TO THE COMMITTEE OF PUBLIC
SAFETY OF ALGERIA AND THE SAHARA, BROADCAST OVER RADIO
ALGIERS AT 1:20 P.M., JUNE 7, 1958.

For more than three weeks, with an unshakeable faith, an unfailing courage and resolution, you have consecrated yourself entirely to French Algeria and to France.

In close communion with the army you have carried out an exceptional work which is going to allow General de Gaulle to rally the full energy of the nation to bring the revival of our country to a successful end.

With generosity and disinterestedness, you have placed yourself entirely at the service of the head of government. He has made you his companions and he has told you at Oran, whatever community you belong to: "There is your duty: to become united in your hearts and souls. There is our greatest task for tomorrow that I ask you to fulfill . . . "

I thank you for the work that you have accomplished. It has been crowned by the arrival among us of General de Gaulle, the head of the government of the Republic.

I count on all of you, on your patriotism, your desire to serve, your faith in a revived and renewed France to aid me in the mission which General de Gaulle has conferred upon me.

Together we will realize a French Algeria.

[signed]

> General R. Salan, Delegate-General of the Government and Commander in Chief of the Armed Forces in Algeria, Commander of the 10th Military District (*L'Écho d'Alger*, June 8–9, 1958, p. 12)

COLONEL VAUDRAY, VICE-PRESIDENT OF THE CPS OF ALGIERS: THE PROVISIONS OF THE LOI-CADRE ARE DISAPPEARING BEFORE THE FACT OF INTEGRATION

Saturday [June 7] at 6 p.m., at the new city hall, the Committee of Public Safety of the city of Algiers held a briefing session. In the absence of Colonel Godard, the president, detained by the obligations which the organization of the *Sûreté nationale* in Algeria force upon him, Colonel Vaudray, the vice president, took over the presidency. . . .

Having recalled the declarations made by General de Gaulle in the course of the three great days of glory which marked his journey to Algeria, Colonel Vaudray analyzed these declarations and stated in particular the answers that could be furnished to those who still show some misunderstanding. . . .

"Here are the responses," he continued, "which have been made to the principal demands formulated by our committees of public safety:

"First. The army to power has been demanded: Salan has been appointed. A total liaison is established between the civilian domain and the military domain.

"Second. We cried 'Vive l'Algérie française': Algeria has indeed definitely become French through integration, the only valid way of proving that there are truly ten million Frenchmen in Algeria, henceforth having the same rights and also the same duties. Moreover, following the referendum, Algeria will elect its representatives to the new Constituent Assembly.

"Third. In regard to the committees of public safety the General has approved this great national movement and stated his thoughts: these committees are to prepare the integration of hearts and minds and consequently to establish the necessary contacts between the Algerian communities. General Salan has also said that he expects much from these committees."

Colonel Vaudray then answered the questions some of his listeners put to him. His answers could be thus summarized:

The presence of officers on the committees of public safety has not been questioned and has not been disapproved by General de Gaulle.

The referendum—we will discuss it when the moment has come.

The FLN is counting on aid from abroad to exploit domestic divisions. These divisions will be neutralized. Through his strongly defined position General de Gaulle had closed the door to independence. The FLN is counting on the conciliatory attitude of the English and the Americans, but they have answered through a tribute of confidence addressed to General de Gaulle.

On the military side the reinforcement of the effectives will be continued, as well as the defense of the frontiers and the strengthening of certain dispositions.

On the psychological side the participation of all Moslems in the national movement is another answer to the FLN. De Gaulle is opening a way out to those of its members who have had enough.

Arrangements will certainly be made in France to mitigate the lying and destructive campaign of a certain part of the press.

The provisions of the *loi-cadre* are disappearing before the fact of integration.

(*L'Écho d'Alger*, June 8–9, 1958, p. 12)

The French Constitution

Adopted by the Referendum of September 28, 1958,
and Promulgated on October 4, 1958.

Preamble

The French people hereby solemnly proclaims its attachment to the Rights of Man and the principles of national sovereignty as defined by the Declaration of 1789, reaffirmed and complemented by the Preamble of the Constitution of 1946.

By virtue of these principles and that of the free determination of peoples, the Republic hereby offers to the Overseas Territories that express the desire to adhere to them, new institutions based on the common ideal of liberty, equality and fraternity and conceived with a view to their democratic evolution.

ARTICLE 1

The Republic and the peoples of the Overseas Territories who, by an act of free determination, adopt the present Constitution thereby institute a Community.

The Community shall be based on the equality and the solidarity of the peoples composing it.

Title I
On Sovereignty

ARTICLE 2

France is a Republic, indivisible, secular, democratic and social. It shall ensure the equality of all citizens before the law, without distinction of origin, race or religion. It shall respect all beliefs. . . .

ARTICLE 3

National sovereignty belongs to the people, which shall exercise this sovereignty through its representatives and by means of referendums.

No section of the people, nor any individual, may attribute to themselves or himself the exercise thereof.

Suffrage may be direct or indirect under the conditions stipulated by the Constitution. It shall always be universal, equal and secret.

All French citizens of both sexes who have reached their majority and who enjoy civil and political rights may vote under the conditions to be determined by law.

.   .   .

Title II
The President of the Republic

ARTICLE 5

The President of the Republic shall see that the Constitution is respected. He shall ensure, by his arbitration, the regular functioning of the governmental authorities, as well as the continuance of the State.

He shall be the guarantor of national independence, of the integrity of the territory, and of respect for Community agreements and treaties.

ARTICLE 6

The President of the Republic shall be elected for seven years by an electoral college comprising the members of Parliament, of the General Councils and of the Assemblies of the Overseas Territories, as well as the elected representatives of the municipal councils. . . .

ARTICLE 7

The President of the Republic shall be elected by an absolute majority on the first ballot. If this is not obtained, the President of the Republic shall be elected on a second ballot by a relative majority.

The voting shall begin at the summons of the Government. . . .

ARTICLE 8

The President of the Republic shall appoint the Premier. He shall terminate the functions of the Premier when the latter presents the resignation of the Government.

On the proposal of the Premier, he shall appoint the other members of the Government and shall terminate their functions.

ARTICLE 9

The President of the Republic shall preside over the Council of Ministers.

ARTICLE 10

The President of the Republic shall promulgate the laws within fifteen days following the transmission to the Government of the finally adopted law.

He may, before the expiration of this time limit, ask Parliament for a reconsideration of the law or of certain of its articles. This reconsideration may not be refused.

ARTICLE 11

The President of the Republic, on the proposal of the Government during [Parliamentary] sessions, or on joint motion of the two assemblies, published in the *Journal Officiel*, may submit to a referendum any bill dealing with the organization of the governmental authorities, entailing approval of a Community agreement, or providing for authorization to ratify a treaty that, without being contrary to the Constitution, might affect the functioning of [existing] institutions.

When the referendum decides in favor of the bill, the President of the Republic shall promulgate it within the time limit stipulated in the preceding article.

ARTICLE 12

The President of the Republic may, after consultation with the Premier and the Presidents of the assemblies, declare the dissolution of the National Assembly.

General elections shall take place twenty days at the least and forty days at the most after the dissolution. . . .

There may be no further dissolution within a year following these elections.

.   .   .

ARTICLE 16

When the institutions of the Republic, the independence of the nation, the integrity of its territory or the fulfillment of its international commitments are threatened in a grave and immediate manner and when the regular functioning of the constitutional governmental authorities is interrupted, the President of the Republic shall take the measures commanded by these circumstances, after official consultation with the Premier, the Presidents of the assemblies and the Constitutional Council.

He shall inform the nation of these measures in a message.

These measures must be prompted by the desire to ensure to the constitutional governmental authorities, in the shortest possible time, the means of fulfilling their assigned functions. The Constitutional Council shall be consulted with regard to such measures.

Parliament shall meet by right.

The National Assembly may not be dissolved during the exercise of emergency powers [by the President].

.   .   .

Title III
The Government

ARTICLE 20

The Government shall determine and direct the policy of the nation. It shall have at its disposal the administration and the armed forces.

It shall be responsible to Parliament under the conditions and according to the procedures stipulated in Articles 49 and 50.

ARTICLE 21

The Premier shall direct the operation of the Government. He shall be responsible for national defense. He shall ensure the execution of the laws. Subject to the provisions of Article 13, he shall have regulatory powers and shall make appointments to civil and military posts. . . .

.   .   .

Title IV
The Parliament

ARTICLE 24

The Parliament shall comprise the National Assembly and the Senate.

The deputies to the National Assembly shall be elected by direct suffrage.

The Senate shall be elected by indirect suffrage. It shall ensure the representation of the territorial units of the Republic. Frenchmen living outside France shall be represented in the Senate.

.   .   .

Title V
On Relations Between Parliament and the Government

ARTICLE 38

The Government may, in order to carry out its program, ask Parliament to authorize it, for a limited period, to take through ordinances measures that are normally within the domain of law.

The ordinances shall be enacted in meetings of the Council of Ministers after consultation with the Council of State. They shall come into force upon their publication, but shall become null and void if the bill for their ratification is not submitted to Parliament before the date set by the enabling act.

At the expiration of the time limit referred to in the first paragraph of the present article, the ordinances may be modified only by law in those matters which are within the legislative domain.

.   .   .

ARTICLE 47

Parliament shall pass finance bills under the conditions to be stipulated by an organic law.

Should the National Assembly fail to reach a decision on first reading within a time limit of forty days after a bill has been filed, the Government shall refer it to the Senate, which must rule within a time limit of fifteen days. The procedure set forth in Article 45 shall then be followed.

Should Parliament fail to reach a decision within a time limit of seventy days, the provisions of the bill may be enforced by ordinance.

Should the finance bill establishing the resources and expenditures of a fiscal year not be filed in time for it to be promulgated before the beginning of that fiscal year, the Government shall immediately request Parliament for the authorization to collect the taxes and shall make available by decree the funds needed to meet the Government commitments already voted. . . .

.   .   .

The Premier, after deliberation by the Council of Ministers, may pledge the responsibility of the Government to the National Assembly with regard to the program of the Government, or with regard to a declaration of general policy, as the case may be.

The National Assembly may question the responsibility of the Government by the vote of a motion of censure. Such a motion shall be admissible only if it is signed by at least one tenth of the members of the National Assembly. The vote may only take place forty-eight hours after the motion has been filed; the only votes counted shall be those favorable to the motion of censure, which may be adopted only by a majority of the members comprising the Assembly. Should the motion of censure be rejected, its signatories may not introduce another motion in the course of the same session, except in the case provided for in the paragraph below.

The Premier may, after deliberation by the Council of Ministers, pledge the Government's responsibility to the National Assembly on the vote of a text. In this case, the text shall be considered as adopted, unless a motion of censure, filed in the succeeding twenty-four hours, is voted under the conditions laid down in the previous paragraph.

The Premier shall be entitled to ask the Senate for approval of a general policy declaration.

ARTICLE 50

When the National Assembly adopts a motion of censure, or when it disapproves the program or a declaration of general policy of the Government, the Premier must submit the resignation of the Government to the President of the Republic.

.   .   .

Title XIV
On Amendment

ARTICLE 89

The initiative for amending the Constitution shall belong both to the President of the Republic on the proposal of the Premier and to the members of Parliament.

The Government or Parliamentary bill for amendment must be

passed by the two assemblies in identical terms. The amendment shall become definitive after approval by a referendum.

Nevertheless, the proposed amendment shall not be submitted to a referendum when the President of the Republic decides to submit it to Parliament convened in Congress; in this case, the proposed amendment shall be approved only if it is accepted by a three-fifths majority of the votes cast. The Secretariat of the Congress shall be that of the National Assembly.

No amendment procedure may be undertaken or followed when the integrity of the territory is in jeopardy.

The republican form of government shall not be subject to amendment. . . .

Address by Premier Charles de Gaulle Outlining the Draft Constitution on September 4, 1958

It was at a time when it had to reform or be shattered that our people first had recourse to the Republic. Until then, down the centuries, the *ancien régime* had achieved the unity and maintained the integrity of France. But, while a great tidal wave was forming in the depths, it showed itself incapable of adapting to a new world. It was then—in the midst of national turmoil and of foreign war—that the Republic appeared. It was the sovereignty of the people, the call of liberty, the hope of justice. That is what it was to remain through all the restless vicissitudes of its history. Today, as much as ever, that is what we want it to remain.

Of course, the Republic has assumed various forms during the successive periods when it has held sway. In 1792, we saw it—revolutionary and warlike—overthrow thrones and privileges only to succumb, eight years later, in the midst of abuses and disturbances that it had not been able to master. In 1848, we saw it rise above the barricades, set its face against anarchy, prove itself socially minded within and fraternal without, but soon fade away once more through its failure to reconcile order with the enthusiasm for renewal. On September 4, 1870, the day after Sedan, we saw it offer its services to the country to redeem the disaster.

In fact, the Republic succeeded in putting France back on her feet again, reconstituting her armies, recreating a vast empire, renew-

Major Addresses, Statements and Press Conferences of General Charles de Gaulle, pp. 13–16.

ing firm alliances, framing good social laws and developing an educational system. So well did it do all this that, during the First World War, it had the glory of ensuring our safety and our victory. On November 11, when the people gather and the flags are dipped in commemoration, the tribute that the nation pays to those who have served it well is paid also to the Republic.

Nevertheless, the regime contained functional defects which might have seemed tolerable in a more or less stable era, but which were no longer compatible with the social transformations, the economic changes and the external perils that preceded the Second World War. Had not this situation been remedied, the terrible events of 1940 would have swept everything away. But when, on June 18, the struggle for the liberation of France began, it was immediately proclaimed that the Republic to be rebuilt would be a new Republic. The whole Resistance Movement constantly affirmed this.

We know, we know only too well what became of these hopes. . . . We know, we know only too well, that once the danger had passed, everything was turned over to the discretion of the parties. We know, we know only too well, what were the consequences of this. By reason of inconsistency and instability—whatever may have been the intentions and, often, the ability of the men in office—the regime found itself deprived of authority in internal affairs and assurance in external affairs, without which it could not act. It was inevitable that the paralysis of the state should bring on a grave national crisis and that, immediately, the Republic should be threatened with collapse.

The necessary steps were taken to prevent the irreparable at the very moment that it was about to occur. The disruption of the state was, by a narrow margin, prevented. They managed to save the last chance of the Republic. It was by legal means that I and my Government assumed the unusual mandate of drafting a new constitution and of submitting it to the decision of the people.

We have done this on the basis of the principles laid down at the time of our investiture. We have done this with the collaboration of the Consultative Committee instituted by law. We have done this, taking into account the solemn opinion of the Council of State. We have done this after very frank and very thorough discussion with our own Councils of Ministers. These Councils were formed of men as diversified as possible as to origin and inclination, but resolutely united. We have done this without meanwhile doing violence to any right of the people or any public liberty. The nation, which alone is the judge, will approve or reject our work. But it is in good conscience that we propose this constitution to them.

Henceforth what is primordial for the public powers is their effectiveness and their continuity. We are living at a time when titanic forces are engaged in transforming the world. Lest we become a people out of date and scorned, we must evolve rapidly in the scientific, economic, and social spheres. Moreover, the taste for progress and the passion for technical achievements that are becoming evident among the French, and especially among our young people, are equal to this imperative need. These are all facts that dominate our national existence and that, consequently, must order our institutions.

The necessity of renovating agriculture and industry; of procuring—for our rejuvenated population—the means of livelihood, of work, of education, of housing; and of associating workers in the functioning of enterprises: the necessity to do all this compels us to be dynamic and expeditious in public affairs. The duty of restoring peace in Algeria, next of developing it, and finally of settling the question of its status and its place in our great whole, impels us to arduous and prolonged efforts. The prospects offered us by the resources of the Sahara are magnificent indeed, but complex. The relations between metropolitan France and the Overseas Territories require profound adjustment. The world is crossed by currents that threaten the very future of the human race and prompt France to protect herself while playing the role of moderation, peace, and fraternity dictated by her mission. In short, the French nation will flourish again or will perish according to whether the state does or does not have enough strength, constancy, and prestige to lead her along the path she must follow.

Therefore, it is for the people we are, for the century and the world in which we live, that the proposed constitution was drafted. The country effectively governed by those to whom it gives the mandate and to whom it grants the confidence that makes for lawfulness. A national arbiter—far removed from political bickering—elected by the citizens who hold a public mandate, charged with the task of ensuring the normal functioning of the institutions, possessing the right to resort to the judgment of the sovereign people, accountable, in the case of extreme danger, for the independence, the honor, and integrity of France and for the safety of the Republic. A Government made to govern, which is granted the necessary time and opportunity, which does not turn to anything other than its task and which thereby deserves the country's support. A parliament intended to represent the political will of the nation, to enact laws, and to control the executive, without venturing to overstep its role. A Government and parliament that work together but remain separate as to their responsibilities, with no member of one being at the same time a member of the other.

Such is the balanced structure that power must assume. The rest will depend upon men.

A social and economic council, appointed outside politics by the business, professional and labor organizations of France and the Overseas Territories, that gives advice to parliament and to the Government. A constitutional committee, free of any attachment, empowered to judge whether the laws that have been passed are constitutional and whether the various elections have been properly held. A judicial authority assured of its independence which remains the guardian of individual liberty. Thus will the competence, the dignity, the impartiality of the state be better guaranteed.

A community formed between the French nation and those of the Overseas Territories that so desire, within which each territory will become a state that governs itself, while foreign policy, defense, the currency, economic and financial policies, use of raw materials, the control of justice, higher education, long-distance communications will constitute a common domain over which the organs of the Community —the President, Executive Council, Senate, and Court of Arbitration— will have jurisdiction. Thus, this vast organization will renovate the human complex grouped around France. This will be effected by virtue of the free determination of all. In fact, every territory will have an opportunity, through its vote in the referendum, either to accept France's proposal or to refuse it and, by so doing, to break every tie with her. Once a member of the Community, it can in the future, after coming to an agreement with the common organs, assume its own destiny independently of the others.

Finally, during the four months following the referendum, the Government will be responsible for the country's affairs and, in particular, will establish the system of elections. In this way, through a mandate from the people, the necessary measures may be taken for the setting up of the new institutions.

Here, women and men of France, is what inspires and what makes up the constitution which, on September 28, will be submitted to your vote. With all my heart, in the name of France, I ask you to answer "Yes."

If you do not vote thus, we shall return, that very day, to the bad old ways with which you are familiar. But if you do, the result will be to make the Republic strong and effective, provided that those in positions of responsibility know, hereafter, the meaning of determination. But there will also be, in this positive display of the national will, the proof that our country is regaining its unity and, by the same token, its opportunity for grandeur. The world, which understands full well what importance our decision will have for it, will draw the inevitable conclusion. Perhaps it is already drawing the conclusion.

A great hope will arise over France. I think it has already arisen. *Vive la République! Vive la France!*

Press Conference of Premier Charles de Gaulle Held in Paris at the Hôtel Matignon on October 23, 1958

QUESTION: The FLN is making overtures concerning the possibilities of peace in Algeria. What attitude does the Government plan to take toward this?

ANSWER: The organization of which you are speaking started the fight on its own initiative. It has continued it for four years. I leave it to the future to determine what purpose this struggle may have served. But, in any case, it no longer really serves any purpose. Of course, they can, if they wish, continue the outrages, lie in ambush on the roads, hurl grenades in market places, and sneak into villages at night to kill a few unfortunate people. They can hide in mountain caves, go in groups from *djebel* to *djebel*, and hide weapons in rock crevices to be used when the opportunity arises. But the issue does not lie there. Nor is it in the political dreams and the propaganda oratory of refugees abroad. In truth and in all conscience, the issue is now clear. It is made clear by the fact that the forces of law and order are little by little gaining control of the terrain. But above all, it is made clear by the decisive demonstration that took place on September 28. However, I say unequivocally that, as for most of them, the men of the insurrection have fought courageously. Let the peace of the brave come, and I am sure that all hatred will fade away and disappear.

I have spoken of the peace of the brave. What does this mean? Simply this: let those who opened fire, cease fire, and let them return without humiliation to their families and their work. People say to me: but what can they do to end the struggle? My answer is: wherever they are organized for combat, their leaders need only enter into contact with the French command. The old warrior's procedure, long used when one wanted to silence the guns, was to wave the white flag

Major Addresses, Statements and Press Conferences of General Charles de Gaulle, pp. 25–6.

of truce. And I answer that, in that case, the combatants would be received and treated honorably. . . .

As for the external organization of which we were just speaking, which, from the outside, strives to direct the struggle, I repeat openly what I have already made known. If delegates were designated to come and negotiate with the authorities the end of hostilities, they would have only to address themselves to the French Embassy at Tunis or at Rabat. Either one would ensure their transportation to metropolitan France. There, they would be assured of complete safety, and I guarantee them the freedom to depart.

Some say: but what would be the political conditions that the French government would be willing to discuss? I reply: the political destiny of Algeria is Algeria itself. Opening fire does not give a man the right to determine that destiny. When the democratic way is open, when the citizens have an opportunity to express their will, then there is no other way that is acceptable. Now, this way is open in Algeria. The referendum has taken place. In November the legislative elections will be held; in March, the elections to the municipal councils; in April, the election of senators. What will be the outcome? That is a matter of evolution. In any case, a vast physical and spiritual transformation is under way in Algeria. France, because it is her duty and because she alone is capable of doing it—France is bringing about this transformation. As and when developments occur, political solutions will take shape. I believe, as I have already said, that future solutions will be based—because that is the nature of things—upon the courageous personality of Algeria and upon its close association with metropolitan France. I believe also that this ensemble, completed by the Sahara, will link itself, for the common progress, with the free states of Morocco and Tunisia. Sufficient unto the day is the burdensome evil thereof. But who will win out in the end? You will see that it will be the fraternal civilization that wins.

Address by President Charles de Gaulle on the Future of Algeria Broadcast over French Radio and Television on September 16, 1959

. . . France is still faced with a difficult and bloody problem: that of Algeria. This we must solve. We will certainly not do so by tossing at each other empty and oversimplified slogans, on one side or the other,

Major Addresses, Statements and Press Conferences of General Charles de Gaulle, pp. 52–6.

both of which are blind to everything save their conflicting passions, interests, or daydreams. We will solve it as a great nation should do, choosing the only path worthy of being followed. I mean the free choice which the Algerians themselves will make for their future.

As a matter of fact, much has already been done to pave the way for this solution. Through pacification first of all, for nothing can be solved against a background of shooting and assassination. From that point of view, I do not claim that we have reached the end of the road. But I say that there is no comparison, in terms of the safety of persons and property, between the situation which prevailed two or three years ago and that which prevails now. Our army is accomplishing its mission both courageously and skillfully, fighting its opponents while maintaining with the population deeper and broader contacts than had ever existed before. If our soldiers, and in particular, the 120,000 Moslems among them, had faltered in their duty or if the Algerian masses had turned against France, that indeed would have spelled disaster. But since this has not occurred, the restoration of public order, although it may not be imminent, is now in sight.

The second requisite for a settlement is that all Algerians should have the means of expressing themselves through truly universal suffrage. Up to last year they have never had it. They have it now, thanks to the institution of equal rights, a single college, and the fact that the larger communities, those of the Moslems, are sure of obtaining at the polls the largest numbers of representatives elected. This was a change of the greatest significance, actually a revolution. On September 28 of last year, the Algerians, by referendum, adopted the Constitution and signified their intention that their future should be shaped along with France.

On November 30 they elected their deputies, on April 19, their municipal councils, and on May 31, their senators. No doubt there are some people who claim that, in the situation in which the voters found themselves, under pressure from the forces of law and order and the threats of the insurgents, these elections could be sincere only to a limited extent. They were held, however, in towns and rural areas, and with a large mass of voters; and even at the time of the referendum, participation was widespread, spontaneous, and enthusiastic.

At all events the path is open. As soon as violence has subsided, the path may be used even more broadly, and more freely. Next year, the General Councils will be elected, from which, later, will be drawn a number of administrative, economic, and social councils, which will discuss with the Delegate General the development of Algeria. . . .

Thanks to the progress of pacification, to democracy, and to social advancement, we can now look forward to the day when the men and women who live in Algeria will be in a position to decide their own destiny, once and for all, freely and in the full knowledge of what is at stake. Taking into account all these factors—those of the Algerian situation, those inherent in the national and the international situation —I deem it necessary that recourse to self-determination be here and now proclaimed. In the name of France and of the Republic, by virtue of the power granted to me by the Constitution to consult its citizens —if only God lets me live and the people listen to me—I pledge myself to ask the Algerians, on the one hand, in their twelve *départements*, what, when all is said and done, they wish to be; and, on the other hand, all Frenchmen, to endorse that choice.

The question, obviously, will be put to the Algerians as individuals. For since the beginning of the world there has never been any Algerian unity, far less any Algerian sovereignty. The Carthaginians, the Romans, the Vandals, the Byzantines, the Syrian Arabs, the Cordova Arabs, the Turks, the French have, one after the other, penetrated the country without there being—at any time, under any shape or form —an Algerian state. As for the time of the elections, I will decide upon it in due course, at the latest four years after the actual restoration of peace; that is to say, once a situation has been established whereby not more than two hundred persons a year will lose their lives, either in ambushes or isolated attacks. The ensuing period of time will be devoted to resuming normal existence, to emptying the camps and prisons, to permitting the return of exiles, to restoring the free play of individual and public liberties, and to enabling the population to become fully aware of what is at stake. I would like to invite, here and now, observers from all over the world to attend, without hindrance, the final culmination of this process.

But what will this political destiny finally be, for the men and women of Algeria who will choose it, once peace is restored? Everyone knows that in theory it is possible to imagine three solutions. Since it is in the interest of all concerned—and especially of France— that the question be answered without ambiguity, the three conceivable solutions will be put to the vote:

—Either secession, where some believe independence would be found. France would then leave the Algerians who had expressed their wish to become separated from her. They would organize, without her, the territory in which they live, the resources which they have at their disposal, the government which they desire. I am convinced personally that such an outcome would be incredible and disastrous. Algeria being what it is at the present time, and the world what we know it to be, secession would carry in its wake the most appalling poverty, frightful political chaos, widespread slaughter, and, soon after, the warlike dictatorship of the Communists. But this demon must be exorcised, and this must be done by the Algerians themselves. If it should appear through some inconceivable misfortune that such is indeed their will, France would undoubtedly stop devoting so many assets and so many billions of francs to a cause shorn of any hope. It goes without saying that, on this assumption, those Algerians, regardless of origin, who might wish to remain French would do so in any case and that France would arrange, if need be, for their regrouping and resettlement. On the other hand, everything would be arranged so that the operation of oil wells, the handling and shipping of Saharan oil—which is the result of French efforts and which is of interest to the whole Western world—would be ensured in any event.

—Or out-and-out identification with France, as is implied in equality of rights: Algerians can accede to all political, administrative, and judicial functions of the state and have free access to the public service. They would benefit, as regards salaries, wages, social security, education, and vocational training, from all measures provided for in metropolitan France; they would live and work wherever they saw fit, throughout the territory of the Republic; in other words, they would be living, from every point of view, regardless of their religion or the community to which they belonged, by and large on the same footing and at the same level as other citizens and become part and parcel of the French people who would then, in effect, spread from Dunkirk to Tamanrasset.

—Or the government of Algerians by Algerians, backed up by French help and in close relationship with her, as regards the economy, education, defense, and foreign relations. In that case, the internal regime of Algeria should be of the federal type, so that the various communities—French, Arab, Kabyle, Mozabite—who live together in the country would find guarantees for their own way of life and a framework for co-operation.

But since for a year now it has been settled that—through the institution of equal voting rights, the single college, and the emergence of a majority of Moslem representatives—the political future of Algerians is to depend on Algerians; since it has been officially and solemnly emphasized that, once peace has been restored, the Algerians will let it be known what fate they want for themselves, to the exclusion of any other, and that all of them, whatever their program may be, whatever they might have done, wherever they come from, will take part, if they wish to do so, in this vote: what then could be the meaning of rebellion?

If those who lead it claim for all Algerians the right to self-determination, all paths are wide open. If the insurgents fear that in stopping the combat, they will be turned over to justice, then it is entirely up to them to settle with the authorities the conditions for their unhindered return, as I suggested when I offered the peace of the brave. If the men who represent the political organization of the insurrection intend not to be excluded from the debate, or later from the polls, or finally from the institutions which will determine the fate of Algeria and ensure its political life, I proclaim that they will have the same place as all the others—no more, no less—a hearing, a share, a place which will be granted them by the votes of the citizens. Why, then, should the odious strife and the fratricidal murders, which are still drenching the Algerian soil with blood, continue?

Unless it is the work of a group of ambitious agitators, determined to establish by brute force and terror their totalitarian dictatorship and believing that they will one day obtain from the Republic the privilege of discussing with it the fate of Algeria, thus building up these agitators into an Algerian government. There is not a chance that France would lend herself to any thing so arbitrary. The future of Algerians rests with Algerians, not as forced on them by knife and machine gun, but according to the will which they will legitimately express through universal suffrage. With them and for them, France will see to the freedom of their choice.

During the few years which will pass before the deadline we have set, there will be much to do so that Algeria, when pacified, can weigh all the factors and consequences of its own decision. I intend to concern myself personally with the task. Furthermore, the procedures of the future vote must in due course be elaborated and specified. But the road is open. The decision is taken, the stakes are worthy of France.

TWO GROUPS OF INSURGENTS ARE STILL ENTRENCHED IN THE
CENTER OF ALGIERS

GENERAL DE GAULLE TERMS THE UPRISING "AN EVIL BLOW
LEVELED AT FRANCE."

The uprising that the "activists" unleashed Sunday in Algiers has left
twenty-one dead, including eleven in the security forces.

According to most accounts and corroborated by the Ministry of
Information, the first shots aimed against the security forces who
were forcing back the crowd came from a window of the insurgents'
headquarters.

If definitely established, this fact would prove that the leaders
of the "activist" movements wittingly provoked Sunday's bloody
incidents.

The armed insurgents, who were being heavily reinforced on Monday
morning, occupy two "entrenched camps" in the university quarter at
the center of Algiers.

At 2:40 a.m., however, General de Gaulle issued a declaration
describing the uprising as "an evil blow leveled at France" and calling
on the insurgents "to return to the ranks of the nation."

M. Michel Debré* conferred early Monday morning with the Army
Minister, the Chief of State, and finally with General Ely. No action
then seemed contemplated against the "entrenched camp" which a
cordon of paratroopers was surrounding, without preventing, however,
the provisioning of the insurgents after nightfall and the arrival of
new demonstrators at the periphery. But in the course of Monday
morning the paratroopers began to push back the gathering crowd.
Moreover, reinforcements arrived at the gates of Algiers. Several
thousand people in Oran also demonstrated calmly and the situation
was tense at Constantine.

On the mainland, where order reigns, all public meetings and
demonstrations have been forbidden.

A Council of Ministers has been summoned for 3:30 p.m. at the
Élysée to approve the instructions given to M. Delouvrier [Delegate-
General in Algeria, successor to General Salan] and to General Challe,
instructions bearing primarily on the execution of new measures designed to reduce the "activists'" insurrection in Algiers.

(*Le Monde*, January 26, 1960, p. 1)

*[Premier, 1958–62—Eds.]

Although Algiers has known violent bouts of fever in the past five years, this Sunday, January 24, was the first time that demonstrators and police fired on one another. To reach this climax, which previous clashes had been able to avoid, the Algerian crisis had to assume an intensity or take on a nature different from that of February 1956 or the month of May 1958.

It is appropriate to remember first of all that a psychological climate ever more hostile to the Chief of State and to the government had been created, especially since the sixteenth of September, and that tracts denouncing General de Gaulle and those responsible for Algerian policy in the most violent terms have been distributed daily since then.

The announcement of a conference devoted to the Algerian problem on January 22 provoked a frantic agitation against the initiatives, willingly attributed to General de Gaulle. Against this political background, an impassioned climate was created by the rebel terrorist campaign in the Algiers area, which incited a natural indignation that swelled about the cadavers of the aged and the funerals of the slain. The uneasiness that spread in the political circles of Algiers took on a new dimension with the broadcasting of news concerning the reshuffle of the FLN "government," which was interpreted as facilitating possible negotiations.

Then intervened the publication of the interview with the General commanding the army corps in Algiers and the punishment he thereby incurred.* But for weeks certain political circles in metropolitan France already knew what Algerian activists had divulged: that January 24 or 25 could be an important date.

The new elements which gave an insurrectional character to the twenty-fourth of January were on the one hand the creation of a paramilitary formation—the militia of the French National Front, more ready for immediate action than the peasant phalanxes of M. Martel or even the students of MM. Lagaillarde and Susini; on the other hand, the relative isolation of the insurgents, who did not succeed in winning either the immediate adherence of the army or the support of the Moslems, which despite its controversial origins, had provided [in 1958] a characteristic style and a relative tranquility.

[*The government had relieved General Massu of his command at Algiers, following a German journal's publication of Massu's remarks to the effect that the army would not allow de Gaulle to abandon French Algeria—Eds.]

Conflict broke out because this time the rebels found themselves confronted by resistance (despite the virtually "neutral" attitude of certain units). And this deadly collision occurred also because this time the insurgents were armed and organized.

Notice has been taken now for months of the growth and development of this singular phalanx that is the French National Front, obviously linked with the Young Nation movement. It was known that they were increasing their arms and reinforcing their organization. And M. Ortiz was able to preserve an almost clandestine character for his organization until last month.

The Algiers opposition had found a chief more determined than M. Lagaillarde, better armed than M. Martel, more his own master than M. Susini, more attached to immediate action than Dr. Lefèvre. It is no accident if, as things degenerated Sunday, it was M. Ortiz whom General Challe received at length in his headquarters, not fearing to bestow on the café owner a representative status he could thereafter boast of.

It is certain, however, that the men of the FNF were prepared for another form of action than this one, and that their plans were laid for a silent and technically adept "putsch" permitting them to seize the strategic points of their adversaries in a few hours.

Must one predict that since they had to wage battle differently from what they prepared for, the forces constituting the nucleus of the insurrection have been taken at cross purposes? What seems clear in any case is that they had counted on another attitude on the part of the army, that they were disoriented by the coolness shown them; furthermore, that the failure of M. Kaouah, M. Lagaillarde's electoral partner who was assigned to recruit Moslem demonstrators, isolated the movement and prevented it from appearing as what one Algiers daily calls it this morning—a "unanimous uprising."

Jean Lacouture
(*Le Monde*, January 29, 1960, p. 1)

PARIS: SEARCHES AMONG EXTREME RIGHTIST GROUPS
DEPUTY LE PEN INTERROGATED BY THE POLICE
EIGHTY WARRANTS DELIVERED

ALGIERS: TOTAL FAILURE OF ATTEMPTS TO ASSOCIATE THE
MOSLEMS WITH THIS MORNING'S DEMONSTRATIONS

The goals of the insurrection unleashed Sunday in Algiers emerge more clearly every hour.

It is not only aimed at obliging the government and the Chief of State to renounce his Algerian policy as defined September 16. In this respect the insurgents are benefiting from the at least benevolent neutrality of a segment of the military leaders. But as the UNR declared, and as the government believes, the insurrection "is part of a vaster plan" which aims at obtaining a change of regime and the eviction of General de Gaulle.

In this regard, this plan—announced, moreover, several weeks ago —was to have extensions in metropolitan France. Large-scale police operations were begun Thursday morning among the circles of the extreme right. Eighty warrants have been issued and searches made at the quarters of various formations that support the Algiers insurgents and at their leaders' homes. M. Le Pen, Independent deputy of Paris, has been taken to police headquarters for interrogation.

In Algiers: The demonstration organized Thursday morning at the edges of the Casbah by the Veterans' Committee of Entente to gather together Europeans and Moslems has been a total failure. A new attempt is planned for 5 p.m.

The supporters of M. Lagaillarde are publishing a bulletin, *Forces de l'Algérie Française,* whose program includes among other points the immediate execution of all rebels condemned to death. . . .

(*Le Monde,* January 29, 1960, p. 1)

REACTIONS OF ORGANIZATIONS ON THE MAINLAND

THE SFIO: ORGANIZE A REFERENDUM QUICKLY ON
SELF-DETERMINATION

At the conclusion of deliberations Wednesday evening the executive committee of the SFIO published the following declaration:

"The Socialist Party (SFIO) supports the President of the Republic with all its might in order to have the state's authority in Algeria respected unconditionally. . . .

"The government must immediately begin legal prosecutions against those responsible for the uprising and their accomplices, and dissolve their organizations.

"In order to make the national will clear for everyone and definitively to shut the door on any attempts at civil war, the Socialist Party demands the quickest possible organization of a referendum that will allow the country to decide on self-determination. . . ."

THE INDEPENDENTS OF THE DÉPARTEMENT OF THE SEINE: TOTAL SOLIDARITY WITH "THOSE WHO ARE FIGHTING THROUGHOUT ALGERIA"

Meeting Wednesday evening at the [Paris] city hall, the Independent office holders of the *département* of the Seine—deputies, senators, *département* representatives, and city councillors of Paris, mayors and city councillors in the *département*—have published a communiqué in which they declare that remaining "faithful to the ideal of French Algeria which they have always upheld," they "bow to those who have died for this ideal and express their total solidarity with those who are fighting throughout Algeria to remain French on this French land."

(*Le Monde*, January 29, 1960, p. 4)

Address by President Charles de Gaulle on Algerian Policy Broadcast over French Radio and Television on January 29, 1960

If I have put on my uniform today to address you on television, it is in order to show that it is General de Gaulle who speaks, as well as the Chief of State.

In Algeria, we are fighting against a rebellion which has lasted more than five years. France is valiantly continuing to exert the necessary efforts to put down that rebellion.

But she wants to arrive at a peace that is peace; to do what has to be done so that the tragedy does not begin all over again; to act in

Major Addresses, Statements and Press Conferences of General Charles de Gaulle, pp. 71-4.

such a way so as not—when all is said and done—to lose Algeria, which would be a disaster for us and for the West. The world, a prey to vast crises and movements which are well known, is watching this struggle which disturbs it and in which the various opposing camps seek to take a hand. It is obvious that the unity, progress, and prestige of the French people are at stake, and that the future of this people is blocked so long as the Algerian problem remains unsolved.

Taking all this into consideration, I, in the name of France, made the following decision: the Algerians shall have free choice of their destiny. When, one way or another—through the conclusion of a cease-fire or through total defeat of the rebels—we shall have put an end to the fighting, when later, after a prolonged period of restored peace, the populations will have had a chance to understand what is at stake and, moreover, thanks to us, to achieve the necessary progress in the political, economic, social, educational, and other fields—then it will be the Algerians who will say what they want to be. This will not be dictated to them. For if their response were not really *their* response, then while for a time there might well be military victory, basically nothing would be settled. On the contrary, everything can be settled and, I believe, settled in France's favor, when the Algerians will have had an opportunity to make known their will in all freedom, dignity, and security. In short, self-determination is the only policy that is worthy of France. It is the only possible outcome. It is the policy which has been defined by the President of the Republic, decided upon by the Government, approved by the Parliament, and adopted by the French nation.

Now, then, there are two categories of people who do not want any part of this free choice.

First, the rebel organization, which maintains that it will cease fire only if I negotiate with it beforehand, by special prerogative, on the political destiny of Algeria, which would be tantamount to building it up as the only valid representative and to elevating it in advance to being the Government of the country. That I will not do.

On the other hand, some persons of French descent demand that I renounce the idea of self-determination, that I say that everything has been done and that the fate of the Algerians has already been decided. That I will not do either. Self-determination is the only means by which the Moslems can themselves cast out the demon of secession. As to the terms of this or that French solution, I mean to have them worked out at leisure, when peace has been restored. After which, I reserve the right to commit myself—when the right time comes—for whatever I shall consider good. You may be sure that I will do this thoroughly.

It was then that, trying to force their pretended claims on the nation, on the state, and on myself, certain people in Algiers started an insurrection; it was then that they fired on the forces of law and order and killed fine soldiers, and they are now rising up in arms against the authority of France. Aided in the beginning by the accommodating uncertainty of various military elements, and profiting from the fears and feverish passions stirred up by agitators, they have thus far obtained the support of part of the European population; they have instigated a forced strike, the halting of transportation and the closing of stores. Because of them, there is danger that a disruption of the national unity may occur, to the indignation of the French nation and in the very midst of the struggle being waged against the rebels. There is not a man with any common sense who does not see what the inevitable consequences would be if this dreadful secession carried the day.

In the face of the foul blow that has thus been struck against France, I speak first of all to the community of French descent in Algeria. This community has known me for many years. It has seen me many times in its midst, especially during the war when its sons, in great numbers, were serving in the ranks of the Army of Liberation, or else when, following the upheaval of May 1958, I once again assumed leadership of France in order to rebuild the unity of Frenchmen on both shores of the Mediterranean. Whatever any agitators are trying to make this community believe, there are, between it and myself, very special ties that are very dear to me and very much alive. I know perfectly well what services this community renders France through its century of toil in Algeria, what cruel trials it is undergoing, what moving sorrow it has for the victims it mourns. But I must speak to this community in plain and unmistakable words.

Frenchmen of Algeria, how can you listen to the liars and the conspirators who tell you that in granting a free choice to the Algerians, France and de Gaulle want to abandon you, to pull out of Algeria and hand it over to the rebellion? Is it abandoning you, is it wanting to lose Algeria, to send there and to maintain there an army of five hundred thousand men equipped with tremendous amounts of matériel; to consent to the sacrifice there of a good many of our children; to pay out there, this very year, civil and military expenditures amounting to two billion dollars, to undertake there a tremendous program of development; to draw from the Sahara, with great difficulty and at great expense, oil and gas in order to bring them to the sea?

How can you doubt that if, some day, the Moslems freely and formally decide that the Algeria of tomorrow must be closely united with France—how can you doubt that anything would bring greater joy to our country and to de Gaulle than to see them choose, between one solution or another, the one that would be the most French? How can you deny that all the work for the development of the Moslem populations, which was initiated eighteen months ago, and is now still being pursued and which, after pacification, will have to be expanded yet more—how can you deny that this work tends precisely to create new and manifold ties between France and the Algerians? Above all else, how can you fail to see that, in rising up against the state and against the nation, you are surely heading toward ruin and at the same time you are running the risk of causing France to lose Algeria at the very moment when the decline of the rebellion is becoming evident? I solemnly appeal to you to return to law and order.

Next, I speak to the army, which, thanks to its magnificent efforts, is in the process of winning the victory in Algeria; however, some of the elements of this army might be tempted to think that this war is their war, not France's war, and that they have a right to a policy which would not be France's policy. To all our soldiers I say: in your mission there is no room for equivocation or interpretation. You must liquidate the rebel force, which is seeking to drive France out of Algeria and to impose upon that land its dictatorship of want and sterility. At the same time that you are conducting the battle, you must contribute to the material and spiritual transformation of the Moslem populations so as to win their hearts and minds to France. When the time comes for the people to vote, it will be your responsibility to guarantee the complete freedom and sincerity of this vote.

Yes, that is your mission, as France gives it to you, and it is France that you serve. What would the French army become but an anarchic and absurd conglomeration of military feudalisms if it should happen that certain elements made their loyalty conditional? As you know, I have the supreme responsibility. It is I who bear the country's destiny. I must therefore be obeyed by every French soldier. I believe that I shall be obeyed, because I know you, because I have a high regard for you, because I feel affection for you, because I have confidence in General Challe whom I have placed at your head, soldiers of Algeria, and, finally, because I have need of you for France.

This having been said, listen to me carefully. In the presence of the insurrection in Algeria and in the midst of the agitation—bordering on a paroxysm—the Delegate-General, M. Paul Delouvrier, who is France in Algeria, and the Commander in Chief may, on their own responsibility, not have wanted to give the signal themselves for a pitched battle, but no soldier, under penalty of being guilty of a serious fault, may associate himself at any time, even passively, with the insurrection. In the last analysis, law and order must be re-established. The methods to be employed so that law and order will prevail may be of various sorts. But your duty is to bring this about. I have given, and am giving, this order.

Finally, I speak to France. Well, my dear country, my old country, here we are together, once again, facing a harsh test. By virtue of the mandate that the people have given me and of the national legitimacy that I have embodied for twenty years, I ask all men and women to support me, no matter what happens.

And while the guilty ones, who dream of being usurpers, take as a pretext the decision that I have made concerning Algeria, let it be known everywhere, let it be clearly understood, that I do not intend to go back on that decision. To yield on this point and under these conditions would be to destroy the trump cards that we still hold in Algeria, but it would also be to make the state bow before the outrage that is being inflicted on it and the threat that is aimed at it. Thus France would become but a poor broken toy adrift on the sea of hazards.

Once again, I call upon all Frenchmen, wherever they may be, whoever they may be, to reunite themselves with France.

Vive la République! Vive la France!

AFTER THE "SURRENDER" OF THE TWO "ENTRENCHED CAMPS"
THE INSURRECTION HAS ENDED IN ALGIERS

In Algiers the insurrection ended late Monday morning after a night of discussions between its leaders and military authorities.

At noon M. Lagaillarde was evacuating his barricaded camp surrounded by more than six hundred and fifty of his supporters, tricolor flags at their head, arms on their shoulders. While they passed in front of the paratroopers forming the cordon around the entrenched camp, the crowd, which was kept behind the soldiers' trucks, cried: "Vive l'Algérie française, Vive Lagaillarde!" After filing down Boulevard Laferrière the men in the column were placed in twenty-seven military trucks ranged at the bottom of the Plateau des Glières.

The Ortiz "redoubt" had already been emptied by the supporters of the leader of the armed activist organization, the French National Front.

All the men who left the entrenched camp at noon have been taken to Zeralda, the depot of the first Foreign Legion Paratroop Regiment, twenty-five kilometers from Algiers. They will be enlisted there and later used against the fellaghas.

Lagaillarde, ex-deputy Demarquet, and Jean-Jacques Susini, president of the General Association of Students, are among them. It is not known what the fate of Lagaillarde will be.

As for Ortiz, Radio Algiers confirmed at 1:45 p. m. that he was in flight. But the impression prevails that no effort had yet been made to arrest him.

In all of Algeria order is re-established but the war continues. . . .

In Paris the Council of Ministers has been called for 3 p.m. at the Élysée. Its deliberations will continue the numerous conversations which took place during the weekend and on Monday at the Élysée and the Hôtel Matignon.

A reshuffling of the government is envisaged. Parliament is to be called into extraordinary session in order to decide on a request for delegation of powers according to Article 38 of the Constitution.

(*Le Monde*, February 2, 1960, p. 1)

AFTER SUNDAY'S DRAMATIC HOURS (65 DEAD AND HUNDREDS WOUNDED)

GENERAL DE GAULLE IS ADVANCING BY A DAY HIS RETURN TO PARIS WHERE HE WILL TAKE STOCK OF EVENTS

PRO-FLN DEMONSTRATIONS RESUME MONDAY IN ALGIERS AND NEW VICTIMS ARE COUNTED

General de Gaulle is shortening his trip to Algeria by a day. He will return to Paris Tuesday afternoon, twenty-four hours earlier than planned. . . .

The President of the Republic, we are assured, was not informed of the character taken by events in Algiers until late Sunday afternoon. The silence he observed in the following hours and on Sunday morning is explained by his desire to be completely informed of what happened before publicly taking stock of its consequences.

According to whether he decides in the final analysis that the situation was exploited by agitators whose action does not correspond to the true feeling of the populations, or, on the contrary, that the minority has expressed with violence the views of the majorities of the different communities, the actions of the Chief of State will evidently be quite different.

If he adopts the first thesis he could content himself with words of pacification without changing any plans. If, on the other hand, the second explanation prevails, constitutional and political measures must be envisaged, as well as an acceleration of certain stages of his Algerian plans, more clearly directed toward the search for peace.

The first total of the bloody days of Saturday and Sunday in Algiers and Oran was made public Sunday by M. Morin, Delegate-General: sixty-five dead—fifty-nine Moslems, including four in Oran, five Europeans, and a police officer. But during the course of Monday the French Radio and Television gave the figure as eighty-one dead. . . .

In Algiers, the debauch of violence that on Sunday put Moslem groups in opposition with Europeans and then the army does not seem to have exhausted the reservoirs of anger in the two communities. Monday morning, while the strike was at least partially under way, and public transport was not functioning, new Moslem demonstrations were observed, especially in the Casbah, the Randon Market, and the Boulevard de la Victoire. . . .

In Oran, where Moslems started counter-demonstrations on Saturday, pacification appeared to be well under way on Monday. The strike orders have been maintained by the Front de l'Algérie Française and are being observed. The Moslems are being contained by troops in the "Village Nègre," their quarter, where there is still much turmoil.

At Tunis M. Ferhat Abbas [Head of the FLN "Provisional Government"] declared in a press conference that the events of Algiers were the evident sign that the colonial regime had definitely lost the game. . . .

(*Le Monde*, December 13, 1960, p. 1)

First Address by President Charles de Gaulle Informing the Nation of the Referendum on Algeria, Broadcast over French Radio and Television on December 20, 1960

In the midst of a disrupted world, France finds herself confronted by great problems which are also great tests. She would not be France if it were otherwise. She must become wedded to her times and adapt herself to the circumstances, full of hope but cruel, that are reshaping our world.

France at the time of the last war and in spite of an initial disaster, having safeguarded her independence, unity, and integrity; next bending her efforts to a thoroughgoing economic, technical, and social transformation; two years ago reforming her administration in order to make it more stable and more effective; playing an important part in organizing the defense of the free world; embarking with fervor on the construction of Europe; beginning the creation of her nuclear power; changing, as we have just seen, the outworn system of colonization into fruitful and friendly co-operation with twelve African republics and the Malagasy Republic—France is thus evidently a modern nation, enterprising and sure of herself. In order to open the door to the future yet wider for herself, she must now solve the question of her relations with Algeria and of peace in that strife-torn land.

As it is my role, and as it is my duty, I have chosen the road to follow and, as proposed to me by the government, I am asking the French people to give me their approval. Twice before I have appealed to them in this manner: in 1945, at the end of the tragedy, in order to decide upon a course of political renewal while rejecting totalitarian servitude; in 1958, in order to provide us with a constitution which would make it possible for us to rebuild the state and, at the same time, give our Overseas Territories the right of self-determination. Now, for the third time, I am turning directly to the nation.

The French people are thus called upon to say, on January 8, through the referendum, whether they approve—as I ask them to—that, as soon as peace reigns, the Algerian populations choose their own destiny. That means: either to break with the French Republic, to be a part of it, or to be associated with it. It is understood in advance that France, for her part, will validate the choice.

There can be no mistaking the extreme importance of the country's

Major Addresses, Statements and Press Conferences of General Charles de Gaulle, pp. 104–7.

answer. For Algeria, the right granted to the populations to determine their own destiny will signal the beginning of a totally new life. Some may regret that routine, fear, and prejudices have, in the past, hindered the assimilation, pure and simple, of the Moslems—supposing that were possible. But the fact that the Moslems form eight-ninths of the population and that this percentage is constantly increasing in their favor; the evolution of people and of things brought about by events and, especially, by the insurrection; and, finally, the past and present course of world events—all this makes these considerations unrealistic and these regrets superfluous.

The Algeria of tomorrow, then, will be Algerian. The Algerians will conduct their own affairs, and it will be up to them alone to found a state with its own government, its own institutions, and its own laws.

France will solemnly take the decision to consent to this. She will take it according to her own special genius, which is to liberate others —when the time has come and provided that, after liberation, these others are not going to oppress anyone. She will take it in the hope— in accordance with her interest—of dealing, in the future, by no means with a disunited and rebellious Algeria, but with a calmed and responsible Algeria.

However, when, in a peaceful climate, it will one day be up to the Algerian populations to make their decision, it is on realities that they must base their choice, unless they blindly follow the people who would lead them into hopeless chaos. What are these realities?

First of all, the fact that there are, alongside the Moslems, more than a million inhabitants of European origin who also have their roots there and who have every right to be there, who, taken all together, are essential to the life of Algeria and whom—come what may—France, whose children they are, is determined to protect, as well as those Moslems who would, in any case, wish to remain French. Whatever may have been the abuses, the clashes, the incitements, it is thus only common sense for the Moslem communities and the French community to live together, work together, co-operate unhesitatingly within the same institutions, each one having, however, special guarantees as to its rights, its way of life, and its security.

On the other hand, in order to live, to develop, and to become prosperous and modern, Algeria must have help. France is giving her the necessary help. During 1960, we shall have invested in Algeria, in all sorts of forms, more than $800 million. The administrative, economic, technical, and social task accomplished in Algeria by the French does not suffer in comparison with that which any other people of the world has accomplished in this regard in any other region. In the administration, the courts, education, and the army, on both sides of the Mediterranean, two hundred and fifty thousand Moslems are already serving in or being trained for the government service. In the universities, technical schools, and vocational centers, one hundred thousand others are being trained as leaders or advisors for the various activities. In metropolitan France, four hundred thousand earn a living for themselves and for their families whom they have left in Algeria, unless they have come to join them. During the past three years the number of Moslem children enrolled in school has doubled; it will double again during the next three years. What power other than France would be so unsparing with such aid? But who can imagine that she would continue to do so in the case of a break?

In truth, everything demands that the Algeria of tomorrow be associated with France. Now, France is, in advance, fraternally disposed toward this in the name of the many bonds woven during more than a century; by reason of what she expects, as I see it, from an Algeria which would be prosperous and friendly, in spite of and even because of the wounds and the sorrows of these last six years, wounds and sorrows which we must now heal. But it is with an Algeria such that the co-operation of the communities is ensured there; with an Algeria in which each of them has, organically, the appropriate guarantees; with an Algeria joined with us in precisely the domains in which we must aid it—it is with such an Algeria that France, for her part, conceives of association.

It is in order to prepare for this that if, by virtue of the referendum, the people's answer is in the affirmative, Algerian public powers—an executive and assemblies—will be organized without any further delay for the whole territory, pending self-determination; that public life and action will be decentralized, thanks to a regional and departmental organization corresponding to the geographic and ethnic diversity of Algeria; and finally, that, between metropolitan France and Algeria, organs will be created having jurisdiction in the common domains, as for example, the Constantine Plan. Certainly these institutions will be valid only until the day when the future decisive consultations of the populations will either confirm, modify, or reject them. But in the meantime they will help Algeria to set forth along the road leading to the solution of common sense.

As this solution comes into focus, France appreciates better the services that her army is rendering and will continue to render in Algeria. What a sea of killing and woe would this country have been

plunged into had our soldiers—metropolitan French, Moslem, African
—faltered in their duty to maintain law and order. Henceforth, on the
contrary, we can see an end to the tragedy, for these soldiers have,
through their brave and long-enduring efforts, restored security in all
parts of the territory; so much so that, in this last week, fewer people
were killed in the insurrection than in accidents on the highway or at
work. And, regarding the possibilities of future association between
Algeria and France, how valuable are the innumerable personal contacts which have arisen between our troops and the populations! It is
because all this was done that, today, France can propose peace.

Yes, we are proposing peace. We are ready at any time to receive
the delegates of the people who are fighting against us. As soon as the
last skirmishes and terrorist attacks have come to an end, the government will be able to arrange—with the various Algerian factions, and
especially with the leaders of the rebellion—all the conditions under
which the right of self-determination can be exercised openly. That
is why the affirmative answer of our people in the referendum will also
take on the character of an appeal for an end to the fighting and for
a peaceable confrontation.

Women and men of France, the frank and massive "yes" that General de Gaulle, President of the Republic, asks of you will be France's
decision. It will give Algeria an opportunity for a free future. It will
prove to the world that the French nation, today as much as ever,
stands united, clear-sighted, and generous. And to me, whose task is
arduous, what support it will lend.

Vive la République! Vive la France!

THE "YESSES" WIN 75.25 PER CENT OF THE VOTES IN MAINLAND
FRANCE; 69.09 PER CENT IN ALGERIA, WHERE THERE ARE 40.2
PER CENT ABSTENTIONS (URBAN MOSLEMS)

In metropolitan France—The results of the referendum constitute a
clear and important success for General de Gaulle, whose Algerian
policy has been widely approved.

The "yesses" received 15,196,668 votes, that is, 75.25 per cent of
the votes cast or 55.89 per cent of the registered voters. In 1958 the
two figures were respectively 79.26 and 66.41.

The "noes" thus represent, with 4,995,912 votes, 24.74 per cent
of the votes and 18.37 per cent of those registered. In 1958, 20.74
per cent of all those who voted and 17.38 per cent of the registered

voters voted "no. . . . " The principle of self-determination is thus ratified, and the legislative bill concerning the provisional organization of the public powers in Algeria is adopted.

In Algeria the third day of the voting did not produce the same electoral participation as the two earlier days: in the large cities, above all Algiers and Oran, the FLN instructions to abstain were largely followed by the Moslem populations. In total, throughout all of Algeria, there were 40.2 per cent abstentions (a percentage about that of the municipal and district elections). Europeans for their part massively voted "no," making the negative vote prevail in several centers, including Algiers (72.2 per cent "no"), as well as Oran, Philippeville, and Bône. Of 4,414,636 registered voters, 1,747,529 "yesses" and 782,052 "noes" were counted.

Various incidents disturbed the balloting Saturday and Sunday, notably in the South and West of the Oran region: twenty dead were allegedly counted.

FAILURE OF ALGÉRIE-FRANÇAISE SUPPORTERS IN PARIS AND THE PROVINCES

. . . Abstentions are more numerous than in the six legislative elections that have taken place since the liberation and in three of four of the constitutional referendums of the past fifteen years. Only the referendum of October 13, 1946, which decided on the definitive adoption of the Fourth Republic, saw greater abstention (31.42 per cent). About 10 per cent of the registered voters who cast ballots two years ago did not return to the ballot boxes.

Abstentions occurred especially in the Massif Central. . . . Abstentions also touched certain Alpine and Pyrenees *départements*. . . . The large wine-growing *départements* of the South, where the mayors' and vintners' associations called for abstentions, partially observed this attitude. On the other hand the voting was heaviest in the northern region (Pas de Calais, Nord, and Somme), in Lorraine, Alsace, Normandy, and the Breton West, surpassing 80 per cent of the electorate.

(*Le Monde*, January 10, 1961, p. 1)

THE ALGERIAN VOTE CONFIRMS THE POSITIONS OF THE TWO COMMUNITIES, BUT SETTLES NO ISSUES

Never perhaps has the index of refraction which transforms or inverts proposals, intentions, and policies between one shore of the Mediterranean and the other been so visible as on the occasion of this unique referendum. One could predict this, to be sure, as soon as General de Gaulle had decided to put his Algerian policy to the test of a referendum. But the results of the voting exceed the prognostications. . . .

It was not expected that the Algerian populations would observe discipline, so much more scrupulously than those of the mainland in respect to the organizations grouping them. It is clear that, insofar as the terms of the election permitted, the FLN on one side, the Front de l'Algérie Française on the other, have drawn their troops in the directions they prescribed.

For the first time, moreover, the army seems to have played a discreet role in many sectors. Military men had received orders to consider the referendum of 1958 as a battle and to win at all costs. Yesterday, especially in the Algiers region, and in that army corps which so vigorously continues the tradition and influence of General Massu's staff, the officers exerted hardly any pressure in favor of the government's program.

Another essential element intervened in the vote: the memory of the events of last December 9 and 10. The impressive mass of abstentions that emerged from Algiers to Tlemcen and from Oran to Sétif, as well as the processions with FLN banners at their head that sometimes accompanied the voting . . . could not have been foreseen before the demonstrations of last month. It appears more and more that the parade of Moslem crowds in Algiers and Oran constitutes a sort of May 13 in reverse, that it has opened a new phase in the conflict, and that it gives it new perspectives. . . .

What appears in the results of the Algerian voting even more than the protest movement on the part of the European population against the policies of the Chief of State, is the strength of the abstentionist movement in the Moslem urban milieu which testifies to the FLN hold over the city masses. Thus emerges the opposition, almost the symmetry between the two aspects of the vote on both sides of the Mediterranean. M. Masmoudi, Tunisian State Secretary for Information, declared Monday morning that there were in fact two referendums, and that if the one on the mainland gave General de Gaulle more strength and liberty to put his policies into effect, the other one in Algeria designated the mediator he had to use. This formula is worth remembering. Whatever disdain he had displayed for the vote, Ferhat Abbas will not fail to make use of its results.

If it is true that on Sunday the Chief of State received a broad new mandate from the mainland—and the mainland alone—to put into effect his Algerian policy, it seems that the vote cannot fail to add to the authority of the leader of the FLN. Thus the referendum has assembled the nation less than it has clarified the reciprocal positions and distinguished their respective spokesmen. Perhaps we are still far from face-to-face discussions, but Sunday's vote should favor the resumption of contacts, if on the two sides there is a willingness to move in this direction.

Jean Lacouture
(*Le Monde*, January 10, 1961, p. 1)

Fourth Press Conference Held by General de Gaulle as President of the French Republic in Paris at the Elysée Palace on April 11, 1961

Algeria

Question: Mr. President, after simultaneous announcements from Paris and Tunis of the meeting at Evian, the FLN has abruptly changed its mind. Is there a new factor in the situation? How can this change of position be explained? What are the present possibilities of opening discussions? Could these be undertaken or pursued if, in the absence of a cease-fire, a de facto truce were at least announced?

Answer: If you will permit, we shall take up at once—since the whole world is waiting for it—the question of Algeria, which I should like once again to discuss thoroughly. In defining France's policy toward Algeria it can, of course, be said first of all that France intends to see to it that, by one means or another, the fighting and the terrorist attacks are stopped, for nothing constructive can be accomplished while the war continues. It can also be said that France intends to let the Algerian populations freely determine their own destiny, for nothing is or will be valid unless the populations are given the right to determine their own fate.

But, as France sees it, what is primarily at stake is the future of Al-

Major Addresses, Statements and Press Conferences of General Charles de Gaulle, pp. 113–18.

geria. The cease-fire, self-determination—these are preliminaries that are designed to open the way for Algeria.

What the Algeria of tomorrow will be, what its future relations with France will be—that is what I want to talk about and outline, once again, what my country's policy is.

It is a fact that at the moment Algeria is a country in which war rages. It is also a fact that its future is not at all clear. I should like it to be well understood that in France's policy toward Algeria, the following essential idea must be faced squarely: in the world of today and in the times in which we live, France has no interest whatsoever in maintaining under her jurisdiction and under her dependence an Algeria which would choose another destiny, and it would not be in France's interest to be responsible for the population of an Algeria which would have become master of its own fate and would have nothing to offer in exchange for what it would ask. The fact is that, to say the least, Algeria costs us much more than it is worth to us. Whether in the matter of administrative expenses, economic investments, social welfare, cultural development, or the many obligations with regard to the maintenance of law and order—what we furnished to it in effort, money, and human ability has no counterpart that anywhere nearly approaches it.

It must in the same way be realized that France's present responsibilities in Algeria constitute heavy military and diplomatic burdens for her. And that is why France would consider today with the greatest calm a solution whereby Algeria would cease to be a part of France—a solution which in former times might have seemed disastrous for us but which, I say it again, we consider with a perfectly calm mind. It would be quite different, of course, if the Algerian masses were bent on remaining part of the French people for, in that case, it would be worth any sacrifice to retain within the mother country a fraction of her children. But it is difficult to claim that the Algerian masses, as a whole, wish to be a part of the French people. Consequently, when it is a matter of its fate in relation to us, we will first have to consider our interest and that is why—I repeat it—France has no objection and intends to raise no obstacle to the fact that the Algerian populations would decide to form a state which would be in charge of their country. This state will be such as the Algerians want. For my part, I am convinced that it will be a sovereign one within and without.

And, once again, France will raise no obstacle to this. There are people who will say: "But it is the rebellion which leads you to think in this way." I do not deny that the rebellion has confirmed, affirmed in my mind what was already my thought well before the rebellion broke out. In any case, it is not the present situation of the fighting which induces me to speak as I do, for at no time during the past six years have the army and the police had, as it is said, things better in hand, although numerous information organs—is this a liking for catastrophe?—continually bring up the "fresh outbreaks" of the skirmishes and terrorist attacks. It is a fact that the rebellion, which, in the past, took a daily toll of about fifty civilians and soldiers, now takes an average of only seven or eight a day, four or five of whom are Moslems. It is not this that makes me speak as I do; I do not deny that the events which have occurred, which are occurring in Algeria have confirmed what I have thought and demonstrated for more than twenty years, without any joy of course—and you can well understand why—but with the certainty of serving France well.

Since Brazzaville, I have not ceased to affirm that the populations dependent on us should have the right to self-determination. In 1941, I granted independence to the mandated states of Syria and Lebanon. In 1945, I gave all Africans, including Algerian Moslems, the right to vote. In 1947, I approved the Statute of Algeria which, if it had been applied, would probably have led to the progressive institution of an Algerian state associated with France. At that time, I agreed that the protectorate treaties concerning Tunisia and Morocco should come to an end. In 1958, having resumed leadership, I, along with my government, created the Community and later recognized and aided the independence of the young states in Black Africa and Madagascar. Not having returned to power in time to prevent the Algerian insurrection, immediately upon my return I proposed to its leaders to conclude the peace of the brave and to open political talks. In 1959, I proclaimed the right of the Algerian populations to self-determination as well as the determination of France to accept the solution, whatever it might be, which would result from this. In 1960, I affirmed many times over that Algeria would be Algerian, I spoke of the birth of its future republic and renewed our offer of discussions. It was not our fault that the Melun contacts did not have any results; at the same time I broke the plots intended to force me to support integration. In 1961, I asked the French people to give me their approval, which was done through a massive "Yes" vote in the referendum, and, once again, I invited the men of the rebellion to get in touch with our representatives.

And, during these same three years, I and my Government have not ceased to act in order to promote a Moslem leadership in Algeria and to put the Moslems in a position to take local affairs into their own hands, until such time as they are able to take over on the government level. Thus, the single college was instituted, numerous deputies and senators were elected—a great majority of whom were Moslems—many communes were established, a great number of Moslems have come to hold most of the mayors' offices, and general councils have been re-elected or instituted. At present the chairman of each of these thirteen councils is a Moslem. Thus, the commissions of elected representatives have been set up, composed for the most part of Moslems. Thus, a large number—a number which will be further increased—of Moslem prefects and subprefects have been appointed in Algeria, and the proportion of Moslems in all ranks and levels of the army, the police force, the administration, and the magistrature has grown. In short we are proving every day that an Algeria belonging to itself would in no way be contrary to the policy of France.

In conclusion what does this add up to: to decolonization. But if I have undertaken and pursued this task for a long time, it is not only because we could foresee and later because we witnessed the vast movement toward freedom which the world war and its aftermath unleashed in every corner of the globe, and which the rival bids of the Soviet Union and America did not fail to emphasize. I have done it also, and especially because it seemed to me contrary to France's present interests and new ambition to remain bound by obligations and burdens which are no longer in keeping with the requirements of her strength and influence.

Moreover, this is true for others as well. It must be recognized that in the great transformation which is taking place from one end of the universe to the other, the itching for independence of erstwhile dominated peoples and also the incitements thrown out by all the demagogies of the world are not the only motivating forces. There is another which is not always very clearly perceived because of habits of mind, but which is nonetheless a very positive factor, one that is growing and tending to become the predominant one, especially in France. I mean that the reasons which once led certain civilized peoples to take under their direct control certain other peoples which were not—these reasons are disappearing even from the minds of the ex-colonizers. It now seems to the most powerful nations that their future, their welfare and the potentialities of their world action depend on their own development and on the co-operation of the formerly colonized countries, much more than on domination imposed on dissimilar peoples.

It was not always like that. We French built our empire at a time
when our internal activities had reached a sort of ceiling—an industry
which was not breaking any new ground, and agriculture which was
not making any changes, trade channels which were fixed, salaries and
wages unchanged, practically stereotyped budgets, gold currency,
interest rates at 3 per cent, etc. On the other hand, our old ambitions
of European hegemony and natural frontiers were countered by the
treaties of 1815 and, after 1870, by the unity and strength of a threatening Germany. Then we sought in distant extensions a new role for
the surplus of our enterprising abilities, a complement to our prestige,
and soldiers for our defense.

France does not have to be at all sorry for what she has achieved
overseas in this capacity and in this form. I have said it often and I
repeat: it constitutes a great human accomplishment which—notwithstanding certain abuses and errors and despite all the endless
spouting of all sorts of worthless demagogues—will forever be a
credit to France. But how many things have changed today.

Now our great national ambition is our own national progress, constituting a real source of power and influence. Now the modern era
permits us, compels us, to undertake a vast development. Now for
this development to succeed we must first of all employ the means and
resources at our disposal on our own behalf, in our own country. All
the more so as we need these means and resources to ensure our own
defense and that of our neighbors against the greatest imperialism that
the world has ever known—the imperialism of the Soviet Union. We
also need these means to win out in the tremendous economic, technical, and social struggle now under way between the forces of humanity and the forces of slavery.

It is a fact: our interest, and consequently our policy, lies in decolonization. Why should we continue to cling to costly, bloody, and
fruitless domination when our country has to undergo complete renovation, when all the underdeveloped countries, beginning with those
which yesterday were our dependencies and which today are our
favorite friends, ask for our aid and our assistance? But this aid and
this assistance—why should we extend them if it is not worthwhile,
if there is no co-operation, if what we give finds no return? Yes, it is
a matter of exchange, because of what is due us, but also because of
the dignity of those with whom we are dealing. . . .

This is the basis of France's policy with regard to her future relations with Algeria. If in the final analysis the Algerian populations

are willing to let themselves be led to a break with France, such that we will no longer have any part to play in their destiny, we shall not oppose this in any way. Naturally, we shall cease immediately to sink in a henceforth hopeless enterprise our resources, our men, and our money. . . .

But it is also possible that the Algerian populations—through self-determination, while deciding on the institution of a sovereign state—will express their desire to see the new Algeria associated with the new France. In such an event, it would have to be known on both sides what this actually meant. That is why a solution should be submitted to the vote of the Algerian people—pending ratification by the French people—a solution agreed upon beforehand by the government and the different political elements in Algeria, the rebels in particular. France would undoubtedly be willing to lend her economic, administrative, financial, cultural, military, and technical aid to the young Mediterranean state, provided the organic co-operation between the Algerian communities, preferential conditions for economic and cultural exchange, and finally the bases and facilities necessary for our defense, are assured and guaranteed. . . .

One can be astonished that the leaders of the rebellion have not, until now, felt they could answer the invitation addressed to them. But one can also think that, up to now, they have been diverted from adopting a constructive position by their prolonged exile, by the composition of their own organization, by the influences exercised over them by various outside imperialistic forces, finally by the illusions with regard to the French situation instilled in them by certain partisan factions or press clans in metropolitan France—with whom they have had contact and for whom the Algerian affair is only a ground for opposition. I admit that it is difficult for an essentially insurrectional organism to tackle, with the minimum necessary serenity and on the desired level, questions such as those of peace, of the organization of a state and of the economic development of a country. But these leaders—since they will not win on the military field where our army at present, I repeat, has the situation in hand; since, on the other hand, they have great responsibilities because of the influence they exercise and the audience they find among a large number of Moslems; since, finally, a number of them seem to be called upon to play an outstanding role in the first stages of the new Algeria—the question is, will these leaders, in the final analysis, be capable of adopting a positive stand. . . .

WITH THE SUPPORT OF PARATROOPERS—
MILITARY COUP IN ALGIERS FRIDAY NIGHT

GENERALS CHALLE, JOUHAUD, AND ZELLER SEIZE POWER

A military coup has taken place in Algiers Friday night and early Saturday morning. Shortly after midnight, elements of the First Foreign Legion Paratroop Regiment surrounded Government House, the official buildings, the radio station, and telephone and telegraph switchboards. M. Jean Morin, Delegate-General, M. Robert Buron, Minister of Public Works, who was the guest of the Delegate-General, and General Gambiez [were taken prisoner].

The mutiny is directed by retired Generals Maurice Challe, Jouhaud, and André Zeller, who have proclaimed a state of siege. General Salan, whose name also figures in the proclamations broadcast in Algiers, was still in Madrid at the end of Saturday morning, as was M. Pierre Lagaillarde.

According to news reaching Paris, Generals de Pouilly and Gouraud, who were commanding the army corps of Oran and Constantine and were said to have received an "ultimatum" from the generals in Algiers, have allegedly refused to join the movement.

M. Louis Joxe, provided with the most extensive powers, and General Olié, named Commander in Chief, have been sent to Algeria. They arrived shortly after 12:30 at an undisclosed location.

No other incident was reported on the mainland where feverish activity reigned in the centers of government. The government has let it be known that it has taken all necessary measures to have the law enforced. In a broadcast speech, M. Michel Debré said at the beginning of the afternoon, "The government is resolved to have the will of the nation respected." A Council of Ministers has been summoned at the Élysée for 5 p. m.

The UNR, the parties of the left and the unions have raised sharp protests against the coup and are consulting on what form of action would be appropriate, mentioning the words "General Strike."

(*Le Monde*, April 23–24, 1961, p. 1)

Address by President Charles de Gaulle Broadcast over French Radio and Television on April 23, 1961

An insurrectional power has set itself up in Algeria by a military pronunciamento. Those guilty of this usurpation have exploited the passion of officers of certain special units, the inflamed support of one part of the population of European origin, misguided by fears and myths, the impotence of authorities overwhelmed by the military conspiracy.

This power has an appearance: a quartet of retired generals. It has a reality: a group of partisan, ambitious, and fanatical officers. This group and this quartet possess a limited and expeditious ability, but they see and know the nation and the world only as deformed by their fanaticism.

Their venture cannot but lead to a national disaster. For the immense effort of recovery in France—begun at the depths of the abyss on June 18, 1940; continued later despite everything until victory was gained, independence assured, the Republic restored; resumed three years ago in order to remake the state, maintain the national unity, rebuild our power, restore our position in the world, pursue our task overseas through a necessary decolonization—all this risks being made useless, on the very eve of success, by the odious and stupid adventure in Algeria.

Now the state is flouted, the nation defied, our power degraded, our international prestige lowered, our role and our place in Africa jeopardized. And by whom? Alas! Alas! By men whose duty, honor, and reason for being was to serve and obey.

In the name of France, I order that all means—I say all means—be employed everywhere to bar the route to these men, until they are subjugated. I forbid any Frenchmen, and first of all any soldier, to execute any of their orders. The argument that it might be locally necessary to accept their command under the pretext of operational or administrative obligations can fool no one.

The civil and military leaders who have the right to assume responsibilities are those who have been legally named and precisely those the insurgents prevent from doing so.

The future of the usurpers should only be that provided for them by the rigor of the law.

In the face of the misfortune which looms over the country and

Major Addresses, Statements and Press Conferences of General Charles de Gaulle, pp. 127–8.

of the threat that hangs over the Republic, I have decided, having formally consulted the Constitutional Council, the Premier, the President of the Senate, the President of the National Assembly, to put into force Article 16 of our Constitution. As of today, I will take, if necessary directly, the measures that appear to me to be required by the circumstances.

In this way, I confirm myself in the French and republican legality which was conferred upon me by the nation and which I will maintain no matter what happens until the end of my term, or until I lack either force or life; and I will take measures to make sure that this legality remains after me.

Frenchwomen, Frenchmen, see where France risks going, compared with what she was again becoming.

Frenchwomen, Frenchmen, help me.

IN THE FACE OF THE SITUATION'S DEVELOPMENT AND GRAVITY GENERAL DE GAULLE PLANS TO BRING INTO PLAY ARTICLE 16 RESPECTING FULL POWERS

GENERAL CHALLE SEEKS TO EXTEND THE SEDITION TO THE WHOLE OF ALGERIA

Faced with the development of the Algerian situation, General de Gaulle plans to bring into play Article 16 of the Constitution, which lets him assume all powers when "there exists a serious and immediate threat to the institutions of the Republic, the independence of the nation, the integrity of its territory. . . ." Concerning this matter he has consulted successively this Sunday morning MM. Debré, Monnerville, and Chaban-Delmas, and is to receive at the beginning of the afternoon the President of the Constitutional Council, Léon Noël.

According to the same provision of the Constitution the President must address a message to the nation to inform it of his decision. Parliament, which was to open its session Tuesday, thus convenes fully in accordance with the law, and the National Assembly cannot be dissolved.

This recourse to exceptional powers will permit taking measures more rapidly and completely than did the state of urgency decreed Saturday evening by the Council of Ministers, who have moreover turned over Generals Challe, Salan, Jouhaud, and Zeller and Colonel Godard to military jurisdiction.

On the mainland, order has not been disturbed except by new plastic bomb attacks. Order reigns in all *départements*. . . .

In Algiers, the leaders of the mutiny are announcing over the air waves of "Radio France" that they control the major part of Algerian territory, notably Oran, Constantine, and the base of Télegerma. It is true that General de Pouilly, commanding the Oran Army Corps, has had to fall back on Tlemcen. On the other hand, it is hard to estimate the situation exactly for the rest of the country, especially the area of Constantine. Communications with Algiers are still interrupted, and the concern, if not the intoxication with propaganda, of the military who control the broadcasts of Radio Algiers is evident. . . .

At Tunis, according to declarations of M. Ferhat Abbas, calling the Algerian people to "resist provocations," the spokesmen of the FLN have taken a position against the insurgents and indicated that their intentions to negotiate remained unchanged. . . .

(*Le Monde*, special edition, April 24, 1961, p. 1)

ANSWERING APPEALS ISSUED SUNDAY EVENING BY GENERAL DE GAULLE AND M. DEBRÉ

VOLUNTEER CORPS—TO REMAIN ON ALERT—JOIN THE SECURITY FORCES TO COUNTER A POSSIBLE COUP D'ÉTAT ON THE MAINLAND

The readying of the capital for defense and the formation of regular units composed of reservists and volunteers resolved to oppose by arms any attempted coup d'état were actively pursued Monday morning.

Broadcast hourly, the appeal of M. Michel Debré awakened intense emotion in Paris during the course of the night, but the excitement eased at daybreak.

Important official security measures were taken immediately. Tanks, whose passing drew Parisians to their windows, entered the capital and some took up positions in front of the Palais-Bourbon.

Answering the appeal of the Prime Minister, numerous volunteers crowded Place Beauvau, the Grand Palais, and the headquarters of unions to enroll in defense groups. Ministers and top functionaries responsible for public order sat practically in permanence at the Hôtel Matignon. . . .

The message of the Chief of State announcing his decision [to assume full powers] has received an almost unanimously favorable reception, and expressions of confidence and loyalty continue to flood the Élysée. . . .   (*Le Monde*, April 25, 1961, p. 1)

Here is the film of events that have taken place in Algeria since Tuesday [April 25] p.m. . . .

5 p.m. The paratroopers leave Oran

The paratroop units who Sunday evening had occupied the city of Oran leave in the direction of Algiers. General Gardy and Colonel Argoud also leave Oran. . . .

8:30 p.m. The entire Oran region is in the hands of the legal authorities. . . .

9:10 p.m. Radio Algiers broadcasts an appeal to the territorial units

Radio Algiers broadcasts the following proclamation by ex-Generals Challe, Salan, Zeller, and Jouhaud.

"To Frenchmen of every origin: four days have passed that France will remember a long time. A magnificent spirit of patriotism has answered the appeal of April 22. In view of the success of pacification we have decided to demobilize all the soldiers who have served eighteen months and over, therefore to reduce the term of service to eighteen months. Before their departure we congratulate all the soldiers who have fought to defend the honor and the liberty of France, whose loyal sons they have demonstrated themselves to be. The population thanks them. . . . "

9:44 p.m.

The French News Agency announces that ex-Generals Challe, Zeller, Jouhaud, and Salan as well as ex-colonel Godard left Algiers at the beginning of the evening, but the news is not confirmed by an official source.

10:15 p.m. Thousands of people in the streets of Algiers

Forces including mobile gendarmes, the 7th Zouave Regiment, CRS, and armored cars move to converge on the center of Algiers. *10:30 p.m.* Mobile gendarme units and armored cars take position above Government House. They rapidly make an enveloping move; meanwhile the paratroopers retreat toward Government House.

11:15 p.m. Thousands of people in the streets of Algiers

Several thousand people—many women and children—invade the Forum. Hundreds of autos furrow down the streets of Algiers honking [the rhythm of] *"Algérie française"* on their horns, while large crowds climb the stairs to Government House. Armed young men hide in the thickets and orders are given to women to block the road crossings. At Rue Berthezène several automobiles are placed across the roadway. Green berets and mobile gendarmes stand face to face forty meters apart. The crowd shouts the usual slogans: "Algérie française," "Vive l'armée," and "De Gaulle to the wall," (for the first time in four days).

Wednesday: from midnight on everything collapses . . .

12:45 a.m. Last appearance of Challe and Salan

Ex-generals Challe and Salan appear a last time at the balcony of Government House. They prepare to speak but there are no more microphones. . . . They are frantically applauded, wave their hands, and slowly return to the offices of Government House. (At the same time in Paris it was being announced that ex-General Maurice Challe had told the government that he was at the disposition of the courts while rumor circulated in the capital that ex-General Salan had committed suicide.)

1:20 a.m. MM. Buron, Morin, and General Gambiez are freed . . .

The Forum is now empty. Suddenly bursts of fire ring out near the large post office: Zouaves crouch and point their rifles toward a group of about one hundred people. But they do not fire. Two vehicles carrying machine guns arrive to reinforce the soldiers. It is the end. The residents of Algiers return to their homes, stupefied, stunned, fists clenched. Some have tears in their eyes. They cannot understand. . . .

1:50 a.m. Challe, Salan, and Jouhaud leave Government House for Zeralda

. . . To a journalist who asks him if he will surrender, Salan, smiling, answers, "No."

(Le Monde, April 27, 1961, pp. 2–3)

"GENERAL DECLARATION" OF THE FRENCH AND FLN DELEGATIONS
ISSUED AT EVIAN-LES-BAINS, MARCH 18, 1962

The French people by the referendum of January 8, 1961, recognized the right of the Algerians to choose by consultation of direct and universal suffrage their political destiny in relation to the French Republic.

The negotiations that took place at Evian from March 7 to 18, 1962, between the government of the Republic and the FLN reached the following conclusion:

A cease-fire is concluded. Military operations and the armed struggle throughout Algerian territory will come to an end March 19.

The guarantees relative to the application of self-determination and the organization of the public powers in Algeria during the transition period have been defined in common agreement.

The formation after self-determination of an independent and sovereign state appears to conform to Algerian realities, and in these conditions, co-operation between France and Algeria responding to the interests of the two countries, the French government considers with the FLN that the solution of the independence of Algeria in co-operation with France is the one which corresponds to this situation.

The government and the FLN have therefore defined in common agreement this solution in the declarations which will be submitted to the approval of the electors at the time of the self-determination vote.

Chapter I

Organization of public powers during the transition period and self-determination guarantees:

A. The self-determination vote will permit the electors to make known whether they want Algeria to be independent and in that case whether they want France and Algeria to co-operate in the conditions defined by the present declarations.

B. This consultation will take place throughout the whole of the territory of Algeria, that is to say in the fifteen following *départements*: Algiers, Batna, Bône, Constantine, Medea, Mostaganem, Oases, Oran, Orléansville, Saida, Saoura, Sétif, Tiaret, Tizi-Ouzou, Tlemcen.

The results of the different voting offices will be totaled and proclaimed for the whole territory.

C. The freedom and the sincerity of the consultation will be guaranteed in conformity with the regulation fixing the conditions of the self-determination consultation. . . .

I. The FLN will be considered as a legal political formation.

J. Persons interned both in France and Algeria will be released within a maximum period of twenty days from the cease-fire.

K. The amnesty will be proclaimed immediately. Detained persons will be released. . . .

Chapter II

Independence and co-operation:

If the solution of independence and co-operation is adopted, the contents of the present declarations will be binding on the Algerian state.

Independence of Algeria

The Algerian state will exercise its full and complete sovereignty both internally and externally. This sovereignty will be exercised in all spheres, notably defense and foreign affairs.

The Algerian state will freely decide on its own institutions and will choose the political and social regime which it deems most suitable to its interests. In the international fields it will draw up and apply in full sovereignty the policy of its choice.

The Algerian state will unreservedly subscribe to the Universal Declaration of Human Rights and will base its institutions on democratic principles and on equality of political rights among all citizens without discrimination of race, origin, or religon. It will apply the recognized guarantees notably to citizens of French civilian status.

Co-operation Between France and Algeria

2. In the existing departments of the Oases and Sahara, the development of sub-soil wealth will be carried according to the following principles.

A. Franco-Algerian co-operation will be insured by a technical body of Sahara co-operation. This body will have parity. Its role will notably be to develop the infrastructure necessary for the exploitation of the subsoil, to give advice on mining bills and regulations, to examine demands concerning the granting of mining concessions. The Algerian state will deliver the mining titles and will enact ministerial legislation in full sovereignty.

B. French interests will notably be assured by the exercising of rights attached to mining concessions granted by France in accordance with the rules of the Sahara oil code such as it exists at present.

French companies will be given preference in the case of equal offers in the granting of new mining permits, according to provisions provided for by Algerian mining legislation.

Payment in French currency for Sahara hydrocarbons to meet requirements of France and other franc-zone countries. . . .

(Le Monde, March 20, 1962, p. 4.)

Transcript of the Trial of General Raoul Salan, May 1962 (Excerpts)

HEARING OF MAY 21, 1962. TESTIMONY OF COLONEL JEAN THOMAZO, RETIRED COLONEL AND DEPUTY FROM BASSES-PYRÉNÉES.

M. TIXIER-VIGNANCOUR: Colonel Thomazo, both by himself and through his children, belongs to the category of those who have given everything. He served under General Salan both in Indochina and Algeria. I would appreciate if he could tell us, with the authority given him by his sacrifices, what he thinks were the motives which might have moved General Salan.

COLONEL THOMAZO: I served under General Salan: in Indochina from 1951 to 1953 and in Algeria from 1956 to November 1958.

If I speak of Indochina at the beginning of my testimony, it is because I believe that the army's crisis of conscience began in Indochina and that it is impossible to understand the motives of many commanders—and especially the motives for the actions of General Salan in Algeria—if one does not go back to the deep and real causes of this fearsome drama of conscience which many of my comrades and I myself lived through.

To lead men into battle, to risk one's life, there have to be motives. People never shed their blood *gratis*: they die to defend a cause which they believe just; they die to help a friend who is in danger. If the cause is hopeless, they die to salvage honor.

In Indochina as, alas, later in Algeria, thousands and thousands of men were killed for a cause which people knew was lost and which people wanted lost. We were forced to abandon our friends whom we had promised to protect; we were forced to leave in dishonor.

Those who like myself—and there are many of us in the army—lost sons in the Indochinese and Algerian campaigns, artillery lieutenants or parachutists, perhaps more than others we have the duty to tell you—having known the mentality of these young officers under our orders—what they thought in the depths of their hearts of this fearful divorce between the government and its army, between the nation and its army. It was in Algeria that the gulf between the nation and its army began to widen.

Le Procès de Raoul Salan, Compte Rendu Stenographique, 371–5. From the series "Les Grands Procès Contemporains," under the direction of Maître Maurice Garçon of the Académie Française, reprinted by permission of the publisher, Éditions Albin Michel, Paris.

Permit me to mention a personal experience:

Once in Indochina, in Tonkin, on General Salan's orders which were transmitted to me by General de Linarès, I was given the mission to negotiate with the Catholic bishops of Fat-Diem and of Bouchou. This meant for us to rally the populace of these two bishoprics which had fought against the Communist Vietminh with great courage, but which were soon going to lose the revolutionary war the Vietminh was fighting against them. I was commissioned to negotiate agreements with the two bishops and in the name of France, with the agreement of the government, to give the pledge that French troops would stay in these two bishoprics to protect the Catholic minorities against the raids of Vietminh troops.

You know what happened.

On the orders of the government, on orders from Paris, our troops had to leave. Then came the heart-rending exodus of this Catholic populace—men, women, and children in droves sought refuge in South Vietnam. And it was even worse: these people, hooking onto the ships which were taking away our troops, tried to follow them in sampans and junks loaded with women and children, some of them sinking amid prayers to the heavens—these prayers which our missionaries had taught them—these tortured people, lost by our fault.

When one has seen and lived through these things, one cannot help holding in his heart a feeling of reprobation for the authorities who tolerated them. One cannot help, when one is a soldier, swearing to do all he can never to let them happen again.

This was the state of mind of this young army which fought for five years in Indochina, when it came back to Algeria to fight the same battle, the same revolutionary war with the same leader as commander in chief: General Salan.

In Algeria I served as deputy to the commander of the army corps of Algeria, General Allard, and in my duties, in addition to commanding certain operations in the region of Algiers, I served as a liaison officer with the organizations of students who were in military studies, with organizations of reserve officers, and with patriotic associations such as *Souvenir Français*. In the course of these missions I had frequent personal contact with General Salan, who tried to keep well informed of the state of mind of the European and Moslem population of Algeria.

He always listened to me with great attention and asked me precise questions. I should say and I can attest that in the course of all these numerous conversations General Salan always gave me directives and orders to calm down the hotheads and the "ultras" of Algeria, and to make the Europeans understand that Algeria could only be saved through the integration of the two communities, that it was absolutely necessary to re-establish confidence between the two communities. These were his orders; they were the same ones he had given us in Indochina. He never changed on that point.

No one can talk about political ambition on the part of General Salan! If General Salan had had political ambitions he could have realized them with ease. And here I want to speak to you a little about May 13.

These people of Algeria had to be convinced—especially the European populace—that they had to make sacrifices in the cause of integration, to abandon all racial prejudice, and to treat Moslems and Europeans as equal in rights and duties. This was our goal, that of our General and of all the army. May 13 had no other motive.

To convince these people the psychological branch of the army was given the task of spreading this word, in conferences with military students, with reserve officers, with territorial reserve units, with patriotic veterans' societies.

During the months which preceded May 13 this psychological branch, under the direction of General Salan, and with a group of officers as talented as Commander Cogniet, succeeded in convincing the Algerian populace that there was no other solution than loyal and fraternal integration with the Moslem populace. This was the work of the army, under the direction of its chief: General Salan.

We prepared May 13 entirely in this spirit: to preserve the territory of Algeria for the Republic, because, concerned solely with the defense of our country—which was our mission—we knew what kind of danger it would be, not only for France but for Mediterranean Europe and for all of Europe, if, under the guise of a supposedly "independent" FLN government, Asiatic-Soviet influence and power were established in Algeria.

Concerned with this defense, we succeeded in convincing the *colons* and the French officials in Algeria that the hour of integration had sounded, for in the face of the Communist menace everyone had to unite to save Algeria for the mother country. It was in this spirit that May 13 took place.

A few weeks previous, in April 1958, I received a visit from Léon Delbecque, then one from Neuwirth, then one from M. Biaggi at my office at the army corps of Algiers. They came from Paris, from metropolitan France to set up a listening post in Algeria for the

Ministry of National Defense, directed at that time by M. Chaban-Delmas.

They had been received without great enthusiasm at the quarters of the Commander in Chief, and they came to visit me to facilitate their getting a place to stay and to negotiate the installation of this listening post with General Salan. During the private conversations which Léon Delbecque, Neuwirth, and I had that day in my office, they told me: "Actually we have come here to speak to those of you who are preparing to save Algeria by desperate acts; to tell you: 'You can only save French Algeria if you overturn the system and if you replace the Republic by General de Gaulle!' "

This was said to me one morning in April 1958.

The emissaries were coldly received both by me and—if I am to believe what I have been told—by the entourage of General Salan. We found it astonishing and shocking that they wanted to politicize a problem which for us was only a problem of the defense of territorial integrity and the security of the country. Things being what they were, though, they were right.

After the magnificent upsurge of the populace on May 13—an upheaval I will speak to you about in a few moments—the Fourth Republic indeed collapsed . . . and General de Gaulle came to power.

And we who knew him and had served in the Resistance—for I was in the Resistance in North Africa from 1940 on—we could not conceive that this leader, General de Gaulle, who had been our leader during the harsh years of the German Occupation, would ever sacrifice the security of our country to ideas which were doubtless humanitarian, and not see the Communist danger which we had confronted in Indochina and which we knew very well could win North Africa and all of Africa.

Thus, May 13 took place. General Salan was really triumphant on the evenings of May 15, May 16, and May 17 and the days that followed, for he had received from a unanimous populace the reward for his tenacity and his forthrightness in his efforts to bring the two communities together.

[These demonstrations took place] in the presence of numerous journalists, foreign and French, who filled the terrace of Government House watching this poignant spectacle and who said to us: "Well, we are no longer merely drifting with history. The fraternization has taken place."

It was sincere. It wasn't comedy or a myth.

When one saw the *colons* and their daughters holding their agricultural workers by the hand, when one saw the Algerians following the French flag and singing with us—for those who knew Moslems the fraternization was accomplished.

This fraternization which we had desired, General Salan and ourselves, was realized. If the course we had opened had been followed, if the integration of the Moslem populace with the French populace and the integration of Algeria into the Republic had been continued, we would not have witnessed the drama we are living through today.

Others besides me have told you of the fearful dramas of conscience, from 1958 until today, in the army which is fighting in Algeria. I did not return, for then I was no longer an active soldier but a modest deputy in the National Assembly, who continued to defend the same cause, but on political ground.

My General (the witness turns to the accused), you were victorious on May 13; your victory was stolen from you. The whole army had its victory and its long, bloody, and painful sacrifices stolen from it. They killed the soul of the army. If it still exists, it is because of men like you and those who followed you! My General, whatever may be the judgment of men, we know that the judgment of history will recognize you as the magnificent leader whom we served.

We are sure—knowing you as a man—that you have nothing to fear from the judgment of God.

I have finished, Mr. President.